LATE ARCHAIC CHINESE

LATE ARCHAIC CHINESE

A Grammatical Study by

W. A. C. H. DOBSON

Professor of Chinese and Head of the Department
of East Asiatic Studies, University of Toronto

UNIVERSITY OF TORONTO PRESS

Copyright, Canada, 1959, by
University of Toronto Press

Reprinted in paperback 2015
London: Oxford University Press

SCHOLARLY REPRINT SERIES
ISBN 978-0-8020-7003-6 (cloth)
ISBN 978-1-4426-3992-8 (paper)
LC 59-38059

*Chinese type courtesy of the Harvard-Yenching Institute of
Harvard University*

A la mémoire de

HENRI MASPERO

Savant orientaliste et fervent patriote

Mort à Buchenwald

1945

PREFACE

In this work the results of an analysis, made by a system based upon certain stated postulates, are reported. The system and its results are to be taken as a whole, as self-explanatory within the system. In a work of this kind, however, the problems arising from the nature of the material are very considerable. I have had the benefit of the advice of a number of scholars who have read the manuscript and proffered criticism and suggestion. I would particularly like to acknowledge the help given by Dr. Arthur Waley, and by Professor Walter Simon and Dr. Angus Graham of the School of Oriental and African Studies, University of London, by Professor E. Pullyblank and Dr. M. Halliday of Cambridge University, by Dr. Raymond Dawson of the Department of Oriental Studies, University of Durham, and by Dr. David Hawkes of the University of Oxford. To Drs. Hawkes and Graham, I am particularly indebted for lengthy personal communications and for making available to me material on matters in which they are particularly knowledgeable. I am similarly indebted to Professor A. F. P. Hulsewé and Dr. E. Zürcher of the Sinologische Instituut of the University of Leiden, and to Professor Lü Shu-shiang, Vice-director of the Institute of Linguistics and Philology, Academia Sinica, Peking, and his colleagues. I owe a particular debt of gratitude to the members of the Harvard-Yenching Institute at Harvard University and especially to Professor Edwin O. Reischauer, its Director, for placing the very considerable resources of the library at my disposal, and to Professor Lien-sheng Yang, Dr. Ch'iu K'ai-ming, and Professor William Hung for bibliographical help and advice. To Professors Francis Cleaves and Robert Hightower of Harvard, I am indebted not only for criticism and encouragement, but for congenial entertainment during my stay at Harvard. To Professor George A. Kennedy of Yale, I am especially beholden not only for criticism but for generously placing at my disposal the results of his own considerable researches in LAC. Professor Murray Emeneau, Professor of Linguistics at the University of California to whose work on *Annamite* I am indebted for a number of linguistic techniques, also kindly read the manuscript, and has guided me on a number of technical points. My colleagues in the University of Toronto, Professor Shih Ching-cheng and Mr. Richard Robinson, in ways too many to mention, have contributed in bringing this work to fruition. To Professor Paul Demiéville, Professor of Chinese at the Collège de France, I owe thanks not only for kindly criticism, but for his work *Le Chinois* which, together with the pioneer work of

Henri Maspero, first suggested the possibility of a work of this kind. I would like to record my thanks to the Harvard-Yenching Institute who most generously made possible the use of the Chinese type in the text and to Dr. Glen Baxter of Harvard who kindly read the proofs. Finally, I would like to acknowledge the assistance of the Publications Fund of the University of Toronto Press.

W.A.C.H.D.

CONTENTS

PREFACE	vii
INTRODUCTION	xv
(i) Aims and Objects	xv
(ii) Late Archaic Chinese	xvi
(iii) Method and Analysis	xvii
(iii.a) Units	xvii
(iii.b) Elements	xviii
(iii.c) Classes	xviii
(iii.d) Limitations of the Material	xviii
(iv) Method and Statement	xix
(iv.a) Levels of Analysis and Statement	xix
(iv.b) Organization of the Statement	xx
(iv.c) Systems of Transcription	xx
(iv.d) System of References	xxi
(iv.e) Translation	xxii
(iv.f) Terminology	xxii
(v) Features of the Analysis	xxii
(v.a) Distributional or Word Classes	xxii
(v.b) Use of Phonological Data	xxiv
(v.c) Maximal and Minimal Forms	xxv
(v.d) The Paradigm and the Rule of Economy	xxvi
(vi) Features of the Statement	xxvi
(vii) Summary	xxviii
I. THE LEXIC AND THE WORD	3
1. The Lexic	3
1.1. The Word	4
1.1.1. Cenematic and Plerematic Words	4
1.2. Word Derivation	5
1.2.1. Classes of Compound Words	6
1.2.2. Reduplication	7
1.2.2.1. Distributives	7
1.2.2.2. Frequentatives and Iteratives	8
1.2.2.3. Intensives	8
1.2.2.4. Emotive Words	8
1.2.2.5. Similatives	9
1.2.2.6. Imitatives	10
1.2.2.7. Miscellaneous Reduplicatives	11
1.2.3. Parataxis	11
1.2.3.1. Contrastive Meaning—Simple Connection	11
1.2.3.2. Contrastive Meaning—Alternative Connection	12
1.2.3.3. Identical Meaning—Simple Connection (tautological hendiadys)	12

CONTENTS

1.2.3.4. Partial Identity of Meaning—Simple Connection (morphological hendiadys)	12
1.2.4. Hypotaxis	13
1.3. Words and Grammatical Word-classes	13
1.3.1. Classes of Cenematic Words	13
1.3.2. Plerematic Words and Grammatical Word-classes	14
1.3.3. Grammatical Quality and Plerematic Words	16
II. SYNTAGMA	**18**
2.1 Introduction	18
2.2. Morphological Functions of Syntagma	19
2.2.1. Syntagma and the Rule of Economy	19
2.3. Syntagmas and Grammatical Quality	20
2.4. The Processes of Syntagmatic Formation	20
2.5. The Parataxical Syntagma	20
2.6. The Hypotaxical Syntagma	21
2.6.1. Determinative	21
2.6.2. The Determinant Word	23
2.6.3. The Determinant Word—Possessive	24
2.6.3.1. The Determinant Word (quasi attributes)	24
2.6.3.2. The Determined Word	25
2.6.3.3. Determination and Spatial Relations	26
2.6.4. Determinant Words with Grammatical Class-meanings	27
2.6.4.1. Pronominal Determinant Words	27
2.6.4.2. Demonstrative Determinant Words	28
2.6.4.3. Privatives	29
2.6.4.4. Determinants of Number	29
2.6.4.4.1. Definite Number	30
2.6.4.4.2. Indefinite Number	30
2.6.4.4.3. Units of Measure	31
2.6.4.5. Collective and Restrictive Determinant Words	31
2.6.5. Directive	33
2.6.6. Substitutes in Syntagma	33
2.7. Syntagma and Sentential Forms	34
2.7.1. The Use of the Particle of Syntagma	34
2.7.2. The Use of the Particle of Determination *jy* in Syntagma	36
2.8. Concluding Remarks on Syntagma	36
2.9. Conspectus of the Syntagmatic Particles, and Specialized Forms	37
III. THE VERBAL SENTENCE	**38**
3. Introduction	38
3.1. The Verbal Sentence	38
3.2. The Verb	39
3.2.1. Verbal Sentences in Minimal Form	40
3.2.2. Verbal Sentences at Maximal Form	40
3.3. The Verbal Syntagma	41
3.3.1. Modal Determinants of the Verb	41
3.3.1.1. Indicative	42
3.3.1.2. Injunctive and Hortatory	44

3.3.1.3. Subjunctive	45
3.3.1.4. Mood Contextually Imposed	47
3.3.2. Aspect and the Verbal Syntagma	48
3.3.2.1. Potential Aspect	49
3.3.2.2. Desiderative Aspect	50
3.3.2.3. Momentary Aspect	50
3.3.2.4. Durative or Continuative Aspect	52
3.3.2.5. Perfective Aspect	52
3.3.2.6. Resultative Aspect	53
3.3.2.7. Customary Aspect	54
3.3.2.8. Aspects of Incidence	55
3.3.2.9. Miscellaneous Aspects	56
3.3.2.10. Miscellaneous Notes on Aspect	58
3.3.3.1. Determinations of Manner	59
3.3.3.2. The State of the Agent	60
3.3.4. Conspectus of the Verbal Syntagma	62
3.4. The Post-verbal Elements	62
3.4.1. Transitive and Intransitive	63
3.4.2. Transitive Verbs in Causative Voice	63
3.4.3. The Directive—Active Voice	65
3.4.4. The Directive—Passive Voice	66
3.4.5. Periphrastic Treatment of Voice	67
3.4.5.1. Periphrastic Treatment of Direction	68
3.4.6. Attributive Verbs and the Post-verbal Elements	69
3.4.7. Special Cases of Post-verbal Distribution	69
3.4.8. Polarity of Mood and the Post-Verbal Elements	73
3.4.9. Summary of the Post-verbal Elements	76
3.4.10. Conspectus of Voice and the Two Post-verbal Positions	76
3.5. The Agent	76
3.5.1. Introduction	76
3.5.2. Pronominal Agents	77
3.5.3. Agential Distributives	78
3.5.3.1. Agential Distributives (cont'd)	82
3.5.3.2. Agential Distributives (substantival)	84
3.5.4. Two or More Agents and Reciprocity	84
3.5.4.1. One Agent and the Reflexive	85
3.5.4.2. Reciprocity and the Reflexive	85
3.5.5. Delegation of Agency	86
3.5.6. Conspectus of Agency	87
3.6. The Instrumental	87
3.6.1. Description, Particles, Distribution	87
3.6.2. Ingressive and Resultative Instrument	88
3.6.3. The Ingressive Instrument and the Continuative Form	90
3.6.4. Conspectus of the Instrumental	90
3.7. The Subordinate Clause	90
3.7.1. *Erl* and the Integral Clause	90
3.7.2. *Erl* as a Conjunction	93
3.7.2.1. The Emphatic Form of Conjunctive *Erl*	94
3.8. Anaphora in the Verbal Sentence	94
3.9. Sentential Mood	97
3.9.1. Interjections	99
3.10. Time and Place	99

CONTENTS

3.11. Emphatic Exposure	101
3.11.1. Syntax of Exposure	102
3.11.2. Proper Names and Pronouns in Emphatic Exposure	104
3.12. Accentuation	104
3.12.1. Stress and Meaning	106
3.13. The Verbal Sentence in Summary	107
IV. THE DETERMINATIVE SENTENCE	108
4.1. Definition and Description	108
4.2. Syntax	108
4.3. The Properties of the Two Terms	109
4.3.1. The Determinant Term	109
4.3.2. The Determinant Term in Summary	111
4.4. Qualifications of the Predication	111
4.4.1. Negation of the Unqualified Categorical	111
4.4.2. Emphasis or Restriction upon the Unqualified Categorical	112
4.4.3. Qualified Categorical	113
4.5. The Properties of the Two Terms (cont'd)	114
4.6. Total Inclusion of Terms and Common Inclusion in a Third Term	114
4.6.1. Common and Total Inclusion	116
4.7. Modal Use of the Determinative Sentence Form	116
4.8. Occurrence or Presence	118
4.8.1. *Yeou* and *Wu* as Determined Terms	119
4.8.2. *Yeou* as the Determinant Term	119
4.9. The Use of *Shyh* and *Fei*	120
4.9.1. *Shyh* and *Fei* as Determined Terms	120
4.9.2. *Shyh* and *Fei* as Determinant Terms	121
4.9.3. *Shyh* and *Fei* in Plerematic Usage	121
4.10. The Properties of the Two Terms (cont'd)	122
4.10.1. Grammaticized Determinant Terms	122
4.10.2. The Non-status Personal Pronouns	122
4.10.3. The Demonstratives and Anaphora in the Determinative Sentence	122
4.10.4. Number as the Determinant Term	123
4.11. The Instrumental and the Determinative Sentence	124
4.12. Distributives and the Determined Term	126
4.13. The Determinative Sentence in Summary	127
V. SENTENCES IN DISTRIBUTION	128
5. Introduction	128
5.1. Co-ordinate Sentences in Sequence	128
5.2. Subordinate Sentences in Sequence	129
5.3. Conditioned Sequence	130
5.3.1. Fulfilled Condition	130
5.3.2. Unfulfilled Condition	131
5.4. Concession	132
5.4.1. Simple Concession	132
5.4.2. Conditioned Concession (i)	134
5.4.3. Conditioned Concession (ii)	134

VI. SUBSTITUTION 136

6.1. Substitution 136
6.2. The Personal Pronouns 136
  6.2.1. The Non-status Personal Pronouns 137
  6.2.2. Status Pronouns 139
6.3. The Demonstratives 141
6.4. Anaphoric Pronouns 141
6.5. The Interrogative Substitute 141
  6.5.1. Interrogative Substitution in Syntagma 143
  6.5.2. Interrogative Substitution in the Verbal Sentence 144
    6.5.2.1. Substitution in the Time Position (column 1) 145
    6.5.2.2. Substitution in the Place Position (column 2) and in the Second Post-verbal Position (column 10) 146
    6.5.2.3. Interrogative Substitution in the Agential Position. 1. The Agent (column 3) 148
    6.5.2.4. Substitution in the Agential Position. 2. Agential Distributives (column 4) 149
    6.5.2.5. Substitution in the Instrumental Position (column 5) 149
    6.5.2.6. Substitution for the Subordinate Clause (column 6) 150
    6.5.2.7. Substitution in the Verbal Syntagma (column 7). 1. Determinations of Manner 150
    6.5.2.8. Substitution in the First Post-verbal Position 150
  6.5.3. Interrogative Substitution in the Determinative Sentence 151
    6.5.3.1. Total Inclusion of the Terms (line 1) 151
    6.5.3.2. Partial Inclusion (line 2) 152
    6.5.3.3. Occurrence and Presence 152
    6.5.3.4. Substitution for *Fei* and *Shyh* (line 4) 153
    6.5.3.5. Substitution in Cause and Consequence Sequences (line 5, columns 1 and 3) 153
    6.5.3.6. Substitution in Cause and Consequence Sequences (cont'd) (line 5, column 2) 154
  6.5.4. Interrogative Substitution in Conditioned Sequences 156
6.6. The Indefinite Substitute 157
  6.6.1. Types of Occurrence 157
    6.6.1.1. Substitution for Post-verbal Elements 157
    6.6.1.2. Substitution for the Agent 158
    6.6.1.3. Substitution for the Instrument 159
    6.6.1.4. Substitution in the Agential Syntagma 160
6.7. Levels of Distribution 160
  6.7.1. In Syntagma 160
  6.7.2. In the Verbal Sentence 161
  6.7.3. *Suoo* in the Determinative Sentence 161
  6.7.4. *Suoo* and *Her* in Complementary Distribution 162
6.8. Interrogative and Indefinite 163

VII. MISCELLANEOUS 164

7.1. Degrees of Comparison 164
7.2. Status 165
7.3. The Use of *Meei* and *Shi* 166

CONTENTS

7.4.	Inversions of Word Order	167
7.5.	The Allegro Form	167
7.6.	Number	168

VIII. TEXTS FROM LAC AUTHORS — 170

8.1.	Introduction	170
8.2.	List of Conventional Signs and Abbreviations	170
8.3.	"On Justice and Humanity" (*Mencius*)	172
8.4.	"The Pleasures of Kings" (*Mencius*)	178
8.5.	"Half-measures in Government" (*Mencius*)	182
8.6.	"The Love that Embraces All Things" (*Micius*)	186
8.7.	"The Perennial Philosophy" (*Chuang Tzu*)	195
8.8.	"Chapped Hands" (*Chuang Tzu*)	199
8.9.	"The Mystical Journey" (*Chuang Tzu*)	202
8.10.	"The Feudal States Abolish the Resort to Arms" (*Tso Chuan*)	206
8.11.	"The Politician's Reward" (*Tso Chuan*)	212

APPENDIXES

I.	Orthography	221
II.	Phonological Affinities among Cenematic Lexics	227
III.	The Second Person Pronouns *Ruu*, *Ruoh*, and *Eel*, *Erl*, *Nae*	229

LIST OF WORKS MENTIONED — 231

LEXICON AND INDEX OF WORDS TREATED AT SOME LENGTH — 237

INTRODUCTION

(i) Aims and Objects

The present work is a descriptive grammar of Late Archaic Chinese (hereafter abbreviated as LAC), a literary language of the fourth and third centuries B.C. in use in North China. LAC is the language in which certain works which later became canonical are written. The literature of the period as a whole became classical in the sense that it has been regarded in later periods as a model of both style and usage.

The work has been undertaken with certain objectives in view. It is first of all an attempt to isolate a body of material from the vast corpus of "classical Chinese" (the language about which most Chinese grammars make statements) and to treat it exhaustively, that is, to account for all of the grammatical data in the material. It is secondly an attempt at strictly formal grammatical analysis, in which a categorical system is set up which is self-evident within and intrinsic to the material itself. No category has been recognized which is identifiable only by exterior criteria (e.g., by prior translation into a "reference language" or the relegation of words to grammatical word-classes *a priori*).[1] It is thirdly an attempt to resolve the problem in statement (though not in analysis) of describing the "source language" (LAC) in terms of the "target language" (English).[2] Hence, while analysis is purely formal, statement takes account of certain linguistic features of the language of description.[3] The work thus seeks to exploit the techniques of modern formal linguistics, and to apply them to a particular need, that of the occidental sinologist concerned primarily with reading and translating LAC texts. Modes of description have been used and, where choices of procedure offered, selected with this purpose in mind. The statement is grammatical. It treats comprehensively grammar only, introducing phonological, orthographical, and other linguistic phenomena only in so far as such matters make for clear grammatical exposition. With suitable selection and rearrangement of material, this work might form the basis of a primer but that is beyond its present purpose which is purely descriptive.

[1] See *Firth* (3), p. 79. [2] See *Firth* (2), p. 18.

[3] In chapter 8 examples of purely formal analysis, described extra-lingually by conventional symbols, will be found. Formal analysis throughout has been by this method. In statement, however, account has been taken of certain features of English.

(ii) Late Archaic Chinese

LAC is an abstraction. The term is a convenient descriptive label, nothing more. It represents a hypothetical norm for the literary language in use in North China in the fourth and third centuries B.C. and has been set up for the purposes previously mentioned. More specifically, it is the language of certain portions of the texts of *Mencius*, *Micius*, *Chuang-tzu*, and the *Tso Chuan*, assumed here to be typical of the language of the period.[4]

Furthermore, the statement only claims to account exhaustively for the features of four samples taken from these authors, each of some two thousand "characters" in length. The statement has, however, been tested over a wide range of authors and material of the period and found to be generally valid. In this description of LAC no account is taken of possible dialectical, regional, or social stratifications of the language, though the presence of such features is hinted at in the material itself. Citations from works of earlier periods within the material, where such can be identified, have also been excluded from consideration, though the possibility remains that the material contains archaisms.[5]

---

[4] In selecting this material, I should like to echo some recent observations of Karlgren (see Karlgren (4), p. 117): "It may seem bold and uncritical to treat a text like the present *Chuang-tzu*, or the present *Mo-tzu* or the present *Tso-Chuan* as a homogeneous and authentic whole and register the auxiliaries in *Chuang tzu* etc. I ought on the one hand to know that certain chapters are spurious or, in part at least, later interpolations, and I ought to know on the other hand that a text like *Tso Chuan* is made up of several earlier texts boiled down together to make new soup. The former reproach leaves me quite unconcerned. It is fashionable among both Chinese and Western scholars to indicate such and such a chapter in *Chuang tzu* or *Mo-tzu* as 'spurious' or such and such a passage as an 'interpolation'. It looks very scholarly and critical. But with few exceptions such condemnations are based on flimsy insufficient and subjective arguments, and it is my firm conviction (after decades of work with pre-Han texts) that in nine cases out of ten such criticisms are unfounded or exaggerated."

[5] "Archaic Chinese" is used here for the language of all pre-Ch'in literature. Late Archaic Chinese is used in contrast to Early Archaic Chinese (EAC), for example, *The Book of Songs* and authentic *Shu Ching*, and Middle Archaic Chinese (MAC), for example, *The Spring and Autumn Annals*, and the early *Analects*. The division is, of course, arbitrary but it is useful. It makes possible, for example, the observation of very considerable changes that occur within the limits of "classical Chinese" even when "classical Chinese" is restricted to mean the language of the Chinese classics. A system of periodization of the language for grammatical purposes has been suggested by Jou (3), p. 44, who gives a suggestive sketch of the characteristic particle usages of each period.

The material has been assumed to be "literary." The extent to which it departs from the vernaculars of the period is uncertain, and it cannot be assumed always to have done so simply because the literary language and the vernaculars of later periods diverge.[6]

Since LAC represents a stage in the evolution of the language (i.e., it is the language of a period) no account has been taken of the peculiarities of individual authors. Statement is made in the matter of usage as a series of alternatives occurring within the LAC period.[7]

(iii) Method and Analysis

The scheme of grammatical categories set up, and the criteria by which they are set up, is described in detail as the statement proceeds. But something should be said about the scheme itself. The categories recognized are units, elements, and classes.

(iii.a) Units

The first type of category, that of "units," is designed to account for the several levels of distribution of groupings in which the morpheme occurs. The unit is the category corresponding to a segment of the material about which statements are made. The units recognized are lexic, word, syntagma, clause, and sentence.

Lexic is a general term for that linguistic unit which is at once (a) the unit of the script, (b) the phonological unit, and (c) the morpheme (the grammatical unit). In the script system in which LAC texts are written the lexic is the only unit represented, and its representation (the "character" of popular description) is called a "sign." For each lexic there is a unique sign. In phonological analysis, the lexic represents that unit within which occurs the distribution of the segmental phonemes of the language. It is marked by juncture and characterized by a single peak of sonority. In grammatical analysis the lexic is the minimal distributable unit—the morpheme. The morpheme occurs in distribution in word-formation, and word group construction (syntagma) and also occurs in free state in larger units (clause and sentence).

[6]While certain of the material bears plainly the marks of artifice (rhyme, metre, parallelism, the formal archival entry, and so on), the maxims of the sophists used in open debate, and depending for their intelligibility upon the literal transcription of the *thing said*, at the very least must be examples of the spoken language.

[7]For example, the determinant form of the demonstrative is stated as being *sieg *tiəg and *dieg, though *tiəg in this usage occurs almost exclusively in *Chuang-tzu* (see 2.6.4.2). The negative injunctive *wu* does not occur in *Mencius* (see 3.3.1.2). A number of observations of this kind have been noted in footnotes, but the description does not take account of them otherwise.

The "word" may be either a free morpheme (a simple word) represented in the script by a single sign, or a compound of two morphemes (a compound word) represented in the script by two signs. Thus "words" (empirically—dictionary entries) may comprise one or more morphemes and be represented in the script by one or more signs.

Syntagma is a unit intermediate between word and sentence and is set up to account for the distribution of the "elements" (see iii.b) of the clause and sentence. The elements of the sentence are segregated and treated as units, irrespective of whether the elements of this unit are simple words, compound words (customary groups), or groups of words (syntagmas) made as it were *ad hoc.*

The sentence is a unit defined arbitrarily in LAC as an element in the "piece" characterized as a unit by the occurrence (or possibility of occurrence) of particles in final position of the "class" (see iii.c) of "particles of sentential mood."

The clause is a unit set up to account for the occurrence of a formal sentence as an element in a sentence.

(iii.b) Elements

The second type of category are "elements," set up to describe the constituents of units. Certain units are themselves the elements of higher units (e.g., the lexic as an element in the compound word, and the lexic, when it is itself a word, as an element in the sentence).

(iii.c) Classes

The third type of category is "class." Classes have been set up among lexics, words, syntagmas, clauses, and sentences.

Certain classes have been set up by purely formal criteria (e.g., the cenematic and plerematic classes among words which in the first instance occur in fixed or limited positions in distribution, and in the latter instance are operationally ambivalent). Other classes have been set up by functional criteria (e.g., the class among particles set up as "directive particles"). Still others have been set up by class-meaning (e.g., the classes set up among compound words formed by reduplication), while certain classes have been set up purely in terms of the target language (e.g., the distinction made between interrogative and indefinite substitutes), since the purpose for which the statement is made involves taking into consideration such distinctions made in the target language.

(iii.d) Limitations of the Material

The nature of the material (printed texts) imposes certain limitations upon both linguistic procedure and statement. Little is known,

INTRODUCTION

or at least little can be deduced directly from the material, about the phonological features of LAC. Little is known of its prosodic features; even punctuation comes down from later tradition. A hypothetical statement is possible about the values of its segmental phonemes, but phonological research even at this level is at a far from conclusive stage.[8]

The script system used in the texts preserves phonological indications of a kind.[9] One of the processes by which signs are formed is that by which the sign for lexic "x" is formed upon the analogy of the sign for lexic "y" when both x and y are homophonous. (Homophonous, that is, at the time of orthographic formation; the script takes no account of subsequent phonological divergence.) But the system does not provide for the identification and segregation of segmental phonemes. All that is preserved of the phonology of any given sign is its value in an evolved form in modern dialects. On the other hand, the script-system is such that it isolates the morphemes of the language in discrete form. No process of segmentation or of deduction is required to identify them. This allows, within the material itself, the observation of their distribution quite objectively. These features are of the nature of the material, and linguistic analysis must proceed as far as it can, exploiting such advantages as the material offers and accepting its limitations.

(iv) Method and Statement

(iv.a) Levels of Analysis and Statement

Procedure in analysis has been undertaken at varying levels and dimensions; procedure in statement, however, has been governed ultimately by the objectives described in (i). For example, in setting up the classes of *aspect*, *mood*, and *sentential mood* there are cross distributions among the classes. The negatives have been classed as modal, but they operate in certain cases both at the aspectual and modal level (e.g., *wey* combines both polarity of mood and experential aspect). *Jiang* and *chiee*, treated as aspectual, occur indifferently as aspect (e.g., *jiang chiuh* (將去) "about to go") and as modal (e.g.,

---

[8] See Bodman (1), p. 341: "The phonology of Ancient Chinese is well enough known to be phonemicized, whether it was an absolutely homogeneous language or not. It is probably still too early to attempt the same for Archaic Chinese. There is still too much disagreement and uncertainty concerning the phonological facts." Bodman gives a résumé of the principal theories current at present. He also goes on to say that "the time is now ripe for early Chinese texts to be grammatically analyzed with this point in mind." Since Bodman wrote, Martin's *The Phonemes of Ancient Chinese* has appeared.

[9] A brief description of the script system is given in Appendix 1.

jiang yinq jy (將應之) "I would answer him"). The interrogative mood, which in LAC pertains to the polar modal system, is treated in part as sentential mood and considered independently of the mood of the verb. In synthesizing and identifying in this way there is both economy in statement and descriptive advantage. The advantage in the instances cited is that the words so segregated occur in contrasting types of distribution and are, therefore, readily and formally identifiable.

As has already been mentioned (iii.c) the description occasionally takes cognizance of classes not warranted by formal analysis, but imposed by the purposes for which the statement is made.[10]

(iv.b) Organization of the Statement

The description proceeds in an "upward" direction of procedure (from the smaller unit to the larger). This procedure is suggested by the purpose for which the work has been undertaken. The western sinologist in his approach to a text proceeds in practice from the minimal unit, the lexic, to the larger units. In the description, therefore, the lexic is considered first, the description proceeding to its distribution as an element in the word (chapter 1) and then as an element in syntagma (chapter 2). The sentence is treated in chapters 3 and 4, sentential elements being analysed as the description of each sentential type proceeds. The distributions of sentences as elements in larger segments is considered next (chapter 5). Classes are identified and described at the unitary or elemental level at which they occur. Words of the class "substitutes" are, however, treated separately (chapter 6) since substitution occurs at all levels of distribution. Chapter 7 contains a miscellany of notes and observations which, while falling outside the general descriptive framework, present by way of either summary or rearrangement, observations relating to the material which either augment or clarify the description. Chapter 8 contains extracts from the test material, exemplifies the analytical methods used, and demonstrates the results in application. The appendixes contain material too long or involved to be included as footnotes. The indexes contain a lexicon and index of words treated at some length (p. 256), and a bibliography of works cited in the description (p. 251).

(iv.c) Systems of Transcription

Formal analysis has been undertaken independently of phonological data. But, since LAC texts are customarily read giving to each sign

[10] Cf. the remarks of Emeneau (1), p. 59, upon the fluctuation between interrogative and indefinite substitutes in Annamite (cf. here 6.8), "This causes one to wonder whether the attempt to make a difference is not due to some Indo-European bias."

its phonetic value in Modern Standard Chinese, this value has been given throughout the text. The system of transcription used is the "Official Chinese Latin Script" (Gwoyeu Romatzyh) used in the standard Chinese dictionary *Tsyr-hae* (辭海) and made familiar to, and described for the western student in the dictionaries of Simon (see Simon (1)) and Chao Yuan-ren and Yang Lien-sheng (see Chao (1)). In the cases of grammatical words, an entry marked with an asterisk gives a phonetic transcription of the reconstructed phonological value in Archaic Chinese given in *Grammata Serica* (Karlgren (3)). Further, in the lexicon (p. 256), references are given to the appropriate entry in *Grammata Serica*[11] (a paragraph number preceded by "K") and to the entry in Yang Shuh-dar's *Particle Lexicon* (a number preceded by YST; see Yang (1)) and also to the classification number used in the Harvard-Yenching Concordances.

(iv.d) System of References

References to the examples cited from the works of LAC authors are made as follows. For citations from *Mencius, Micius, Chuang-tzu, Hsun-tzu* and *Tso Chuan*, reference is to the text printed with the Harvard-Yenching Concordance of the works of each author. For *Mencius*, reference is given to chapter and verse and to the line number of the verse. For *Micius, Chuang-tzu, Hsun-tzu* and *Tso Chuan*, reference is to page and line number as given in the Concordance text, but in the case of *Tso Chuan* the line number is calculated from the top of the page. Reference to the *Shih Ching* (*The Book of Songs*) is to the number of the ode as it occurs in a consecutive numbering of the traditional arrangement (e.g., as in the Harvard-Yenching Concordance). References to the *Shu Ching* (*The Book of Documents*) are to the page and line number of the text published by Karlgren, *The Book of Documents* (reprinted from BMFEA 22 [Stockholm, 1950]. References in *Shih Chi* are to the volume, page, and line number of *Guh Jye-gang's Bair-wen Shyy-jih* (Peking, 1937). References to *Han Shu* and *Hou Han Shu* are to the chapter and page numbers of Wang Shian-chian's *Hann-shu Buu-juh* and *How Hann-shu Jyi-jiee* (Shiu-show tarng ed.). References to *Analects, Great Learning* and *Doctrine of the Mean* are to the chapter and verse respectively, as given in Legge, *The Chinese Classics*, vol. I.

Most of the examples cited are taken arbitrarily from a "piece" and a wider context is often necessary for a proper understanding of their meaning. This brevity is regrettable, but it is imposed purely from considerations of economy. However, the references will, in part, make up this deficiency.

[11]Karlgren's notation has been simplified for typographical reasons, but his own form can be quickly verified by the use of these references.

Though many examples could be given for most statements, where possible examples have been restricted to *Mencius*.

References to the works of scholars are given in the text by name and page number only. Full bibliographical details are given in the bibliography.

(iv.e) Translation

A free or literary translation of examples appears between quotation marks and a "literal" translation appears between soliduses. The nature of a "literal" translation should be fully understood. There is no word-for-word correspondence between source and target language. The LAC word is uncommitted to such matters as mood, aspect, and number, and tense is not a grammatical division at all. This uncommitedness often cannot be rendered in "literal" translation. Many of the grammatical words of LAC have no counterpart, even within the rough terms of "literal" translation in the language of description. "Literal" translations are merely offered as a means of identifying elements in the structure and of illustrating their distribution. On the other hand, free or literary translations are often the only way by means of which an accurate account of meaning can be conveyed. They should not be thought to be any less "accurate" than "literal" translations.[12]

(iv.f) Terminology

One cannot adopt the methods of formal linguistics without adopting (and in this work adapting) its technical vocabulary. But such a procedure is not without its problems. In the event, terms used in contemporary linguistics have been adopted, and have been supplemented by new terms where necessary, but in either case such terms have been defined or redefined, at their first occurrence. The terms are not meant to convey any implications beyond the immediate context of this description.

(v) Features of the Analysis

(v.a) Distributional or Word Classes

The principal observable variety in the linguistic material of LAC as it has survived is the variety of distribution, and the sets of distributions in which the morpheme occurs. Since, in the material, each

---

[12] The remarks of Emeneau (1), p. 65, on translation from Vietnamese are equally applicable to LAC: "However it should be clear that the absence of any obligatory voice category in the Vietnamese verb in general makes all English translations only approximate at best, and at worst very misleading."

morpheme is represented by a unique sign, the sign offers no formal features, in isolation, for classification. The observation and classification of forms of distribution are, therefore, the main divisions of this analysis. Thus, a morpheme in distribution may be said to have grammatical quality since it then shares in a class with other morphemes similarly distributed, but undistributed its quality is uncertain. Upon this basis, morphemes fall into two classes: those which occur in fixed or limited distribution, and those which are freely distributed. Those occurring in fixed distribution are well institutionalized as a class among Chinese scholars, as "empty words" (i.e., "form" or "cenematic" words). The identification of such a class was first made as an observation in poetics, such words being elided or unstressed in the reckoning of metre. It is possible to exhaust the varieties of distribution of such words in each individual case and to make comprehensive statements about their occurrence and function. This can be done with economy as their number is limited. The "full" words of Chinese tradition (i.e., "content" or "plerematic" words), which compose the major part of the lexicon, are not so limited or fixed. It is a feature of this description that "content or plerematic words" are not segregated into word-classes;[13] rather, analysis is made of the types of distribution and environment in which they occur, such types of distribution being classified. It would be possible to go further and to give statistical accounts in the case of each word. One could proceed as follows. If distribution type A = an environment in which a word so found will have the grammatical value V, and if distribution type B = an environment in which a word so found will have the grammatical value S, then any given word can be said to occur in the material x times at A and y times at B. But it cannot usefully be said to be "of the class V, but used also as S" except as an observation of preponderance. This would simply be a statement of statistical probabilities. Further, if grammatical analysis is based on word-classes so segregated, the alternative possibilities of

---

[13]The question as to whether Chinese "has parts of speech" or whether the "parts of speech exist" in Chinese, has been so lengthily discussed that it is important here to point out that such metaphysical problems are foreign to the spirit of scientific linguistics. The question is, "Can these classes usefully be set up?" The answer, of course, depends partly upon the purpose for which analysis is made, and partly upon the canons of scientific analysis for setting up any class or category. We are not here dealing with eternal verities but with analytical and descriptive conveniences.

Speaking of linguistic systems, W. S. Allen (1), p. 53, observes that "the aim should be a theory (in the Hjelmslevian sense) rather than a hypothesis; for whilst the latter may, as the subject progresses or further material is considered, be shown to be true or false, no such contingency applies to the former; it is to be judged only by its adequacy or otherwise to handle particular material...."

the word occurring outside of its word-class are such that to each formal statement made, for example, about "verbs," secondary statements about "nouns acting as verbs, adjectives acting as verbs, adverbs acting as verbs," and so on must be added.

Since both V and S are environmentally determined, and are not intrinsic properties of the given word, a more economical statement is to say that a word found at A has the value V, but if found at B it has the value S. In grammatical statement this makes for economy since one statement only is required for each type of environment, whereas analysis based upon word-classes involves as many statements as there are word-classes set up for each type of environment.[14]

(v.b) Use of Phonological Data

LAC material, or rather the orthographic system in which it is written, provides the linguist with a feature of particular interest, since, as has already been observed (iii.d), the script isolates and provides a separate symbol for each morpheme, but does not, of intent, give phonological data.[15] The material thus presents a clear and unambiguous morphology but deprives the linguist of phonological assistance in analysis. The problem here has been to set up an analytical system which is independent of phonological considerations since the material is silent upon such matters. However, in three cases in this description prosodic or phonological features have been hypothetised, and are stated as hypotheses.

The first is the *allegro form*. Formally it might be stated that certain pairs of grammaticized words occur regularly in complementary distribution (i.e., interchange with no change in meaning reference) with certain single grammaticized words. The inference is that the single word is simply an allegro form of the pair—the product of customary association and perhaps rapid enunciation with loss of stress, resulting in a word with a single peak of sonority. The inference is not unjustified.[16] In certain cases the paired form has dropped out of usage and the allegro form is predominant (e.g., *Yan* (焉) = allegro form of *yu jy* (於之), though *yu jy* never occurs); in other cases, the complementary distribution occurs (e.g., *hwu* (胡) and *her*

[14]In lexicography, of course, a statement of the environmental occurrences of each word is essential, and the formal methods here employed provide a method for scientific lexicography. This has not so far been undertaken for the LAC lexicon. See Halliday (1), p. 212, for an excellent discussion and demonstration of this point in the case of Modern Standard Chinese.

[15]That is, it is not a phonetic script, but a script in which phonology in part enters into the processes of orthographic formation.

[16]It could, for example, be inferred from modern Chinese dialectology where the allegro form is well recognized. (See Chao (2), p. 57.)

guh (何故); in other cases still, the paired form occurs in one author, and the allegro form is used by another (e.g., *yu* (與) in *Mencius* and *yee hu* (也乎) in *Tso*). A conspectus of allegro forms is given in 7.5.

The second is the inference of a prosodic feature (stress) to account for the otherwise complementary distribution of two forms of the formal indicative negative, and the two forms of the injunctive negative. An emphatic and unemphatic form has been proposed.

The third is the segregation of a class of grammaticized words, as "particles of accentuation." This is, of course, again pure hypothesis, offered simply as a plausible explanation of their occurrence *faute de mieux*. While formally such explanations may seem inadmissible, for the purposes of this work a plausible hypothesis (stated to be such) is preferable to no explanation at all in cases where the data is silent or does not yield to the formal methods of analysis employed.

(v.c) Maximal and Minimal Forms

In accounting for the distribution of the unit within a segment, at the various levels of distribution which have been segregated, the method has been paradigmatic. That is to say, since in the material all elements are not always and simultaneously present in any one given type of distribution in a segment, a paradigm has been built up of the maximal form.[17] Similarly, the two main classes within the segment "sentences" are delimited by the features of their minimal forms.[18]

Thus an adequate account is given of the formal features of the sentence without introducing the hitherto ubiquitous, though frequently inapplicable, division of all sentences into subject/predicate.[19] In the case of the verbal sentence this division is inapplicable, and in the case of the determinative sentence, the predication is essentially of a class with the determinative process in morphology and recognition is given to this.[20]

[17] For example, a simple illustration is given at 7.6 where the maximal form for stating a fraction has five elements though it may be stated with varying degrees of economy with four, three, or two elements.

[18] See 3.2.1 where the minimal form of the "verbal sentence" is given as one term, since, when stated with the maximum economy, such sentences can be stated with one term; when stated with more than one term, the other terms are taken to be subordinate, or secondary. The determinative sentence, on the other hand, can be stated only with a minimal form of two terms. The two terms are therefore taken to be co-ordinate, or equally primary.

[19] A not dissimilar procedure has been adopted by Halliday (1) for Modern Standard Chinese (see p. 188).

[20] Halliday's "given" and "new" adequately accounts for determination at both the syntagma and the sentential levels (Halliday (1), p. 188).

(v.d) The Paradigm and the Rule of Economy

A further use of the paradigmatic method has been imposed by one of the most distinctive linguistic features of LAC, namely, the non-obligatoriness of the use of many of its grammatical devices. A lexic used as a verb may be invested environmentally with mood, voice and aspect, but the verb may equally occur uncommitted, or neutral in any or all of these regards. Similarly, a lexic in nominal usage may be invested with number, or occur uncommitted to number. The language is not governed by rules which require the introduction of such indications as a matter of prescribed necessity. Statements are made with the minimum of grammatical indications consistent with clear statement. This feature is here described as the "rule of economy." In describing the distributions of the elements of a verb group, therefore, a paradigm is built from a verb group at its maximal form. The statement is then made that the distribution of elements is as distributed in the maximal form. When a verb group is used with the rule of economy operating, no matter which element is suppressed for economy, the remaining elements will be found to be in the distributional order of the maximal form. Similarly, certain formations are formally characterized in the description by the occurrence of certain particles distinctive to that type of formation. But when these diagnostic particles are dropped under the operation of the rule of economy, their presence or possibility of occurrence must be inferred from the paradigm.[21] Such inference may be alien to the spirit of objective analysis, and may introduce statements of possibilities and probabilities where certainties are preferable, but it is imposed by the operation of this disconcerting rule. It might seem to those accustomed to the obligatory grammatical indications of Indo-European languages that such selectivity in their use would make for ambiguity or lack of clarity, but in practice this is rarely so, though the feature poses problems for translators from LAC into languages where such categories are obligatory.

(vi) Features of the Statement

The description of LAC here set down is governed in its form, and the analytical observations are selected and described, ultimately,

---

[21]For example, two classes of elements are placed post-verbally, which when occurring simultaneously are separated by the particle *yu* (於) (particle of the second post-verbal position.). The second element may occur without the first but still diagnostic is the occurrence of the particle of the second post-verbal position. Examples, however, are encountered where both first element and diagnostic particle are dropped, so that there are no formal criteria for deciding whether the element is in the first or second post-verbal position.

by the needs of the occidental sinologist.[22] Though a variety of purposes can be served by descriptive grammars, the form and the selection of observation will vary with the purpose for which they are written. The purposes governing the form of this description are those of the needs of the reader and translator of LAC texts. This is, in short, a "translational grammar."[23] It provides a system for the reading of texts which is based upon observable criteria within the material. The main problem has lain hitherto with the so-called particles (strictly form or cenematic words). However loose or vague the "meanings" of this class of word may seem from dictionaries, they occur in practice, with precise function, in an exhaustible range of distributions. Their functions and types of distribution are set out comprehensively here so that, once the type of distribution is identified, the function is immediately clear. Types of distribution are identifiable by a convergence of diagnostic features so that by a process of elimination, in the preponderating number of cases, one solution, and one solution only is possible. The seeming ambiguities arising from the ambivalence of function of many content or plerematic words (full words) is more apparent than real, since, in texts, such words occur predominantly in distribution, and are then committed to precise function. Here the cenematic words offer clues to the type of distribution or environment in which they occur, an environment which imposes those precisions of function which the plerematic word, standing alone, does not indicate. It is thus possible, by purely formal criteria, to eliminate most of the translational solutions, which a word-for-word translation made with the aid of dictionaries might suggest as possible.[24]

[22]Cf. here the observation of Hjelmslev, p. 145: "Donc, si la linguistique structurale de nos jours peut paraître à certains esprits trop théorique, il ne faut pas oublier que la théorie est faite pour faciliter le travail pratique, et qu'elle est née d'un besoin pratique."

[23]See Firth (2), p. 18.

[24]As an example of the application of the system in translation, the opening verse of *Mencius* contains the sentence "*soou buh yeuan chian lii erl lai*" (叟不遠千里而來)/Old man/not/distant/thousand/mile/-/come/. The cenematic words are *erl* and *buh*. *Erl*, particle of the subordinated clause, indicates at once that: (*a*) the single word following could only be the main verb *lai* "come," and (*b*) the clause preceding it is verbal. The verb of the clause is identified by the formal modal negative *buh*, and therefore must be *yeuan*. *Yeuan*, "distant," is of the class of verb that may occur in factitive or putative usage (see 3.4.6): "to think distant" or "to put at a distance." *Chian* is a numerical determinant in syntagma, so that therefore *chian lii* is a syntagma "thousand miles." *Lii* is thus committed to number. As an element in the clause it is in the first post-verbal position; it is thus the affectee of the verb, in this case of *yeuan*, thus "not to regard as distant a thousand miles." Since this is the subordinated

(vii) Summary

The general characteristic of LAC as it emerges from this analysis is one of rigorous syntactical regularity. Its grammatical categories (properly identified) are well defined, and distinguish a remarkable range of nuance. The language has a complex but consistently observed syntax, but makes provision for a wide variety of mood and emphasis. There is both richness and subtlety in the language. Masters of LAC prose cleverly exploit the resources of their language, namely, that many of its grammatical forms are not obligatory, that the rule of economy permits great metrical flexibility, and that the absence of form classes among words permits of a high mobility among the units of its vocabulary.

---

clause, subordinated clause and main clause must be joined as follows "not having regarded as distant a thousand miles, have come." *Soou* is of the class of substitutes (personal status pronoun), used as a polite form of address to elderly men, and thus "Venerable Sir, you have come [here] not having thought a journey of a thousand miles too far."

LATE ARCHAIC CHINESE

I. The Lexic and the Word

1. The Lexic

The material presented by an LAC text requires no segmentation or process of inference to identify the morphemes of the language other than that already provided by the script in which it is written. The script system is one which isolates and demarks morphemes and represents them each with a single and unique sign. This sign (the "character" of popular description, and the *tzyh* (字) of Chinese usage) provides therefore a clear point of departure for grammatical analysis.[1] But, since each sign is unique, it offers in itself no criteria for setting up form-classes among morphemes.[2]

Each sign is given a phonetic value when read. In modern practice this value is the value currently given to the sign in Modern Standard Chinese, or in the vernacular of the reader.[3] In the fourth and third centuries B.C. this value was different from the modern value.[4]

The phonetic value of any given sign in Late Archaic Chinese is a matter now for inference only since the script-system is not a phonetic one, in the sense that segmental phonemes are represented, or one from which their values can be deduced. The sign symbolizes the morpheme. Upon the analogy of our knowledge of later and modern Chinese phonology, and from deductions that can be made from the processes of orthographic formation, it is clear that what the sign represents is not only the morpheme (the unit of grammatical analysis), but also a phonological segment (a unit of phonological analysis). This segment occurs with a maximal distribution of elements of initial consonant (consonantal clusters have been inferred for Archaic

[1] See Hockett (1) p. 84: "Since Chinese characters constitute essentially a morphemic writing system, they also represent a centuries-old, slowly but constantly evolving folk-analysis of the language. One might suspect that the identifications thus arrived at would be as valid as any the modern analyst might discover."

[2] The sign has common formal features for setting up classes of orthographic formation and for setting up classification systems for signs (e.g., for dictionary arrangement), but this is a matter of orthography, and not of morphology. A brief description of the script system is given in Appendix 1.

[3] There is a convention that certain signs are given a "literary" reading, when occurring in classical literature, but their number is limited to a few instances.

[4] For example, rhymed verse, when given modern reading values, no longer rhymes.

Chinese) vowel(s) (including consonantal vowels), and final consonant. No segmental phoneme occurs outside of this distribution. This segment also has a single peak of sonority, and is delimited by juncture (in the phonetician's sense).[5] The phonological value of any given sign does not extend beyond this maximal distribution. The sign therefore provides the phonetician with a unit for phonological analysis and is thus a triple analytical unit.

In this description, the term "sign" is used for orthographical observation, "morpheme" for grammatical observation, and "phonological unit" for phonological observation, but for a term which is not committed specifically to any one of these analytical aspects, the term "lexic" is used. "Lexic," therefore, denotes all that is represented orthographically, phonologically, and morphologically by the sign. Since each sign is a unique form, no formal characteristics offer for a classification of lexics by common formal features.[6] But since lexics occur in LAC texts in differing forms and sets of distribution, distribution can be formally observed and classified.

1.1. The Word

The lexic occurs in distribution as an element in the formation of "compound words" (see 1.2); as an element in the formation of word-groups (themselves elements in higher forms of distribution, and called "syntagmas"; see 2.1); but also as a single element in higher formations—clauses and sentences. As a single element in formations above the compound word, the lexic is a "word." Thus "words" (empirically —dictionary entries) may be either single lexics, when in a higher form of distribution than in the compound word, or two lexics, when occurring in the compound word.[7]

1.1.1. Cenematic and Plerematic Words

Two classes are formally identifiable among "words" by the manner of their distribution, that is, those which occur in fixed or limited distribution, and those which are not so restricted. The former, though formally defined, are also well institutionalized as a class among

---

[5] See Hockett (2), p. 261.

[6] Neither have "words" (see 1.1) morphological inflexion, so that even if use were made of phonological data, no word-classes can be set up by formal features alone.

[7] In current Chinese linguistic usage, *tzyh* (字) designates indifferently the lexic as a sign, as a morpheme, and as the phonological unit (as defined in 1). *Tsyr* (詞) is used in the sense in which "word" is used here. This use of *tsyr* is confined to technical usage. In popular usage it is less precise. For example, see *Yang Bor-jiunn* (1), 2.1.

Chinese classical scholars,[8] and are known to them as *shiu tzyh* (虛字) empty words (i.e., form or "cenematic" words[9]). They provide the grammatical repertory of the lexicon. The latter class of *shyr tzyh* (實字) the full words of Chinese tradition (i.e., content or "plerematic" words[9]) provide the remaining and substantial portion of the lexicon. Certain words are members of both classes, and this is noted in the lexicon (see p. 256). The "word" as used in this description therefore, falls into the following sub-categories:

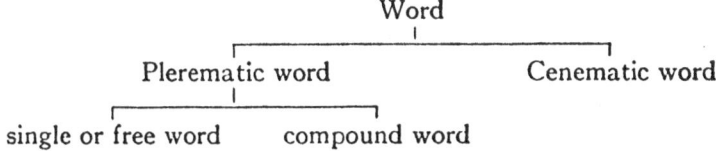

1.2. Word Derivation

Single lexic words of the plerematic class enter as elements in the processes of word-formation by which compound words[10] are formed. The processes of derivation[11] are simply additive, and when a compound word is so formed, no liaison is marked in the script.[12] Com-

---

[8] For example, special lexicons have been compiled for them. Recent lexicons are those of Yang Shuh-dar (see Yang (1)), and Peir Shyue-hae (see Peir (1)).

[9] For the terms "plerematic" and "cenematic," see Demiéville (1), p. 130. Some words recognized to be *shiu tzyh* (e.g., certain substitutes) would not be included among "form" words by linguists who use the terms "form" and "content." Since cenematic and plerematic have no such association they better represent, and are used here to represent, the Chinese phenomenon exclusively.

[10] The term "compound word" is used with reservation, bearing in mind the precise criteria set down by grammarians of Sanskrit for compounding, and the morphological implications generally, of the term.

[11] "Derivation" and "derived" are used throughout this description in a descriptive not in a historical sense (see Bloch and Trager, p. 54).

[12] This is not to say that some prosodic feature, such as close rather than open juncture, might not characterize them, but the material is silent upon such matters. In reduplication, however, a hint is given of some such feature since reduplication sometimes leads to phonological dissimilation in one member (see 1.2.2). This may well take place under the influence of some such feature as force or length of utterance. Since compound words are created by varying structural modes (e.g., by parataxis and hypotaxis—see 1.2.3 and 1.2.4), and these are not formally differenced, Kennedy ((1), p. 1), on the analogy of modern dialect evidence, has proposed contrastive stress patterns. These, as Kennedy observes, are not deducible from the material, but he is surely right in suspecting the presence of some contrastive prosodic feature now irrecoverable except by inference from such comparative studies.

pound words are formed by the same structural principles that govern syntagmas (see 2.1 ff.). Compound words differ merely in being customary associations of lexics, in contrast to the spontaneous associations of syntagma made as it were *ad hoc*. An empirical observation is that compound words are characterized by specializations of sense, and as such are found as dictionary entries.[13] The proportion of compound words to single or free words as they occur in the control material of LAC was never higher than three per cent.[14]

1.2.1. Classes of Compound Words

Compound words are classified according to the processes by which they are formed. Compound words are formed by reduplication (see

---

[13]Specialization of sense, that is, technical usage. Cf., for example, the formally comparable *tian-shiah* (天下)/sky/below/ and *jao-shang* (沼上)/pool/above/ as used in *Mencius*. The former occurs 174 times (a customary association), the latter once only. Both belong to a characteristic form class (see 2.6.3.3) and the "natural" interpretation of either would be "of the sky, the below part," that is, "below the sky" and "of the pool, the above part," that is, "above the pool," respectively. *Jao-shang*, in fact, occurs in this natural sense "standing above the pool," while *tian-shiah* is specialized in meaning, and refers to "all below the skies" > "the world of men" > "society" > "the Empire." *Tian-shiah* is thus a compound word, *jao-shang* a syntagma. The compound word is characterized, therefore, by a technical rather than a natural sense.

[14]Excluding proper names. I know no comparable statistics for any subsequent period of the language, but the proportion rises perceptibly in Han usage (second cent. B.C.—second cent. A.D.), and is very much higher in Modern Chinese. Emeneau ((1), p. 3) gives, for a basic Vietnamese vocabulary, the proportion of 1 to 5. There is also no occurrence in LAC of the non-free morpheme (with the exception of the dissimilated member of the broken reduplicative—see 1.2.2). The non-free morpheme is the morpheme which occurs in no higher unit, in free state, than the compound word (see Yang Lien-sheng (1)). This is a marked feature of Modern Chinese (see Halliday (1), p. 211). An example in LAC which seemed to offer is *fu* (夫) "individual, man, husband" occurring in *Dah-fu* (大夫) /great/individual/ "a noble"; *Pii-fu* (匹夫) /mean/individual/ "commoner"; *Fu-fuh* (夫婦) /husband/wife/ "married couple"; *Fu-ren* (夫人) "wife"; *Nong-fu* (農夫) /farming/person/ "farmer"; *Kwang-fu* (狂夫) /mad/person/ "madman"; *Lao-fu* (老夫) /old/man/ "elderly person"; *Pann-fu* (叛夫) /revolt/man/ "a rebel"; *Tzae-fu* (宰夫) /slaughter/man/ "a butcher"; *Yih-fu* (役夫) /servant/man/ "a servant," etc. The term *i fu* (一夫) /one/person/ occurs in *Der i fu erl shy i gwo* (得一夫而失一國): "We may save one person but lose the entire State" (*Tso* 60.11), but *i fu* is perjorative in "*Wey jy i fu*" (謂之一夫): "We call him a mere fellow" (*Mencius* 1b.8.2). *Fu* however does occur in free state in *Ren jinn fu yee, fuh i erl-yii* (人盡夫也父一而已): "Any man might be her husband, but one only is her father" (*Tso* 42.6).

1.2.2), by parataxis (see 1.2.3), and by hypotaxis (see 1.2.4). Within these three broad classes, sub-classes (of class-meanings) have been distinguished.

1.2.2. Reduplication

Compound words created by reduplication occur in identical reduplication (gemination), and with phonological dissimilation[15] in one member (broken reduplicative).[16] Certain well-defined class-meanings are created by reduplication.

1.2.2.1. Distributives

Words are derived by reduplication with the common class-meaning of "a totality, conceived as a series of given instances."

EXAMPLES

I (一) "one, the whole," etc., and so *i-i* "one by one, individually."
Wuu (五) "five" and so *wuu-wuu* "in groups of five, five by five."
Ren (人) "man, mankind" and so *ren-ren* "men as individuals" as, for example, in *Ren-ren yeou guey yu jii jee fwu sy eel yii* (人人有貴於己者弗思耳矣) "Each man individually has within himself a capacity for nobility, it is merely that he does not set his mind upon it" (*Mencius* 6a.17.1).

---

[15]The broken reduplicate sets up a unique class of morpheme about which a special statement must now be made. It is a derivative from the lexic and thus operates at a somewhat lower level than the morpheme as described in 1.1. It is non-free, occurring uniquely in the reduplicative form. In orthography it is given a distinct sign. In traditional lexicography "meanings" are sometimes given to such signs, giving rise to such folk etymologies as *Guoo-luoo* (果蓏), *klwar-glwar (also occurring as *gua-lou* (栝樓), *gua-lou* (瓜蔞) and *guoo-luoo* (果蓏)) "a fruit or nut" from *guoo* "fruit of trees" and *luoo* "fruit of plants," or from *guoo* "fruit with a stone" and *luoo* "fruit without a stone"; whereas *guoo-luoo* is simply a derivative by reduplication from *guoo* "fruit." The sign for *guoo-luoo* also occurs for the homophonous reduplicative (sometimes written 蜾蠃) "the solitary wasp" (see Tarng Lan (1), p. 27).

[16]That the latter is but a variant of the former is shown by Emeneau (1), p. 159, in the case of Annamite. An example of historical transition from one form to the other in Chinese is the word for "camel," the camel being introduced to China during the LAC period (for which, see Schafer). In *Chan-kuo Ts'e* (戰國策), *Shan-hai Ching* (山海經), and *Shih Chi* (史記) (c. third to first cents. B.C.) the word occurs as *two-two* *tak-tak, and is written variously as 駝駝 and 橐駝; while in *Po-wu Chih* (博物志), *Yi Yuan* (異苑), and *Hou-Han Shu* (後漢書) (c. third to fourth cents. A.D.), it occurs as *luoh-two* *lak-tak (駱駝); cf. also *hwang-hwang* (皇皇) "as though gone, lost, bereft, distrait," and *parng-hwang* (written variously 彷徨, 方湟 etc.) "distrait, abstracted, in trance."

Shyh (世) "a year, a generation" and thus *shyh-shyh* "year by year, generation by generation, hereditarily."
Chyr (遲) "slow, late" and so *chyr-chyr* "by and by," as, for example, in *Chyr-chyr wu shyng yee* (遲遲吾行也) "I will be going shortly" (*Mencius* 5b.1.10).
Ryh (日) "the sun, a day" and so *ryh-ryh* "day by day."

1.2.2.2. Frequentatives and Iteratives

Words are derived by reduplication with the common class-meaning of "actions or states in a repetitive pattern, succeeding each other."

EXAMPLES

Shuh (數) "a number, many" and so *shuu-shuu* "to number, to count."
Yun (云) (cf. *yunn* (運) "to turn") and so *yun-yun* "twisting and turning."
Tah (沓) "talk, conversation" (cf. *tah* (諮) "garrulous") and so *tah-tah* "to chatter, to ramble on and on, tittle-tattle."
Hwu-suh (觳觫) "to shudder, to tremble."
Nah-nah (吶吶) "to stutter or mutter."
Bih-bih (弊弊) "to busy oneself about this and that, to fuss."
Mang-mang (芒芒) "busy about this and that, hurriedly, fussily."
Jiuann-jiuann (睊睊) "to glance from side to side."
Pwu-fwu (匍匐) "to creep, to crawl, to toddle" as, for example, in *Chyh-tzyy pwu-fwu jiang ruh jiing* (赤子匍匐將入井) "a baby crawling about about to fall into a well" (*Mencius* 3a.5.7).

1.2.2.3. Intensives

Words are derived by reduplication with the common class-meaning "in an intense degree."

EXAMPLES

Pyng (平) "level, flat" and so *pyng-pyng* "very flat."
Tsang (蒼) "the blue-green of nature" and so *tsang-tsang* "deep blue" as, for example, in *Tian jy tsang-tsang, chyi jenq seh ye* (天之蒼蒼其正色邪) "Is the deep blue of the sky its real colour?" (*Chuang* 1.4).
Charng (常) "always, constantly," and so *Yuh charng-charng erl jiann jy, guh yuan-yuan erl lai* (欲常常而見之故源源而來) "He was constantly wanting to see him, so he was for ever coming" (*Mencius* 5a.3.7).
For *yuan-yuan* "on and on" from *yuan* "a fountain or spring" and thus "perpetually, like a spring," see Similatives 1.2.2.5.

1.2.2.4. Emotive Words

Words are derived by reduplication with the common class-meaning "to experience the emotion of, to have a feeling of."

EXAMPLES

Chi (戚) "a relative, kinsfolk" and thus *chi-chi* "to have a feeling of affinity with, a sense of familiarity with, or recognition of," as in *Yu woo, shin yeou chi-chi yan* (於我心有戚戚焉) "Within me, in my heart there was a sense of familiarity with what you said" (*Mencius* 1a.7.13) (said by a Prince, who, on failing to recall his previous state of mind, had it suggested to him by another—the suggestion proffered "struck a familiar chord").

Shin (欣) "happiness" and so *shin-shin* "to feel happy" as in *Jeu shin-shin ran yeou shii seh erl shiang gaw iue*...(舉欣欣然有喜色而相告) "Everyone feeling happy, with pleased expressions turned to each other and said..." (*Mencius* 1b.1.10).

Shinq (悻) "anger" and thus *shinq-shinq* "to feel angry" as in *Jiann yu chyi jiun erl bwu show, tzer nuh. Shinq-shinq ran jiann yu chyi miann* (諫於其君而不受則怒悻悻然見於其面) "When, having remonstrated with their Prince, the Prince refuses to accept their censure, they are resentful. Feeling anger [anger] is betrayed on their faces" (*Mencius* 2b.12.7).

Yu (俞) "to agree, to concur, yes" and so *yu-yu* "to feel acquiescent, to have a feeling of acceptance with things as they are, resignation, concurring with things as they are"; as in *Wu-wei tzer yu-yu. Yu-yu jee, iou huann buh neng chu* (无爲則俞俞,俞俞者憂患不能處) "He who practises *wu-wei* ["actionless activity"] has a feeling of acceptance of things as they are. A person who feels in this way is unaffected by grief or by sorrow" (*Chuang* 33.6).

1.2.2.5. Similatives

Words are formed by reduplication with the common class-meaning of "giving the impression of, appearing to be." Such words are used metaphorically, that is, as attributes transferred from one object for which they are proper, to another to which their application is merely figurative.[17]

EXAMPLES

Jwo (濯) "to wash, to scrub, to scour" and thus *jwo-jwo* "as though scoured or washed"; used of deer in *You-luh jwo-jwo* (麀鹿濯濯) "The deer are sleek"

---

[17]Reduplicatives form a technical vocabulary in ritual literature and describe conventional postures, prescribed poses, and so on, proper in polite conduct on formal occasions. They describe "feelings" and "attitudes" which protocol requires should be simulated, and are perhaps most closely akin to the class-meaning of 1.2.2.4 and 1.2.2.5. These poses are often accompanied by symbolic gestures.

EXAMPLES

Wanq-wanq "as though gazing at some distant object" (see above), is said also to be the name of a pose proper to mourners following a coffin.

Chih-chih (仡仡) is a pose in which one appears to be terrified and struck dumb, appropriate, for example, when being ushered into the presence of a Prince.

Jiuh-jiuh (且且) is a pose in which one appears to be "awe-inspiring and majestic."

(*Mencius* 1a.2.3 quoting *Songs*); of armour in *gou-ing jwo-jwo* (鉤膺濯濯) "with accoutrements glistening" (*Songs* 259.); and of hills cropped clean by sheep, in *Ren jiann chyi jwo-jwo yee* (人見其濯濯也) "Men observing its [the mountain's] scoured-like appearance, . . ." (*Mencius* 6a.8.2).

Liang (涼) "cold" and thus *liang-liang* "as though cold to the touch, chilly, remote," as, for example, in *Shing her-wey jeu-jeu liang-liang* (行何爲踽踽涼涼) "Why was their conduct so singular, so impersonal?" (*Mencius* 7b.37.8) (here see also *jeu* (踽) "alone, single, odd" and thus *jeu-jeu* "odd-like, singular").

Tsy (孳) "to give birth to, to bear" and thus *tsy-tsy* "as though in child-labour, with great effort," as, for example, in *Ji-ming erl chii, tzy-tzy wei shann jee, Shuenn jy twu yee* (鷄鳴而起孳孳爲善者舜之徒也) "He who, rising at cock-crow, with great effort seeks to become good, is a true follower of Shun" (*Mencius* 7a.25.1); and also in *Her buh shyy bii wei kee jii-jyi erl ryh tzy-tzy yee* (何不使彼爲可幾及而日孳孳也) "Why do you not make [your teachings] attainable, so that they may be attained by daily unremitting effort?" (*Mencius* 7a.41.1).

Yeu (圉) "a prison, a corral" and thus *yeu-yeu* "as though fettered, bound," as in *Shyy, shee jy, yeu-yeu yan, shao, tzer yang-yang yan* (始舍之圉圉焉少則洋洋焉)

"When first I released it [a fish that had previously been caught] it did not move [i.e., it seemed "bound"], but after a short time it swam freely away" (*Mencius* 5a.2.9) (*yang* (洋) "the ocean" and thus "free as the ocean," in contrast to rivers and dikes which are restricted by their banks).

Wanq (望) "to gaze, to peer" and thus *wanq-wanq* "as though peering into the distance, to look through someone, aloof, disdainful," as in *Wanq-wanq ran chiuh jy, ruoh jiang meei yan* (望望然去之若將浼焉) "Disdainfully he dismissed him as though he would be defiled by him" (*Mencius* 2a.9.3).

Joong (腫) "tumour" and thus *Iong-joong* (擁腫) "as though with tumours, bumpy, uneven;" used, for example, of a tree in the sense of "knotted and gnarled": *Chyi dah been iong-joong erl bwu jonq sherng-moh* (其大本擁腫而不中繩墨) "Its great trunk being knotted and gnarled, it does not measure up to the inked-string [a carpenter's tool for drawing straight lines]" (*Chuang* 3.43).

1.2.2.6. Imitatives

Words are formed by reduplication from words imitative of sounds, with the common class-meaning "sounds and noises which are continuous repetitions" (cf. Frequentatives 1.2.2.2).

EXAMPLES

Ling-ling (令令) "tinkling of bells, jingling of jade jewels."
He-he (呵呵) "sound of laughter."
Huen-huen (混混) "sound of waves pounding, of thunder rumbling, or of drums booming" as in *Yuan-chyuan huenn-huenn, buh shee jow-yeh* (源泉混混不舍晝夜) "The fountain rumbles forth, ceasing neither day nor night" (*Mencius* 4b.18.1).

1.2.2.7. Miscellaneous Reduplicatives

Many of the (perhaps familiar or diminutive) names of animals and plants are formed by reduplication.[18]

EXAMPLES

Jiau-liau (鷦鷯) (*tsiog-liog) "the tailor-bird."
Shi-syh (犀兕) (*dzier-sier) "the rhinoceros."
Iuan-iang (鴛鴦) (*iwan-iang) "the mandarin duck."
Cf. with 1.2.2.6: *woh-woh* (鶃鶃) said to be the "noise made by geese" and its use in *shyh woh-woh jee* (是鶃鶃者) "this thing that cackles," that is, "this goose," in *Mencius* 3b.10.8.

1.2.3. Parataxis

Compound words formed by parataxis[19] are composed of single words of contrastive or similar meaning in simple or alternative connection.

1.2.3.1. Contrastive Meaning—Simple Connection

Pairs of words with contrastive meaning and in simple connection (A and B) create a class of compound words with the class-meaning "denoting a generic or abstract concept." Each member denotes a species of which the resulting compound word is the generic name, or concrete instances of which the resulting compound word is the abstraction.

EXAMPLES

Tian-dih (天地) /sky/earth/ "the universe."
Tsao-muh (草木) /grass/trees/ "vegetation, flora generally."
Guei-jeu (規矩) /arcs/squares/"measuring gauges," and in metaphorical and specialized senses "criteria of behaviour, good manners."
Horng-yann (鴻鴈) /swan/goose/"wildfowl generally."
Jin-fuu (斤斧) /kind of axe/kind of axe/"axes generally."
Kuenn-kuu (困苦) /restraint/bitter/"suffering generally."
Fuh-day (負戴) /carry on back/carry on head/ "to carry (generally)."

---

[18] In Modern Chinese many animals have a familiar name, formed by prefixing *lao* "old," as, for example, *lao-huu* "tiger"; *lao-diau* "kite"; *lao-gua* "crow"; *lao-ing* "eagle." (See Chao (2), p. 40.)

[19] The terms "parataxis" and "hypotaxis" as used in this work designate a relationship between words as elements in the formation of compound words and syntagmas. In parataxis the meaning reference of both elements is primary and immediate. In hypotaxis, by contrast, the relationship imposes upon one element a modification of meaning reference by virtue of its juxtaposition to the other. The meaning of one element, therefore, is secondary or derived.

Gwo-jia (國家) /feudal city or state/feudal estate/ "a Feudal State," "the State."
Daw-luh (道路) /highway/connecting road/"roads generally."
Shiong-dih (兄弟) /older brother/younger brother/"brothers."
Fuh-muu (父母) /father/mother/"parent, parents."

1.2.3.2. Contrastive Meaning—Alternative Connection

Pairs of words with contrastive meaning and in alternative connection (A or B) create a class of compound words with the class-meaning "denoting an abstraction." The contrastive meaning in this class is usually antonymic in some sense.

EXAMPLES

Chyr-suh (遲速) /late/early/"appointed time."
Gau-bei (高卑) /high/low/"height."
Charng-doan (長短) /long/short/"length."
Ching-jonq (輕重) /light/heavy/"weight."
Yih-torng (異同) /difference/similarity/"difference."
Shyng-jyy (行止) /go/stop/"advancement, progress."
Pyn-fuh (貧富) /poor/rich/"financial circumstances."
Duo-goa (多寡) /much/little/"quantity, amount."

1.2.3.3. Identical Meaning—Simple Connection (tautological hendiadys)

Pairs of words with identical or similar meaning in simple connection create a class of compound words, tactically interchangeable with either member used singly. This form is rare in LAC and appears to be used *metri causa*.

EXAMPLES

Huan-yaw (歡樂) /enjoy/enjoy/"enjoy."
Faa-liuh (法律) "law."
An-jinq (安靖) "peace, to pacify."
Chiin-woh (寢臥) "to sleep."
Jyh-huey (智慧) "wisdom."

1.2.3.4. Partial Identity of Meaning—Simple Connection (morphological hendiadys)

Pairs of words with identical or similar meaning, but which vary in the total extensions and intensions of their meanings, create a class of compound words the meaning of which is confined to that of the meanings shared in common by its elements.

EXAMPLES

Li-saan (離散) "dispersed" from *li* "to leave, depart from, *dispersed*, separated, divided" and *saan* "loose, broken up, *dispersed*, scattered."

Shih-leei (係累) "to bind as with chains, ropes, etc." from *shih* "*bind*, connect, succeed" and *leei* "*bind*, involve, implicate, embarrass, accumulate, augment."
Chuh-tih (怵惕) "apprehensive" from *chuh* "fear, *apprehension*, timidity, shy" and *tih* "fear, *apprehension*, awe, respect, reverence."

1.2.4. Hypotaxis

Compound words formed by hypotaxis[20] fall into two sub-classes, depending upon whether the modifying term precedes or follows the term it modifies. The tactical processes are identical with those employed in syntagma (see 2.6: Determination), and with those governing the relationship of the verb and its post-posited elements (see 3.4: Post-verbal Elements) and are described in detail later. The two classes are determinative compounds where the modifying element precedes, and directive compounds where the modifying element follows the modified element.

EXAMPLES

Determinative Compounds
Tian-shiah (天下) /sky/below/"the world, the world of men, society."
Dah-fu (大夫) /great/individual/"a nobleman."
Ju-hour (諸候) /various/marquises/"the Feudatory."
Fu-nau (膚橈) /skin/disturb/"to flinch."
Muh-taur (目逃) /eye/jump/"to blink."

Directive Compounds
Dang-luh (當路) /hit upon/road/"to achieve an ambition" (more specifically "to obtain official preferment").
Wei-gwo (爲國) /control/state/"to govern, to obtain the government."
Chyong-faa (窮髮) /impoverished of/hair [i.e., growth]/"the tundra."
Sha-ren (殺人) /kill/man/"murder" as in *sha-ren jy tzuey* (殺人之罪) "the crime of murder" (*Mencius* 1b 2.5).

1.3. Words and Grammatical Word-classes

The two main classes among words described in 1.1.1 (cenematic and plerematic words) are divided into sub-classes as follows:

1.3.1. Classes of Cenematic Words

Cenematic words are classed as: (1) *particles* when their function is to indicate a tactical relationship between plerematic words in syntagma or between elements in the sentence (see, e.g., the particles of co-ordination (2.5), the particle of determination (2.6.2) in syntagma, and the particles of the second post-verbal position (3.4), the particles of the instrumental (3.6), etc.) in the verbal sentence; (2) *grammatical determinants* when their function is to impose gram-

---
[20]See 1.2.3 footnote 19.

matical quality upon the word they determine (see, e.g., the determinants of mood (3.3.1) and of aspect (3.3.2) in the verbal syntagma, and the determinants of number (2.6.4.4), and the determinants of pronominal possession (2.6.4.1) in the substantival syntagma); (3) *conjunctions* when their function is to indicate a tactical relationship between elements at the level of sentential distribution (see 5.1 ff.); and (4) *substitutes* when their function is to substitute for plerematic words (see 6.1 ff.).

1.3.2. Plerematic Words and Grammatical Word-classes

No word-classes are set up for plerematic words (see Introduction v.a). Grammatical quality is said to be imposed upon the plerematic word when in distribution, since it is useful to proceed as though any plerematic word may occur in any type of distribution in which a cenematic word is not found.[21]

Undistributed, a plerematic word might be said to represent a notion undifferentiated by grammatical quality[22] and it is the syn-

---

[21]This is not to say that a statistical statement of *actual* occurrences would not be useful or meaningful, but that for the purposes of this work such a task would be not only formidable and time-consuming, but also unnecessary. Kennedy has undertaken some important statistical work of this kind upon the text of *Mencius*. He observes (Kennedy (1), p. 1), "The project had proceeded upon the assumption that word-classes can and must be defined before the relationship between words can be grammatically treated. It has now reached the conclusion that in the final analysis word-classes cannot be defined, hence that Chinese grammar must start from different premises." The procedural assumption in this work is that any plerematic word may occur in any form of distribution. In practice it is not difficult to isolate certain words that do not occur in all the types of distribution identified. But the number of words that are tactically ambivalent is sufficient (as Kennedy has shown) to make a classification by word-classes, at this stage, uneconomical as a grammatical analytical device.

[22]It might be useful to speak about the "field of meaning" of a word. For example, the word *yeu* (與), the sign for which depicts two pairs of hands holding a (?) tray (?) boat, has the basic notion of "association, togetherness, exchange." In context, and without formal change, *yeu* occurs with the meanings "an association, a caucus, an ally," "to associate with, accompany, join with, or ally oneself to" and in cenematic usage "particle of simple connection in syntagma" (A *and* B). Like the word *show* (授) the sign for which has common features with the sign for *yeu* (see Tarng Lan (1), p. 47) *yeu* means "to receive, to accept, to concede," and causatively "to grant, to bestow." If its "field of meaning" is said to cover "association and interchange" unencumbered by grammatical assignation, then selectivity within that field of meaning, and the imposition of grammatical quality, may be said to be environmentally determined, and not inherently present.

Verbal Sentence

Sentential elements	T/P	Agent		Verb		First Post-verbal Position γ¹	Second Post-verbal Position γ²	References
Syntagmatic elements	Det.	α	Dist.	Det.	β			
1	[—]	國			慕	之		Mencius 4a.6.1
2	[—]	齊人			得	之		Mencius 3b.6.2
3					正			Analects 5.19
4				[—]	正	君		Mencius 4a.21.2
5			孰	能	定	之		Mencius 1a.6.2
6					治		于[—]	Mencius 1a.6.2
7	[—]/[—]				亂		[—]邦	Mencius 3b.9.2

Determinative Sentence

	DT		Dt	References
8	晉之乘楚之檮杌魯之春秋	[—]	也	Mencius 4b.21.2
9	能不龜手	[—]	也	Chuang 3.40

tactical situation, rather than any inherent grammatical meaning, that invests the word with that quality.

1.3.3. Grammatical Quality and Plerematic Words

Environmental classes in which plerematic words occur are divided into two main classes and given the grammatical value nominal and verbal. The classes are mutually exclusive, and are characterized (*i*) by classes of cenematic words which occur as elements within them (the classes of such cenematic words are also mutually exclusive classes); (*ii*) by classes of distribution as elements in the sentence. Thus, when verbal quality is imposed upon a word, the word so governed will occur in a word-group (the verbal syntagma) with determinants of mood and of aspect, and will occur as an element in the sentence in a characteristic position (e.g., pre-posed by instrumental and agential word-groups, and post-posed by elements with particles occurring exclusively in that position). When nominal quality is imposed the word so governed will occur in prescribed elements in the sentence and will be governed by an exclusive class of cenematic words.

Verbal quality is classified as transitive and intransitive, and by voice into active, passive, and causative. These classes are characterized by contrastive varieties of distribution of the post-posited elements.

Nominal quality distinguishes proper names (which are never used as determined terms—see 2.6.3.2) and common nouns.[23] Among

---

[23]The varieties of grammatical quality imposed environmentally upon a word can be illustrated by setting out a series of the occurrences of *i* (—) "one" arranged by types of distribution.

The varieties of distribution of *i* are not exhausted in this schema, but in it *i* occurs as a number determinant "one," and thus "one instance of, one" (example 2: "If one man from Ch'i taught him..."); "an indefinite instance of, an, another" (example 3: "arriving in another State"); "many conceived of as one, the whole, the entire" (example 1: "the entire state desires him"); "of one species, similar" (example 8: "The Ch'eng of Tsin, the T'ao-wu of Ch'u, and the Ch'un Ch'iu of Lu are works of a similar kind"); "of one piece, identical" (example 9: "The ability, on the part of both parties, not to get their hands chapped, was identical"); "one occasion," and thus "once, as soon as" (example 4: "As soon as the ruler is corrected..."); and "one moment, one moment," "Now...Now..." (example 7: "now well governed, now in disorder"); "to make one, to unite, to unify" (example 5: "Which ruler can unite it, [i.e., the world]"); and "made as one, united, unity, unification" (example 6: "It will be pacified by unification"). As a sentential element or as the principal term in a sentential element i has the value T/P, Dt, and γ^2 (in this work assigned the grammatical quality of *nominal*), and β (in this work

common nouns are distinguished (when used in the determinative position), nouns of attribute and of genus (see 2.6.2).

---

assigned the grammatical quality of *verbal*); as an element in syntagma *i* occurs as the determinant element (grammatical value nominal) and as the determinant element of the class "grammatical determinants" (of number) in a nominal syntagma, and (of aspect) in the verbal syntagma.

II. Syntagma

2.1. Introduction

"Syntagma" is a unit intermediate between "word" and "sentence." The elements of the clause or sentence may be either "words" (single morpheme or free words, or compound words) or groupings of words which are interchangeable syntactically with "words" as elements in the clause or sentence. In observing the distributional behaviour of the elements of the sentence, therefore, some unit is required that takes account of this feature of the language. For word-groups at this analytical level the term "syntagma" is employed. The levels of distribution recognized may be represented as follows:

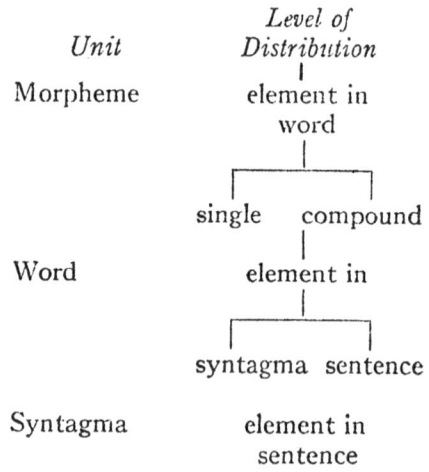

The word thus operates as an element at two levels, that is, singly as an element in the sentence, or in groups as elements in syntagma. Syntagma operates at one level only, that is, as elements in the sentence.

A syntagma is constructed by syntactical rules peculiar to syntagma and to compound words, and has particles peculiar to it ("syntagmatic particles"). Such rules are called "syntagmatic," the unit "a syntagma" and the grammatical phenomenon in general "syntagma." In this description the term "syntax" is hereafter reserved to describe the relationships between sentential units, and "syntagma" for the relationships of words in tactical word-groups.

2.2. Morphological Functions of Syntagma

Syntagma is a morphological process. The plerematic word undistributed may represent a very broad "field of meaning" (see 1.3.2 footnote 22) and is uncommitted to grammatical quality (see 1.3.2). In syntagma it is invested with both material modifications in meaning and with certain grammatical qualities (i.e., it becomes "committed"). The processes of formation of syntagmas are the same as those used for compound words (1.2). Syntagmas differ from compound words in being spontaneous groupings, or groupings made as it were *ad hoc* in contrast to the customary groupings of compound words. Unlike compound words they are not institutionalized within the language and given specialized meanings (see 1.2).

2.2.1. Syntagma and the Rule of Economy

It is a peculiarity of the language that many of the modifications (both material and grammatical) made not only at the syntagma, but also at other levels, are not made of prescriptive necessity. In syntagma, therefore, a verb *may* be invested with both mood and aspect, or a noun be invested with number, but the language is not governed by rules which make such indications matters of required or prescribed usage. A word may, therefore, occur without such qualification and is then said to be "uncommitted" or "neutral" (for example, to mood or aspect or number). Propositions occur in the language stated at a high level of generality and uncommittedness in this regard. Such particularities are introduced only when they are thought to be material to the sense of the information to be conveyed. Similar economy is employed in the use of particles. A particle which in this description is stated to be "characteristic of" or "diagnostic of" a given structure, does not necessarily always occur (as a matter of prescription) in that structure. The statement must be taken to mean that the particle will occur, and be characteristic, only when a minimum of economy is employed, but that when economy is employed the particle may be dropped. In other words, the particle will occur in the paradigm, though not always in the structure as encountered in usage in the material. This feature of the language is here called the rule of economy.[1]

In syntagma, therefore, many grammatical features may be intro-

---

[1] See Introduction (v.d) for a fuller discussion of the rule of economy. Illustrations of the rule in practice will be found in 2.5, 2.6.2, 2.6.2 footnote 7, 2.6.3, 2.6.3.3, 2.7.1, 3.1, 3.3, 3.3.1.4, 3.4, etc.

duced, but are not introduced obligatorily, and particles restricted to syntagma may (though not always) be present.²

2.3. Syntagmas and Grammatical Quality

With one exception all syntagmas are given the grammatical quality or value of *nominal*. The exception is the syntagma occurring as β in the verbal sentence (see 3.3). For economy in nomenclature, therefore, the term "a syntagma" without further qualification will be used hereafter for "nominal syntagma," but for the exception mentioned above the term "verbal syntagma" will be used consistently.

2.4. The Processes of Syntagmatic Formation

Syntagmas are formed by parataxis and hypotaxis (see 1.2.3 and 1.2.4). Sub-classes of formation are distinguished among these two major classes by formal features.

2.5. The Parataxical Syntagma

The parataxical syntagma may be formed from two words or groups of words, in simple connection (A together with B) or in alternative connection (A or B) (conventional symbol A + B, and A/B). When syntagmatic particles are used, the sub-classes are differentiated formally. Without particles (i.e., stated with economy; see 2.2.1) the sub-classes are not formally distinguished. The syntagmatic particles of parataxis are (for simple connection) *yeu* (與) (*zio), or *jyi* (及) (*g'iəp),³ and (for alternative connection) *ruoh* (若) (*ńiak).⁴ In the parataxical syntagma both elements are given the value *nominal*.

EXAMPLES

(*a*) Simple connection—no particle
Ren yih (仁義) "humanity and justice" (*Mencius* 1a.1.5).
Shang shiah (上下) "superiors and inferiors" (e.g., *Mencius* 1a.1.3) "major and minor powers" (e.g., *Tso* 318.10), etc.
Tair chyr neau show (臺池鳥獸) "towers, fishpools, birds and beasts" (*Mencius* 1a.2.6).

---

²Cf. Emeneau (1), p. 208, on the use of *mà* in Annamite: "The degree of arbitrariness of selection of any particular word in this language seems amazingly great to those who are accustomed to the obligatoriness of the categories carried by morphological systems, and the amount of free option exercised by speakers in choosing to use *mà* is undoubtedly only one example of this feature of the language."

³Karlgren (1) observes that *jyi* (及) does not occur in this usage in *Analects* and *Mencius* (p. 40), or in *Chuang-tzu* (p. 58).

⁴*Ru* (如) occurs in *Analects* (two occurrences in 11.24) in a similar sense.

(b) Alternative connection—no particle

Ryh yueh chu yii (日月出矣) "when *the sun or the moon* comes out" (*Chuang* 2.22).
Fey shing tswen wang huen ming (廢興存亡昏明) "dismissal or promotion, preservation or destruction, obscurity or recognition" (*Tso* 318.13).
Syy shii wu chu shiang (死徙無出鄉) "on *an occasion of death, or of a change in residence* they [the serfs] should not leave the village" (*Mencius* 3a.3.18).

(c) Simple connection with syntagmatic particle

Tiing yeu renn (梃與刃) "a cudgel and a knife" (*Mencius* 1a.4.1).
Dih tzyy yeu chern (弟子與臣) "younger brothers, sons and subjects" (*Micius* 22.9).
Guu jy ren yeu min (古之人與民) "men of ancient times and the commoners" (*Mencius* 1a.2.5).
Sonq jyi Jenq pyng (宋及鄭平) "*The States of Sung and Cheng* made peace" (*Tso* 15.24).
Jaw-menq jyi Tzyy-shii meng (趙孟及子皙盟) "*Chao-meng and Tzu-hsi* swore a solemn covenant" (*Tso* 316.23).

(d) Alternative connection with syntagmatic particle

Biing-tzyy ruoh ren-wu (丙子若壬午) "the *pingtzu or the jenwu* day" (*Tso* 393.20).
Chiing wei Ling ruoh Lih (請為靈若厲) "I request that my [posthumous name] might be *Ling or Li*" (*Tso* 277.11).
Chiing jiun ruoh tay-tzyy lai (請君若太子來) "I beg *you sir, or your eldest son* to come" (*Tso* 495.7).
Yeu and *jyi* occur together in *Gong yeu dah-fu jyi Jeu-tzyy meng* (公與大夫及莒子盟) "The Duke and his great officers and the Viscount of Chü swore a solemn covenant" (*Tso* 305.14).

2.6. The Hypotaxical Syntagma

The hypotaxical syntagma may be of two classes, the first the *determinative* (see 2.6.1 ff.) and the second the *directive* (see 2.6.5).

2.6.1. Determinative

The determinative syntagma may be formed from two or more words or groups of words. The final word is modified in meaning-reference by all words that precede it. (Conventional symbol A→B or A(A→B)→B etc.) The grammatical value given to its elements is nominal.[5] The structure most frequently occurring in the material is A→B, for example, *dah been* (大本) "great trunk," but A(A→B)→B, for example, *lin gwo jy jenq* (鄰國之政) /neighbour/states/→/government/ "the governments of neighbouring states," is almost as frequent, and more complex structures occur such as A(A→B(A→B

[5] An important observation must be made here about nominal usage in LAC. A word used nominally denominates indifferently both *species* and *a specimen* or

specimens of the species. Thus, *ren* (人) in nominal usage is indifferently "homo sapiens," "man" as a species, or "a man, the man, men" as a specimen or specimens of the species. It is not merely that number (the difference between one, two, or more than two instances of) is not differentiated, but that both class and member are comprised within the one term. Certain of these distinctions are imposed in determination, and the noun is then said to be "committed"; otherwise it remains neutral in its indications as to these distinctions. A noun determined by, for example, a numeral or a unit of measure becomes immediately "an enumerated instance of" or "a quantified unit of" the thing it signifies. In a later stage of the language (as a common feature, post-Hann; see Yang Bor-jiunn 4.29), between numeral and noun is interposed one of a class of words with the class-meaning "a numerable instance of" or "quantified unit of." (For a detailed description see Gau (1), p. 347 ff.) For example, LAC has *yih maa* (一馬) "one horse" and Modern Standard Chinese has *yih pi maa* (一匹馬) "one horse" (the interposed *pi* being a word of the class "a numerable instance of" and is used for "horses" and "cloth," the latter in the sense "one, two, or more pieces of cloth").

The lack of distinction between class and member ("universal" and "particular") and between numbered and unnumbered members in the noun is a linguistic feature of which logicians of the LAC period were well aware, as the following propositions show:

(1) *Yih maa maa yee* (一馬馬也).
(2) *Ell maa maa yee* (二馬馬也).
(3) *Maa syh tzwu jee, yih maa erl syh tzwu yee, fei leang maa erl syh tzwu yee* (馬四足者一馬而四足也非兩馬而四足也).
(4) *Yih maa maa yee* (一馬馬也).
(5) *Maa huoh bair jee, ell maa erl huoh bair yee, fei yih maa erl huoh bair* (馬或白者二馬而或白也非一馬而或白).

(1) "Any given horse [unnumbered particular] is of the class horse [universal]."
(2) "Any two horses [numbered particular] are of the class horse [universal]."
(3) "But in the proposition 'horses have four feet,' four feet is a property of any given horse [unnumbered particular] and not a property of two horses as such [numbered particular]."
(4) "Any given horse is of the class horse."
(5) "But in the proposition 'some horses are white' white is the property of some horses [numbered or distributed particulars] and not of any given horse [unnumbered or undistributed particular]" (*Micius* 78.28).

In the above, the word *maa* occurs undetermined, as universal in (1), as an unnumbered particular in (3), and as a numbered or distributed particular in (5). But in formal restatement as logical propositions, these three distinctions may be made by determination, that is, *yih maa* (an unnumbered particular), *ell maa* (numbered particulars), *maa huo* (distributed particulars—of necessity numbered).

(I take it that the use of *yih maa* contra *ell maa* is technical here, and is not a distinction between singular and plural, but between differentiated and undifferentiated number. On "One is no number in East and West," see Solomon (1).)

(A→B)))→B, that is, *shann wei buh jiun shoou jy yaw* (善為不龜手之藥) /effective/cause to become/not/chapped/hands/→/medicine/ "an effective salve for preventing chapped hands" (*Chuang* 2.38). No attempt is made here to enumerate all occurring structures, but all structures have the common feature "proceeding from greatest degree of specificness to greatest degree of generality."[6] The elements of a determinative syntagma (A→B) are designated (at A) *determinant word*, and (at B) *determined word*.

2.6.2. The Determinant Word

The determinant word (A in the structure A→B) may be used in one of two classes of nominal usage (excepting here the classes described in 2.6.4 ff.). In the first class, the determinant word denominates the *species-class* to which the determined word is said to pertain, and in the second class it denominates an *attribute* in which the determined word is said to partake. The *particle of determination*[7] *jy* (之) (*tiəg) (conventional symbol →) has the possibility of occurrence only in the first class.

EXAMPLES
Class 1 (without particle)
Gong minq (公命) "a ducal decree" (*Tso* 142.24).
Wang daw (王道) "the Way of Kings" (*Mencius* 1a.3.8).
Ren chyng (人情) "the feelings of men" (*Chuang* 2.28).
Gwo-du (國都) "State capitals" (*Micius* 25.12).
Class 1 (with particle)
Guu jy ren (古之人) "men of antiquity" (*Mencius* 1b.10.3).
Shian wang jy daw (先王之道) "the way of the Former Kings" (*Mencius* 4a.1.3).

---

[6] A useful pedagogical device is to proceed in construing from the final element backwards as follows (taking the example above from *Chuang*): medicine—medicine for the hands—medicine for causing non-chapping of hands—effective medicine for causing non-chapping of hands.

[7] The occurrence, or possibility of occurrence (see 2.2.1), of the particle of determination distinguishes the first from the second class. No mutually exclusive word-classes can be set up by this criteria. "Gods," "Dukes," and "Kings" share a common class-meaning, but in the examples given *gong minq* is "the decree of a Duke" and not "a decree with ducal attributes," *wang daw* is "the way of a King" and not "ways with regal attributes"; conversely *shern ren* are "men with godlike attributes" and not "men of the gods," that is, "gods." *Yee maa* is "a wild [i.e., untamed] horse" (*yee* "the country-side, wild places," and thus "having the attributes of wild places," "uncultivated," "wild") but *Yee ren* (野人) are "men of the country-side" but not "wild men." *Guu jy ren* are "men of antiquity" but not "antique men." One and the same word may thus operate in both classes. The class in which it is operating is formally determined by the occurrence or otherwise of the particle of determination.

Tian-tzyy jy minq (天子之命) "a decree of the Son of Heaven" (*Tso* 101.1).
Ren jy chyng (人之情) "the feelings of men" (*Mencius* 6a.8.7).

Class 2
Feir row (肥肉) "fat meat" (*Mencius* 1a.4.2).
Shern ren (神人) "spiritual men" (*Chuang* 90.3.).[8]
Yee maa (野馬) "wild horses" (*Chuang* 1.4).
Dah been (大本) "the great trunk" (*Chuang* 3.43).
Nan-wuh (難物) "troublesome things, difficulties" (*Micius* 23.16).

2.6.3. The Determinant Word—Possessive

No formal difference is made between categorical determinations (B of the class A) and determinations of possession (B possessed by A). So that, for example, *Ren jy jyi* (人之疾) may indifferently mean "[this particular] man's disease" and "the diseases of man."[9] In the first class described in 2.6.2 must be included, therefore:

With particle
Ren jy jyi (人之疾) "a man's illness" (*Micius* 21.2).
Tzyy-muh jy shinn (子木之信) "the integrity of Tzu-mu" (*Tso* 339.2).
Feng shyh jy tiau (豐氏之祧) "The Ancestral Temple of the Feng Family" (*Tso* 338.18).

Without particle
Tian chyr (天池) "The Fishpool of Heaven" (*Chuang* 1.2).
Min lih (民力) "the labour of the people" (*Mencius* 1a.2.4).
Lin gwo (鄰國) "the States of neighbouring rulers" (*Mencius* 1a.3.2).
Yang jeau (羊角) "ram's horns" used in specialized sense "spirals" (*Chuang* 1.14).

2.6.3.1. The Determinant Word (quasi attributes)

Words describing the tools of or the materials pertaining to a vocation are used as determinant words in formations creating vocational names (no particle).

EXAMPLES
Yuh-ren (玉人) /Jade/man/"a lapidary" (*Mencius* 1b.9.3).
Goan-ren (館人): /Hostel/man/"a hostel-keeper" (*Tso* 338.18).
Muh-gong (木工): /wood/workman/"carpenter" (*Li Chi, Chiu Lii* 2.2).
Shyy-ren (矢人): /arrow/man/"an arrowmaker" (*Mencius* 2a.7.1).
Harn-ren (函人): /armour/man/"an armourer" (*Mencius* 2a.7.1).

---

[8]*Shern ren* also occurs as a parataxical syntagma "Gods and men," for example, in *Tso* passim.

[9]However, the difference between "specific" and "generalized" is usually clear in a given context.

Words describing the materials of which objects are made are used as determinant words with the class-meaning "made of...."

EXAMPLES

Pyi guan (皮冠) "a fur cap" (*Mencius* 5b.7.10).
Jin guu (金鼓) "a bronze drum" (*Tso* 120.5).
Muh ji (木雞) "a chicken carved in wood" (*Chuang* 50.48).

2.6.3.2. The Determined Word

Except where committed (e.g., by determination by a numeral) the determined word is neutral as to number. It is also formally uncommitted to specific and generalized reference (see 2.6.3), such references usually being contextually deducible in a given instance. Proper names never occur as a determined word in a determinative syntagma, except as the elements in the composition of a compound proper name.[10] In such compositions the order of determination is place name[11]/family name/personal names/rank or title.[12]

EXAMPLES

Liang Huey Wang (梁惠王) = *Liang* "Name of State Capital" u.f. "Name of State"/*Huey* given name/*wang* title "King," and thus "King Huey of the State of Liang."
Menq-tzyy (孟子) = *Menq* proper name/*tzyy* title of nobility ("viscount") and in depreciated sense "title of respect," "Master," "Sir," etc., and thus "Master Meng."
Jenq Tzyy-chaan (鄭子產) "Tzū-ch'an of the State of Cheng."

---

[10] A rare exception is the use of a proper name in a generic sense, for example, *Mencius* 3b.6.4, which speaks of "Shiue Jiu-jou" (薛居州) in the plural, "If everyone were Shiue Jiu-jou[s]" and of "a Shiue Jiu-jou,"; in the sense of "a man of the class or type of Shiue Jiu-jou."

[11] With possibility of occurrence of determinative particle *jy* between place name and family name but not elsewhere.

[12] A variant of this determining order occurs, for example, in the titles of the Premiers of Ch'u, where it is "place/title/personal name," as in *Chuu Linq-yiin Tzyy-yuan* (楚令尹子元) "Tzu-yuan, the Premier of Ch'u," and as in references to the sons of Dukes and Kings, in which the title *wang-tzyy* (王子) "prince," *tay-tzyy* (太子) "heir apparent," and *gong-tzyy* (公子) "Duke's son" occur before the personal name. Fraser and Lockhart (1), s.v., say of *gong-tzyy* "practically a surname," and *wang-suen* (王孫) "King's grandson," "a surname." A number of Chinese family names derive from titles of rank and of official position (at one time held hereditarily), and such titles may have been borne as family names, in which case this would not be a variant.

Chuu Ling-yiin (楚令尹) "The Premier of Ch'u."
Sonq Tzuoo-shy (宋左師) "the Master of the Left of the State of Sung."

2.6.3.3. Determination and Spatial Relations

Plerematic words with the class-meaning "denoting a spatial relationship"[13] occur both as determinant and as determined words. As determinant words they are attributive (no particle).

EXAMPLES

Dong-yi (東夷) "The Eastern Barbarians" (*Mencius* 4b.1.1).
Jong-gwo (中國) "The Central States" (*Mencius* 3a.4.28).
Shi-men (西門) "The West Gate" (*Tso* 232.19).
Way-ren (外人) "Outsiders" (*Mencius* 3b.9.1).
Nan-hae (南海) "The Southern Sea" (*Chuang* 44.58).

As determined words they provide, in syntagma, for certain particulars of direction that the directive particle *yu* (於) (see 3.4) does not distinguish.[14] The determining order is "object in relation to which the spatial position exists/the spatial relation." The particle of determination may occur.

EXAMPLES

Shi-men jy way (西門之外)/in relation to the West Gate, the beyond space/that is, "beyond the West Gate" (*Tso* 232.20).
Fern-shoei jy yang (汾水之陽) "on the sunny side [i.e., the side facing south] of the Fen River" (*Chuang* 2.35).
Chyong-faa jy beei (窮髮之北)/in relation to the Tundra, north/that is, "North of the Tundra" (*Chuang* 1.13).
Syh-hae jy ney (四海之內) "within the Four Seas" (in specialized sense "the world") (*Mencius* 3b.5.6).
The particle may be omitted:
Tian-shiah (天下) "under the sky" that is, "the world" (*Mencius* 1a.3.13).
Sheng-shanq (牲上) "upon the sacrifice" (*Tso* 339.10).
Jao shanq (沼上) "at the pool" (*Mencius* 1a.2.1).
Her-dong (河東) "east of the [Yellow] River" (place name) (*Mencius* 1a.3.1).

[13] That is, *shanq* (上) "top," *shiah* (下) "bottom," *ney* (內) "inside," *way* (外) "outside," *jong* (中) "middle"; the four directions, viz. *beei* (北) "north," *nan* (南) "south," *dong* (東) "east," and *shi* (西) "west"; *yang* (陽) "the sunlit side," and *in* (陰) "the shady side."

[14] *Yu* is not committed to such distinctions as "upon, within, in, at, on" but is indicative of general direction only. Certain of these distinctions are made by the use of the syntagma type here described. (See 3.4 and 3.4.4, footnote 27.)

2.6.4. Determinant Words with Grammatical Class-meanings

Four classes are distinguished among determinant words which are used either exclusively as determinant words (e.g., the determinant forms of the pronouns and demonstratives) or with grammatical implications (e.g., the numerals since they impose grammatical number). These are: (1) *pronominal determinants* (see 2.6.4.1); (2) *demonstrative determinants* (see 2.6.4.2); (3) *privatives* (see 2.6.4.3); (4) *determinants of number* (see 2.6.4.4); and (5) *determinants of collectivity and restriction* (see 2.6.4.5).

2.6.4.1. Pronominal Determinant Words

The personal non-status pronouns (see 6.2) are *woo* (我) *ngâ (person or persons speaking) and *ruu* (汝 or 女) *ńio (person or persons addressed). These never[15] occur as determinant words and are replaced by *wu* (吾) *ngo (for person(s) speaking) and *eel* (爾) *ńiar, with variants *erl* (而)[16] *niəg and *nae* (乃) *nəg (for person(s) addressed). The anaphoric pronoun *jy* (之) *tiəg (see 3.8) is similarly replaced by *chyi* (其) *kiəg as a determinant word in syntagma.[17]

EXAMPLES

Wu gwo (吾國) "my state" (*Mencius* 1a.1.1).
Wu shen (吾身) "our-selves" (*Mencius* 1a.1.3).
Eel lih (爾力) "your strength" (*Mencius* 5b.1.15).
Eel choou (爾醜) "your ugliness" (*Chuang* 42.7).
Erl tzuu (而祖) "your ancestor" (*Tso* 183.8).
Nae shiun (乃勳) "your merit" (*Tso* 105.15).
Nae jyr (乃職) "your duties" (*Tso* 105.16).

---

[15]Blunting in the distinction between determinant and pregnant forms occurs somewhat after the LAC period for pronouns, though sporadic examples of earlier blunting occur (see Karlgren (1), p. 50). Leu Shwu-shiang (see Leu (1), p. 181) gives examples of blunting in the use of *chyi* by Han times, and observes that "only Pre-Chin literature [i.e., prior to the end of the third cent. BC] provides correct models for the use of *chyi*."

[16]Jou Faa-gau (Jou (4), p. 249) points out that *erl* (而) is the determinant form used in Eastern Chou bronze inscriptions, and suggests as an etymology for the determinant form, an allegro form of *ruu jy* (汝之), that is, of the pregnant form of the pronoun plus the particle of determination *jy*. See Appendix 3 for a note on the relative roles of *ruu* and *eel*.

[17]The EAC form of the determinant anaphoric pronoun is *jyue* (厥) *kiwat. It is supplanted by *chyi* in MAC and LAC. It occurs sporadically in LAC (e.g. in *Tso*) and is then archaistic (See Jou (1).) *Jyue* in EAC has been treated at length by Karlgren (5) and Bodman (2). For a description of the tendency to archaism in the pronouns of Modern Chinese, see Demiéville (2).

Chyi min (其民) "their peoples" (*Mencius* 1a.5.5).
Chyi tair (其臺)) "his tower" (*Mencius* 1a.2.4).
Chyi dah been (其大本) "its great trunk" (*Chuang* 3.43).

Where status relationships are involved (see 6.2), status determinant words, self-deprecatory on the part of the speaker, and adulatory towards the person addressed, are substituted for the non-status personal pronouns.

EXAMPLES

Goa, "single, lonely," etc. and so, *goa-jiun* (寡君) "my ruler" (*Tso* 11.4); *goa dah-fu* (寡大夫) "our nobles" (*Tso* 338.15); *goa-ren* (寡人)/lonely/person/"I, myself" (used by kings; passim).
Bih "worn-out, tattered"; *bih yih* (敝邑) "our city" (*Tso* 257.16); *bih fuh* (敝賦) "our levies" (*Tso* 418.2).
Dah "great, large"; *dah gwo* (大國) "your State" (*Tso* 350.19).

2.6.4.2. Demonstrative Determinant Words

The demonstratives are deictic in type and distinguish relative nearness to the point of reference. They are *tsyy* (此) *ts'iar "this" and *bii* (彼) *pia "that" (see 6.3). The demonstratives occur as determinant words, as, for example, *tsyy jyi* (此極) "these extremities" (*Mencius* 1b.1.7); *tsyy shyr* (此時) "at this time" (*Mencius* 2a.1.15); *bii min* (彼民) "those people" (*Mencius* 5a.3.7); but more commonly the determinant function is restricted to determinant forms. These are *sy* (斯) *sieg, *jy* (之) *tiəg which occur only as determinant forms, and *shyh* (是) *dieg occurring in both forms, but predominantly as the determinant form. (In such customary formations as *shyh-yii* (是以) "for this reason" and *shyh-guh* (是故) "therefore" *shyh* predominates, *tsyy* rarely occurs.[18])

[18] Blunting of the distinction between determinant and pregnant forms of the demonstratives takes place somewhat earlier than in the case of the pronouns (see 2.6.4.1, footnote 15). In individual works, the following have been noted. (*a*) Determinant *jy* is almost entirely restricted to *Chuang Tzu* in LAC but is regular in the Oracle Bones (noted by Jou (1), p. 1). (*b*) *Sy* does not occur in *Tso* in determinant usage (noted by Karlgren (1), p. 39). (*c*) *Tsyy* does not occur in *Analects* (Dr. A. C. Graham in a personal communication). Dr. David Hawkes (in a personal communication) informs me that in *Ch'uu Tsyr* the pregnant forms are *tzy* (茲) in *Li Sao*, and *shyh* in *Chiu Chang*, and the determinant forms are *tsyy* in *Li Sao*, *tsyy*, *tzy* and *sy* in *Chiu Chang* and *tsyy* in *Chiu Pien*. The important observation is that here (as with the pronouns) contrast (irrespective of the nature of the contrast) marks the two forms. In my own material it is between forms with a common point of articulation in the initial *t— *d— *s—/ *ts— and contrast in the vowel *a/*eə. We may have here dialectical differences (the view of Karlgren (1), passim),

EXAMPLES

Shyh yeh (是夜) "this night" (*Tso* 316.23).
Shyh shin (是心) "these thoughts" (*Mencius* 1a.7.6).
Sy min (斯民) "these people" (*Mencius* 1a.4.5).
Sy shyr (斯時) "this time" (*Mencius* 5a.4.2).
Jy ell chorng (之二蟲) "these two insects" (*Chuang* 1.10).
Jy ren (之人) "this man" (*Chuang* 2.32).

2.6.4.3. Privatives

Certain words with the class-meaning of "negation" when used as determinant words in syntagma create privatives. These are the formal indicative negative *Bu*[19] (不) *pwət (see 3.3.1.1), and the material negative *Wu*[20] (無 and 无) *miwo "not to possess, to lack." The former creates a privative form of states, processes and actions, and the latter of qualities and abstractions. The difference is not always apparent, but the first might be thought of as a failure to take some action, and the second the non-possession of some attribute. *Fei* (非) *piwər, the copula/demonstrative (see 4.4.1 and 4.9ff.), creates privatives in the sense of "contrary to."

EXAMPLES

Wu-yonq (無用) "uselessness" (*Chuang* 2.37).
Wu-lih (無力) "effortlessly" (*Chuang* (1.5).
Wu-jyi (无極) "limitlessness" (*Chuang* 27.43).
Bwu-shiaw (不孝) "unfilial behaviour" (*Micius* 22.13).
Bwu-shinn (不信) "faithlessness" (*Tso* 339.1).
Buh-goei (不軌) "lawlessness" (*Tso* 318.12).
Fei-yih (非義) "contrary to justice" as in *Ru jy chyi fei-yih* ... (如知其非義) "if you know it is unjust ..." (*Mencius* 3b.8.3).

2.6.4.4. Determinants of Number

It is not characteristic of "nominal quality" that it differentiates "number" (see 2.6.1 footnote 5). Number, when number is material to the information to be conveyed, is imposed upon the noun by the

---

or, in the case of the initials, allophones of a common phone articulated supradentally together, with vowel grade, imposed under the influence of differences in the force and length of utterance, of a common morph in contrastive environmental conditions.

[19]*Bu* in Modern Standard Chinese is read *buh* before first, second, and third tone morphemes, and *bwu* before the fourth tone.

[20]Both signs occur in *Chuang*; the second is a hapax legomenon in *Tso*, and does not occur in *Mencius* or *Micius*.

determinants of number. These are the numerals used as determinant words (see 7.6 on numbers and their syntax), and certain words having quantitative implications.

2.6.4.4.1. Definite Number

Definite number is imposed by the use of the numerals as determinant words. A form is preserved in LAC (perhaps from an earlier stage of the language?) in which the enumerated noun occurs before the number, for example, *yih liow-shyr* (邑六十), /city/six/tens/ in *yeu jy yih liow-shyr* (與之邑六十) "gave to him sixty cities" (*Tso* 318.9), but the form typical of LAC is "number/enumerated noun."

EXAMPLES

Bae buh (百步) "one hundred paces" (*Mencius* 1a.3.4).
Wuu muu (五畝) "five acres" (*Mencius* 1a.3.8).
Ell chorng (二蟲) "two insects" (*Chuang* 1.10).
San yueh (三月) "three months" (*Chuang* 1.10).[21]
Syh Tzyy (四子) "The Four Adepts" (*Chuang* 2.35).

2.6.4.4.2. Indefinite Number

The determinants of indefinite number are *shuh* (數) *sliu "a number, several, many," and *jii* (幾) *kiər "a few," which determine numbers or units of measure,

EXAMPLES

Shuh chian lii (數千里) "several thousand miles" (*Chuang* 1.13).
Shuh renn (數仞) "several fathoms" (*Mencius* 7b.34.1).
Shuh koou jy jia (數口之家) "a family of many mouths [i.e., a large family]" (*Mencius* 1a.3.9) (*koou* "mouths" is a unit of measure for population).
Shuh chyy (數尺) "several feet" (*Mencius* 7b.34.1).
Jii chian ren (幾千人) "several thousand men" (*Mencius* 1b.12.3).
Jii ryh (幾日) "a few days," for example, in *Jii ryh erl buh woo tsorng* (幾日而不我從) "Will you not be following me in a few days time?" (*Tso* 261.11).

and *jonq* (眾) *tiông "many, all," and *goa* (寡) *kwå "a few, single," which determine enumerated nouns only.[22]

---

[21]Distinguishing between the cardinals and ordinals by prefixing a numeral with *dih* (第) "rank" to form an ordinal is later than LAC. *San yueh*, therefore, in other contexts might equally be "the third month."

[22]*Jonq* and *goa* also occur in pleromatic usage "the many," "the few," for example, in *Goa guh buh kee yii dyi jonq* (寡固不可以敵眾) "The few certainly cannot oppose the many" (*Mencius* 1a.7.33).

EXAMPLES

Jonq min (眾民) "many people" (*Mencius* 7a.21.1).
Jonq ren (眾人) "many, most men" (*Mencius* 6b.6.11).
Jonq Chuu-ren (眾楚人) "many men from Ch'u" (*Mencius* 3b.6.2).
Goa yuh (寡欲) "few desires" (*Mencius* 7b.35.1).

2.6.4.4.3. Units of Measure

Units of measure, which can be determined by numerals and by indefinite number (see, e.g., *renn* "a fathom," and *lii* "a mile" in 2.6.4.4.2) occur also as determinant words quantifying the noun they determine; for example, *chyy dih* (尺地) "one foot of land" (*Mencius* 2a.1.11). Certain other words (i.e., apart from units of measure) occur as quasi-measures.

EXAMPLES

Yu (輿) "a wagon, a cart" but "a wagon-full or cartload" in *Bwu jiann yu shin* (不見輿薪) "I do not see a cartload of faggots" (*Mencius* 1a.7.15).
Bei (杯) "a cup or bowl," but "a cupful" in *Fuh bei shoei yu aw tarng jy shang* (覆杯水於坳堂之上) "pour a cupful of water in a depression in the floor of the hall" (*Chuang* 1.6).
Dan (簞) "a basket," *hwu* (壺) "a bowl" and thus *dan shyr hwu jiang* (簞食壺漿) "baskets of rice and bowls of broth" (*Mencius* 1b.10.4).

2.6.4.5. Collective and Restrictive Determinant Words

Two further classes of words having quantitative implications occur as determinant words. They are: (1) a group of words with the class-meaning "all instances [of the species denominated by the determined noun] conceived as a totality," "all," "the entire," called here "collectives," and (2) a group of words with the class-meaning "the denominated species to the exclusion of all others," "only," "nothing but," called here "restrictives."

Words with these class-meanings occurring as determinant words contrast with words with the same class-meaning occurring as distributives (see 3.5.3). The contrast is one of (*a*) distribution (the determinant series occurring as A in the form A→B, and the distributive series occurring as x in the form B←x); and (*b*) of orthography, determinant and distributive having different signs. A series is suggested by (i) partial similarity of phonological shape (see 3.5.3 note), and (ii) common class-meaning. The determinant series are:

(*a*) Identifying collectives. *Farn* (凡) *b'iwam; *Jiuh* (具) *g'iu; and *Jeu* (舉) *kio with the class-meaning "a series of identical instances conceived as a totality," "all."

EXAMPLES

Farn Ju-hour sheau gwo (凡諸侯小國) "all of the Feudatory's satellite states" (*Tso* 318.10).

Farn Ju-hour (凡諸侯) "All of the Feudal Lords" (*Tso* 253.12).

Farn woo torng meng jy ren (凡我同盟之人) /All/we/together/covenant/→/men/ "All of us who here together covenant . . ." (*Tso* 101.3, *Mencius* 6b.7.9).

Tzyy-shiah, Tzyy-you, Tzyy-jang jie yeou Shenq-ren jy i tii, Raan Niou, Minn-tzyy, Yan Iuan tzer jiuh tii erl uei. (子夏子游子張皆有聖人之一體。冉牛閔子顏淵則具體而微) "Tzu Hsia, Tzu Yu, and Tzu Chang each possessed one characteristic of the Sage [i.e., Confucius], but in the case of Jan Niu, Min Tzu and Yen Yuan, they possessed *all of the characteristics* though in a lesser degree" (*Mencius* 2a.2.27).

Jeu shyh (舉世) "all generations" (*Chuang* 2.18).

Chii wei goa jiun, jeu chyun chern shyr show chyi kuanq (豈惟寡君舉群臣實受其貺) "It is surely not only our Prince, *but all of his subjects* that will in fact reap the benefit of your gift" (*Tso* 348.16).

(b) Synthesizing collectives. *Ju* (諸) *tio; *Chyun* (群) *giwən with the class-meaning "a series of varied instances conceived as a totality," "various."²³

EXAMPLES

Ju-hour (諸侯) /various/marquises/ "the Feudatory" (all texts passim).

Ju dah-fu (諸大夫) "the nobles of varying rank" (*Tso* passim).

Ju jiun-tzyy jie yeu Huan yan . . . (諸君子皆與驩言 . . .) /All/prince-sons = gentlemen/all/with/Huan [P.N.]/speak/ "Every gentleman present has spoken with me" (*Mencius* 4b.27.2).

Chyun chern gaan wang jiun hu (群臣敢忘君乎) "Dare subjects forget their ruler?" (*Tso* 474.10).

Chyun Gong-tzyy ben Shiau (群公子奔蕭) "All the sons of Dukes fled to Hsiao" (*Tso* 60.7).

(c) Restrictives. *Wei* (惟唯) *diwər; and *twu* (徒) *d'o with the class-meaning "to the exclusion of all else," "only," "nothing but."

EXAMPLES

Wei shyr wei neng (惟士為能) "*only gentlemen* would be able to" (*Mencius* 1a.7.38).

Wei tsyy-shyr wei ran (惟此時為然) "*only* of these times would that be true" (*Mencius* 2a.1.18).

Wei ren jee wei neng yii dah shyh sheau (惟仁者為能以大事小) "*Only one* who is truly humane would be able to serve a small state, his own state being large" (*Mencius* 1b.3.1).

---

²³*Chyun* and *ju* distinguish status (see 6.2 and 7.2). *Ju* is used for nobles, feudal lords and the like, and *chyun* for subjects, servants, children, etc. In either case the determination is one of "in all their variety, as a totality."

Twu shann buh tzwu yii wei jenq (徒善不足以爲政) *"Goodness by itself* is not enough to govern a state" (*Mencius* 4a.1.3).
Chii twu Chyi-min an (豈徒齊民安) "Surely it would not be *only the people of Ch'i* that would be comforted?" (*Mencius* 2b.12.6).

2.6.5. Directive

The *directive syntagma* (A←B) is formed upon the analogy of the verbal syntagma (β) and its post-posited elements (γ^1 and γ^2) (see 3.3 ff. and 3.4 ff.). The verb (β) in the verbal syntagma is determined by the determinants of mood and of aspect, etcetera, which *precede* the verb. It is also restricted in both scope and direction by elements which occur *after* it. The meaning-reference of the verb therefore is conditioned both by words that precede it (determinative) and by words that follow it (directive). In the verbal sentence a verb with its determinations composes a verbal syntagma, and as such is distributed as an element in the sentence, with the value "verbal." Its post-posited elements (γ^1 and γ^2) are also distributed as elements in the sentence. In syntagma, verb and post-posited elements ($\beta\gamma$) occur as a single element in the sentence, or as elements in syntagma, for example (A($\beta\gamma$)→B). In syntagma ($\beta\gamma$) has the value *nominal*.

EXAMPLES

Examples have occurred in the preceding pages.

Buh jiun shoou (see 2.6.1) at sentential level would be (Md $\beta\gamma^1$) "does not chap the hands," but at syntagma level ⟩ (A(Md $\beta\gamma^1$)) in *buh-jiun-shoou jy yaw* (A(Md $\beta\gamma$) →B) "a not-chapping-the-hands kind of medicine."

Torng meng (see 2.6.4.5) at sentential level would be (⟨α⟩ As β) "[they] covenanted together," but at syntagma level ⟩ A (As β) in *torng meng jy ren* (A (As β)→B) "together-covenant men" "men who have covenanted together."

Pyng-pih kuanq (see 2.7.1) at sentential level would similarly be $\beta(\beta+\beta)\gamma'$ "bleach silk," but at syntagma level "the bleaching of silk" in *yii pyng-pih kuanq wei shyh* /take/bleaching of silk/make it/occupation/ "They engaged in the occupation of silk-bleaching."

Ay ren (愛人) "love others" ($\beta\gamma^1$) becomes in *buh kee bwu chiuann ay ren* (see 2.7.1) $\gamma^1(\beta\gamma^1)$, a syntagma, and thus nominal "love of others, love for others," thus: "One cannot but preach love for others."

2.6.6. Substitutes in Syntagma

Words of the general class *substitutes* (see 6.1ff.) which have forms peculiar to, or characteristic of, syntagmatic distribution (e.g., the pronominal and demonstrative determinants) have already been described (see 2.6.4.1 and 2.6.4.2). *Suoo* (所) *indefinite substitute* and *her* (何) *interrogative substitute* also occur in syntagmatic distribution, but are not restricted to this form of distribution and are treated at length in 6.5ff. and 6.6ff.

2.7. Syntagma and Sentential Forms

Syntagmas are elements in the sentence (see 2.1). Certain elements occur which in their internal structure are verbal sentences, but which are distributed as single elements in a sentence. Such structures are said to be "in syntagma form." They are given the grammatical value of nominal.

2.7.1. The Use of the Particle of Syntagma

Syntagma form is characterized by the use of the *particle of syntagma* (conventional symbol—syn) *Jee* (者) *tiǎ which is placed after, and demarks the syntagma form.²⁴ Thus, a verbal sentence governed by *jee* becomes a syntagma—a single element, nominal in quality, in the sentence in which it occurs. As an illustration, the formula "yii . . . wei . . ." /take/[activity]/make it/[occupation]/ "to engage in the vocation of" occurs in both of the following:

(1) (a verbal sentence) *Shyh-shyh yii pyng-pih kuang wei shyh* (世世以洴澼絖爲事) /generation-by-generation/take/wash-bleach/silk-floss/make it/occupation/ "They had hereditarily followed the occupation of silk-floss bleachers" (*Chuang* 2.38) and

(2) (a syntagma) *Shenq-ren yii jyh tian-shiah wei shyh jee yee bih jy luann jy suoo tzyh-chii* (聖人以治天下爲事者也必知亂之所自起) /Sage-person/take/govern/world/make it/occupation/syn/st./must/know/disorder/→/that which/from/arises/ "*The wise man concerned with the government of the world,* must know that from which disorder arises" (*Micius* 21.1).

In (1) the form "(agent)/instrument/verb" is a verbal sentence; in (2) the comparable form "agent/instrument/verb" but with postposited *jee* is a single element (here the agent) in a verbal sentence. As such it is tactically interchangeable with any single lexic or compound-word occurring as the agent in a verbal sentence. Syntagma is

---

²⁴On the etymology of *jee* *tiǎ, cf. the collective *ju* *tio (諸 and cf. 都) and the demonstrative *tsyy* *ts'iar. Is there here a process of derivation from a common semanteme (a word-family)? (See Appendix 1.) (See Karlgren (2), and cf. comments of Demiéville (2), p. 2, footnote 3.) Have we here three instances of "specializations of sense" from a parent morpheme, specializations indicated by phonological change, made under the influence of the differing environmental circumstances in which they occur in serving contrastive grammatical purposes? Is there a common history for *ju* "these [the following] in their entirety," *jee* "this [the preceding] in its entirety" and *tsyy* "these, this"? *Gau* (1), p. 275, notes the use of 者 for 此 in *Tang* authors, and the survival of *jee* in this usage in Modern Fukienese.

thus distinguishable from clause (see iii.a) in that the syntagma is tactically interchangeable with the single lexic, and freely distributable in the sentence, whereas the clause is neither.

EXAMPLES

Tian-shiah jy yuh jyi chyi jiun jee (天下之欲疾其君者) "Those in the world who wish to criticize their rulers . . ." (*Mencius* 1a.7.36).

Wann cherng jy gwo shyh chyi jiun jee (萬乘之國弒其君者) "He who in a large state [i.e., one capable in feudal duty of raising a thousand chariots] kills his sovereign")*Mencius* 1a.1.3).

Bih syy jee (比死者) /overtake/death/ "by the time that I die" (*Mencius* 1a.5.2).

Jyh luann jee (治亂者) /set-in-order/disorder/ and thus "the setting in order of disorder . . ." (*Micius* 21.3).

Yang-hu wey bwu jiann Raan-meeng jee (陽虎僞不見冉猛者) "Yang Hu pretended *not to see Jan Meng*" (*Tso* 451.1).

Jee is used with formations stated with considerable economy. But the grammatical quality of all ". . . *jee*" formations is "verbal forms in nominal usage."

EXAMPLES

Wuu-shyr jee (五十者) /fifty/ "those who are fifty years of age" (*Mencius* 1a.3.8).
Ban bair jee (斑白者) /streaked-white/ "the grey headed ones" (*Mencius* 1a.3.10).
Chwu-rau jee (芻蕘者) /straw/kindling/ "those who gather straw kindling "(*Mencius* 1b.2.3).
Jyh-tuh jee (雉兔者) /pheasant/hare/ "those who hunt for small game" (*Mencius* 1b.2.3).
Juanq jee (壯者) /strong, adult/ "the able-bodied" (*Mencius* 1a.5.3).
Jianq jee (匠者) /carpenter/ "those who are carpenters" (*Chuang* 3.43).

Jee is also used to demark, and to set off, a quoted remark, or cited passage, when the remark or citation occurs as a single element in the sentence.

EXAMPLE

Guh Tzyy Moh-tzyy iue "buh kee yii bwu chiuann ay ren" jee tsyy yee (故子墨子曰不可以不勸愛人者此也) /therefore/our Master/Micius/say/no/can/not/preach/love others/particle of syntagma/[is, i.e., refers to]/this.st./ "Therefore it was this that our Master Micius was speaking about when he said 'One cannot but preach love for others' " (*Micius* 22.19).

Again, in this form considerable economy occurs, so that in the following example *ren* (仁) "humane" suffices to stand for the citation appearing at *Micius* 22.1, though it is merely the first word of the quotation, which in full is "Our Master Micius had a saying 'The humane man in the conduct of his affairs must promote the world's commonweal, and eradicate its ills.' "

EXAMPLES

Shyh-yii "ren" jee yuh jy (是以仁者譽之) "Therefore [the saying of Micius, beginning with the word] 'ren' commends it"; "it" being here an exposition of the means of bringing about the ends envisaged in the citation (*Micius* 23.15).

Cherng yeou "bae-shing" jee (誠有百姓者) /Indeed/there was/"the common-people"/syn./. "*Bae-shing*" refers to a remark in the previous context "*bae-shing jie yii wang wei ay yee*" (百姓皆以王爲愛也) "The common people thought Your Majesty was mean," and thus "It is indeed true [as you said] 'the common people [thought me mean]' " (*Mencius* 1a.7.7).

Jee is also used to set off and demark words when used in the sense of "the word 'x.' " It indicates a word's "citation form."

EXAMPLES

Fwu "ming-tarng" jee, wang jee jy tarng yee (夫明堂者王者之堂也) "The word 'Ming-tarng' [The Hall of Immanences] just referred to is by definition a hall of those who rule as Kings" (*Mencius* 1b.5.1).

Ren jee ren yee . . . Yih jee yi yee (仁者人也義者宜也) "The word *ren* [humaneness is *ren* [man]. . . . The word *yih* [justice] is *yi* [right, proper]" (*Chung Yung* 20.5).

2.7.2. The Use of the Particle of Determination *jy* in Syntagma

The particle of determination *jy* (see 2.6.2) occurring between agent and verb of a verbal sentence, occurring as a single element in a sentence, also creates a syntagma form.[25]

EXAMPLES

Wu wanq (min jy duo yu lin gwo) yee (無望民之多於鄰國也) "You would not expect your population to be greater than your neighbour's" (*Mencius* 1a.3.5).

Chern tzyy jy bwu shiaw jiun fuh (臣子之不孝君父) "A subject's or a son's failure to behave filially to his prince or father" (*Micius* 21.4).

The particle of syntagma *jee* and the particle of determination *jy* occur together in:

EXAMPLE

Ru (i jy gong ren jy jyi) jee (如醫之攻人之疾者) "It resembles a doctor's treating a man's illness" (*Micius* 21.2).

2.8. Concluding Remarks on Syntagma

It has been convenient for the purpose of this description to distinguish, as analytical units, between "single" and "compound" words and "syntagmas." However, it is important to observe that in LAC morphology does not stop short at "words" but carries over into

[25]See, for example, 3.4.2 Note and 3.4.7 paragraph 4.

syntagma (see 2.2), so that a degree of arbitrariness is introduced in making the distinction in formal grammatical analysis, though the distinction is important for lexicography. If "words" are what dictionaries talk about, it is "words" and "syntagmas" that the language talks with. Though words in LAC have no accidence, when "talked with" they have grammatical value, and these values are imposed in part, in syntagma. That many of these grammatical values are only optionally imposed (and not, as with accidence, imposed of necessity) should not obscure the real morphological function of syntagma. Operationally speaking, it is only by a disregard of the division "free word/compound word/syntagma" that the elements of the sentence can be separated and their behaviour objectively observed.

2.9. Conspectus of the Syntagmatic Particles, and Specialized Forms

Process of formation	Type	Particle or form	Symbol
Parataxis	Simple connection	與及	A+B
	Alternate connection	若	A/B
Hypotaxis	Determinative	之	→
	Pronominal	吾爾而乃	
	Demonstrative	斯是之	
	Privative	不無非	
	Number	see 2.6.4.4ff.	
	Collective and restrictive	see 2.6.4.5	
Reductions from verbal forms		者	β(syn)
		之	α→βγ

III. The Verbal Sentence

3. Introduction

The elements in a "piece,"[1] however complex the piece and regardless of the intricacies of dependence and independence of its elements one with another, can be placed in two major classes—the verbal sentence and the determinative sentence—by purely formal means. The sentence is formally demarked as a unit by the occurrence in absolute final position of the particles of sentential mood (see 3.9). These particles occur outside of the internal structure of the sentence and provide an objective criterion for determining the extent of a formally complete sentence. The sentential classes (verbal and determinative) are structurally defined by the paradigm of their minimal forms (see Introduction v.c; 3.1; and 4.1).

3.1. The Verbal Sentence

The verbal sentence has as its principal word, and its irreducibly minimal form, a single word (conventional symbol β). It has the grammatical value "verbal." All other elements in the sentence are qualifications of some kind or another of this verb and are subordinate to it.[2] The verb may be a simple or a compound word. It may be used without further qualification and is then uncommitted to mood, to aspect, and to voice. None of these qualifications is introduced as a matter of prescription. When thought by the user to be relevant to the information he wishes to convey, the verb is determined in syntagma. Each of these qualifications is made by a series of grammatical determinants which occur in characteristic distributions in the verbal syntagma. The verbal syntagma is a single element in the sentence.

Other elements in the verbal sentence are the agent (conventional symbol α; see 3.5); the instrument (conventional symbol Ins; see 3.6) or (tactically interchangeable with it), the integral subordinate clause (see 3.7). These precede the verb or verbal syntagma in that order. After the verb occur two elements (conventional symbols $\gamma^1 \gamma^2$) which restrict the scope and govern the voice of the verb (see 3.4).

[1] "Piece," that is, the unit in which the sentence as an element is distributed.
[2] Cf. Mundy, p. 279.

THE VERBAL SENTENCE 39

The mood and the aspect of the verb, and certain other qualifications, for example, that of manner, are incorporated in the verbal syntagma (see 3.3.1; 3.3.2; 3.3.3). The voice of the verb is governed by the distributions of the two post-verbal elements (see 3.4.2; 3.4.3; 3.4.4).

The agent precedes the instrument and the two are clearly distinguished. The agent is a determination of the verb; it is *not* the "subject" of the sentence. Where the agent is indicated by the use of pronominal forms, the determinant form is used.

Certain "moods" of the speaker (see 3.9) are indicated by a class of grammaticized words, placed absolutely at the end of the sentence.

Certain indications (e.g., time and place) are stated initially and absolutely (see 3.10; 3.11).

3.2. The Verb

Any word occurring in the environmental conditions described in 3.1 is a "verb." Such words do not conform to patterns of class-meanings, nor does the segregation of words occurring in the verbal position set up an exclusive word-class. In speaking of the "verbal value" of such words, the following should be noted:

(1) A word used as a determinant word (attribute) in syntagma (see 2.6.2 class 2) occurring at β may be used factitively or putatively.

EXAMPLES

Sheau (小) "small"; *sheau gwo* (小國) "petty states"; and thus, factitive, "to make small": *Jianq-ren jwo erl sheau jy* (匠人斲而小之) "The carpenter having cut it [the wood] up, made it too small" /smalled/it/ "too small" is inferred from context (*Mencius* 1b.9.2). And putative, "to think small": *Koong-tzyy deng Dong-shan erl sheau Luu* (孔子登東山而小魯) /Confucius/climb/Eastern/Hills/subordinating particle/regard-as-small/Lu/ "When Confucius climbed the Eastern Hills, the State of Lu looked small to him" (*Mencius* 7a.24.1). By extension, "to think small" > "to think lightly of" > "to treat with contempt": *Gwo buh kee sheau* (國不可小) "The State is not to be slighted" (*Tso* 396.10).

Yeuan (遠) "far," "distant"; and thus, putative, "to think distant": *Soou buh yeuan chian lii erl lai* (叟不遠千里而來) "You Sir have come, not thinking [too] distant a journey of a thousand miles" (*Mencius* 1a.1.1). And factitive, "to make distant," "keep at a distance from," etc.: *Jiun-tzyy yeuan³ paur-chwu* (君子遠庖廚) "The gentleman keeps clear of kitchens" (*Mencius* 1a.7.12).

(2) A word used as a determinant word (species) in syntagma (see 2.6.2 class 1) occurs in verbal usage with the following class-meanings:

³Mathews (1) gives for *yeuan* s.v. the reading "*yuann*" for factitive usage in Modern Standard Chinese. This is idiosyncratic. No series can be established whereby, for example, tone 3 regularly > tone 4, where putative > factitive.

(*a*) "to treat affectee as a member of the species x is, or should be, treated"; (*b*) "to cause affectee to become a member of the species x"; (*c*) "to use species x."

EXAMPLES

Keh (客) "a guest," *keh jy bwu how* (客之不厚) "treated them as guests but not lavishly" (*Micius* 79.16.)

Lao (老) "aged," *lao wu lao yii jyi ren jy lao* (老吾老以及人之老) "treating our own aged, as the aged should be treated, so that [the example set] might thereby reach to the aged of others" (*Mencius* 1a.7.20).

Guu (鼓) "a drum," *guu jy* (鼓之) "signal them with a drum" (*Mencius* 1a.3.3).

Wang (王) "a king," *kee yii wanq* (可以王) "[One] could thereby rule as a king" (*Mencius* 1a.5.3).

Sheh (舍) "a hut," *sheh yu jiau* (舍於郊) "built a hut in the suburbs" (*Mencius* 1b.4.11).

Yih (邑) "a city," *yih yu Chyi-shan jy shiah* (邑于岐山之下) "built a city beneath Mt Ch'i" (*Mencius* 1b.15.5).

Wuu-wang (吳王) "P.N. 'The King of Wu.'" *Eel yuh Wuu-wang woo hu* (爾欲吳王我乎) /You/wish/King Wu/me?/ "Do you want to treat me as the King of Wu was treated?" (*Tso* 456.22).

3.2.1. Verbal Sentences in Minimal Form

The verb is the principal element and the irreducible minimal form of the verbal sentence. The verbal sentence occurs in minimal form in:

Yeou (有) "There is a (way)" (*Mencius* 1b.4.1).
Chu (出) "He got out" (*Mencius* 5a.2.5).
Ran (然) "It is as you say" (*Mencius* 2b.9.5).
Nuoh (諾) "I agree" (*Mencius* 1b.16.3).
Foou (否) "It is not so" (*Mencius* 5a.2.8).

but such sentences occur rarely in isolation.[4] They are common in distribution as elements in the "piece," for example, in *Ruh nih erl chu* (入逆而出) "[He] entered [the city], took possession of [his bride], and having done so [he] departed" (*Tso* 338.19).

3.2.2. Verbal Sentences at Maximal Form

Forms higher than the minimal form of the verbal sentence are made

---

[4]In unpunctuated texts, the occurrence of such sentences sometimes evokes comment. The example cited above (*Mencius* 1b.4.1) is glossed by *Her Yih-suen* (何異孫) in *Shyr-i Jing Wenn-duey* (十一經問對), with *Yeou tzyh shyh jiuh* (有字是句) "the sign *yeou* is here a sentence."

(i) at the syntagma level by determinations of the verb in the verbal syntagma, and

(ii) at the sentential level by the qualification of the verb or verbal syntagma with the remaining elements of the sentence.

3.3. The Verbal Syntagma

The determined element of the verbal syntagma (β in ($\ldots \beta$)) occurs as a simple word, for example, *lai* (來) "to come," or as a compound word, for example, *shuu-shuu* (數數) "to count," *parng-hwang* (彷徨) "to go into trance," *bao-tsarng* (保藏) "to cherish," *kuenn-kuu* (困苦) "to suffer."

Certain material determinations occur with this element, and take precedence over all grammatical determinations. They are:

(1) Determinations of species.

EXAMPLES

Jann (戰) "to fight a battle"; and *hae-jann* (海戰) "to fight a naval battle."

Gaw (告) "to announce to"; *yan gaw* (筵告) /straw-mat/announce/ "to announce to the ancestors while kneeling in obeisance upon a straw mat."

Dann (誕) "to boast"; and *bey-dann* (背誕) /back/boast/ "to be disloyal."

(2) Determinations of attribute.

EXAMPLES

Dah (大) "large, great"; *dah bay* (大敗) "to impose an overwhelming defeat upon."

Jinn (盡) "total," and thus *jinn fern jy* (盡焚之) "burned it out completely" (*Tso* 235.22).

Shao (少) "few" and thus *shao nuoh* (少懦) "to be somewhat weakened," for example, in *Jinn shao nuoh* (晉少懦) "Tsin is somewhat weakened" (*Tso* 340.22); and *shao an* (少安) "a little more relaxed" (*Tso* 308.12).

Sheau (小) "small" and thus "to a small degree" as in *sheau buu jy* (小補之) "helps it slightly" (*Mencius* 7a.13.2).

By these compounding and material determinative processes the verb is given the degree of specificness required by the user. The verb is then determined by the grammatical determinants of mood, aspect, manner and so on.

3.3.1. Modal Determinants of the Verb

Three moods are distinguished: (i) Indicative; (ii) Injunctive or Hortatory; and (iii) Subjunctive.[5] When undetermined by a modal determinant the verb is neutral as to mood. When determined the moods are distinguished as follows.

[5] These three modal classes account for the occurrence before the verb of three contrastive forms of the negative. The distinction between the indicative and non-

3.3.1.1. Indicative

The verb is indicative when negated with *Bu* (不) *pwət or with the stressed form *Fwu* (非) *piwət.[6]

---

indicative moods (i.e., between the use of the *p- initial series of negatives and the *m- initial series of negatives) is sufficiently clear. The border-line separating the non-indicative moods is, however, not so clearly demarked. In the imperative form there occur direct commands (an unambiguous imperative) but there are also urgings, statements of duty or of obligation. In the subjunctive form there are statements that are clearly hypothetical or potential (e.g., in unfulfilled conditional statements), but there also occur statements of wishing, and willing. But whatever the divisions of usage, apart from the dissimilarity of forms (viz. 毋 and 無), 毋 like 不 is a purely formal negative. *Bwu jiann* (不見) "I do not see" has polarity with *jiann* (見) "I do see"; and *wu ting* (毋聽) "do not listen" with *ting* (聽) "listen." *Wu* (無) on the other hand is a material negative with a positive reflex counterpart *yeou* (有) ("not to possess, not to have, not to be," contra "to possess, to have, to be") and since *wu* and *yeou* appear in series as modal determinants of the verb (*yeou* never in any sense imperative), its modal quality is better deduced from its polarity with *yeou*, rather than supposing it interchangeable with 毋. Thus, while the terms "indicative," "injunctive," and "subjunctive" serve well enough as names for form-classes, too much should not be read into them as terms for modal class-meanings.

On the connection between the negatives and mood, see also Leu Shwu-shiang (1), p. 12 and Gau Ming-kae p. 519 ff., p. 612 ff.; on the negatives in general see Kennedy (5), p. 1 ff.

[6]The suggestion, first advanced by Gabelentz (1), p. 452 and developed by Ding Sheng-shuh (1) (in the case of *fwu*) and by Graham (1) (in the case of *wuh*; see 3.3.1.2), that *fwu* and *wuh* are allegro forms of the indicative and imperative negatives with the anaphoric pronoun *jy* substituting for the direct object, fails to account for the occurrence of *fwu* and *wuh* before intransitive verbs, and for the possibility of occurrence of the object after the verb. (See examples above and 3.4.8 footnote 36.)

However, it is observable, as Dr. Graham points out in a private communication, that *fwu* and *wuh* occur predominantly before transitive verbs where the object is omitted. But it is also observable that *bu*, where polarity "negative/positive-reflex" is present, behaves in precisely the same way: for example, *yaw tsyy . . . bwu yaw yee* (樂此 . . . 不樂也) "does enjoy this . . . does not enjoy [this]", *yeu jy . . . buh yeu* (與之 . . . 不與) "join him . . . not to join [him]", *neng gong jy . . . buh neng gong* (能攻之 . . . 不能攻) "can cure it . . . cannot cure [it]"; *yonq jy . . . bwu yonq* (用之 . . . 不用) "use it . . . not to use [it]"; (see also 3.4.8 footnote 37), so that the feature is not a contrast between *fwu* and *bu*, but a feature common to both. (It might also be said that the rate of incidence of occurrence before transitive and intransitive verbs is only significant when the ratio of transitive to intransitive verbs is known. The intransitive verb is a small class (see 3.4.1 and 3.4.6).)

The contrast between *bu* and *fwu*, and between *wu* and *wuh*, seems to me to have

THE VERBAL SENTENCE

EXAMPLES

Buh shyan jee swei yeou tsyy bwu yaw yee (不賢者雖有此不樂也) "He who *is not worthy* though he may possess these things, does not enjoy [them]" (*Mencius* 1a.2.2).

Buh jyi shyh (不及是) "It *will not* come to this" (*Tso* 317.10).

Jea erl buh faan (假而不反) "Having borrowed it, you *will not* return it" (*Tso* 339.14).

Buh jy luann jy suoo tzyh chii tzer buh neng jyh. . . . Buh jy jyi jy suoo tzyh chii tzer fwu neng gong (不知亂之所自起則不能治, 不知疾之所自起則弗能攻) "When we *do not* know from whence disorder arises, we cannot bring about good order. . . . When [the doctor] *does not* know from whence the illness arises, then he cannot effect a cure" (*Micius* 21.1ff.).

Ji jee fwu shyr, lau jee fwu shyi (飢者弗食勞者弗息) "The hungry *do not* eat, and the weary *do not* rest" (*Mencius* 1b.4.8).

Shyy wu jinq Tzyy . . . jin wu fwu jinq Tzyy (始吾敬子 . . . 今吾弗敬子) "At first, I respected you Sir! Now I do *not* respect you" (*Tso* 59.10).

The verb is indicative when negated with *Wey* (未) *miwəd but, whereas with *bu* one particular instance of the act is envisaged and negated, in *wey* all conceivable instances envisaged are negated. The difference is between particular denial (an envisaged instance), and universal denial (all envisaged instances).[7]

---

more to do with the prosodic system of the language, and not with its morphology. For example, in the following, where *bwu shinn* (不信) "not to be trusted" and *fwu shinn* (弗信) "not to be trusted" occur in the same piece, the non-emphatic form occurs in the protasis, and the emphatic form occurs in the apodosis. There is, in this example, no question of a "direct object." *Huoh yu shanq yeou daw. Bwu shinn yu yeou fwu huoh yu shanq yii. Shinn yu yeou, yeou daw. Shyh chin fwu yueh fwu shinn yu yeou yii* (獲於上有道,不信於友,弗獲於上矣.信於友有道, 事親弗悅弗信於友矣) "There is a teaching upon the subject of 'being acceptable to one's superiors.' If one is *not trusted* by one's friends, one *will not* be acceptable to one's superiors. There is a teaching on the subject of 'being trusted by one's friends.' If in serving one's parents, one *is not* pleasing to them, then one *will not be trusted* by one's friends." (*Mencius* 4a.13.1).

The theory of an allegro form for *fwu* and *wuh* has been examined by Leu Shwu-shiang (1), p. 12 who rejects it on historical and phonological grounds, suggesting that the difference is one of "different degrees of strength."

[7] The universality of the denial of *wey* and the particularity of the denial of *bu* may be modified for emphasis by determining *bu* with *jong* "end, to the end"— thus *jong bwu wang* (終不忘) "I will not forget it as long as I live" (*Mencius* 3a.2.1) —and by determining *wey* with *shyr*, thus *wey jiann niow yee* (未見牛也) "had never seen an ox" (*Mencius* 1a.7.11); but in a paraphrase of *Jaw Chyi* (趙岐), *Shyr wey jiann niow yee* (時未見牛也) "up to that time he had never seen an ox."

EXAMPLES

Jiann niou wey jiann yang yee (見牛未見羊也) "It was because you had seen an ox [in such a predicament] but had at no time seen a sheep [in a similar predicament]" (*Mencius* 1a.7.11).

Ta ryh jiun chu tzer bih minq yeou-sy suoo jy, jin cherng-yu yii jiah yii, yeou-sy wey jy suoo jy. (他日君出則必命有司所之今乘輿已駕矣有司未知所之) "When on other occasions My Lord is going out he invariably tells his courtiers where he is going, but today, his carriage is already prepared [and he is therefore presumably going out without informing the Court]. His courtiers will never know where he has gone" (*Mencius* 1b.16.1).

Wey yeou (未有) "There has never been . . ." (Texts passim).

Bu and *wey* negate verbs describing situations of actual or declared fact.

3.3.1.2. Injunctive and Hortatory

The verb is injunctive or hortatory when negated with *Wu* (毋) *miwo[8] or with its stressed form *Wuh* (勿) *miwət.

EXAMPLES

Wu: *Dah wu chin sheau* (大毋侵小) "Great States should not invade small States" (*Tso* 289.6); *Wu fey wang minq* (毋廢王命) "You should not disregard a royal command" (*Tso* 197.20); *Farn woo torng meng, wu uen nian, wu iong lih, wu bao jian, wu liou teh* (凡我同盟毋蘊年毋壅利毋保姦毋留慝) "All of us who thus together covenant agree that we should not hoard grain, should not exclude each other from advantages we possess, should not protect traitors, or harbour criminals" (*Tso* 273.23).

Wuh: *Wang chiing wuh yi* (王請勿疑) "I beg Your Majesty, do not doubt it" (*Mencius* 1a.5.6); *Wuh dwo chyi shyr, shuh koou jy jia kee yii wu ji yii* (勿奪其時數口之家可以無飢矣) "Do not take from the peasants their labour in the farming seasons, and then large families need not starve" (*Mencius* 1a.3.9); *Wang yuh shyng wanq jenq, tzer wuh hoei jy yii* (王欲行王政則勿毀之矣) "If Your Majesty intends to pursue the policies of a true king, then you should not destroy it" (*Mencius* 1b.5.2); *Huoh wey goa-ren wuh cheu, huoh wey goa-ren cheu jy* (或謂寡人勿取或謂寡人取之) "Some say I should not take [Yen], others say I should take it" (*Mencius* 1b.10.1).

The verb is injunctive when determined by *der* (得) *tək.

EXAMPLES

Tzyy-kuay buh der yeu ren Ian. Tzyy-jy buh der show Ian yu Tzyy-kuay (子噲不得與人燕子之不得受燕於子噲) "Tzu-k'uai ought not to have given the State of Yen to another, and Tzu-chih ought not to have accepted it from him" (*Mencius* 2b.8.1).

Buh der show yu chyi jia (不得受於其家) "The gentleman ought not to receive it in his own house" (*Mencius* 3b.7.3).

---

[8] The unstressed form does not occur in *Mencius* (see Graham (1)).

The verb is injunctive when determined by *Dang* (當) *tâng.

EXAMPLES

Ju yee dang yuh (朱也當御) "I Chu, ought to deal with this" (*Tso* 309.5).
Dang wuh jy wei jyi (當務之爲急) "What should be taken seriously would be the most important" (*Mencius* 7a.46.1).

A verb is injunctive when determined by *Shanq* (尙) *diang in requests made in divination in the sense of "should we?" "ought we?" "might we?"

EXAMPLES

Yuan shanq sheang Wey-gwo (元尙享衞國) "Might Yuan enjoy [i.e., succeed to] the State of Wei?" (*Tso* 367.4).
Yu shanq lih Chyr (余尙立縶) "Should we enthrone Ch'ih?" (*Tso* 367.5).
Yu shanq der tian-shiah (余尙得天下) "May I become ruler of the world?" (*Tso* 382.7).
Shanq dah keh jy (尙大克之) "Ought we to impose a great defeat upon them?" (*Tso* 394.5).

3.3.1.3. Subjunctive

The verb is subjunctive (i.e., describing non-real, hypothetical or imagined situations) when negated with *wu* (無无) *miwo[9] or determined by *yeou* (有) *giug (its antonym).

EXAMPLES

Wu: *Wang ru jy tsyy, tzer wu wanq min jy duo yu lin gwo yee* (王如知此則無望民之多於鄰國也) "If the King really understood this, then *he would not expect* his population to be any larger than that of his neighbour" (*Mencius* 1a.3.5); *Char lin gwo jy jenq, wu ru goa-ren jy yonq shin jee* (察鄰國之政無如寡人之用心者) "If you were to examine the governments of neighbouring states, they *would not compare* to mine in devotion" (*Mencius* 1a.3.2); *Wang wu tzuey suey, sy tian-shiah jy min jyh yan* (王無罪歲斯天下之民至焉) "If the King *would not blame* the harvest [for the starvation prevailing in his state, but take precautionary measures] then the peoples of the whole world would come to him" (*Mencius* 1a.3.12); *Jonq-ni jy twu, wu daw Hwan Wen jy shyh jee, shyh-yii how shyh wu chwan yan* (仲尼之徒無道桓文之事者是以後世無傳焉) "It was because the disciples of Confucius *would not* speak about the affairs of Duke Huan of Ch'i and Duke Wen of Tsin that their successors *would not* tradite them" (*Mencius* 1a.7.1); *Wuh wu hai* (物无害) "that which living things would not harm" (*Chuang* (3.47); (see also 3.3.2.6 footnote (20) *buh-der-yii* and *wu-yii*).
Yeou: *Dah-fu yeou tsyh yu shyh, buh der show yu jia* (大夫有賜於士不得受於家) "A noble might make a gift to a gentleman, but the gentleman ought not to

---

[9] See 2.6.4.3 footnote (20).

receive it in his own home" (*Mencius* 3b.7.2); *Guh jiun-tzyy yeou bwu jann, jann bih shenq yii* (故君子有不戰戰必勝矣) "Therefore, though a gentleman might refrain from fighting, if he fights he invariably wins" (*Mencius* 2b.1.6). (On this passage, the Han paraphrast *Jaw Chyi* has *Jiun-tzyy jy daw, guey bwu jann* (君子之道貴不戰) "In the code of gentlemen it is thought honourable not to fight," and the Ch'ing scholar *Jiau Shyun*, sensing a modal import in *yeou*, says *Yeou bwu jann dang bwu jann* (有不戰當不戰) "*Yeou bwu jann* means ought not to fight.") *Shianq buh der yeou wei yu chyi gwo* (象不得有爲於其國) /Hsiang/did not/bring successful conclusion/might/do/in/his/state/ "Hsiang did not do what he might have done in his State" (*Mencius* 5a.3.6); *Wu wey neng yeou shyng yan, nae suoo yuan tzer shyue Koong-tzyy yee* (吾未能有行焉乃所願則學孔子也) "I might never have attained to it, but had I had my wish, it would have been to study with Confucius" (*Mencius* 2a.2.31).

The verb is subjunctive when determined by *wei* (爲) *gwia "to become."

EXAMPLES

Jiun wei lai jiann ... buh guoo lai (君爲來見 ... 不果來) "My Lord would have come to see you ... but he did not come" (*Mencius* 1b.16.7).

Goou wei how yih erl shian lih (苟爲後義而先利) "If indeed you were to put profit first and justice last ..." (*Mencius* 1a.1.4).

Jie gaw yu sheau gwo, wei huey yu Sonq (皆告於小國爲會於宋) "[The major states] all announced to the minor states that they would meet in Sung" (*Tso* 316.16).

Ji jee yih wei shyr, kee jee yih wei yiin (飢者易爲食渴者易爲飲) "The hungry might easily be fed, and the thirsty given drink" (*Mencius* 2a.1.16).

Wei tsyy-shyr wei ran (惟此時爲然) "Only of these times would [this] be true" (*Mencius* 2a.1.18).

A verb determined by *Ru* (如) *ńio, *Ruoh* (若) *ńiak, or *You* (猶) *ziôg "to resemble, to be like, as though," is subjunctive in the protasis of an unfulfilled conditional.

EXAMPLES

Wang ru jy tsyy ... (王如知此) "If the King were to understand this ..." (*Mencius* 1a.3.5).

Wang ru shy ren jenq yu min ... (王如施仁政於民) "If the King were to reveal to the people a humane governmental policy ..." (*Mencius* 1a.5.3).

Ruoh jinq shyng chyi lii ... (若敬行其禮) "If we were reverently to conduct the ceremonials accorded to them ..." (*Tso* 306.16).

Chuu Jiun ruoh neng shyy Chyn Jiun ruu yu bih yih (楚君若使能秦君辱於敝邑) "If the Lord of Ch'u were able to make the Lord of Ch'in demean himself in our capital, then ..." (*Tso* 316.21).

Woo you shy jy (我猶尸之) "If I were to preside over it ..." (*Chuang* 2.24).

Woo you day jy (我猶代之) "If I were to take your place ..." (*Chuang* 2.24).

THE VERBAL SENTENCE

The subjunctive use of *ruoh, ru,* and *you* is typical of but is not confined to the conditional.

EXAMPLES

Jin yan wanq ruoh yih ran tzer Wen Wang buh tzwu faa yu (今言王若易然則文王不足法與) "If you say true kingship *would be* easy, then King Wen is an inadequate example of it, is he?" (*Mencius* 2a.1.8).

Muh ruoh yii meei ran (木若以美然) "The wood *I would have thought* was too elegant" (*Mencius* 2b.7.2).

Fu-tzyy ruoh yeou bwu yuh seh (夫子若有不豫色) "You Sir seem displeased" (*Mencius* 2b.13.1).

Goa-ren ru jiow jiann jee yee (寡人如就見者也) "*I would have come* to see you, but..." (*Mencius* 2b.2.1).

Wei ji jy sang, you yuh yu yii hu (爲朞之喪猶愈於已乎) "Were you to put into effect a one-year mourning period, would that not be better than stopping it altogether?" (*Mencius* 7a.39.1).

Chyi chern-gow bih-kang jiang you taur-juh Yau Shuenn jee yee (其塵垢粃糠將猶陶鑄堯舜者也) "His 'dust and siftings' might have fashioned a Yao or a Shun" (*Chuang* 2.33).

NOTE. *Wuh* determined by *ru* occurs in: *Tian yuh sha jy, tzer ru wuh sheng* (天欲殺之則如勿生) "If Heaven intends you to murder him, then it were better that he had not been born" (*Tso* 117.3). *Ruoh ay chorng shang tzer ru wuh shang* (若愛重傷則如勿傷) "If you would be reluctant to inflict a second wound, then it were better that you did not inflict a wound at all" (*Tso* 120.4).

3.3.1.4. Mood Contextually Imposed

Some qualification must be made to the statement in 3.3.1 that "undetermined by a modal determinant the verb is neutral as to mood" since, where contrast is involved, the contextual situation imposes mood, though it is formally unmarked. For example, in *Huoh wey goa-ren wuh cheu, huoh wey goa-ren cheu jy* (或謂寡人勿取或謂寡人取之) "Some say to me 'do not take it' and some say to me 'take it'" (*Mencius* 1b.10.1) *wuh cheu* "do not take it" and *cheu jy* "do take it" are in parallel distribution, and the mood, though formally marked in one term only, is common to both. Mood here is contextually imposed. Except in the case of *wu* (which has a reflexive-positive, *yeou*), the modal negatives have formal polarity with zero.

EXAMPLES

Negative	Positive[10]
bwu jiann (Md β) "does not see"	*jiann* (Zero β) "does see"
wuh ting (Md β) "do not listen"	*ting* (Zero β) "listen!"

---

[10] *Jiann* and *ting* here are only modal in context of situation described above.

The injunctives *der, dang, shanq* and the subjunctives *wei, ru, ruoh,* etc. do not occur in situations vis-à-vis *wuh wu* and *wu,* but provide, out of such situations, some means of marking mood in positive and contrastive assertion. Similarly, since in the indicative *bu* is polar with zero, the reflex-positive indicative may be marked with determinants (other than zero) where the context is one of contrast between indicative and some non-indicative mood. These determinants are:

guoo (果) *klwar "fruit, fruition, realization, real," and
guh (固) *ko "ancient, established, assured, true."

EXAMPLES

Jiun wei lai jiann ... *buh guoo lai* (君爲來見 ... 不果來) "My Lord *would have come to see you,* but *did not come* ..." (*Mencius* 1b.16.7).

Woo fwu sheu, tzer guh shi wu min yii (我弗許則固攜吾民矣) "If we do not agree, then we will in fact have to drag our people into war" (*Tso* 316.15).

Wu guh yuann jiann (吾固願見) "I did wish to see him" (*Mencius* 3a.5.1).

Guh jiang chaur (固將朝) "You were going to court" (*Mencius* 2b.2.10).

Polarity[11] is combined in the modal determinant *Huoh* (或) *g'wəd (which occurs also in the agential distributive series *huoh* "of the agents, some," and *moh* "of the agents, none" (see 3.5.3.1)) in the sense of "whether to or not."

EXAMPLES

Jiang huoh mii jy (將或弭之) /about to/do or not do/abolish/it/ "whether or not we are to abolish them" (*Tso* 316.12).

Goou huoh jy jy (苟或知之) /if indeed/do or not do/know/it/ "whether we knew of it or not ..." (*Tso* 339.15).

3.3.2. Aspect and the Verbal Syntagma

"Aspect" in this description[12] is used of a class of determinants, occurring in the verbal syntagma, the purpose of which is to define

---

[11] Polarity is further discussed in 3.4.8 and 6.5 footnote (9).

[12] In contrast to the use of the term "aspect" for the aspectual systems of Modern Standard Chinese (e.g., by Frei p. 138 ff.; Průsek and Halliday p. 193) in which aspect is set up by other than contrastive distributional classes. Frei, for example, operates with "adverbs aspectif," "auxiliare," and "particule aspective" (three contrastive distributional classes). In this description the use of the category "aspectual" is confined to the class of words occurring in the verbal syntagma, with the class-meaning defined above. In a synthetic treatment of aspect in LAC, account would have to be taken, for example, of the *resultative* treated here, on formal grounds, as a class of instrumentation (see 3.6.2, and also see the role of *erl* in 3.7.2), and of the grammatical meanings of accentuation (see 3.12).

THE VERBAL SENTENCE

(i) a point in the progress of the action of the verb as envisaged by the user[13] which may be: the point of conception (desiderative aspect), a point prior to realization (potential aspect), a point or span in the period of realization (durative), the point of completion (perfective), the point of successful completion (resultative);

(ii) degrees of incidence of the act, which may be once, several or many times repeated (iteratives), or occur in sequence for the first, or second time, and for consecutive times;

(iii) the distinction between the act of a precise moment (momentary aspect), or a customary act (customary aspect).

3.3.2.1. Potential Aspect

A verb determined by *jiang* (將) *tsiang or *chiee* (且) *ts'iă has potential aspect. Whether the verb is indicative (as in examples 1 and 2 of *jiang*) or subjunctive (as in examples 5 and 6 of *jiang*) is a matter of general context.

EXAMPLES

Jiang: Ju-hour jiang mou jiow Ian (諸侯將謀救燕) "The Feudal Lords are going to discuss the rescue of Yen" (*Mencius* 1b.11.1); *Chyi-ren jiang jwu Shiue* (齊人將築薛) "Ch'i are going to fortify Hsueh" (*Mencius* 1b.14.1); *Jiang jiann Menq-tzyy* (將見孟子) "I am going to see Mencius" (*Mencius* 1b.16.2); *Jou Gong jy chyi jiang pann erl shyy jy yu* (周公知其將畔而使之與) "The Duke of Chou sent him knowing that he would rebel, did he?" (*Mencius* 2b.9.5); *Gwo-jiun jinn shyan ru buh-der-yii, jiang shyy bei yu tzuen* (國君進賢如不得巳將使卑踰尊) "A ruler promotes a man of worth only when he has no other course since he would be placing a commoner over a noble" (*Mencius* 1b.7.2); *Tzer jiang yinq jy* (則將應之...) "... then I would answer him" (*Mencius* 2b.8.5); *Jin jiang shyng ren jenq tzer...* (今將行仁政則...) "If you would put into practice humane governmental policies, then..." (*Mencius* 3b.5.1).

Chiee: Jou Gong fang chiee ing jy (周公方且膺之) "The Duke of Chou was, at that very moment, about to strike them" (*Mencius* 3a.4.34); *Chiee wey jaang jee yih hu, jaang jy jee yih hu* (且謂長者義乎長之者義乎) "Would you call the elderly person himself righteous, or the person righteous who treated him as an elderly person should be treated?" (*Mencius* 6a.4.4); *Ran tzer shenq-ren chiee yeou guoh yu?* (然則聖人且有過與) "If that is so, then [even a] sage might err?" (*Mencius* 2b.9.5); *Binq yuh, woo chiee woang jiann* (病愈我且往見) "When I am better, I will go and see him" (*Mencius* 3a.5.1); *Woo chiee jyr jy* (我且直之) "I would correct him" (*Mencius* 3a.5.2); *Chiee ruh jiing fei ruh jiing* (且入井非入井) "To be going to fall into a well, is not falling into a well" (*Micius* 78.19); *Chiee*

---

[13]Envisaged by the user, irrespective of its occurrence in real time (see 3.3.2.5 footnote 18). Time of occurrence is not treated as a determination of the verb. Tense is not a grammatical distinction in LAC (see 3.10). (See also *Gau* p. 377 ff.)

cheu yu Gong-suen Duann shyh (且娶於公孫段氏) "He was going to marry into the family of Kung-sun Tuan" (*Tso* 338.11).

3.3.2.2. Desiderative Aspect

A verb determined by *yuh* (欲) *giuk has desiderative aspect. In LAC usage it is confined to acts of intention and will, but in Han usage this is blunted and *yuh* becomes potential.[14]

EXAMPLES

Fwu ren yow erl shyue jy, juanq erl yuh shyng jy (夫人幼而學之壯而欲行之) "If being young a man studies something, on reaching maturity, he will want to practise it" (*Mencius* 1b.9.2).

Luu yuh shyy Shenn-tzyy wei jianq-jiun (魯欲使慎子爲將軍) "Lu intended to make Shen-tzu a general" (*Mencius* 6b.8.1).

Wang yuh shyng wanq jenq, tzer wuh hoei jy yii (王欲行王政則勿毀之矣) "If the King intends to pursue the policies of a true king, then he should not destroy it" (*Mencius* 1b.5.2).

3.3.2.3. Momentary Aspect

A verb determined by *fang* (方) *piwang has momentary aspect. The act is conceived as taking place at one moment rather than another. If the act is envisaged in retrospect *fang* indicates "at that moment," if happening at present "at this moment," or (with two acts) "the moment x happens, that moment y happens too."[15]

EXAMPLES

That moment

Chern Tsay fang muh yu Wey (陳蔡方睦於衞) "The States of Ch'en and Ts'ai were at that moment on friendly terms with Wei" (*Tso* 10.7).

Fang shuu, chiueh dih, shiah bing erl chwang yan (方暑闕地下冰而牀焉) "At that time it was hot, so having dug a pit and placed ice in it, he slept in it" (*Tso* 293.16).

Fang chiee ing jy (方且膺之) "At that very time he was just about to smite them" (*Mencius* 3a.4.34).

This moment

Chern Hwan Gong fang yeou choong yu Wang (陳桓公方有寵於王) "Duke Huan of Ch'en is at the moment in favour with the King" (*Tso* 11.3).

---

[14] Cf. the use of *yaw* (要) "to want" in Modern Standard Chinese (see *Chao* (2), p. 53) which has a similar aspectual usage.

[15] In Han usage *fang* "at this moment" is used in an extended sense "in a moment, in a short while," for example, in *Ju-hour wey Gong-tzyy, fang yuh gonq lih jy* (諸侯畏公子之威方欲共立之) "Fearful of the prince's prestige, the Feudal Lords intend shortly to set him up as King" (*Shih Chi* 3.167.85).

Tian fang show Chuu (天方授楚) "Heaven is now giving power to Ch'u" (*Tso* 203.9).

Chuu shy fang juanq (楚師方壯) "The army of Ch'u is at present powerful" (*Tso* 199.1).

Any precise moment

Fang sheng fang syy, fang syy fang sheng (方生方死方死方生) "The moment we are born we die, the moment we die we are born" (*Chuang* 4.28).

(A clear example of momentary aspect is in EAC:

Ryh jy fang jonq (日之方中) /of the sun/the precise moment/hit the centre/ "When the sun is at its meridian" [*Songs* 38].)

A verb determined by *Jah* (乍) *dz'ag has aspectual indications similar to those of *fang*.

EXAMPLES

Jin ren jah jiann ru-tzyy jiang ruh yu jiing . . . (今人乍見孺子將入於井 . . .) "Now the moment a man sees a small child about to fall into a well . . ." (*Mencius* 2a.6.3). With which compare:

Fei jah gau jah shiah yee (飛乍高乍下也) "Its flight is now high, now low" (*Ta Tai Li Chi* 47).

Jah jiann jah moh (乍見乍沒) "The boat was one moment visible, the next, inundated" (*Han Shu* 53.6).

A verb determined by *shyh* (適) *śiek has momentary aspect, but has greater precision than *fang*, that is, "at this or that very moment . . ."[16]

EXAMPLES

Wang shyy shyh jyh, suey jyy jy (王使適至遂止之) "The King's envoy at that very moment arrived and so prevented him" (*Tso* 161.5).

Wu mou shyh bwu yonq yee (吾謀適不用也) "Because my advice is not, at this precise moment, being followed" (*Tso* 165.9).

Fenq-neau shyh jyh (鳳鳥適至) "A phoenix appeared at that very moment" (*Tso* 392.23).

A verb determined by *Gu* (姑) *ko has momentary aspect. The act is conceived as taking place "for the moment, for the time being," etc.

EXAMPLES

Gu shuh der yan, yii dai neng jee (姑樹德焉以待能者) "For the moment, let us implant virtue in the state, thus to await an able ruler" (*Tso* 111.4).

---

[16]*Shyh* is also used to determine the verb in the sense of "it chanced that, it so happened that, by coincidence," etc. For example, *Chyi shyh yuh yn jiun* (其適遇淫君) "if by chance they happen upon a profligate ruler . . ." (*Tso* 402.8).

Gu shee shyh (姑舍是) "For the moment let this be" (*Mencius* 2a.2.28).
Gu wuh shiou der, yii dai shyr hu (姑務修德以待時乎) "Should we not, for the time being, concentrate upon cultivating our virtue and abide our time?" (*Tso* 54.12).

Gu is also used in extended sense "in a moment," "in a short while," "shortly."

EXAMPLE

Tzyy gu iou Tzyy-shi jy yuh bey-dann yee (子姑憂子皙之欲背誕也) "You, Sir, will regret before long, the intention of Tzu-Hsi to be disloyal" (*Tso* 339.13).

3.3.2.4. Durative or Continuative Aspect

A verb determined by *you* (猶) *ziôg, *shanq* (尚) *diang, or *shanq-you* (尚猶) has continuative aspect. The act is conceived as in process or continuing, but not terminated.¹⁷

EXAMPLES

Dang Yau jy shyr, tian-shiah you wey pyng . . . (當堯之時天下猶未平) "In the days of the Emperor Yao, when the world was still unsettled . . ." /still/at no time/pacified/ (*Mencius* 3a.4.15).
Ruenn-yueh bwu guh yueh, you chaur yu miaw (閏月不告月猶朝于廟) "An intercalary month—the Duke did not perform the appropriate calendrical ceremonies but continued to present himself before the ancestral shrines" (*Ch'un ch'iu* 154.19).
Wen Wang jy der, bae nian erl-how beng, you wey shya yu tian-shiah (文王之德百年而後崩猶未洽於天下) "The virtues of King Wen, though he lived to a hundred, still had not permeated the entire world" (*Mencius* 2a.1.8).
Woei-jea shanq yow (蔿賈尚幼) "Wei Chia was still young" (*Tso* 129.20).
Shi-syh shanq duo (犀兕尚多) "Rhinoceros were still prolific" (*Tso* 180.7).
Jin wu shanq bing (今吾尚病) "I am still ill today" (*Mencius* 3a.5.1).
Shyr nian shianq-you yeou chow (十年尚猶有臭) "And ten years hence it will still stink" (*Tso* 93.17).

3.3.2.5. Perfective Aspect

A verb determined by *jih* (既) *kiəd, *yii* (已) *ziəg, or *jih-yii* (既已) has perfective aspect. The act is envisaged as completed.¹⁸

---

¹⁷*Shanq* and *you* are also used in a form of concession "contrary to expectation, even so, yet, still" (see 5.4.3).

¹⁸That aspect is relative to the speaker, and not to fixed points in time, is referred to in the Mohist Canons of Logic. *Tzyh chyan iue "chiee," tzyh how iue "yii," fang ran yih chiee* (自前曰自自後曰既方然亦且) "Though we say for an event in front of us 'chiee,' and for an event behind us 'yii,' in fact, the event of any given moment, is an event about to be [i.e., it is both in being and coming into being—a matter of viewpoint]" (*Micius* 68.14). (This was first brought to my attention by Dr. Raymond Dawson.)

EXAMPLES

Cherng-yu yii jiah (乘輿已駕) "Your carriage is ready" (*Mencius* 1b.16.1).
Bing renn jih jie (兵刃既接) "The sword blades had clashed" (*Mencius* 1a.3.3).
Yau Shuenn jih moh (堯舜既沒) "Yao and Shun are dead" (*Mencius* 3b.9.5).
Farn woo torng meng jy ren, jih meng jy how, yan guei yu haw (凡我同盟之人既盟之後言歸于好) "All of us who thus covenant, having covenanted, declare that we return to our homes in amity" (*Mencius* 6b.7.9).
Yu jih-yii jy jy yii (予既已知之矣) "I already know that" (*Mencius* 6b.13.4).
Tian-shiah jih-yii jyh yee (天下既已治也) "The world is already well-governed" (*Chuang* 2.24).

3.3.2.6. Resultative Aspect

A verb determined by *der* (得) *tək has resultative aspect.[19] The act is viewed as not only being complete, but also brought to a successful conclusion. It is the *result* that is in view. (*Der* is used plerematically in the sense of "to obtain, to get"; cf. here English "get to know, see," etc.)[20]

[19] *Der* thus operates in two forms in the verbal syntagma: *der yeu* (得與) "ought to give," *der show* (得受) "should receive" (see 3.3.1.2) but *der jiann* (得見) "succeed in seeing," *der mean* (得免) "manage to rid" (as above). (The distinction is recognized in Modern Standard Chinese, where the modal *der* is read *deei*.) But *der* contrasts with all other determinants classified here as aspectual, in occurring not only in the form "aspect/verb" (in which it conforms with the class), but also occurring with an interposed *erl* (而), aspect/*erl*/verb. In this *der* differs from all other grammatical determinants of the verb in LAC. Simon (8), p. 441, in an article discussing the occurrence in Analects of "*der jiann*" and "*der erl jiann*" suggests that *erl* here is anaphoric, with the class-meaning "a person, thing, etc. of this kind or class" and proposes the meaning "such." A further peculiarity of *der* is noted by Gau p. 441, who observes that *der* is the only verbal determinant of its class that transposes to the post-verbal position in Mediaeval Chinese.

[20] *Der* with *yii* "to finish," negated with *bu*, that is, *buh-der-yii* (不得已) means "inevitable, to have no other recourse, to have no alternative but . . ." etc. /not/ succeed/finish [otherwise]/.

EXAMPLES

Fei tzer erl cheu jy, buh-der-yii yee (非擇而取之不得已也) "It was not that he took it from choice, but that he could not do otherwise" (*Mencius* 1b.14.2).
Buh-der-yii erl jy Jiing-shyh, suh yan (不得已而之景氏宿焉) "He had no alternative but to go to the Ch'ing family residence, and stay the night with them" (lit: having no alternative/he went/ . . .) (*Mencius* 2b.2.5).
A shift from indicative *bu* to subjunctive *wu* is found in
Shyh mou fei wu suoo neng jyi yee, wu yii tzer yeou i yan (是謀非吾所能及也無已則有一焉) "Advice of this kind is not the sort I aspire to give, but were I pressed to do so, then there is one piece of advice I have to offer" (*Mencius* 1b.13.1).

EXAMPLES

Shyy buh der geng-now, yii yang chyi fuh-muu (使不得耕耨以養其父母) "It would bring about their not being able to conduct successfully their farming operations that thereby they might maintain their parents" (*Mencius* 1a.5.5).

Jye lih yii shyh dah gwo tzer buh der mean yan (竭力以事大國則不得免焉) "Even if I did my utmost to serve the Great States, I would not get rid of them" (lit: succeed/being rid/of them) (*Mencius* 1b.15.1).

Ian der jyh (焉得智) "When will he become wise!" (*Mencius* 2a.7.2).

Bwu shyh kee shyy goa-ren der jiann hu (不識可使寡人得見乎) /not/know/can/cause/self/manage/see/mood/ "Will it be possible for me to manage to see you?" (*Mencius* 2b.2.1).

Gaw tzer buh der cheu (告則不得娶) "If he had informed his parents he would never have managed to marry" (*Mencius* 5a.2.2).

Tzer buh der chih jiann jy (則不得亟見之) "... then they did not manage to see them often" (*Mencius* 7a.8.2).

Yu wey der wei Koong-tzyy twu yee (予未得為孔子徒也) "I would never have succeeded in becoming a disciple of Confucius" (*Mencius* 4b.22.1).

3.3.2.7. Customary Aspect

A verb determined by *charng* (嘗) *diang has customary aspect. The act is viewed as being one of habit rather than of a specific occurrence. Since habitual action is not "one instance of the act" (see 3.3.1.1) a verb determined by *charng* cannot be negated with *bu* but is negated with *wey*. (*Charng* is used plerematically for "to taste" and thus by extension "to experience.")

EXAMPLES

Shyi jee, Menq-tzyy charng yeu woo yan yu Song yu shin jong bwu wang (昔者孟子嘗與我言於宋於心終不忘) "Formerly, when we were in Sung, Mencius used to talk with me, and in my heart I have never forgotten [the things he said]" (*Mencius* 3a.2.1).

Wu charng wen dah yeong yu Fu-tzyy yii (吾嘗聞大勇於夫子矣) "I used to hear about great feats of valour from the Master ..." (*Mencius* 2a.2.8).

Gay shang-shyh charng yeou bwu tzang chyi chin jee (蓋上世嘗有不葬其親者)

Woo ian der-yii (我焉得已) /we/when?/succeed/finish [otherwise]/ "What alternative have we?" (*Tso* 316.14).

Der with *jyh* "to will, to determine to," that is, *der-jyh* "to succeed in one's wishes," "to get one's own way," occurs in

Goou der-jyh yan (苟得志焉) "If indeed we manage to get our own way in this ..." (*Tso* 317.4).

Chuu-ren der-jyh yu Jinn (楚人得志於晉) "The Ch'u [delegates] got their way at the expence of Tsin" (*Tso* 339.1).

"No doubt in time past there used to be [the custom] of not burying one's dead relatives" (*Mencius* 3a.5.8).
Ju-hour jy lii, wu wey jy shyue yee, swei-ran wu charng wen jy yii (諸侯之禮吾未之學也雖然吾嘗聞之矣) "I have not studied the rituals of the Feudal Princes but still, I used to hear about them" (*Mencius* 3a.2.4).
Guu jy ren wey charng bwu yuh shyh (古之人未嘗不欲仕) /no time/experience/ not to/want/to be in office/ "Men of old always desired to be in office" (*Mencius* 3b.3.9).

3.3.2.8. Aspects of Incidence

A number of words occurring in the aspectual position before the verb define aspects of incidence. These aspects have to do with the number, sequence, or degrees of incidence of the act envisaged.

(*a*) Number or sequence of incidence.

In one act
I (一) "one": *Yuann bih syy jee, i saa jy* (願比死者一洒之) "I wish before I die, to expunge it [i.e., the disgrace] in one fell swoop" (*Mencius* 1a.5.2).

An act repeated
Tzay (再) "twice": *Tzay her Ju-hour, san her dah-fu* (再合諸侯三合大夫) "Twice he convened the Feudal Lords, and three times he convened the Nobles" (*Tso* 339.3). (S.W. definition of *tzay* s.v. *i jeu erl ell* (一舉而二) "having acted once, to act for a second time." See 7.6.)

For the first time
Chu (初) "first": *Yu-shyh, chu shiann liow yeu, shyy yonq liow yih* (于是初獻六羽始用六佾) "Whereupon, for the first time the Duke used six feather-dancers in the shrine ceremonies, and for the first time employed six rows of dancers" (*Tso* 13.11).
Shyy (始) "begin" (see previous example) and cf. *Yu shyh shyy shing-fa buu buh tzwu* (於是始興發補不足) "from that time Ch'i began to issue [grain] from the State granaries to help the needy" (*Mencius* 1b.4.11).

For the second time, once again
Fuh (復) "to return, to repeat": *Jiang yii fuh jinn yee* (將以復進也) "He intended to bring them in again" (*Mencius* 4a.20.5).
Jonq (重) "heavy" (read in this usage *chorng*) *Chuu chorng der-jyh yu Jinn* (楚重得志於晉) "If Ch'u once again get their way at Tsin's expense" (*Tso* 339.3).
Yow (又) "once again": *Jin yow chih goa-ren erl guei* (今又棄寡人而歸) "Now once again you are leaving me to return home" (*Mencius* 2b.10.1).
Meei (每) "each time": *Meei chaur, chyi chi bih jich jy* (每朝其妻必戒之) "Each time he attended Court, his wife invariably warned him" (*Tso* 239.10).

In alternate sequence
Dye (迭) "alternately": *Dye wei bin juu* (迭爲賓主) "He acted alternately as guest and host" (*Mencius* 5b.3.9).

(b) Degrees of incidence (iterative and frequentative aspect).

Shuh (數) "number" (read *shuoh*) and cognates *lou* (婁) (read *leu*) and *leu* (屢) "many times, repeatedly, often": *Shann yu jee shuoh neng* (善游者數能) "good swimmers often can [learn to handle boats well]" (*Chuang* 49.23); *Shuoh cheng Chi Gong* (數稱絡工) "often spoke approvingly of Ch'i Kung" (*Chuang* 54.1); *Wu buh ru dah gwo jy shuoh ben yee* (吾不如大國之數奔也) /we/not/like/ your/state/→/often/flee/st./ "We don't compare with your State in the frequency with which we retreat" (*Tso* 199.5); with which cf. MAC and Han examples; *Leu tzeng yu ren* (屢憎於人) "is often hated by others" (*Analects* 5.5); *Leu tzau shiong jiow* (屢遭凶咎) "We have frequently encountered baneful calamities" (*Han Shu* 9.9).

Duo (多) "many" and thus *Sonq duo tzer luh yu Jenq* (宋多責賂於鄭) "Sung was constantly importuning Tseng for bribes" (*Tso* 40.8).

Chih (亟) and *chow* (驟) (grammatical forms of *jyi* "fast, quick," and *tzow* "fast, quick," respectively) "often, frequently": *Muh-gong jy yu Tzyy-sy yee, chih wenn, chih kuey diing row* (繆公之於子思也亟問亟饋鼎肉) "Duke Mu frequently enquired after, and frequently sent presents of cooked meat to Tzu Szu" (*Mencius* 5b.6.5); *Chow shy yu gwo erl duo jiuh shyh* (驟施於國而多聚士) "Having frequently made gifts in the State, he had gathered a large number of supporters" (*Tso* 166.23); *Shiuan-tzyy chow jiann, Gong huann jy* (宣子驟諫公患之) "[Chao] Hsuan-tzu frequently remonstrated with the Duke, and the Duke was vexed with him" (*Tso* 181.4).

Haan (罕) "infrequently": *Tzyy haan yan ...* (子罕言 ...) "The Master rarely spoke of ..." (*Analects* 9.1).

Shao (少) "few" and so "in slow sequence, little by little, gradually": *Bing, chyi shao mii yii* (兵其少弭矣) "They might gradually bring to an end the resort to arms" (*Tso* 306.16).

Sheau (小) "small" (used here in same sense as *shao*): *binq sheau yuh* (病小愈) "his illness is gradually getting better" (*Mencius* 2b.2.4).

Shau (稍) (*sog cognate with 小 śiog) has a Han example: *Shang nuh shau jiee* (上怒稍解) "The Emperor's anger gradually subsided" (*Shih Chi* 2.549.35).

Ryh (日) "day" and so "daily," for example, in *Jin yeou ren ryh raang chyi lin jy ji jee* (今有人日攘其鄰之雞者) "Now suppose there was a man who day after day stole his neighbour's chickens" (*Mencius* 3b.8.2). *Ryh* is also used in a geminated form, for example, in *"Ryh-ryh shin"* (日日新) "Daily renew it" (*Great Learning* 2.1).

3.3.2.9. Miscellaneous Aspects

A number of words occurring in the aspectual position before the verb define aspects which do not fall within the classes previously set up.

(1) Comparable to momentary aspect are:

Shin (新) "new" and thus "recently": *Chyi Tsuei Chinq shin der jenq* (齊崔慶新得政) "Ts'ui [Chu] and Ch'ing [Feng] of Ch'i have recently gained control of the government" (*Tso* 306.16).

I (一) "one" and thus *I jenq jiun erl gwo dinq yii* (一正君而國定矣) "Once the ruler is corrected, the state will be peaceful" (*Mencius* 4a.21.2).

Shian (先) "previous, first": *Chuu Gong-tzyy Hei-hong shian jyh* (楚公子黑肱先至) "Hei-hung, Prince of Ch'u arrived beforehand" (*Tso* 316.19).

Shao (少) "few" and thus "for a few days, months, etc., only just, hardly, barely": *Tsyy ren shao juanq, chii neng wanq chyi fuh tzai* (此人少壯豈能忘其父哉) "This man has barely reached manhood, he surely cannot have forgotten his father" (*Han Shu* 48.34). Here "but recently, beforehand, immediately" simply define with greater specificness the moment of action.

(2) A restrictive aspect is imposed by:

Dan (單) "single" in the sense of "one act to the exclusion of others, merely": *Dan bih chyi syy* (單斃其死) /only/cause to become a violent death/his/death/ "He will only be ensuring for himself a violent death" (*Tso* 317.7).

Juan (專) "alone, entire" in the sense of "applying to one affectee to the exclusion of all others": *Chii juan tzay Jinn* (豈專在晉) "Surely it need not exclusively lie with Tsin?" (*Tso* 317.14).

Teh (特) "single" in the sense of "applying to one agent in a unique way": *teh wenn* (特聞) "particularly famous" (*Chuang* 1.12). *Teh, dan* and *juan* derive from the common notion "one, single, sole, entire."

From the notion of "straight, exact, precise, just, only" is derived a similar form of restriction:

Jyy (祇) (cf. *jyr* (直) restrictive copula): *Jinn wey kee mieh erl sha chyi jiun, jyy yii cherng eh* (晉未可滅而殺其君祇以成惡) "Since Tsin cannot be destroyed, to kill its prince would merely result in calamity" (*Tso* 110.4); *Shyh wey kee jy, jyy cherng eh ming, jyy yee* (事未可知祇成惡名止也) "The outcome of this affair is unpredictable, and it will only result in giving us a bad name [I propose that we] desist [from it]" (*Tso* 315.18).

(3) Aspects in which the number of agents, or the number of affectees is involved, are:

Torng (同) "together" (one act, many agents), and thus "unanimously": *Jonq suoo torng chiuh* (衆所同去) "that which the commonalty unanimously rejects" (*Chuang* 3.44), and "together, in concert": *Buh yeu min torng yaw yee* (不與民同樂也) "It was because the King and his people did not share their pleasures in common" (*Mencius* 1b.1.9).

Dwu (獨) "one, single" and thus "alone, in private": *Chii neng dwu yaw tzai* (豈能獨樂哉) "Surely he cannot take his pleasures by himself" (*Mencius* 1a.2.6).

Binq (並) "together, as one" and thus "equally, without discrimination" (one act, all affectees): *Min binq yonq jy* (民並用之) "The common people use all [of the five basic materials] equally" (*Tso* 318.12).

Shenq (勝) "to conquer, to obtain victory over," "to be fully equal to," (read *sheng*): *Fuu-jin yii shyr ruh shan-lin, tsair-muh buh kee sheng yonq yee* (斧斤以時入山林材木不可勝用也) "If forestry is restricted to the proper seasons, then timber will be more than enough for our needs" (lit: not/able/be fully equal/to use/that is, "will never be used up") (*Mencius* 1a.3.6). *Buh kee sheng* . . . occurs in a number of contexts: *Buh kee sheng shyr* (不可勝食) "more than enough to eat"; *buh kee sheng yan* (不可勝言) "indescribable" (more than can be contained in words), etc.

3.3.2.10. Miscellaneous Notes on Aspect

NOTE 1. Many of the words of the class "aspectual determinants" occur also in plerematic usage (e.g., they occur at β in the verbal syntagma, in (. . . β) in addition to their occurrence at *As* in (*As* β). It is the free and non-free forms of distribution that govern their classification as plerematic or cenematic words. Thus *yuh* (欲) occurs plerematically in the sense of "to desire," "desires"; *charng* (嘗) in sense of "to taste" (e.g., a medicine); *jih* (既) and *yii* (已) in sense of "to finish, to complete"; *der* (得) "to get, to obtain." Their aspectual indications are clearly derived from their plerematic meanings. Others are less clearly derived, though *jiang* (將) "about to" and *jianq* (same sign) "to go before, to lead" (cf. 3.3.2.5 footnote 18 where potential aspect is described in the Mohist Canons as "in front of the speaker"), and *fang* (方) "a point or location in time" and *fang* (same sign) "square, region, location" suggest possible connections. *Chiee* (且), *jah* (乍), *you* (猶) and *shanq* (尚), on the other hand, are already institutionalized in the language in their grammatical roles, and their etymology is obscure.

NOTE 2. Words of the class represented, for example, by *binq* (並) "indiscriminately" and *torng* (同) "unanimously" are formally distinguished from words of the class *tsuh* (卒) "abruptly" and *tsuh* (蹙) "frowningly" (see 3.3.3.1) by the occurrence (or possibility of occurrence) of *ran* (然) after the latter. Irrespective of the exigencies of the "target" or "reference" language, the former class has to do with aspect (as defined in 3.3.2), and the latter with manner. The defining characteristic of the latter class is the occurrence or possibility of occurrence of *ran*.

NOTE 3. Certain words used as aspectual determinants occur in a variety of types of distribution, each having a distinctive grammatical role. An analysis by types of distribution gives the following—observe the importance of distinguishing classes among the verbal determinants:[21]

---

[21]See also 3.5.3.1 footnote 47.

THE VERBAL SENTENCE

Time	Agent		Verbal complex			β
	α	Dist.	Coll. and Rest.	Aspect	Degree	
1	日			日		
2	初始			初始		
3	少	少	小 少 稍	小 少 稍	小 少	
4		多	多	多		

(1) *Ryh* (日) in time position: "the other day, on another day"; in aspectual position "daily, day by day."

(2) *Chu* (初) and *shyy* (始) in time position "prior to this, on a previous occasion"; in aspectual position "for the first time."

(3) *Shao* (少) in time position "in a short time, in a little while," and read *shaw* "when young"; as agential distributive "of the agents, few . . ."; as a restrictive (*via* the verb) of post verbal elements, "a few only"; as an aspectual determinant of the verb "gradually, little by little"; ditto "only just, barely"; *shau* (稍) is used both aspectually and as a post verbal restrictive; *sheau* (小) aspectually, and as post verbal restrictive. Both *shao* and *sheau* are determinants of quality or degree of the verb, respectively: "in a small degree, slightly," and "somewhat, a little more."

(4) *Duo* (多) as distributive of the agent "of the agents, many"; as restrictive of the post verbal elements via the verb "much, many"; as aspectual determinant of the verb "frequently, often."

NOTE 4. Economy in the specification of mood, of aspect and of time is nicely illustrated in the following example: *Wu guh yuann jiann, jin wu shanq binq, binq yuh, woo chiee woang jiann* (吾固願見今吾尚病病愈我且往見) "I did wish to see him [yesterday but I was ill]. Today, I am still ill, but when my illness is better, I will go to see him" (*Mencius* 3a.5.1).

3.3.3.1. Determinations of Manner

Determinations of manner occur as elements in the verbal syntagma, characterized as a class by (i) the occurrence of a post-posited *ran* (然) *ńian (an allegro form of *ru-tsyy* (如此)) "like this, in this manner,"[22] or (ii) being in reduplicated form (gemination), or (iii)

---

[22]With this usage of *ran* "in this manner" cf. the use of *nae* (乃) *nəg "in this manner" used for anaphora, in the sense of "in such a manner." For example, *Tzyy-chaan tsuh-ran gae rong geng maw, iue "Tzyy wu nae cheng"* (子產蹵然改容更貌曰"子無乃稱") "Tzu-ch'an, with a frown, altered his stance and changed his expression, [i.e., took up a different ritual posture] and said 'You, Sir, should not have spoken in that way'" Sir/should not/in that manner/speak/ (*Chuang* 13.24).

being both in geminated form and using *ran*. They occur as alternately x/*ran*, xx/*ran*, or xx/o.

EXAMPLES

Shyy-shyy tsorng way lai (施施從外來) "Jauntily, he came in from outside" (*Mencius* 4b.33.6).
Tsuh-ran wenn (卒然問) "Abruptly he asked" (*Mencius* 1a.6.1).
Tian you-ran tzuoh yun (天油然作雲) "Heaven copiously makes clouds" (*Mencius* 1a.6.3).
Pey-ran shiah yeu (沛然下雨) "It rains heavily" (*Mencius* 1a.6.3).
Tserng-shi tsuh-ran iue (曾西蹵然曰) "Tseng Hsi frowningly said" (*Mencius* 2a.1.2).
Mang-mang ran guei (芒芒然歸) "Hurriedly he returned home" (*Mencius* 2a.2.19).
Wanq-wanq ran chiuh jy (望望然去之) "Haughtily he dismissed him" (*Mencius* 2a.9.3).

3.3.3.2. The State of the Agent

A class[23] of determinants of the verb occur in the verbal syntagma with the class-meaning "denoting a state which is a precondition of

---

[23]The cross-distribution of classes at differing levels of analysis provide problems of statement here. The class-meaning given in the statement above, provides a means of segregating words of the *neng, keen, ker, tzwu* type, which is contrastive to the means used for distinguishing modal determinants. Mood has been set up in this analysis primarily on the basis of polarity (since the formal distinction among the negatives provides its clearest observable distinctions). Thereafter the modal paradigm has been filled in by criteria of interchangeability, and contrast within the pattern. However, *mood* overlaps into the class set up above. For example, *kee* (可) "permissibility, what might properly be done" occurs in extended usage to a purely modal "what might, could or may be done," in for example, conditional statements.

EXAMPLES

Tian-shiah kee yunn yu jaang (天下可運於掌) ". . . then the world might be turned in the palm of your hand" (*Mencius* 1a.7.21).
Kee shyy goa-ren der jiann (可使寡人得見) /could/cause/me/manage/see/ "Could I see you?" (*Mencius* 2b.2.2).
Shyh, wey kee jy (是未可知) "this could never be known" (*Mencius* 3b.10.5).

Again *neng* (classed above) and *wei* (classed as modal) occur in contrast in the passage *Wang jy buh wanq, buh wei yee, fei buh neng yee* (王之不王不爲也非不能也) "The King's not acting as a true king, is because he (*buh wei wanq*) 'would not act as a true King' and not because he (*buh neng wanq*) 'could not act as a true King.'" The question then is asked *Buh wei jee, yeu buh neng jee jy shyng, her yii yih* (不爲者與不能者之形何以異) "How can one distinguish between the qualities of the two words *buh wei* [could not] and *buh neng* [would not]?" (*Mencius* 1a.7.17). At the statement level, however, the classes are distinguished as above, this seeming to me the most economical way of resolving in statement this form of cross-distribution.

THE VERBAL SENTENCE

the agency by which the act or state designated by the verb is performed or realized." (Conventional symbol SA.) Words in this class include:

neng (能) *nəng "to be able to be or to act," "can";
kee (可) *k'â "to be permitted to be or to act," "could";
tzwu (足) *tsiuk "to have sufficient resources to be or to act," "adequate to";
gaan (敢) *kâm "to presume or dare to be or to act";
reen (忍) *ńiən "to endure or bear to be or to act";
keen (肯) *k'əng "to be willing to be or to act."[24]

EXAMPLES

Neng: *Shwu neng i jy* (孰能一之) "Who is able to unite it?" (*Mencius* 1a.6.2); *Buh neng jinn yu shyh yii* (不能進於是矣) "I cannot achieve this" (*Mencius* 1a.7.36); *Goa-ren fei neng haw Shian-wang jy yueh yee* (寡人非能好先王之樂也) "I am not one who can appreciate the music of the Former Kings" (*Mencius* 1b.1.3).

Kee: *Her kee fey yee* (何可廢也) "How could we dispense with it?" (*Mencius* 1a.7.6); *Ju dah-fu jie iue "kee sha"* (諸大夫皆曰可殺...) "When all the nobles say 'It is permissible to inflict the death penalty...'" (*Mencius* 1b.7.6); *Ian kee fa yu* (燕可伐與) "Would it be proper to attack Yen?" (*Mencius* 2b.8.1); *Kee wey shiaw yii* (可謂孝矣) "That could with propriety be called filial conduct" (*Mencius* 3a.2.3).

Tzwu: *Tzer Wen Wang buh tzwu faa yu* (則文王不足法與) "Then King Wen would be inadequate as an exemplar, would he not?" (*Mencius* 2a.1.8); *Buh tzwu diaw hu* (不足弔乎) "Is he not inadequately [equipped] to perform the ceremony of condolence?" (*Mencius* 3b.3.5); *Chih buh tzwu yonq yee* (器不足用也) "The vessels would be insufficient for use [i.e., there would not be enough pots]" (*Mencius* 6b.10.2).

Gaan: *Ran-now gaan ruh* (然後敢入) "Then only would he presume to enter" (*Mencius* 1b.2.4); *Bii u gaan dang woo tzai* (彼惡敢當我哉) "How dare he oppose me?" (*Mencius* 1b.3.5); *Gaan chiing* (敢請) "Dare I make a request?" (*Mencius* 1b.16.2); *Shwei gaan wuu jy* (誰敢侮之) "Who dare insult him?"

---

[24]Each of the words of this class occur, not only as SA in the distribution SA/verb, but also as verb in the distribution (———verb), that is,
neng "to be able"; *kee* "to be permitted";
tzwu "to be sufficient or adequate";
gaan "to dare or presume";
reen "to endure, to bear";
keen "to be willing."

Certain of the words also occur at SA in the distribution SA/ins, when the instrumental is resultative (see 3.6.2), for example, *neng-yii* (能以) "one can thereby...";
kee-yii (可以) "one could thereby";
tzwu-yii (足以) "sufficient or adequate whereby to";
and *gaan-yii* (敢以) "one might presume thereby to."

(*Mencius* 2a.4.4); *Gaan wenn* (敢問) "Might I presume to ask . . ." (*Mencius* 5b.3.1).

Reen: *Buh reen jiann chyi syy* (不忍見其死) "could not bear to see it die" (*Mencius* 1a.7.11); *Buh reen shyr chyi row* (不忍食其肉) "could not bear to eat its flesh" (*Mencius* 1a.7.12); *Buh reen jiu yee* (不忍居也) "could not bear to stay" (*Mencius* 5b.1.2); *Buh reen chiuh yee* (不忍去也) "could not bear to go" (*Mencius* 5b.1.8).

Keen: *Wey keen yonq minq* (未肯用命) "never willing to obey orders" (*Tso* 197.4); *Chyi keen tzyh woo hu* (其肯字我乎) "will he be willing to treat us as he would treat his own children?" (*Tso* 220.11); *Chyn Bor buh keen sheh Her* (秦伯不肯涉河) "The Earl of Ch'in was unwilling to cross the Yellow River" (*Tso* 232.7).

3.3.4. Conspectus of the Verbal Syntagma

A high degree of selectivity (see the rule of economy, 2.2.1) occurs in the assembly of the verbal syntagma, so that, varied as the resources for grammatical determination of the verb are in LAC, only one or two are selected in any given instance. It is difficult therefore to build up a paradigm showing the relative ranks of the elements of the verbal syntagma. The constituent elements of the verbal syntagma here summarized in tabular form, are assembled therefore with disregard for their orders of precedence:

The Verbal Syntagma

Grammatical determinations		The Verb	
Mood[4] and Aspect[5]			
Md β	As β	Material determinations[3]	β^1
Manner[6]	Man (然) β	β (A → β)	
State of agency[7] SA β			β ($\beta+\beta$) etc.[2]

[1]See 3.3.　　[3]*Ibid.*　　[3]*Ibid.*　　[4]See 3.3.1.
[5]See 3.3.2.　　[6]See 3.3.3.1.　　[7]See 3.3.3.2.

3.4. The Post-verbal Elements

In the distribution of the elements of the verbal sentence, two elements (conventional symbols γ^1 and γ^2) occur immediately after the verb or verbal syntagma (i.e., β γ^1 γ^2). These elements occur in the distributions β γ^1 γ^2; β γ^1; and β γ^2; but are formally distinguished by the occurrence (or possibility of occurrence) of a particle before γ^2. The purpose of these elements is (i) to restrict the scope of the verb, and (ii) to govern its voice. They are thus determinative of the verb, and subordinate to it. The voice of the verb is governed by varying sets of distributions of these two elements. The scope of the verb (its direction and goal) is defined by them. The particles of the second post-verbal element are *yu* (於) *.io, *yu* (于) *giwo or *hu* (乎) *g'o.[25]

3.4.1. Transitive and Intransitive

The verb is either transitive or intransitive. This is distinguished by the voice of the verb when its affectee or goal is placed in the first post-verbal position. A transitive verb with affectee at γ^1 is *active* (e.g., *tzer* (擇) "to choose," *tzer jy* (擇之) "choose it"; *show* (受) "to receive," *show jy* (受之) "receive it"). An intransitive verb[26] with affectee at γ^1 is *causative* (e.g., *chiuh* (去) "to go out," *chiuh jy* (去之) "cause-to-go-out it [i.e., expel it]," *shyng* (行) "to walk, to proceed," *shyng jy* (行之) "to cause-to-proceed [i.e., to implement] it").

3.4.2. Transitive Verbs in Causative Voice

The affectee or goal of a transitive verb is placed in the γ^2 position when the verb is causative.

EXAMPLES
Hay (害) "to harm, to injure"
(i) with affectee in γ' position
Buh yii wen hay tsyr (不以文害辭) "[Ancient expositors of the Odes] did not do violence to [lit: harm] the line by insisting upon a single word" (*Mencius* 5a.4.9);
Wu yii jiann hay guey (無以賤害貴) "One should not harm the noble, with the ignoble" (*Mencius* 6a.14.3).

---

[25] In LAC *yu* (於) is typical (于) archaistic, occurring most frequently in citations from earlier works or in annalistic style writing, and *hu* (乎) of less frequent occurrence than *yu* (e.g., virtually non-existent in *Tso*). (For a contrary view, see Karlgren (1), p. 41 and contra Karlgren see Jou Faa-gau (2), p. 181.)

[26] Intransitive verbs occur among

(a) words whose meaning content includes some element of direction, for example, *Chu* (出) "to go out," *lai* (來) "to come to, or in," *lih* (立) "to stand up," *fa* (發) "to issue forth," *shing* (興) "to rise up," *jyh* (至) "to arrive at," and thus *chu* "to cause to go out" (i.e., "to issue"), *lai* "to cause to come," *lih* "to cause to stand up" (i.e., "to establish"), *fa* "to cause to issue forth," for example, "to shoot" (as, e.g., an arrow), *shing* "to cause to rise up" (i.e., "to promote, revive," etc.), and *jyh* "to cause to arrive at" (i.e., "to perfect"); and

(b) words which alternate in factative and putative usage (see 3.4.6). Since causative voice may be indicated periphrastically (see 3.4.5) by the use of *shyy* (使) "cause," a further defining characteristic of transitive and intransitive is that the intransitive verb can transpose to this form without violation of sense. *Chiuh jy* (去之) /cause-to-go-out/it/, *shyy jy chiuh* (使之去) /cause/it/to go out/, but the transitive verb cannot. *Tzer jy* (擇之) "choose it," *shyy jy tzer* (使之擇) "cause it to choose."

(ii) with affectee in γ^2 position

Hay yu chyi jenq (害於其政) "That would cause injury to his government" (*Mencius* 3b.9.17);

Hay yu geng (害於耕) "It would cause harm to agriculture" (*Mencius* 3a.4.8).

Yueh (悅) "to please"

(i) with affectee in γ^1 position

Yueh chin yeou daw (悅親有道) "There is a teaching on pleasing parents" (*Mencius* 4a.13.2);

Meei ren erl yueh jy (每人而悅之) "to please everybody" (*Mencius* 4b.2.3).

(ii) with affectee in γ^2 position

Bwu yueh yu chin yii (不悅於親矣) /cause-not-to-be-pleased/parents/ "to be displeasing to parents" (*Mencius* 4a.13.2);

Koong-tzyy bwu yueh yu Luu Wey (孔子不悅於魯衛) "Confucius caused-not-to-be-pleased, the rulers of Lu and Wei," that is, "he was disliked by" (*Mencius* 5a.8.4).

Cheng (稱) "to praise"

(i) with affectee in γ^1 position

Yan bih cheng Yau Shuenn (言必稱堯舜) "In conversation he invariably praised Yao and Shun" (*Mencius* 3a.1.1).

(ii) with affectee in γ^2 position

Jonq-ni chih cheng yu shoei (仲尼亟稱於水) "Confucius frequently caused to be praised water" (*Mencius* 4b.18.1).

This might be represented as follows:

	Verb		Post-verbal elements	
	β	(voice)	γ^1	γ^2
Trans.		active	affectee	
		causative		affectee
Intrans.		active	———	
		causative	affectee	

NOTE. With certain verbs, the element occurring at γ^1 (the affectee) is a formally complete sentence with the particle of determination interposed between agent and verb (see 2.7.2, syntagma form).

EXAMPLES

Wang (望) "to expect": *Wu wanq min jy duo yu lin gwo yee* (無望民之多於鄰國也) "You would not expect your population to be greater than your neighbour's" (*Mencius* 1a.3.5).

Jy (知) "to know": *Bih jy luann jy suoo-tzyh chii* (必知亂之所自起) "[He] must know that from which disorder arises" (*Micius* 21.1).

Chiing (請) "to request, to beg" is exceptional in that the agent of the γ^1 element occurs before the verb. *Chern chiing wey wang yan yueh* (臣請為王言樂) "[I] request that *I* might explain music for you" (*Mencius* 1b.1.5); *Jiun chiing tzer yu sy ell jee* (君請擇於斯二者) "[I] request that *you my Lord* choose from among these two" (*Mencius* 1b.15.6).

3.4.3. The Directive—Active Voice

A restriction is placed upon the scope of the action when its goal or affectee is specified. Thus *tzer* (擇) "choose—in general" (no restriction), *tzer jy* (擇之) "choose *it*—in particular" (restriction). In this sense a further restriction upon the scope of the verb is imposed by directives. These denominate the place, person, object towards which, at which, within which, etc. the action is directed. Thus *tzer yu sy ell jee* (擇於斯二者) "choose [in particular] it, from [in further particular] among these two" (*Mencius* 1b.15.6). The directives occur at γ^2 with both transitive and intransitive verbs. Where the action flows from the verb, *via* the affectee, towards the directive, the voice of the verb is active.

EXAMPLES

(1) Place, person or object towards which action is directed—"to":
Liou Gonq gong yu Iow-jou (流共工于幽州) "banished Kung-Kung to Yu-chou" (*Liou* intransitive "to flow" here causative "cause to flow, to banish" (*Mencius* 5a.3.2).
Yi chyi min yu Her-dong (移其民於河東) "transferred my people to Ho-tung" (*Mencius* 1a.3.1).
Chwan shyr yu Ju-hour (傳食於諸侯) "Send provisions to the Feudal Lords" (*Mencius* 3b.4.1).
Boh chyi eh yu jonq (播其惡於眾) "made known his evil to the populace" (*Mencius* 4a.1.8).
Faan yu Chyi (反於齊) "Returned to Ch'i" (*Mencius* 2b.7.1); *I yu Tzyy-gonq* (揖於子貢) "He bowed to Tzu Kung" (*Mencius* 3a.4.30).

(2) Location at which action takes place—"in" "at":
Shyue yu Jong-gwo (學於中國) "He learned it in the Central States" (*Mencius* 3a.4.28).
Jyh yu jinq (至於境) "arrived at the frontier" (*Mencius* 1b.2.3).

(3) Area in which, objects among which, etc., the action takes place—"among" "in" "within":
Tzer yu sy ell jee (擇於斯二者) "choose from among these two" (*Mencius* 1b.15.6).
Gow yuann yu Ju-hour (構怨於諸侯) "aroused resentment among the Feudal Lords" (*Mencius* 1a.7.25).
Jyi shiann hu tzuey (及陷乎罪) "By the time they have become involved in crime" (*Mencius* 3a.3.3).
Sheh yu jiau (舍於郊) "built a mat shed in the suburbs" (*Mencius* 1b.4.11).
Farn yeou syh duan yu woo jee (凡有四端於我者) "All of those who have these four principles within themselves . . ." (*Mencius* 2a.6.8).

(4) Object or place upon which the action takes place—"on" "upon":
Jiann yu miann (見於面) "appeared on his face" (*Mencius* 7a.21.3).
Lih yu jao-shang (立於沼上) "standing at the pool" (*Mencius* 1a.2.1).
Tzuoh yu twu-tann (坐於塗炭) "sat upon the muddy road" (*Mencius* 2a.9.2).
Bwu fuh-day yu daw-luh yii (不負戴於道路矣) "do not carry heavy burdens upon the highways" (*Mencius* 1a.7.45).

(5) Place from which the action begins—"from":
Chu yu iou guu (出於幽谷) "emerged from the dark chasm" (*Mencius* 3a.4.33).
Shyh you dih-tzyy erl chyy show minq yu shian-shy yee (是猶弟子而恥受命於先師也) "It is like one who, being a student, resents receiving orders from a teacher" (*Mencius* 4a.8.2).
Shyue sheh yu Yih (學射於羿) "He learned archery from Yi" (*Mencius* 4b.24.1).

(6) Miscellaneous—"in between," "into," etc.
Terng sheau gwo yee, jiann yu Chyi Chuu (滕小國也間於齊楚) "T'eng is a minor state, it lies in between Ch'i and Ch'u" (*Mencius* 1b.13.1).
Juann hu gou-huoh (轉乎溝壑) "rolling into the gutters" (*Mencius* 3a.3.9).
Guu yueh yu tsyy (鼓樂於此) "Play music here [at this place]" (*Mencius* 1b.1.6).
Jiu yan (居焉) "He lived there" (*Mencius* 1b.14.2).

3.4.4. The Directive—Passive Voice

Where by contrast the direction of flow of the action proceeds from directive to the verb, the voice of the verb is passive.

EXAMPLES

Jyh (治) "to govern": (active) *Jyh ren* (治人) "to govern others"; (passive) *Jyh yu ren* (治於人) "to be governed by others" as in *Huok lau shin, huoh lau lih. Lao shin jee jyh ren, lao lih jee jyh yu ren. Jyh yu ren jee shyr ren, jyh ren jee shyr yu ren* (或勞心或勞力勞心者治人勞力者治於人治於人者食人治人者食於人) "Some work with their brains, others work with their hands. Those who work with their brains govern others, those who work with their hands are governed by others. Those who are governed provide the food for others. Those who govern are fed by others" (*Mencius* 3a.4.14).

Dinq (定) "to settle, to pacify": (active) *Dinq tian-shiah* (定天下) "to settle the world" (*Mencius* 1a.6.1); (passive) *Dinq yu i* (定于一) "It will be settled by unification" (*Mencius* 1a.6.2).

Gae (改) "to change": (active) *Chiee guu jy jiun-tzyy guoh tzer gae jy* (且古之君子過則改之) "further when a ruler of antiquity transgressed, then [they] corrected him" (*Mencius* 2b.9.6); (passive) *Wu neng gae yu chyi der* (無能改於其德) "They would not be changed by his virtue" (*Mencius* 4a.15.1).

Huann (患) "to worry": *Her huann hu wu jiun* (何患乎無君) "Why be worried [by the fact that you] have no ruler" (*Mencius* 1b.15.4).

Biann (變) "to change": *Wu wen yonq Shiah biann yi jee, wey wen biann yu Yi jee* (吾聞用夏變夷者未聞變於夷者) "I have heard of our civilization changing barbarians, but not of its being changed by barbarians" (*Mencius* 3a.4.27).

THE VERBAL SENTENCE

No formal distinction is made between the active voice (direction towards) and the passive voice (direction from) in the directive.[27] The directive particles are common to both forms. The difference is simply one of directional flow. This might be represented as follows:

$$
\begin{array}{llll}
Verb & (Direction) & (Particle) & \gamma^2 \\
\text{Active} & \rightarrow & 於 & \text{directive} \\
\text{Passive} & \leftarrow & 於 & \text{directive}
\end{array}
$$

3.4.5. Periphrastic Treatment of Voice

Voice, both causative and passive, may be indicated periphrastically. In the periphrastic passive *Jiann* (見) *kian "see" is interposed between agent and verb. In the periphrastic causative *Shyy* (使) *sliəg "cause, send" or *bih* (俾) *pieg "cause, bring about" is interposed between causal and acting agent.[28]

EXAMPLES

(a) *Passive*:
Pern-cherng Kuoh jiann sha (盆成括見殺) "P'en-ch'eng Kuo was murdered" (*Mencius* 7b.29.1).
Bae-shinq jy bwu jiann bao, wey . . ." (百姓之不見保爲 . . .) "The reason why the people are not protected is because . . ." (*Mencius* 1a.7.17).
Ay ren jee bih jiann ay yee (愛人者必見愛也) "He who loves others will be loved by others" (*Micius* 27.71).

(b) *Causative*:
Shyy Wei meng chyi shian-jiun (使圍蒙其先君) "[You] have made me, Wei, deceive my ancestors" (*Tso* 338.15).
Ruoh neng shyy Chyn Jiun ruu yu bih yih . . . (若能使秦君辱於敝邑) "If the Lord of Ch'in can be made to demean himself in our city . . ." (*Tso* 316.22).

---

[27]See 2.6.3.3 footnote (14). The directive particle is purely gestural—a signal of direction. It has none of the semantic content or variety of the prepositions by which it is represented in translation or "defined" in dictionaries.

[28]In LAC the grammatical usage of words is never far removed from their plerematic usage (e.g., see 3.3.2.10 Note 1). For the examples cited under *shyy* "cause, bring about," there is a formally comparable example in which *shyy* is used in the sense "to send," for example, *Tzyh-muh shyy ryh yeh ju Wang* (子木使馹謁諸王) "Tzu-mu despatched a courier to report this to the King." (*Tso* 316.22). Similarly, *tsorng* (從) "to follow" "obey order" substituting for *shyy* gives the meaning "at the behest, or at the instigation of," "acting upon the orders of" etc. *Jinn Shyun-yng tsorng Jaw-wuu jyh* (晉荀盈從趙武至) "Hsun-ying of Tsin arrived, acting under the orders of Chao Wu." (*Tso* 316.18), and *Leh Jenq-tzyy tsorng yu Tzyy-aur jy Chyi* (樂正子從於子敖之齊) "Lo-cheng-tzu, at the instigation of Tzu Ao, went to Ch'i." (*Mencius* 4a.24.1).

Ming-shern jyi jy, bih shy chyi min ((明神殄之俾失其民) "May the Spirits strike him dead, and make him lose his subjects" (*Tso* 274.2).

Shiou Cherng-jou jy cherng, bih shuh-ren wu chyn (修成周之城俾戍人無勤) /repair/Ch'eng-chou/wall/cause/guards/should not be/belaboured/ "Repair the walls of Ch'eng-chou so that my guards need not overwork" (*Tso* 435.3).

3.4.5.1. Periphrastic Treatment of Direction

The directive particle does not distinguish types of direction (see 3.4.4 footnote 27). Neither direction towards or away from the verb (flow of action), nor direction towards or away from the point of reference of the speaker is distinguished. The latter distinction may be made by substituting for the particle of direction, lexical directives, which make this distinction. They are: (towards point of reference, "from") *you* (由) *diôg, with variant *you* (猶) *ziôg, *tzyh* (自) *dz'i, *tsorng* (從) *dz'iung; and (away from point of reference, "towards, to, up to") *jyh-yu* (至於) *tied.io.²⁹ In *jyh yu songq* (至於宋) "arrived at Sung" (*Tso* 316.16) the direction "at" is inferred from context, but in *jyh tzyh Chern* (至自陳) "arrived from Ch'en" (*Tso* 316.24) the direction "from" is lexically specified.

When the lexical directives are used, the directive is not restricted to the second post-verbal position, but may occur pre-verbally.

EXAMPLES

In second post-verbal position:

Jenq-bor guei tzyh Jinn (鄭伯歸自晉) "The Earl of Cheng returned from Tsin" (*Tso* 312.7).

Gong jyh tzyh Jinn (公至自晉) "The Duke arrived from Tsin" (*Tso* 220.9).

In pre-verbal position:

Shyh-tzyy tzyh Chuu faan (世子自楚反) "The Crown Prince returned from Ch'u" (*Mencius* 3a.1.1).

Chyi shiong tzyh way jyh (其兄自外至) "His brother came in from outside" (*Mencius* 3b.10.9).

OTHER EXAMPLES

Tsorng tair shanq tarn ren ... (從臺上彈人) "He was shooting at people from the top of his tower..." (*Tso* 180.21).

Lii yih you shyan jee chu (禮義由賢者出) "The rites and justice derive from worthy men" (*Mencius* 1b.16).

Shy you chin shyy (施由親始) /manifestation/from/parents/begins/ "The manifestation of it begins with parents" (*Mencius* 3a.5.5).

Directives occur simultaneously pre-verbally and post-verbally in the following:

²⁹For the use of the lexical directives in time and place indications, see 3.10 Note.

Chern-hour jy dih, tzyh Chuu guei yu Chern (陳侯之弟自楚歸于陳) "Huang, the younger brother of the Lord of Ch'en, returned to Ch'en from Ch'u" (*Ch'un Ch'iu* 297.24).
Sheu-shyng tzyh Chuu jyh Terng (許行自楚至滕) "Hsu-shing arrived in T'eng from Ch'u" (*Mencius* 3a.4.1).

3.4.6. Attributive Verbs and the Post-verbal Elements

Words that occur as attributive determinant words in syntagma (i.e., class 2 in 2.6.2), occurring in the verbal syntagma, may be used in both factitive and putative senses (see 3.2). They are intransitive. The dispositions and functions of the post-verbal elements are those of intransitive verbs but with one additional function.[30] In the distribution verb/–/γ^2, the directive at γ^2 may indicate a degree of comparison. "Verb" in this distribution then has the class-meaning "to possess the attribute in a greater degree" and the γ^2 denominates "the object in comparison with which, the degree is greater."

EXAMPLES

Chyang (強) "strong, powerful": *Chyang yan* = *yu jy* (強焉 i.e., 強於之) "stronger, more powerful than it," as in *Jinn-gwo, tian-shiah moh chyang yan* (晉國天下莫強焉) /Tsin-state/in world/no state/stronger/ than it [i.e., Tsin]/ "No state in the world was stronger than Tsin" (*Mencius* 1a.5.1).
Dah (大) "great, large" and thus *Tzuey moh dah yan* (罪莫大焉) /of crimes/ no crime/greater/than that/ "No crime is greater than that" (*Tso* 318.14).

The directive at γ^2 conversely, may be a directive as defined in 3.4.3 and 3.4.4 as in *shann* (善) "good" in putative sense "to think good, to think well of, to approve," for example, in *Wang ru shann jy* (王如善之) "If Your Majesty approves of this" (*Mencius* 1b.5.8), but with directive at γ^2 *shann* is passive in *Sonq Shianq Shiu shann yu Jaw Wen-tzyy* (宋向戌善於趙文子) "Hsiang Hsü of Sung was thought well of by Chao Wen-tzu" (*Tso* 316.11) (and not "better than Chao Wen-tzu").

3.4.7. Special Cases of Post-verbal Distribution

Special statements must be made about certain verbs, the dispositions of the post-verbal elements of which do not conform to the distributional pattern hitherto described. These are:

[30] The distinction between factitive and putative usages, the introduction of notions of comparative degree, indeed the segregation of a verb-class (as here) at all, are all instances of "taking into account in statement, features of the language of reference." In formal analytical procedure these are not observable variations. But at the statement level, in view of the purpose for which the statement is made, such variations must be introduced.

(1) Certain verbs with the common meaning "to hand on to," for example, *yi* (貽) "to give," *yeu* (與) "to give, to grant," *yeu* (予) "to give, to grant," *yi* (遺) "to hand over," or "hand on, transmit, bequeath," *tsyh* (賜) "to bestow" (hand to an inferior), *kuey* (饋) "to give a present of food to a superior," occur with the elements of the post-verbal positions distributed as follows: verb/recipient/object given, etc. The particle of direction does not occur ($\beta\ \gamma^1\ \gamma^2$).[31]

EXAMPLES

Yi woo dah huh jy joong (貽我大瓠之種) "He gave to me the seeds of a large gourd" (*Chuang* 2.36).

Yeu jy yih liow-shyr (與之邑六十) "gave to him sixty cities" (*Tso* 318.9).

Gong tsyh jy shyr (公賜之食) "The Duke passed him some food" (*Tso* 3.10).

Kuey Koong-tzyy jeng twen (饋孔子蒸豚) "presented Confucius with a roast pig" (*Mencius* 3b.7.3).

When introduced by *yii* (以) the second post-verbal element may transpose to the pre-verbal position ($yii/\gamma^2/\beta/\gamma^1$):

Yii Tsuei-tzyy jy guan tsyh ren (以崔子之冠賜人) "He gave Ts'ui's hat to someone else" (*Tso* 304.19).

Yii yueh jy bann tsyh Wey Jianq (以樂之半賜魏絳) "He gave half of his musical troupe to Wei Chiang" (*Tso* 274.22).

Yau yii tian-shiah yeu Shuenn (堯以天下與舜) "Yao gave the empire to Shun" (*Mencius* 5a.5.1).

(2) Verbs meaning "to buy" or "to sell," for example, *mae* (買) "to buy" *yuh* (鬻) "to sell," occur with the elements of the post-verbal positions distributed as "verb/object sold/price" (with no directive particle), as well as with the distribution "verb/thing bought or sold/where bought or sold, or from whom bought, or to whom sold" (with directive particle).

EXAMPLES

Mae chyi fang bae jin (買其方百金) "Buy the recipe for one hundred pieces of money" (*Chuang* 2.38).

Yuh jih bae jin (鬻枝百金) "Sell our skill for one hundred pieces of money" (*Chuang* 3.1).

---

[31]With verbs of this class, in addition to the elements "recipient"/"thing given" may occur a further directive. It occurs pre-verbally in *U-chern tzyh Jinn yi ell tzyy shu* (巫臣自晉遺二子書) /Wu-ch'en/from/Tsin/delivered/two/gentlemen/letter/ "Wu Ch'en delivered to the two gentlemen a letter from Tsin" (*Tao* 225.5), and post-verbally in *tsyh meng yu Songq* (賜盟于宋) "Granted us a treaty at Sung" (*Tso* 351.16). The distribution pattern verb/affectee/directive (with the use of directive particle) is found, however, in *Yeou kuey sheng yu yu Jenq Tzyy-chaan* (有饋生魚於鄭子產) "Someone presented a live fish to Tzu-ch'an of Cheng" (*Mencius* 5a.2.8).

THE VERBAL SENTENCE

Compare:

Yuh jy yu Chyi (鬻之於齊) "sold him in Ch'i" (*Chuang* 68.83).
Mae ju (= *jy yu*) *shang-ren* (買諸商人) "bought it from a merchant" (*Tso* 391.3).

(3) Certain verbs with the common meaning "to say, to speak," etc.[32] (e.g., *yan* (言) "to speak, put into words," *yeu* (語) "to speak," *wey* (謂) "to speak to, of, or to describe," *gaw* (告) "to report," *wenn* (問) "to ask about," *suh* (愬) "to accuse, complain of," etc.) occur *typically* with post-verbal elements distributed as follows "verb/thing spoken of/to whom spoken," with the possibility of the directive particle occurring, that is, $\beta\ \gamma^1$ (*yu*) γ^2. The form also occurs as $\beta - (yu)\ \gamma^2$.

EXAMPLES

Wenn ren yu Juang-tzyy (問仁於莊子) "asked Chuang-tzu about Humaneness" (*Chuang* 36.5).
Suh Jeng-bor yu Chuu (愬鄭伯于楚) "complained of the Earl of Cheng to Ch'u" (*Tso* 222.1).
Bwu gaw yu Wang (不告於王) ". . . but did not announce [him] to the King" (*Mencius* 2b.8.2).

The first variant of this pattern is the occurrence of the element at γ^1 (above), after γ^2 and introduced by *yii* (以) or *iue* (曰). The directive particle is typically omitted but may occur.

EXAMPLES

Wenn hu Tzeng-shi iue . . . (問乎曾西曰) "[He] enquired of Tseng Hsi . . ." (*Mencius* 2a.1.2).
Yeu Baw yii haw yueh (語暴以好樂) "[He] spoke to me [Bao] about fondness for music" (*Mencius* 1b.1.1).
Wey Chyi Shiuan wang iue (謂齊宣王曰) "said to Hsuan, King of Ch'i . . ." (*Mencius* 1b.6.1).
Gaw jy yii yeou guoh (告之以有過) "[If anyone] told him he had faults . . ." (*Mencius* 2a.8.1).

The second variant is the occurrence of the element typically at γ^1 *before* the verb and introduced by *yii* (以) (yii $\gamma^1/\beta/\gamma^2$) with possible yii — /β/γ^2.

EXAMPLES

Yii Shyr-tzyy jy yan gaw Menq-tzyy (以時子之言告孟子) "told Mencius what Shih Tzu had said" (*Mencius* 2b.10.4).

---

[32] On *wenn* and *gaw* see Jou Faa-gau, (2), p. 184, and for the special treatment of verbs in the class "give" and "speak" see Yang Bor-juinn 14.20 and Yang (3), 4.184.

Yii lih yan yee (以利言也) "it speaks of profit" (*Mencius* 3b.1.4).
Shyu-tzyy yii gaw Yi-tzyy (徐子以告夷子) "Hsu Tzu told Yi Tzu about it" (*Mencius* 3a.5.4).

The third variant[33] is the occurrence of the element typically at γ^2 before the verb and introduced by *yeu* (與) (yeu/γ^2/β).

EXAMPLES

Yeou jiow Yow-shy jy wey erl yeu Yow-shy yan jee (有就右師之位而與右師言者) "There were some who walked over to the place at which the Master of the Right was standing and spoke to him" (*Mencius* 4b.2.7).
Tzyy-muh yeu jy yan, fwu neng duey (子木與之言弗能對) "Tzu Mu spoke to him but he did not reply" (*Tso* 317.17).

The fourth variant (occurring only when *wey* (謂), *ming* (名) and *yan* (言) are used in the sense of "to name, describe, call"), occurs when the post-verbal elements are distributed as follows: verb/thing named/name. Between "thing named" and "name" may occur *wei* (爲) or *iue* (曰) (i.e., $\beta \gamma^1$ (A *wei* or *iue* B).

EXAMPLES

Wey jy huey (謂之惠) "We call this kindness" (*Mencius* 3a.4.24).
Ming jy iue yih-duo (名之曰益多) "We would call that excessive" (*Chuang* 9.11).
Chuu-ren wey huu u tuh (楚人謂虎於菟) "Ch'u people call hu [a tiger] 'u-tuh'" (*Tso* 185.1).
Fuh-ren wey jiah iue guei (婦人謂嫁曰歸) "A wife calls marriage 'the return home.'" (*Gong-yang* 6.7).

This range of alternances might be summarized as follows:

Typical		β	γ^1	於	γ^2
Variation 1		β	□→		γ^2 以 γ^1 曰
Variation 2	以 γ^1	β	←□		γ^2
Variation 3	與 γ^2	β			←□
Variation 4		β	γ^1(A曰B) 爲		—

(4) Certain verbs with the common meaning "to order, to command, to depute"—for example, *linq* (令) "to command, to order," and *shyy* (使) "to order, to send"—occur with the post-verbal elements distributed as follows: "verb (to order)/recipient of order/the order/."

---

[33]The second and third variants occur together in the following: *Chyi-ren wu yii ren-yih yeu wang yan jee* (齊人無以仁義與王言者) "The reason why, among the men of Ch'i, there is no one who speaks to the King about Justice and Humanity, is ..." (*Mencius* 2b.2.7).

THE VERBAL SENTENCE

The directive particle does not occur. The order may be a formally complete sentence[34] ($\alpha\ \beta\ \gamma^1\ \gamma^2(\beta\ \gamma)$).

EXAMPLES

Linq lih-ren wan keh suoo goan (令吏人完客所館) "[The ruler] has ordered his servants to put into good repair the guest house for visitors" (*Tso* 334.16).

Linq ju-hour san suey erl pinq (令諸侯三歲而聘) "They ordered the Feudatory to make a visit every three years" (*Tso* 347.23).

Wang shyy Yinn shyh Wuu shyh juh jy (王使尹氏武氏助之) "The King deputed the Heads of the Yin and Wu families to assist him" (*Tso* 12.6).

Chyi-hour shyy chyi dih nian lai pinq (齊侯使其弟年來聘) "The Lord of Ch'i sent his younger brother Nien to come [here] on a friendly mission" (*Ch'un Ch'iu* 15.19).

3.4.8. Polarity of Mood and the Post-verbal Elements

The modal forms taken by the negatives have already been described (3.3.1 ff.). The negatives as a class partake in a further modal system, that of polarity. Polarity, in LAC comprises *neutral* (simple assertion—without reference to affirmative or negative), *negative* (and contra negative, the reflex-positive), and *interrogative* (or indefinite). Polarity gives rise to a peculiar form of sentential distribution when the post-verbal elements are represented by substitutes (non-status personal pronouns, and interrogative and indefinite substitutes). In both negative and interrogative polar mood such substitutes appear before the verb and not after it, as is the case when polarity is neutral or when the reflex-positive occurs in contrast to the negative. These substitutes occur between negative and verb. The particles of accentuation *yee* (也) and *yii* (矣) may occur after the verb in the distribution negative/substitute/verb/*yee* or *yii*. Further, where in the reflex-positive the anaphoric pronoun *jy* (之) occurs in the post-verbal positions, it is omitted in the negative, with two exceptions (see para. 5 below).

(1) Where, in the positive-reflex form, the post-verbal elements are represented by the non-status personal pronouns, the negative form occurs as "unstressed negative/pronoun/verb/stress part."[35]

EXAMPLES

Yu buh ruu reen sha ... (余不女忍殺) /I/not/you/bear to/kill/ "I cannot bear to kill you" (*Tso* 342.7).

[34]Cf. 3.4.2 Note.

[35]In the negative both indicative and non-indicative moods occur. The stress particle may occur and the stressed forms of the negatives *fwu* (弗) and *wuh* (勿) do not occur. Among the pronouns both persons occur in both determinant and pregnant forms.

Jii ryh erl buh woo tsorng (幾日而不我從) "Will you not be following me after a few days have passed?" (*Tso* 261.10).

Woo wu eel jah, eel wu woo yu (我無爾詐爾無我虞) "We [of the state of Ch'u agree] that we will not deceive you, and that you should have no anxiety about us" (*Tso* 203.22).

Leu-jiuh buh yu chi yee (僂句不余欺也) "The Lü-chü did not deceive me" (*Tso* 419.10).

(2) Where, in the positive-reflex form, the post-verbal elements are represented by the anaphoric pronoun *jy* (之) the negative form occurs as "negative (stressed or unstressed)/verb/(*yee* or *yii*)."³⁶

EXAMPLES³⁷

Jenq-ren chiing fuh syh Jou-Gong. Gong sheu jy (鄭人請復祀周公公許之) "The [Earl] of Cheng requested that he might once again sacrifice to the Duke of Chou. The Duke granted this request" (*Tso* 23.22).

Yuh chiing woang. Gong fwu sheu (豫請往公弗許) "Yeu requested that he might go. The Duke did not grant his request" (*Tso* 4.13).

Gong chiing shuu Jenq. Jinn-hour buh sheu (公請屬鄭晉侯不許) "The Duke requested that he might annex Cheng. The Lord of Tsin did not grant this request" (but later, in allusion to this request: *Jinn-hour sheu jy* (晉侯許之) "The Lord of Tsin granted this request") (*Tso* 258.5 and 7).

Chyi-hour jiang sheu jy . . . Jiun chyi wuh sheu (齊侯將許之 . . . 君其勿許) "The Lord of Ch'i was going to grant this request" (but was given the advice) "Would that my Lord, would not grant it" (*Tso* 98.9 and 15).

(3) Where the agent is distributed by *moh* (莫) the positive-reflex takes pronouns before the verb, the negated form after the verb.

---

³⁶The feature here discussed is not an inflexible "rule of word order" but a modal device. Its use is not prescriptive. The anaphoric pronoun *jy* occurs after the verb,

(i) when negated by *bu*, for example, in *buh woang jiann jy* (不往見之) "Did not go to see him" (*Mencius* 5b.7.3); *Goou neng chong jy, tzwu yii bao syh-hae. Goou buh chong jy, buh tzwu yii shyh fuh-muu* (苟能充之足以保四海苟不充之不足以事父母) "If one could in fact fulfil them [the requirements of the four principles] one would be adequate to protect the whole world, but if one does not fulfil them one is inadequately equipped to serve one's own parents" (*Mencius* 2a.6.9).

(ii) when negated by *fwu*, for example, in *fwu guoh jy yii* (弗過之矣) "He will not surpass it" (*Tso* 187.11); *fwu shiah jy* (弗下之) "You did not defer to him" (*Tso* 342.6);

(iii) and when negated by *wuh*, for example, in *tzer wuh hoei jy yii* (則勿毀之矣) "Then do not destroy it" (*Mencius* 1b.5.2); *wuh yan jy yii* (勿言之矣) "Do not speak of it" (*Chuang* 11.67).

³⁷*Sheu* (許) "to grant" in these examples is used with high frequency in *Tso* as a verb. *Sheu jy* (許之) "granted it" occurs 75 times, *fwu sheu* (弗許) "did not grant it" 36 times, *buh sheu* (不許) "did not grant it" 18 times, and *wuh sheu* (勿許) "ought not to grant it" 5 times. (See 3.3.1.1 footnote 6.)

THE VERBAL SENTENCE

EXAMPLES

Yii-wei moh jii ruoh jee (以爲莫巳若者) "He thought there was no one like him" (*Chuang* 42.3).
Moh wu neng ruoh yee (莫吾能若也) "No one can compare with me" (*Chuang* 45.70).
Moh yu dwu yee yii (莫余毒也巳) "There is no one now to 'poison' me, at last! [i.e., to affect my happiness]" (*Tso* 133.16).
But *Wuh moh bwu ruoh shyh* (物莫不若是) /things/none/not/like/this/ "All things are thus" (*Chuang* 4.71).

(4) Polarity of mood is present when the restrictive *wei* (唯 or 惟) is used. When *wei* is determinative of elements which, when unrestricted are post-verbal elements, they appear before the verb in the distribution *wei*/affectee/*shyh* or *jy*/verb. The negation of *wei* is "nothing but," "this to the exclusion of all else," "this, not anything else."[38]

EXAMPLES

Wei dyi shyh chyou (唯敵是求) "We seek only for the enemy" (*Tso* 197.16).
Goa-ren shuay yii tinq minq, wei haw shyh chyou (寡人帥以聽命唯好是求) "I will lead them to comply with your orders, seeking only your goodwill" (*Tso* 253.12).
Chyi yih ren juan shin jyh jyh, wei Yih Chiou jy wei ting (其一人專心致志惟弈秋之爲聽) "One of [his pupils] concentrating hard, and setting his mind fully [to learning to play chess] would listen only to the Chess-master Ch'iu" (*Mencius* 6a.9.4).
Wu wei Tzyy jy jiann (吾唯子之見) "I have seen only you [i.e., You are the only exception I have seen]" (*Tso* 461.9).

(5) In certain set forms, when *moh* (莫) and *wey* (未) are used, the post-verbal element, when in the reflex-positive form, is the anaphoric pronoun *jy*; *jy* occurs before the verb.

EXAMPLES

... *Wu wen jy yii* (吾聞之矣) "I have heard of that" (*Mencius* 4a.20.2).
... *Wu wey jy wen yee* (吾未之聞也) "I have never heard of that" (*Mencius* 4a.20.2).
Liang-ren wey jy jy yee shy-shy tsorng way lai (良人未之知也施施從外來) "The goodman, being unaware of this, came swaggering in from outside..." (*Mencius* 4b.33.6).
Moh jy yuh erl buh ren, shyh bwu jyh yee (莫之禦而不仁是不智也) "Being something that nothing can resist, not to be humane is folly" (*Mencius* 2a.7.3).

(6) The interrogative and indefinite substitutes, (*her* (何), *shi* (奚), *shwu* (孰), *shwei* (誰), *suoo* (所), etc.) when substituting for elements

---
[38] See 3.5.3 Note for pre-verbal occurrence of restrictive *dwu*, when determining post-verbal elements.

which, in neutral mood appear after the verb, appear before the verb in interrogative mood.[39] [40]

3.4.9. Summary of the Post-verbal Elements

The varieties of distribution of elements in the two post-verbal positions, and the possibility of alternation in directional flow, are thus the formal resources of LAC by which the voice and the scope of the verb is governed. A further variety is introduced by transitive and intransitive usage. It is by the permutation of the elements in the two post-verbal positions that varieties of voice are imposed upon the verb. The varieties of distribution may now be set out in a conspectus as follows:

3.4.10. Conspectus of Voice and the Two Post-verbal Positions

β		Voice of β	γ^1	Direction	γ^2
transitive	active		affectee	→	directive
	causative		□	→	affectee
	passive		□	←	directive
intransitive (verbs of direction)	active		□	→	directive
	causative		affectee	→	
	passive		□	←	directive
intransitive (attributive verbs)	causative (fact. or put.)		affectee	→	□
	passive		□	←	directive
	comparative degree		□	→	directive

3.5. The Agent
3.5.1. Introduction

The verb of the verbal sentence may be determined as to agency.[41] When agency is indicated by a non-status personal pronoun or by

---

[39] This is fully discussed and illustrated in 6.5 ff.

[40] Detailed discussion of some aspects of these features in Classical Chinese will be found in Yang Shuh-dar (2), Jenq Chyuan-jonq, and Mullie (1).

[41] There are no prescriptive rules requiring the verb to be determined by agency. In most grammars, agency has been treated as the "subject" of the sentence. It then is impossible to account for the occurrence or non-occurrence of the "subject," and since elements other than agents can occur before the agent, such criteria as "logical" and "grammatical" subjects are hypothetized which cannot formally be defined or described. There is no formal division of elements between a line that can be drawn between "subject" and "predicate" which does not have to account for cross distributions of all other elements. (See *Kennedy* (5), p. 15, and *Leu* (2).)

the anaphoric pronoun, the determinant forms are used. Though no distinction is made in the form of the agent, it is useful to distinguish (according to the voice of the verb) an acting agent (when the verb is active), a causal agent (when the verb is causative), and an agent of realization (when the verb is passive).

The agent or the agential syntagma occurs as an element in the sentence at α in α [Ins or S.C] β γ^1 γ^2. The agential syntagma occurs with the elements α ((1) $\rightarrow \alpha$) (2) where at (1) are determinations of the agent at the syntagmatic level, and (2) are particles (distributives, etc.) peculiar to the agential syntagma, a detailed description of which is given at 3.5.3 ff.

Not all sentences have agents, and certain sentences cannot be agentially determined, for example,

Yeu (雨) "It rained" (*Tso* 464.23).
Fang shuu (方署) "It was hot at the time" (*Tso* 293.16).
Ran (然) "It is as you say" (*Mencius* 2b.9.5).
Foou (否) "It is not so" (*Mencius* 1b.16.6).

Verbal sentences capable of being determined by agency frequently are not.

3.5.2. Pronominal Agents

When the verb is determined as to agency by the non-status personal pronouns, or by the use of the anaphoric pronoun, the determinant forms[42] (see 2.6.4.1) are used.[43]

EXAMPLES

Wu sanq woo (吾喪我) "I lost myself" (*Chuang* 3.3).
Wu wen jy (吾聞之) "I have heard it" (*Tso* 132.17).
Wu chyy jy (吾恥之) "I am ashamed of it" (*Mencius* 6b.14.4).
Eel yeou muu yi, i woo, dwu wu (爾有母遺繁我獨無) "You have a mother to give it to, I, alas, have no mother" (*Tso* 3.11).

---

[42]Where the pregnant forms occur, it is indicative of emphatic exposure. See 3.11.1.

[43]See 6.2.1 Note 2. This is a feature of LAC which is peculiar to it. The determinant/pregnant forms of the pronouns are not distinguished in EAC (see, e.g., Jou (1), p. 5) and do not occur after the LAC period except in citation and deliberately archaistic writing.

A similar feature has been observed in *Jyarung*, noted by Kin P'eng: "enfin le pronom possessif s'emploie dans certains cas comme pronom personel sujet" (Kin, p. 271). With this compare Lo Ch'ang-p'ei on *Trung*: "An interesting grammatical feature of this language, like Nung and some Nepalese dialects, is that reduced forms of the personal pronouns except the third are used as prefixes and suffixes of the verb to form verbal conjugations." (*Lo*, p. 343.)

Eel her jy (爾何知) "How do you know?" (*Tso* 140.23).
Chyi wu how hu (其無後乎) "Was not it [the making of grave figures] not without serious consequences?" (*Mencius* 1a.4.5).
Chyi dwu yi woo hu (其獨遺我乎) "Will he abandon me only?" (*Tso* 294.7).
Jou Gong jy chyi jiang pann erl shyy jy yu (周公知其將畔而使之與) "The Duke of Chou sent him knowing that he would rebel, did he?" (*Mencius* 2b.9.6).

3.5.3. Agential Distributives

The grammatical value of the agent is nominal. Nominal usage in LAC does not distinguish between universal/particular, singular/plural (see 2.6.1 footnote 5). In the agent, certain of these distinctions are made in syntagma (see 2.6.4.4 and 5) but others are imposed on the agent by its distributives.[44] The distributives occur at *dis* in α/*dis*. The distributives are

(*a*) collective when all instances are envisaged, and

(*b*) restrictive when all but one agent or one class of agents are excluded.

The collective distributives of the agents are:

(*a*) Collectives with the class-meaning "all given instances conceived as a totality." These are *jie* (皆) *kɛr; *jeu* (舉) *kio; *shyan* (咸) *g'ɛm; *chian* (僉) *k'siam; *bih* (畢) *piet; and *jiun* (盡) *dz'ien.

EXAMPLES

Jie: Tian-shiah jy min jie yiin liing erl wanq jy yii (天下之民皆引領而望之矣) "The people of the world will look to him craning their necks" (*Mencius* 1a.6.5); *Ren jie wey woo hoei ming-tarng* (人皆謂我毀明堂) "Everyone tells me to destroy the Hall of Immanences" (*Mencius* 1b.5.1); *Ju dah-fu jie iue "shyan" wey kee yee* (諸大夫皆曰賢未可也) /various/nobles/all/say/worthy/not ever/possible/stress/ "When all the nobles say he is worthy, he would never do" (*Mencius* 1b.7.3).

Jeu: Jiun jeu bwu shinn chyun chern hu (君舉不信群臣乎) "Do all rulers distrust their subjects?" (*Tso* 475.21); *Jeu shin-shin ran yeou shii seh erl shiang gaw...* (舉欣欣然有喜色而相告...) "Everyone feeling happy, with pleased expressions, will say to one another..." (*Mencius* 1b.1.10).

Shyan: Way ney shyan fwu (外內咸服) "Within and without [the palace] all submitted to him" (*Tso* 258.17); *Syh tzuey erl tian-shiah shyan fwu* (四罪而天下咸服) "These four criminals being dealt with, all men everywhere submitted to him" (*Mencius* 5a.3.3. This is a doublet of *Shu* 6.4). Cf. also, from *Shu Ching Chian* in *Yeou neng bih yih? chian iue "Yu! Goen tzai!"* (有能俾乂僉曰於鯀哉) "Is there anyone I can depute to look after this? Everyone said 'Yes! There is Kun!'" (*Shu* 2.14).

---

[44] A false nuance is sometimes given in translation when these distributives are translated "all," since their function is sometimes merely to distinguish between many instances and one, and there is no emphasis upon "all."

Bih: Jenq shy bih deng (鄭師畢登) /Cheng/army/all of them/climbed up/ "The entire army of Cheng then scaled the wall" (*Tso* 21.7); *Shy bih ruh, jonq jy jy* (師畢入衆知之) "When his troops had all entered the city, the populace became aware of his purpose" (*Tso* 469.13). Cf. also EAC and Han examples, for instance, *Bih lai jih sheng* (畢來旣升) "All have come and have already gone up" (*Songs* 190); *Lieh-hour bih yii show feng . . .*" (列侯畢已受封) "The nobles having all already received fiefs . . ." (*Shih Chi* 2.501.26).

Jinn: Jou Lii jinn tzay Luu yii (周禮盡在魯矣) "The Chou Rites are all preserved in Lu" (*Tso* 346.10); *Ren jinn fu yee, fuh i erl-yii* (人盡夫也父一而已) /man/all/husband/st./father/one/only that/ "Any man might be her husband, but one man only is her father" (*Tso* 42.6); *Daw-jonq jinn syy* (盜衆盡死) "The bandit band all were killed" (*Tso* 271.14); *Fwu fei jinn ren jy tzyy yu* (夫非盡人之子與) "We are, are we not, all somebody's son?" (*Mencius* 7a.36.1).

(*b*) Collectives with the class-meaning "two or more agents, or groups of agents, acting conjointly." These are *jie* (偕) *kɛr and *Jiu* (俱) *kiu.

EXAMPLES

Jie: Chyi muu jie chu (其母偕出) "Their mothers both went out" (*muu* is uncommitted as to number, it is mother/mothers, but the distributive *jie* involves of necessity two, or two groups) (*Tso* 429.1); *Yeu ruu jie yiin* (與女偕隱) "[I] and you, both of us will retire from the world" (*Tso* 123.21).

Jiu: Fuh muu jiu tswen . . . (父母俱存) "When both mother and father are alive . . ." (*Mencius* 7a.20.1); *Shyy jiu iue* (使俱曰) "[She] made them both say . . ." (*Tso* 74.15); *Yeu i ren jiu bih* (與一人俱斃) "[he] and another man both died a violent death" (*Tso* 450.12).

(*c*) Restrictives with the class-meaning "one agent or class of agents to the exclusion of all others," "nothing but, no-one but." *Dwu* (獨) *d'uk.

EXAMPLES

Dwu: Ruu dwu bwu chinq goa-ren (女獨不慶寡人) "You only, did not congratulate me" (*Tso* 194.11); *Tzyy dwu bwu jiann* (子獨不見) "Have you, Sir, alone, not seen . . ." (*Chuang* 3.44); *Dwu her yeu* (獨何與) "That fact alone, how can you allow it to be true?" (*Mencius* 1a.7.16); *Eel yeou muu yi, i! woo dwu wu* (爾有母遺繄我獨無) "You have a mother to give it to, alas! I, myself, have no mother" (*Tso* 3.11). (In the last example, "I alone have no mother," though literal, gives a false nuance in English.)

NOTE. Certain of the above collectives and distributives and their determinant forms occur in other forms of distribution. *Twu* "empty-handed, in vain"; *dwu* "alone"; and *jinn* "totally" occur as material or aspectual determinants of the verb in the following:

EXAMPLES

Chyi shy twu guei (其師徒歸) "The armies of Ch'i returned empty-handed" (*Tso* 304.11).

Jiang dwu chu (將獨出) "I am going by myself" (not "I alone am going") (*Tso* 164.14).

Chii neng dwu yaw tzai (豈能獨樂哉) "Surely he cannot take his pleasures alone?" (*Mencius* 1a.2.6).

Jinn fenn jy (盡焚之) "Burned it out completely" (*Tso* 235.22).

Jinn, *dwu* and *jiuh* occur as determinants of the elements of the two post-verbal positions. Collectives and restrictives in this usage do not occur after the verb, but determine the post-verbal elements, as it were, *via* the verb (i.e., they occur in the distribution (coll/verb/ $\gamma^1\,\gamma^2$) though in fact they determine the post-verbal elements).

In addition to *jinn*, *dwu* and *jiuh* and restricted in this usage, are *shi* (悉) "all the affectees," and *piann* (徧). *Piann* determines the first post-verbal element (in the sense of "all [the affectees]") and with change of reading to *biann*, determines the second post-verbal position (in the sense of "at, in, etc., *all* places," "everywhere").[45] (See also 3.5.3.1 footnote 47 for similar role of *duo* and *shao* and 7.3 for a further feature of *shi* and *meei*.)

EXAMPLES

Jinn:[46] *Gaan jinn buh jy jyr-shyh* (敢盡布之執事) "I have ventured to reveal all of them [my thoughts] to your servants" (*Tso* 235.14); *Jinn chu jy* (盡出之) "He sent forth all of them" (*Tso* 269.4); *Jinn guei chyi yu yih* (盡歸其餘邑) "He returned all of the rest of his cities" (*Tso* 296.12; reading *guei* for *lin*); *Jinn sha chyun gong-tzyy* (盡殺群公子) "He killed all the princes" (i.e., "various princes,"

---

[45] The instrumental is introduced by the particles *yii* (以) and *yonq* (用) (see 3.6). Examples occur where collectives, determining the instrument, occur before the instrumental particle (i.e., as it were, *via* "*yii*").

EXAMPLE

Jinn yii bao shyng (盡以寶行)

"He went with all his treasure" (*Tso* 173.8).

Where the γ^1 element of verbs in the class "to give" occur pre-verbally introduced by *yii* (see 3.4.7), the collective may occur before the *yii*, though it determines the affectee.

EXAMPLE

Jinn yii chyi bao tsyh tzuoo-yow (盡以其寶賜左右) "He gave all of his treasures to his courtiers" (*Tso* 173.10).

[46] The translations given above of *jinn* do not make clear the importance of this distinction, since there might be thought to be little difference between "revealing all of my thoughts" and "totally revealing my thoughts." The difference is however clear in *dwu*, for example, "why bribe *only them*" contra "why only *bribe* them."

"princes of various families") (*Tso* 72.5); *Jinn chih chyi shyue erl shyue yan* (盡棄其學而學焉) "Having abandoned all he had hitherto learned, he went and studied with him" (*Mencius* 3a.4.4).

Dwu: *Shi dwu luh yan* (奚獨賂焉) "Why give bribes only to them?" (*Tso* 332.21); *Chyi dwu yi woo hu* (其獨逌我乎) "Will he abandon me only?" (*Tso* 294.7).

Jiuh: *Hann Wang suoo yii jiuh jy tian-shiah ay-say, huh-koou duo-shao, chyang-ruoh jy chuh, min suoo jyi kuu jee, yii Her jiuh der Chyn twu shu yee* (漢王所以具知天下阨塞戶口多少強弱之處民所疾苦者以何具得秦圖書也) "The reason why the King of Han knew all the strategic passes, the population figures, the strongly and the weakly held points, and the grievances of the populace, was because Hsiao Ho had got hold of all Ch'in's maps and records" (*Shih Chi* 2.499.9).

Shi: *Shi suoo bih fu* (悉索敝賦) "[We] mobilized all our levies" (*Tso* 265.18), and with this compare Han examples *Shi cheu chyi jinn fang-shu, jinn yeu Bean Cheau* (悉取其禁方書盡與扁鵲) "He took all of his proscribed recipe-books, and gave all of them to Pien Ch'iao" (*Shih Chi* 3.445.4); *Shi fuh der chyi guh cherng* (悉復得其故城) "He regained all of his former cities" (*Shih Chi* 2.207.80); for *Shi* see also 7.4.

Piann: *Bwu piann ay ren* (不徧愛人) "did not love all men" (*Mencius* 7a.46.2); *Bwu piann wuh* (不徧物) "did not [know] everything" (*Mencius* 7a.46.2).

Biann: "All places, everywhere, all round." *Biann bay jy* (徧拜之) "bowed to them all round" (*Tso* 298.7); *Biann tsyh dah-fu iue* (徧賜大夫曰) "offering a cup of wine all round to the nobles, he said" (*Tso* 401.8).

The distributions and roles of the collectives and restrictives are set out in the conspectus which follows. A circle shows the series described in 2.6.4.5; a square the series described here.

	Agent	Verb			Post-verbal positions
α	Distributive of the agent	Determinations of post-verbal elements	Determinations of verb	β	γ
Syntagma	←—□		□—→		
○—→	α	□—→		β	—→

Certain of the words in these classes are contrastive in distribution, but of similar phonological shape.

EXAMPLES

Determinant	*g'iu 具	Distributive	*kiu 俱
Determinant	*d'o 徒	Distributive	*d'uk 獨
? Determinant	*dziwan 全	Distributive	*dzien 盡

Determinant	*siet 悉	Distributive	*piet 畢
Determinant γ¹	*pian (piann) 徧	Determinant of direction γ²	*pian 徧 (biann)
Determinant	*t'io 諸	Determinant of direction γ³	*t'o 都

(With the last series *t'io and *t'o cf. *tiǎ 者.)

3.5.3.1. Agential Distributives (cont'd)

Huoh (或) *gwək and *Moh* (莫) *mâk occur as agential distributives. in the sense respectively of "of the agents, some" and "of the agents, none." The agent is not always specified.

EXAMPLES

Huoh: *huoh bae buh erl-how jyy, huoh wuu-shyr buh erl-how jyy* (或百步而止後或五十步而後止) "Of those soldiers, some, having fled a hundred paces stopped, some having fled fifty paces stopped" (*Mencius* 1a.3.4); *Huoh yii feng, huoh buh mean yu pyng-pih kuang* (或以封或不免於洴澼絖) "Some people use their skill to gain a fief, some to remain silk-floss bleachers" (*Chuang* 3.41).

Moh: *Jinn-gwo, tian-shiah moh chyang yan* (晉國天下莫強焉) "Of all the states in the world, none was stronger than Tsin" (*Mencius* 1a.5.1); *Tian-shiah moh buh yeu yee* (天下莫不與也) "Of all the people in the world, none but would join him" (i.e. everyone would join him) (*Mencius* 1a.6.3).

Yeou (有) *giug and *Wu* (無) *miwo occur as agential distributives in the sense respectively of "of the agents, there was one" (or, "there are those") and "of the agents, there is not one" (or, "there are not those").

EXAMPLES

Wu: *Min wu neng ming yan* (民無能名焉) "None of the common people were able to find a name for it" (lit: of the common people/not one) (*Mencius* 3a.4.26).
Chyi-ren wu yii ren yih yeu wang yan jee . . . (齊人無以仁義與王言者...) "The reason why nobody in Ch'i spoke to the King about justice and humanity was . . ." (lit: "of the men of Ch'i/no one . . .") (*Mencius* 2b.2.7).
Tzyh geng jiah taur yu yii jyh wei dih, wu fei cheu yu ren jee (自耕稼陶漁以至為帝無非取於人者) "From the arts of ploughing and sowing, casting pottery and fishing, up to the practice of Kingship, there was no art but that was learned from others" (*Mencius* 2a.8.2).
Yan wu shyr buh shyang (言無實不祥) "No words are really unlucky words" (*Mencius* 4b.17.1).
Yeou: *Song-ren yeou miin chyi miau jy buh jaang erl yah jy jee* (宋人有閔其苗之不長而揠之者) "There was a man of Sung who, worried that his seedlings were not growing, pulled at them in an attempt to make them grow" (lit: of men of Sung/there was one . . .) (*Mencius* 2a.2.19).

Wang jy chern yeou tuo chyi chi tzyy yu chyi yeou erl jy Chuu you jee (王之臣有託其妻子於其友而之楚遊者) "There was one of Your Majesty's subjects who, having entrusted his wife and family to a friend, went on a journey to Ch'u" (*Mencius* 1b.6.1).

Geh (各) *klâk, *Duo* (多) *tâ, and *Shao* (少) *siog occur as agential distributives, in the sense respectively of "of the agents, each, both, all"; "of the agents, many, most"; and "of the agents, a few, some." The agent is not always specified.[47]

EXAMPLES

Geh: *Jinn Chuu geh chuu chyi pian* (晉楚各處其偏) "the delegates of Tsin and Ch'u each occupied one side [of the pavilion]" (*Tso* 317.1); *Dah-fu geh ay chyi jia, bwu ay yih jia* ... (大夫各愛其家不愛異家) "The nobles each caring for their own estates, have no love for the estates of others ..." (*Micius* 22.11); *San tzyy geh hoei chyi chenq* (三子各毀其乘) "The three gentlemen each broke up his establishment of war chariots" (*Tso* 273.5); *Ren geh yeou oou* (人各有耦) "For each man there is a partner in life [that suits him]" (*Tso* 32.10).

Duo: *Fuh suey tsyy-dih duo lay, shiong suey tzyy-dih duo baw* (富歲子弟多賴凶歲子弟多暴) "In a prosperous year, the younger generation are for the most part dependable, but in a bad year many of them are rebellious" (*Mencius* 6a.4.7); *Dah-fu duo shiaw jy, wei Yan-tzyy shinn jy* (大夫多笑之唯晏子信之) "Many of the nobles laughed at him, and none but Yen-tzu believed him" (*Tso* 346.15).

Shao: *Luu duo ru-shyh, shao wei shian-sheng fang jee* (魯多儒士少爲先生方者) "There are many learned gentlemen in Lu, but few of them would compare with you, Sir!" (*Chuang* 56.39).

---

[47] In 3.3.2.10 Note 3, other forms of distribution of *shao* and *duo* are summarized. *Duo* and *shao* are used aspectually (see 3.3.2.8), as a material determinant of the verb (see 3.3), and as verbs (see 3.2). *Duo* and *Shao* also determine the elements of the post-verbal positions *via* the verb (see 3.5.3 Note) as in *Buh tzwu yii hay Wu erl duo sha gwo shyh* (不足以害吳而多殺國士) "The force would be not only insufficient to inflict damage on the Wu forces, but would also result in the loss of many of our knights" (*Tso* 478.14); *Nae duo shee jea yan* (乃多舍甲焉) "accordingly he deployed a large number of guards in armour there" (*Tso* 457.6); *Duo jiuh shyh* (多聚士) "he gathered together many adherents" (*Tso* 166.22); *Wang nuh, shao yeu jy shy* (王怒少與之師) "The king was angry and gave him but few troops" (*Tso* 132.1).

Sheau (小) and *shau* (稍) occur in similar usage. *Sheau yeou tsair* (小有材) "possessed of few talents" (*Mencius* 7b.29.2); *Tzyy-woei duo show yih erl shau jyh ju jiun* (子尾多受邑而稍至諸君) "Tzu-wei having received many cities surrendered but few of them to his prince" (*Tso* 373.9).

3.5.3.2. Agential Distributives (substantival)

Substituting in the agential distributive position for the agential particles, there occasionally occurs a substantival syntagma. This is distributive in the sense of "of the agents, those who . . . ."

EXAMPLE

Shiong-nian ji-suey, Tzyy jy min, lao lei, juann yu gou-huoh, juanq jee, sann erl jy syh fang jee, jii chian ren yii (凶年饑歲子之民老羸轉於溝壑壯者散而之四方者幾千人矣) /[time] evil/harvest/starvation/year/[agent] your subjects/[dist] aged/feeble/roll/into gutters/; [dist] able-bodied/scatter/go to/four/ directions/ jee [those subjects]—several/thousand/men/ "When the harvest fails, those among your subjects who are old and feeble, roll dying into the gutters and those among your subjects who are in good health disperse to the four quarters of the earth. [These subjects lost to you] total some several thousand men" (*Mencius* 1b.12.2).

3.5.4. Two or More Agents and Reciprocity

Where, in the agential syntagma, two or more classes of agency are specified, this may be indicated by the use of the syntagmatic particles of parataxis (see 2.5 with examples).[48] Where the two agents reciprocally engage in the activity of the verb (i.e., they are mutually agent and affectee) the verb is determined by the determinants of reciprocity. These are *shiang* (相) *siang; *jiau* (交) *kog; and (hendiadys) *jiau-shiang* (交相).

EXAMPLES

Shiang: Fuh tzyy bwu shiang jiann (父子不相見) "Fathers and sons do not see each other" (*Mencius* 1b.1.7); *Jiun chern shiang yueh jy yueh* (君臣相說之樂) "Music describing the pleasure that rulers and subjects find in each other" (*Mencius* 1b.4.12); *Buh yu jie erl shiang i yee* (不踰階而相揖也) "[Courtiers] do not break ranks to bow to each other" (*Mencius* 4b.27.3); *Show shiang shyr* (獸相食) "Animals eat their own kind" (*Mencius* 1a.4.3; note here that *show* "animals" is uncommitted to number, but *shiang* implies at least two).
Jiau: Shanq-shiah jiau jeng lih . . . (上下交爭利) "superiors and inferiors contending among themselves over profits . . ." (*Mencius* 1a.1.3; reading 爭 for 征); *Jou Jenq jiau wuh* (周鄭交惡) "Chou and Cheng hated each other" (*Tso* 7.20); *Jou Jenq jiau jyh* (周鄭交質) "Chou and Cheng sent hostages to each other" (*Tso* 7.18).

---

[48]If the second of the two agents specified is denominated by a pronoun distinguishing determinant and pregnant forms (see 2.6.4.1), the pregnant form is used, as in *Fu-tzyy yeu jy you* (夫子與之遊) "[Yet] You Sir and he associate together" (*Mencius* 4b.30.1); and *Wu yeu ruu wei nan* (吾與女爲難) "Let us, you and me, do a difficult thing" (*Tso* 146.23).

Jiau-shiang: *Jinn Chuu jy tsorng jiau-shiang jiann* (晉楚之從交相見) "The States that adhere to Tsin and those that adhere to Ch'u should visit each other" (*Tso* 351.16).

3.5.4.1. One Agent and the Reflexive

Where the agent is itself the affectee of the verb, the verb is determined by *Tzyh* (自) *dz'i.[49]

EXAMPLES

Tzyy tzyh ay bwu ay fuh (子自愛不愛父) "the son loving himself will not love his father" (*Micius* 21.5).
Tzyh faan erl buh suo (自反而不縮) "if on examining myself, I find I am not right . . ." (lit: *tzyh faan* to turn over in my mind myself) (*Mencius* 2a.2.8).
Tzyh wey buh neng jee tzyh tzeir jee yee (自謂不能者自賊者也) "he who describes himself as incapable [of using them] deprives himself" (*Mencius* 2a.6.7).

3.5.4.2. Reciprocity and the Reflexive

The determinants of reciprocity and the reflexive occur in the verbal syntagma, taking precedence over the determinants of mood and aspect. They are described here because of their bearing on agency. They might be summarized as follows:

---

[49]*Tzyh* only occurs in situations in which "agent acts upon himself" (reflexive) and "agent acts in his own behalf" (see 3.5.5 footnote 50). In all other occurrences of "self, oneself, himself," etc. *jii* (己) *kiog is used. For example, as agent in *Ruoh jii tuei erl ney jy gou jong* (若己推而內之溝中) "as though he himself had pushed them into the ditch" (*Mencius* 5a.7.9); *Jii pyn-tsuh iue* (己頻顣曰) "He himself frowningly said . . ." (*Mencius* 3b.10.8); and in post-verbal distribution, for example, in *Min yii wei jiang jeeng jii yu shoei-huoo jy jong yee* (民以為將拯己於水火之中也) "The people thought you were going to rescue them themselves from a great calamity" (*Mencius* 1b.11.6); *Sheh jee jeng jii erl-how fa* (射者正己而後發) "The archer only shoots after having adjusted himself first" (*Mencius* 2a.7.4). This is not simply a matter of contrastive distribution since *buh jii jy* (不己知)/not/self/know/ and *bwu tzyh jy* (不自知) /not/self/know/ both occur in comparable distribution, but the first is "others do not know one" (agent—"other people") (*Analects* 1.16) and the second "do not know myself" (agent—"self") (*Chuang* 81.25). The contrast lies in the nature of the agent, and not in the dispositions of *tzyh* and *jii*. *Jii* is thus plerematic and ambivalent, *tzyh* cenematic, restricted to one form of distribution. Mullie (1) reviewing Shadick (1) observes ". . . il faut noter la différence de position (*ki* après le verbe, excepté dans les propositions négatives et interrogatives, *tsé* toujours avant le verbe)." It is more important to note the nature of the agent. (See Yang Lien-sheng (2), p. 248 commenting on Wang Lih's observations on this point.)

	Agent		Verbal complex	
			→	β
Two agents or groups of agents	←	affect each other	相 交 交相	β
One agent or one group of agents	←	affects itself	自	β

3.5.5. Delegation of Agency

Where the agent is delegated to act on behalf of another, the agential syntagma is composed as follows: acting agent/particle of delegation/delegating agent. The particles of delegation are *Wey* (爲) *gwia (fr. *wei* "to become" > "to become for the time being" > "to act on behalf of"); and *day* (代) **d'əg* (fr. *day* "to substitute for" > "to act on behalf of").[50]

EXAMPLES

Wey: *Wey-ren wey jy fa Jenq* (衞人爲之伐鄭) "the men of Wey attacked Cheng on his behalf" (*Tso* 4.12); *Gong wey wang gong yu Peng* (公爲王宮于邦) "The Duke built a palace for the King at P'eng" (*Tso* 66.19); (*Gong*) *wey tay-tzyy cherng Cheu-woh* ((公)爲太子城曲沃) "[The Duke] fortified the City of Ch'u-wo for the Heir Apparent" (*Tso* 81.22); *Jieh wey jy jou* (芥爲之舟) "a mustard seed would become for it [a small puddle] a large boat" (*Chuang* 1.6). (With the dropping of the particle of delegation) *Min moh jy syy yee* (民莫之死也) /of people/none /[for] them/died/ "no one was willing to die for them" (*Mencius* 1b.12.1).

Day: *Wu day ell tzyy miin yii* (吾代二子憫矣) /I/on behalf of/[you]/two/gentlemen/grieve/ "I grieve for the two of you" (*Tso* 339.14); *Shyh day shuay show ming* (是代帥受名) /this/on behalf of/the Commander/to receive/acclaim/ "this would be to take to myself the acclaim due to the Army Commander" (*Tso* 216.2); *Nae day jy diann* (乃代之殿) "So accordingly they brought up the rear for him" (*Tso* 287.14).

---

[50]When an agent is said to be acting in his own behalf, or interest, the reflexive *tzyh* is used, occurring before *wey*, thus *tzyh-wey*.
EXAMPLES
Chyi tzyh-wey mou yee tzer guoh yii, chyi wey wu jiun mou yee tzer jong (其自爲謀也則過矣其爲吾君謀也則忠) "If he is scheming in his own interest then he is at fault, but if he is scheming in our Prince's interest he is loyal" (*Tso* 215.23).
Wey ren yee ... tzyh-wey yee (爲人也 ... 自爲也) "He works in the interests of others ... he works in his own interests" (*Mencius* 6b.6.1.)
The particle of delegation is not always used, for example,
Sheu-tzyy shi-wey bwu tzyh jy (許子奚爲不自織) "Why does not Hsu Tzu weave for himself?" (*Mencius* 3a.4.8) so that the reflexive (agent acting upon himself, e.g., *Tzyh tzeir* (自賊) "deprive himself" (*Mencius* 2a.6.7)) and delegated agency (agent acting for himself) are not always distinguished.

3.5.6. Conspectus of Agency

Agential complex			Verbal complex	
Grammatical determinations	α	Distributives	Modal position	β
凡舉具 諸群 催徒	Pronouns take determinant forms 吾爾而乃 Delegated agency A 爲 B A 代 B	皆舉咸僉 畢盡 偕俱 獨有無莫 或多名少	Reciprocity 相 交 交相 Reflexive 自	

3.6. The Instrumental
3.6.1. Description, Particles, Distribution

Among the determining elements of the verb in the verbal sentence, the instrument (the thing used) is formally distinguished from the agent (the user). The two are contrasted in the distribution agent /instrument/verb (α/Ins/β) and the instrument is identified by the occurrence of the instrumental particles introducing it. These are *yii* (以) *ziəg "to use, the means, raison d'être," etc. and *yonq* (用) *diung "to use, use." The grammatical value of the instrument is nominal.

EXAMPLES

Wen wang yii min lih wei tair . . . (文王以民力爲臺 . . .) "King Wen, having built a tower with the people's labour . . ." (*Mencius* 1a.2.4).

Shiing, yii ge jwu Tzyy-fann (醒以戈逐子犯) "When he was sober again, he chased Tzu Fan with a spear" (*Tso* 121.20).

Sheu-tzyy yii fuu jinq tsuann, yii tiee geng hu? (許子以釜甑爨以鐵耕乎) "Does Hsu-tzu not cook with cooking pots, and plough with a ploughshare?" (*Mencius* 3a.4.9).

In the examples cited above, *yii* and *yonq* "to use" might be thought to be plerematic verbs, but their grammatization is attested (*a*) by their customary occurrence in the distribution agent/*yii* or *yonq* instrument/verb, and (*b*) by their occurrence before purely grammatical instruments.

EXAMPLES

Chiing yii jann yuh (請以戰喻) "Please allow me to illustrate my answer with warfare" (*Mencius* 1a.3.3).

Yii wuu-shyr buh shiaw bae-buh (以五十步笑百步) "By virtue of their having fled only fifty paces, they derided those who had fled one hundred paces" (*Mencius* 1a.3.4).

Fuu-jin yii shyr ruh shan-lin (斧斤以時入山林) /axes/according to/the seasons/ cause to enter/(them)/into the mountain forests/ "When forestry is carried on according to the seasons" (*Mencius* 1a.3.6).

Juanq jee yii shya ryh shiou chyi shiaw tih jong shinn (壯者以暇日修其孝悌忠信) "if adults could use their spare time to cultivate filial piety, brotherly duty, loyalty and honesty . . ." (*Mencius* 1a.5.4).

Wey wen yii chian lii wey ren jee yee (未聞以千里畏人者也) "I have never heard of a Prince with a thousand miles of territory being afraid of others" (*Mencius* 1b.11.2).

Yii yu guan yu Fu-tzyy (以予觀於夫子) /using/myself/cause to look at/Master/ "As I see it our Master . . ." (*Mencius* 2a.2.35).[51]

Thus, one may cultivate a virtue *by availing* oneself of leisure, create something *by utilizing* the labour of others, illustrate a problem *by taking* a subject, laugh at someone *by virtue of the fact that* he . . . etc., enter timber forests *according to* the proper seasons, need fear no man *because* one possesses a large estate.[52]

3.6.2. Ingressive and Resultative Instrument

Yii (以) occurs at two levels of distribution: (1) as a particle introducing the instrumental element in the verbal sentence, and (2) as a conjunctive and anaphoric element, in the second of two sentences. In (1) the distribution is $\alpha\ [yii \ldots] \beta$. In (2) the distribution is $\beta.[yii]\beta$.[53]

---

[51] In certain of the examples cited, the *occasioning* of the act is treated grammatically as its instrument. Cf. the following: *Chyan yii shyh, how yii dah-fu* (前以士後以大夫) "[Mencius used different rituals to bury his father and mother . . .] on the former occasion because he was a knight only, but on the latter occasion because he held the rank of Great Officer" (*Mencius* 1b.16.5). In a different sentential form (i.e., in the determinative sentence) *yii* (instrument) becomes *yii* (copula of cause) when statements of cause and consequence are made (see 4.11).

[52] The instrumental *yii* and the verb *wei* (爲) "to become, to cause to become, to make, to create" in the distribution *yii* X *wei* Y, occur both in factative and putative sense. For example, as factative in *Yii farn wei jiun* (以藩爲軍) /take/wattle/ make/camp/ "built an encampment with wattle" (*Tso* 317.1), and putative in *Chii yii ren yih wei buh meei yee* (豈以仁義爲不美也) /Surely not/take/humanity/ justice/make them [mentally]/not/beautiful/ "It surely cannot be because they think Humanity and Justice are not admirable?" (*Mencius* 2b.2.8).

From *yii* X *wei* Y the derivative *yii-wei* is formed, with the meaning "to regard as, to think of as," as in *Yii-wei wu-yih erl shee jy jee* (以爲無益而舍之者) "those who, thinking it useless dispense with it . . ." (*Mencius* 2a.2.20).

[53] The observations in 3.3.3.2 footnote 24 should be read in conjunction with the above.

In distribution (1) *yii* serves to introduce the instrument, as described in 3.6.1. In distribution (2) *yii* (i) substitutes for the contents of the previous sentence, (ii) serves to mark the link between the two sentences, and (iii) makes the contents of the previous sentence the instrument of the sentence in which it occurs. These two levels of distribution are distinguished as (*a*) ingressive instrument, and (*b*) resultative instrument.⁵⁴

EXAMPLES OF RESULTATIVE INSTRUMENT

Shyy buh der geng-now . . . yii yanq chyi fuh-muu (使不得耕耨以養其父母) "You make it impossible for them successfully to conduct their farming operations, that they *thereby* might succour their parents" (*Mencius* 1a.5.5).

Ming, yii jiau woo (明以教我) "Explain clearly that *thereby* you may teach me" (*Mencius* 1a.7.37).

Yuh mii Ju-hour jy bing yii wei ming (欲弭諸侯之兵以爲名) "He wished to bring to a close the wars of the Feudal Lords, that *by doing so* he might make a name for himself" (*Tso* 316.11).

---

⁵⁴Two verbs may occur in the resultative relation, without the occurrence of resultative *yii*. For example, *Bor fwu, yau yang-jeau erl shanq jee*, (搏扶搖羊角而上者) /beat [i.e., wings]/[thereby] supports/flaps upon/spirals/subordinate particle/ascends/ "It gains support by flapping its wings, beating upon the thermals [lit: spirals], and then rises" (*Chuang* 1.3).

The verbs *woang* (往) "to go towards," *jiow* (就) "to go to" and *lai* (來) "to come to," occur commonly before other verbs, in the sense of "to come or to go to in order to . . ." The resultative instrumental particle is not used.

EXAMPLES

Chyi tzyy chiu erl woang shyh jy (其子趨而往視之) "His son, running quickly, went to look at it" (*Mencius* 2a.2.20).

Woang sonq jy men (往送之門) "[Her mother] goes to escort her to the door" (*Mencius* 3b.2.3).

Tzer woang bay chyi men (則往拜其門) "then go and bow before his gate" (*Mencius* 3b.7.3).

Buh woang jiann jy (不往見之) "he did not go to see him" (*Mencius* 5b.7.3).

Wang jiow jiann Menq-tzyy (王就見孟子) "The King went to see Mencius" (*Mencius* 2b.10.1).

Bih lai cheu faa (必來取法) "He will certainly come to take an example from you" (*Mencius* 3a.3.12).

Jiun wei lai jiann yee . . . (君爲來見也) "My Lord would have come to see you but . . ." (*Mencius* 1b.16.7).

The resultative relationship also occurs in the distribution βγ¹β.

EXAMPLES

Juh miau jaang yii (助苗長矣) "assisting the seedlings to grow" (*Mencius* 2a.2).

Jyy Tzyy-luh suh (止子路宿) "detained Tzu-lu to spend the night" (*Analects* 18.7).

Guh chieh yih shyh, yii lih chyi shyh (故竊異室以利其室) "Therefore he burgles a stranger's house *in order to* profit his own house" (*Micius* 22.9).

3.6.3. The Ingressive Instrument and the Continuative Form

The occurrence of the ingressive instrument at *ins* in the distribution *agent/verb/ins* . . ./, creates an incomplete or continuative form of the verbal sentence.

EXAMPLES

Shuh jy yii sang (樹之以桑) "being planted with mulberry trees . . ." (*Yii sang shuh jy* (以桑樹之) would be "plant it with mulberry trees") (*Mencius* 1a.3.8).
Shen jy yii shiaw tih jy yih . . . (申之以孝悌之義) "having increased the teaching in the schools with the essential justice of filial piety and brotherly duty . . ." (*Mencius* 1a.3.10).
Sha-ren yii tiing yeu ren . . . (殺人以梃與刃) "Murder committed with a cudgel or with a knife . . ." (*Mencius* 1a.4.1).

3.6.4. Conspectus of the Instrumental

The distributional varieties of the instrument might be summarized as follows:

	Complete form	Incomplete form	Translational aids
Ingressive	$\alpha[yii \ldots]\beta$	$\alpha\beta[yii \ldots]$	"by means of," "by availing oneself self of," "by using, utilizing, taking," "because of," "according to"
Resultative	$[\alpha\beta\gamma] [yii] \beta$		"by its means," "thereby," "therefore," "as a result."

3.7. The Subordinate Clause

3.7.1. *Erl* and the Integral Clause

A clause, the grammatical value of which is verbal, may occur between agent and verb in the verbal sentence. It is predicated of the agent, and is subordinate to the main verb.[55] The particle of sub-

---

[55]The subordinated nature of the verb in the clause governed by *erl* has been illustrated in the literal translation of the examples above by the use of participles. In rendering these examples into literary English, concession, the adversative, instrumentation and the like have been introduced. Such matters are extraneous to the text and should not be read into it. Concession takes a well-defined form in LAC (see 5.4). The adversative, as a distinct grammatical form, does not occur until Han times.

ordination *erl* (而) *ńiəg marks the conclusion of the clause, and serves to introduce the main verb.[56] It occurs in the distribution (α [clause/*erl*] β).

EXAMPLES

Goou wei how yih erl shian lih (苟爲後義而先利) /If indeed/were to/having put-last/justice/*erl*/put-first/profit/ "If indeed, you put profits first, having relegated justice to a secondary place . . ." (*Mencius* 1a.1.4).
Chih jea yih bing erl tzoou (棄甲曳兵而走) "[the soldiers] having abandoned their armour [on the field] and trailing their weapons [behind them] fled" (*Mencius* 1a.3.3).
Dih fang bae lii erl kee yii wang (地方百里而可以王) /territory/being square/hundred/miles/*erl*/could/thereby/rule-as-true-king/ "Even with a kingdom a hundred miles square, one could practise True Kingship" (*Mencius* 1a.5.3).

---

[56] The assumption made here is that *erl* in this form of distribution is purely formal, serving to demark the conclusion of the subordinate clause, and to introduce the main verb. Clauses with *erl* occur with very high frequency in LAC and the functions of the clause vary considerably. In the most general way the clause indicates a secondary, minor, or antecedent consideration to that of the main verb.

In speaking of the "verbal value" of the clause, I have proceeded from a maximal form, for example, *Chih jea yih bing erl tzoou* (棄甲曳兵而走) "having jettisoned [their] armour, [and] trailing [their] weapons, [they] fled" (*Mencius* 1a.3.3), to such forms as *Ren erl yih chyi chyn jee* (仁而遺其親者) "He who, being humane, abandons his own kin" (*Mencius* 1a.1.5), taking here (on the analogy of the paradigm), *ren* "humane" as verbal "to be humane" and subordinated "being humane." Further, and upon the same analogy, *Huoh bae buh erl-how jyy* (或百步而後止) "Some having fled a hundred paces, stopped" (*Mencius* 1a.3.4), taking *bae buh* "one hundred paces" to be a statement with economy of *tzoou bae buh* "having fled a hundred paces" the verb *tzoou* having occurred in the previous context.

Simon, assuming that *erl* is something more than formal, has suggested, in a series of exhaustive studies (see Simon (2), (3), (4), (5), and (6)), certain "meanings" for *erl* which include anaphoric, emphatic, and modal elements and so on. The frequency with which *erl* occurs, for instance, in *Mencius* (769 times) is superseded only by *iue* (曰) "sign of reported speech," *bu* (不) "modal negative," *yee* (也) "particle of accentuation," and *jy* (之) (the figures are from Kennedy (1), p. 3). In such a wide range of contextual situations, it is difficult to distinguish what is inherent in the contextual situation and what is intrinsic to *erl*. In the event I have treated *erl* as I have treated *yii* (以) (the frequency of which is next only to that of *erl* in *Mencius* (632 times)) as purely formal.

LAC has well-defined resources for anaphora, mood, emphasis and the like, and this analysis has proceeded from the postulate that these features are confined to these resources. This is not to say that they are so confined but that the postulate has been found useful, both in analysis and statement.

Jiow jy erl bwu jiann suoo wey yan (就之而不見所畏焉) /approaching/him/*erl*/not/see/that which/respect/in him/ "In advancing towards him, I saw nothing awe-inspiring in him" (*Mencius* 1a.6.1).

Bao min erl wanq (保民而王) "Having provided security for the people, rule as a True King" (*Mencius* 1a.7.3).

Ruoh wu-tzuey erl jiow syy dih . . . (若無罪而就死地) "[It was] like one who, being innocent, is sent to the execution yard . . ." (*Mencius* 1a.7.5).

Faan erl chyou jy (反而求之) /having turned over/*erl*/sought/it/ "Turning the matter over in my mind, I tried to recall my thoughts on that occasion" (*Mencius* 1a.7.13).

Wu lih tzwu yii jeu bae jiun erl buh tzwu yii jeu i yeu (吾力足以舉百鈞而不足以舉一羽) /My/strength/being adequate/thereby/lift/hundred/weight-measure/*erl*/not/adequate/thereby/lift/one/feather/ "Though I am strong enough to lift a hundred-weight, I cannot lift a feather" (*Mencius* 1a.7.14).

Guan shyh ji erl buh jeng (關市譏而不征) /frontier post/market-place/inspecting/*erl*/not/tax/ "At the frontier and in the market place goods were inspected but not taxed" (*Mencius* 1b.5.3).

Huah erl wei neau (化而爲鳥) /having changed/*erl*/became/bird/ "Having metamorphosed, it became a bird" (*Chuang* 1.1).

Nuh erl fei (怒而飛) /being aroused/*erl*/flies/ "Once aroused, it takes to the air" (*Chuang* 1.2).

Fwu Lieh-tzyy yuh feng erl shyng (夫列子御風而行) /Lieh-tzu/riding/wind/*erl*/travels/ "Lieh-tzu travelled, riding on the winds" (*Chuang* 2.19).

The verb of the subordinate clause, and the main verb are in one of two undifferentiated relationships the one to the other. The verb of the subordinate clause may designate an act performed concomitantly with the act of the main verb. Or it may designate acts performed in sequence.

EXAMPLES

(1) *Concomitant action*

Kuei fuh erl tzyh lih (虧父而自利) "While depriving his father, he [at the same time] benefits himself" (*Micius* 21.5).

Linq baur Ju-hour jy bih erl jonq chyi lii (令薄諸侯之幣而重其禮) /Order/make-light/Feudatory/'s/payment/*erl*/make-heavy/their/rites/ "He gave orders to the effect that the contributions exacted from the Feudatory should be lightened, while at the same time the courtesies due to them by protocol should be increased" [*Tso* 306.15].

Fwu Lieh-tzyy yuh feng erl shyng (夫列子御風而行) "Lieh-tzu travelled riding the wind" (*Chuang* 2.19).

(2) *Sequential action*

Huah erl wei neau (化而爲鳥) "Having metamorphosed [it then] becomes a bird" (*Chuang* 1.1).

Nuh erl fei (怒而飛) "Having been aroused [it then] takes to the air" (*Chuang* 1.2).

THE VERBAL SENTENCE

Concomitant and sequential action may be differentiated (though frequently they are not) by the substitution for *erl* of *erl-how* (而後) (*how*—"after").[57] The relationship then between subordinate and main verb is, of necessity, sequential.

EXAMPLES

Huoh bae-buh erl-how jyy, huoh wuu-shyr buh erl-how jyy (或百步而後止或五十步而後止) "Some [of the soldiers] having fled a hundred paces, stopped, while some, having fled fifty paces stopped" (*Mencius* 1a.3.4).

Shyan jee erl-how yaw tsyy (賢者而後樂此) "One who is worthy [already] enjoys these" (*Mencius* 1a.2.1).

NOTE. At the beginning of 3.7 the subordinate clause is stated to be verbal, and in 3.7.1 footnote 56, the nature of this "verbal value" is explained. Economy of statement is conventional when periods of time and locations occur in the subordinate clause. Periods of time occur with the class-meaning "the period designated having elapsed, or having been reached," and location with the class-meaning "the agent having reached, or being present at . . . ."

EXAMPLES

San suh erl-how chu Jou (三宿而後出晝) /three/night-stays/elapsing then/leave /Chou/ "Having passed three nights there, he left Chou" (*Mencius* 2b.12.2).

Jii ryh erl buh woo tsorng (幾日而不我從) /few/days/elapsing/not/me/follow/ "Will you not be following me in a few days' time?" (*Tso* 261.10).

Guh jeou erl-how shy jy (故久而後失之) /therefore/long period/elapsing then/ lost/it/ "Therefore a considerable period of time elapsed before he lost it" (*Mencius* 2a.1.9).

Jong daw erl lih, neng jee tsorng jy (中道而立能者從之) /central/path/being at/ stands up/. Able/those who are/follow/him/ "[The Superior Man] standing firmly in the centre of the [right] path, those who can, follow him" (*Mencius* 7a.41.3).

3.7.2. *Erl* as a Conjunction

When the agent of the subordinate clause is other than the agent of the main verb, *erl* becomes the conjunction of subordination. It is distributed as α β γ *erl* α β γ.

---

[57]*Ran-how* (然後) adds a further nuance, that of "only then." *Ran* (allegro form of *ru tsyy* "like this") is thus both anaphoric and conditional "do x, having done it then only . . ."

EXAMPLES

Chyuan ran-how jy ching-jonq (權然後知輕重) /Weigh/like-that-after/know/ weight/ "It is only by weighing things, that we know their weight" (*Mencius* 1a.7.24).

Jiann shyan yan ran-how yonq jy (見賢焉然後用之) /see/worth/in-him/like-this-after/employ/him/ "It is only when one observes worth in an applicant for the public service that one should employ him" (*Mencius* 1b.7.4).

EXAMPLES

Shanq shiah jiau jeng lih erl gwo wei yii (上下交爭利而國危矣) "Superiors and inferiors contending about profits, the State itself is endangered" (reading 爭 for 征) (*Mencius* 1a.1).

Wen Wang yii min lih wei tair wei jao erl min huan-yaw jy (文王以民力爲臺爲沼而民歡樂之) "King Wen having built a tower with the people's labour, the people delighted in it" (*Mencius* 1a.2.4).

The main verb thus becomes resultative. The distribution of *erl* as a resultative conjunction, differs from that of *yii*, in the resultative instrumental. They are distributed as follows:

Resultative *Yii*   α β γ α   *yii* β γ
Resultative *Erl*   α β γ *erl* α β γ

3.7.2.1. The Emphatic Form of Conjunctive *Erl*

When *erl* is the resultative conjunction, a stressed form *nae* (乃) *nəg may occur, emphasizing the contrastive nature of the two agents.[58]

EXAMPLES

Hwan-gong lih nae lao (桓公立乃老) /Huan/Duke/having come to the throne/ subordinate, with agent changing/[he] pleaded old age [i.e., retired]/ "Duke Huan having come to the throne [he, i.e., Shih Chüeh] pleaded old age and retired" (*Tso* 9.4).

Gong nuh nae jyy (公怒乃止) "The Duke being angry, the operation was halted" (*Tso* 13.16).

Jenq-bor sheu jy nae cherng huen (鄭伯許之乃成昏) "Upon the Earl of Cheng assenting to the proposal, the marriage was consummated" (*Tso* 16.12).

Shie-hour sheu jy nae jaang Terng-hour (薛侯許之乃長滕侯) "With the consent of the Marquis of Hsieh, seniority was accorded to the Marquis of T'eng" (*Tso* 20.22).

3.8. Anaphora in the Verbal Sentence

The anaphoric pronouns (excluding here the personal pronouns) occurring in the verbal sentence are *jy* (之) *tiəg and its determinant form *chyi* (其) *kiəg. They provide for anaphora in the widest sense, substituting for elements of the verbal sentence, with no distinction of number, or person (and neither are they exclusively personal).[59] The

---

[58] It is evidently this that the compiler of *Shuo-wen* had in mind in defining *nae* as *Nae yih tsyr jy nan* (乃曳詞之難) "Nae is the stressed form of the trailing particle." The "trailing particle" being of course "*erl*" which "trails after" the subordinate clause (see *Nae* in s.w. sub. voc.).

[59] The impersonal nature of the anaphoric pronouns has been shown by, among others, Peir (2), p. 49.

pregnant form *jy* substitutes in the two post-verbal positions, and the determinant form *chyi* substitutes in the agential position, and, at a level lower than that of sentential elements, in syntagma.

Jy substitutes in both post-verbal positions but never occurs after the directive particle. Where the directive particle might be expected to occur, it is incorporated in an allegro form. In the first post-verbal position it is *ju* (諸) *tio (i.e., *jy* and *yu*). In the second post-verbal position it is *yan* (焉) *gian (i.e., *yu* and *jy*).[60] An allegro form occurs in which *jy* occurs in both first and second post-verbal positions with *yu*, that is, *jan* (旃) *tian (i.e., *jy* and *yu* and *jy*). An allegro form occurs in which *jy* occurring with the particle of sentential mood *hu* is realized as *chu* (諸).[61]

This may be summarized as follows:

	α	β	γ¹	*yu*	γ²	Md	Allegro form
Sentential level	其		之 (之 (之 (之	於) (於 於	之 之) 之)	乎)	諸 焉 旃 諸
Syntagma level		α(其→)	γ¹(其→)		γ²(其→)		

[60] Opinions are divided among scholars as to the value of the second member of the allegro form *yan*. Wang Yiin-jy (see Wang (2), s.v.) followed by some contemporary scholars thinks that it is a demonstrative (*shyh*—but some think *tsyy*) (see Simon (5), p. 122 footnote). But Kennedy ((2), (3), and (4)) has proposed *jy*, as also has Yang Bor-jiunn (5.16). To the arguments already advanced, the following seems to me to argue conclusively in favour of Kennedy. *Yan* and *jy*, substituting in the second post-verbal position, substitute in precisely complementary roles. They are both anaphoric (i.e., pointing back to some thing or person already mentioned and substituting for it). The demonstrative is deictic (i.e., it points to some object without naming it). Its substitutional role is quite different. *Jy* substitutes anaphorically for directives of place (i.e., in those situations in which *yu shyh* might be thought appropriate) but the demonstrative does not substitute anaphorically in the verbal sentence for person. *Jy* therefore accounts for all of the occurrences of *yan*, *shyh* for only certain occurrences and is here incidental. In the following example, *yan* is clearly an anaphoric substitute, not a deictic demonstrative. *Jiow jy erl bwu jiann suoo wei yan* (就之而不見所畏焉) "Going towards him (i.e., the King), I did not see anything to revere in him (i.e., in the King)" (*Mencius* 1a.6.1). "Him" represented in the example by both *jy* and *yan* is an anaphoric reference to the King previously mentioned, and this role is not performed by deictic demonstratives in the verbal sentence.

[61] As has most recently been shown by Graham (2). For *hu* see 3.9.

EXAMPLES

Chyi—at the sentence level: *Chyi wu how hu* (其無後乎) "was it [i.e., the first making of grave figures, previously referred to] without consequences?" (*Mencius* 1a.4.4); *Chyi ruoh shyh, shwu neng yuh jy* (其若是孰能禦之) "it [i.e., the situation previously described] being like this, who could prevent them?" (*Mencius* 1a.6.4); *Bih chyi faan yee* . . . (比其反也) "by the time that he [the traveller] returned . . ." (*Mencius* 1b.6.1); *Jou Gong jy chyi jiang pann erl shyy jy yu* (周公知其將畔而使之與) "was it that the Duke of Chou appointed him knowing that he [i.e., Kuan Shu] would rebel?" (*Mencius* 2b.9.5).

Chyi—at the syntagma level: *Daw ay chyi shyh bwu ay yih shyh* (盜愛其室不愛異室) "the thief caring for his own house, but caring nothing for a stranger's house . . ." (*Micius* 22.9); *Ren erl yi chyi chin jee* (仁而遺其親者) "one who being humane, neglects his own relatives" (*Mencius* 1a.1.5); *Wey chyi tair iue "ling tair"* (謂其臺曰靈臺) "the people called his [i.e., King Wen's] tower 'Spirit-fraught Tower'" (*Mencius* 1a.2.4).

Jy: *Wu yeou dah shuh, ren wey jy shu* (吾有大樹人謂之樗) "I have a large tree, men call it the 'Shu tree'" (*Chuang* 3.42); *Show shiang shyr, chiee ren wuh jy* (獸相食且人惡之) "animals eat their own kind, furthermore, men despise them" (*Mencius* 1a.4.3); *Sonq-ren yeou shann wei buh jiun shoou jy yaw jee . . . keh wen jy* (宋人有善爲不龜手之藥者客聞之) "a man of Sung had an effective cure for chapped hands . . . a traveller heard about it" (*Chuang* 2.38).

Yan—anaphora in second post-verbal position: *Tian-shiah jy min jy yan* (天下之民至焉) "the people of the world would come to him" (*Mencius* 1a.3.13); *Jiow jy erl bwu jiann suoo wey yan* (就之而不見所畏焉) "walking towards him, I could not see anything to respect in him" (*Mencius* 1a.6.1); *Yeou yu yan* (有魚焉) "there is a fish in it [i.e., the Dark Sea]" (*Chuang* 1.13).

Ju—anaphora in first post-verbal position: *Jeu sy shin, jia ju bii erl yii* (舉斯心加諸彼而巳) "take this attitude of mind and apply it to that [i.e., government]" (*Mencius* 1a.7.22); *Wen ju Fu-tzyy* (聞諸夫子) "I heard it from you Sir!" *Mencius* 2b.13.1); *Jie cheu jy chyi gong jong erl yonq jy* (皆取諸其宮中而用之) "[why does he not with] all of the things he uses, taking them from his own establishment use them? [i.e., why does he not produce at home all of the things he needs?]" (*Mencius* 3a.4.11).

Ju—*jy* and *hu*—(for *hu* see 3.9): *Bwu shyh yeou ju* (不識有諸) "I do not know whether there was such a thing?" (*Mencius* 1a.7.6); *Hoei ju, yii hu* (毀諸巳乎) "shall I destroy it, or stop [the talk of destroying it]?" (*Mencius* 1b.5.1); *Shyy Chyi-ren fuh ju, shyy Chuu-ren fuh ju* (使齊人傳諸使楚人傳諸) "should he depute a man of Ch'i to teach him, or a man of Ch'u?" (*Mencius* 3b.6.2).

Jan—anaphora in both post-verbal positions simultaneously—*Chu Yu-shwu yeou yuh. Yu Gong chyou jan. Fwu shiann.* (初虞叔有玉虞公求旃弗獻) /previous-to-this/Yu/third brother/posses/jade/Yu/Duke/sought/it-from-him/not/present/ "previous to this, the third brother of the Duke of Yu had possessed a jade. The Duke of Yu had asked him for it, but he did not offer it to him" (*Tso* 36.10); *Cherng Miann erl jyh jan* (城緜而寘旃) "they built a wall around the city of Mien, and placed him in it" (*Tso* 328.12).

Notes on Anaphora.

(1) The allegro form *ju* (諸) occurs only in the post-verbal position. *Jy* (之) and *yu* (於) occurring in combination elsewhere remain discrete (see 3.11.1 footnote 72). They also occur in discrete form post-verbally (see examples 2 and 3 in 3.9) as slow speech, that is, deliberate or emphatic forms.

(2) The domestication within the language of these allegro forms is such that occasionally the identity of their constituent members is forgotten, resulting in tautology as, for example, *neng shyh ju hu iue buh neng* (*neng shyh jy hu hu*) (能事諸乎曰不能) "Can you serve him? No!" (*Tso* 146.6). Such occurrences are rare. It is not to be supposed that LAC authors are incapable of "errors of grammar," and such examples cannot be adduced to prove, for instance, that *ju* is not an allegro form of *jy hu*.

(3) See 3.3.3.1 footnote 22 for use of *nae* in anaphora.

3.9. Sentential Mood

A class of grammaticized words occur finally in the verbal (and in the determinative) sentence, and are *absolute* in the sense that they have no relation to the meaning-content of the sentence.[62] They serve to indicate the mood of the speaker using the sentence. By permuting them one with another, no change takes place in the form or meaning of the sentence, other than an indication that the user has changed his "tone of voice." This "tone of voice" may be one indicative of a feeling of surprise, or of indignation, of confident assertion, or of hesitancy and doubt. These particles serve to show the mood of the speaker, in contrast to the grammatical mood, which is imposed upon the verb in the verbal syntagma.

The particles of sentential mood are *hu* (乎) *g'o, tzai* (哉) *dz'eg and *erl-yii* (而已) (*ńiəg-ziəg) or *yii* (已) *ziəg. *Hu* indicates doubt, tentativeness, incredibility (sometimes purely rhetorical, sometimes with an implied invitation to the person addressed to assent or dissent). *Tzai* indicates indignation, wonder (perhaps any heightened emotion), *erl-yii* "a note of finality in the voice" (*yii* is "to finish"). *Erl-yii* occurs invariably with the particle of accentuation *yii* (see 3.12). *Yii* represents the tone of voice roughly corresponding to that used in English in "and that's that!" *Erl-yii* (particle of subordination and "finish") "having said that I finish" differs from *yii* in having the added connotation of "stopping there, adding nothing and subtracting nothing" and thus, "that and that alone" becoming "only that to the exclusion of all else."

[62] An oddity, occurring almost exclusively in the form of the example which follows, is the breaking up of the elements of the sentence into expletives, each followed by a particle of sentential mood. *Shann tzai! Yan hu!* (善哉言乎) /Excellent!/words!/ "Excellent indeed are they not, these words of his!" (*Mencius* 1b.5.5).

Erl-yii is realized as an allegro form in *Eel* (耳 and 爾) (*niəg, *ńiar). *Hu* occurs in an allegro form with *jy* (i.e., *jy hu*) in *ju* (see 3.8), and also with *yee* (也) (i.e., *yee hu*) in *yu* (與 and 歟) *zio, and *ye* (邪 or 耶) *ziȧ.⁶³ *Foou* (否) "It is not so" occurs as *foou hu* (否乎) "Is it not so?" and is realized as an allegro form in *Fwu* (夫)⁶⁴ occurring after a sentence in the sense "isn't it?" "n'est-ce pas?"⁶⁵

Conspectus

slow speech or discrete form		allegro form
乎		
也乎	⟩	與歟 or 邪
之乎	⟩	諸
否乎	⟩	夫
而已	⟩	耳 or 爾

EXAMPLES

Hu (乎); *yu* (與); *yu* (歟); *ye* (邪); *Jiang yeou yii lih wu gwo hu* (將有以利吾國乎) "You may have something by which to profit my state?" (*Mencius* 1a.1.1); *Wang sheu jy hu* (王許之乎) "Would the King concede this!" (*Mencius* 1a.7.15); *Erl Tzyy wey woo yuann jy hu* (而子為我願之乎) "Yet you, Sir, wish that for me!" (*Mencius* 2a.1.5); *Ran tzer fey shinn jong yu* (然則廢釁鐘與) "Quite so, then we dispense with the dedication of the bell, do we not?" (*Mencius* 1a.7.5); *Ran-how kuay yu shin yu* (然後快於心與) "You would be happy in your mind after that would you?" (*Mencius* 1a.7.25). *Chyan yii san diing erl how yii wuu ding yu* (前以三鼎而後以五鼎與) "It was because, having used three tripods on the former occasion, I used five on the latter ocassion, was it not?" (*Mencius* 1b.16.5); *Tian jy tsang-tsang, chyi jenq seh ye* (天之蒼蒼其正色邪) "Is the intense blue of the sky its real colour?" (*Chuang* 1.4); *Yii buh shiang-ay sheng ye* (以不相愛生邪) "Is that begotten of a failure to practise mutual love?" (*Micius* 22.4).

Tzai (哉): *Bii u gaan daang woo tzai* (彼惡敢當我哉) "how dare he challenge me!" (*Mencius* 1b.3.5); *Shi shya jyh lii yih tzai* (奚暇治禮義哉) "what leisure [could they possibly have] to cultivate polite manners and notions of the fitting!" (*Mencius* 1a.7.42); *Chii tzyy suoo yuh tzai* (豈子所欲哉) "it surely cannot be what you want!" (*Mencius* 2b.12.4).

Erl-yii (而已); *eel* (耳); *eel* (爾); etc.: *Yih yeou ren yih erl-yii yii* (亦有仁義而已矣) "after all there is [worth mentioning] only humanity and justice—

---

⁶³*Yu* as an allegro form of *yee hu* has been suggested by Graham (2) who points out that *yu* and *ye* on the one hand and *yee-hu* on the other are mutually exclusive in *Mencius* and *Tso*.

⁶⁴Suggested by Graham (3).

⁶⁵The modal particles occur in combination. Thus both doubt and surprise is expressed in *Ruoh goa-ren, kee yii bao min hu tzai* (若寡人可以保民乎哉) "Could one such as me protect the people?!" (*Mencius* 1a.7.3).

nothing more, nothing less" (*Mencius* 1a.1.2); *Jyr buh bae buh eel* (直不百步耳) "it is simply that they did not flee for a hundred paces—nothing more or less!" (*Mencius* 1a.3.5); *Buh gaan chiing eel* (不敢請耳) "It was nothing more than the fact that I dare not ask it" (*Mencius* 2b.10.2); *Ren-ren yeou guey yu jii jee fwu sy eel* (人人有貴於己者弗思耳) "Each man individually has within himself a capacity for nobility—it is simply that he does not set his mind upon it" (*Mencius* 6a.17.1); *Fwu kee mieh yii* (弗可滅已) "they cannot be destroyed! [and that ends the matter]" (*Tso* 433.23); *Wu buh wei yii* (無不為已) "There is nothing [evil] they would not do [and that is that!]" (*Mencius* 1a.7.38).

Fwu (夫): *Tsair shyh yee fwu?* (才士也夫) "He was a gifted scholar, was he not?" *Chuang* 92.33); *Minq yee fwu* (命也夫) "This is my lot in life, is it not?" (*Chuang* 19.97).

3.9.1. Interjections

A class of signs occurring in LAC texts are used to represent such non-phonemic sounds as sighs, "tut-tuts" and involuntary ejaculations of the "Oh! Ooo!" type. They occur in isolation.

Indicating a groan or a sigh are (咨) *tsiər; (訾) *tsiar or (嗟) *tsia.

Indicating an ejaculation of pain, surprise, or indignation: (噫意) *iəg; (誒) *xiəg; (唉) *.əg; (嘻諰憘) *xiəg; (熙) *.iər; (於) *.io; (呼) *xiwo; (烏) *.o and (惡) *.ak.

(咄) *twət is said to be a "noise made while scolding," while *.əg is said to represent a belch.[66]

3.10. Time and Place

Time of occurrence, and certain indications of place, are stated absolutely (occurring in the distribution, *time or place*//α β γ) when such indications are material to the information to be conveyed. Time of occurrence is not treated as a determination of the verb, and no grammatical divisions of time are recognized.[67] There is no prescriptive

---

[66] The phonology can be at most very approximate.

[67] Distinction is made in the verbal sentence between (a) time of occurrence; (b) time elapsing prior to action; and (c) time of duration of action. (c) Occurs in the distribution time /αβγ (as above); (b) occurs in the distribution α [time erl] β (see 3.7.1 note); and (c) occurs in the distribution αβγ¹γ² (duration) (time of duration).

EXAMPLES OF (c) ARE:

Tzyy jy shiong-dih shyh jy shuh shyr nian (子之兄弟事之數十年) "You Sir and your brothers served him [as students] for several tens of years" (*Mencius* 3a.4.29).

Dwu jiu san nian (獨居三年) "He lived alone for three years" (*Mencius* 3a.4.30).

Ju Jow fa Yean san nian (誅紂伐奄三年) "To punish Chou he attacked Yen for three years" (*Mencius* 3b.9.7).

Tzyy lai jii ryh yii (子來幾日矣) "How long have you been here?" (*Mencius* 4a.24.2).

necessity to introduce considerations of time. Time and place indications may be demarked by the particle of syntagma *jee* (者) or may occur (as with other absolute elements; see 3.11) demarked by the particle of accentuation *yee* (也).

EXAMPLES
Time
Dong yeu Yueh-ren shoei-jann (冬與越人水戰) "In the winter [Wu] and Yueh fought a naval battle" (*Chuang* 3.40).
Jin tzyy yeou dah shuh (今子有大樹) "At the present time, you Sir, have a large tree" (*Chuang* 3.46).
Yuann bih syy jee i saa jy (願比死者一洒之) "By the time that I die [I hope] in one fell swoop to expunge it [the disgrace]" (*Mencius* 1a.5.2).
Tzyh jin yii woang bing chyi shao mii yii (自今以往兵其少弭矣) "Henceforward warfare might gradually cease!" (*Tso* 306.15).
Place
Paur yeou feir row, jiow yeou feir maa, min yeou ji seh, yee yeou eh peau (庖有肥肉廄有肥馬民有飢色野有餓莩) "In your kitchens there are rich meats, in your stables there are sleek horses, among the people there are hungry looks, within the countryside there are starving refugees" (*Mencius* 1a.4.2).
Chyong-faa jy beei yeou Ming Hae jee (窮髮之北有冥海者) "In the barren tundra, there is the Dark Sea" (*Chuang* 1.13).
Time and place together
Jyi goa-ren jy shen dong bay yu Chyi ... (及寡人之身東敗於齊) "By my lifetime in the East we have been defeated by Ch'i ..." (*Mencius* 1a.5.1).

NOTE. Words specialized in, or frequently occurring in the time position are *shyi, shyi jee* (昔;昔者) "yesterday, at some time in the past, in former times," etc. *Guu, guu jee* (古;古者) "in antiquity, in the far past," etc. (*guu* may be further determined e.g., in *jonq-guu* (中古) "in middle antiquity"); *chyan ryh* (前日) "in days past, formerly"; *shianq, shianq yee* (鄉;鄉也) "some time ago, formerly"; *Jin*,[68] *jin yee, jin-ryh, jin-shyr* (今: 今也; 今日; 今時) "today, at present, nowadays, etc." In narrative sequence, transition of time is indicated by *bih* (比)[69] and *jyi* (及) "by the time that, coming to the time when," as in *Bih chyi faan yee* (比其反也) "by the time that he had returned" (*Mencius* 1b.6.1); *Jyi shiann hu tzuey* (及陷乎罪) "by the time that they have become implicated in crime ..." (*Mencius* 3a.3.3). *Chu* (初)[70] in the time position, indicates a retrospection to an event prior to the event of the narrative, a sort of "flashback" parenthesis.

[68] *Jin* (今) "now" is also used to introduce a hypothesis, "now supposing that"; see 5.3.2 Note 2.
[69] For *bih*, see Simon (7).
[70] See 3.3.2.10 Note 3.

EXAMPLES

Chu, gong jwu tair lin Jaang-shyh (初公築臺臨黨氏) "Prior to this [the event being narrated] the Duke had built a tower overlooking the Chang family [residence]" (*Tso* 79.22).

Shyy (始) in the time position indicates "at first, before this": *shyy wu jinq Tzyy . . . jin. . . wu fwu jinq tzyy yii* (始吾敬子 . . . 今吾弗敬子矣) "at first I respected you Sir . . . but now I do not" (*Tso* 59.10).

Dang (當) "to meet with" introduces time phrases in the sense "at, in, or during"; for example, in *Dang Yaw jy shyr* (當堯之時) "during the time of the Emperor Yao" (*Mencius* 3b.9.2).

Yu (於) is used in similar sense, and also for indications of place; *Yu jin chi nian yii* (於今七年矣) "during the last seven years" (*Tso* 339.3), but also in *Yu chuan yeou jy* (於傳有之) "in the traditional records there is such a thing" (*Mencius* 1b.2.1).

Shao (少) in the time position is used for "in a little while, a little later," for example, in *Shao, tzer yang-yang yan* (少則洋洋焉) "a little later he was as free as the sea" (*Mencius* 5a.2.9). *Shao* also occurs in geminated form, for example, *Shao shao yeou shern lai gaw iue* (少少有神來告曰) "Soon after a god came and announced to him . . ." (*Micius* 32.40), but, with reading *shaw* "during youth, when young" *Long shaw shyue shian-wang jy daw* (龍少學先王之道) "I [Kung-sun Lung] in my youth studied the ways of the Former Kings" (*Chuang* 44.66).

The lexical directives (see 3.4.5.1) are used in time indications in the sense "from such and such time, until or up to such and such time."

EXAMPLES

You Tang jyh-yu Wuu-ding (由湯至於武丁) "From the reign of T'ang until the reign of Wu Ting" (*Mencius* 2a.1.8).

Tzyh yeou sheng min yii lai (自有生民以來) "From the birth of the human race until now" (*Mencius* 2a.2.32).

Wen Wang you fang bae lii chii (文王猶方百里起) "From the time that King Wen came into possession of his hundred mile square domain, onwards . . ." (*Mencius* 2a.1.12).

Tsorng guu yii ran (從古以然) "From antiquity it has ever been thus" (*Tso* 352.2).

3.11. Emphatic Exposure

Flexibility is introduced in the otherwise rigid distributional system of the elements of the verbal sentence by the possibility of the occurrence of any sentential element at the beginning of the sentence, stated absolutely, with its accustomed position in the sentence being replaced by the anaphoric pronouns (see 3.8). The "exposure" lifts, as it were, the element from the subordinate position it occupies vis-à-vis the verb, and places it upon a co-ordinate footing. It thus places a special emphasis upon the elements so treated. This syntactical device is used for a variety of rhetorical effects.

3.11.1. Syntax of Exposure

The element exposed may be introduced by *fwu* (夫) and demarked from the sentence proper by *yee* (也) or *yii* (矣). (See particles of accentuation 3.12.) Thus (*fwu*/element exposed/*yee* or *yii*). The element exposed is replaced in the sentence proper by the anaphoric pronouns (the determinant form *chyi* for the agent, and the pregnant form *jy* for post-verbal elements). Where the non-status pronouns are exposed, the pregnant form (even for the agent) is used. Where two elements are exposed, the particles peculiar to the position vacated are also exposed, thus indicating their grammatical role in the sentence proper.

NOTE. Thus, in the example *Goa-ren jy yu gwo yee, jinn shin yan eel yii* (寡人之於國也盡心焉耳矣) the distribution of elements is as follows (// marks the delimitation of exposure): $\alpha \rightarrow \leftarrow \gamma^2 \mathbin{/\mkern-6mu/} \beta\, \gamma^1\, \gamma^2$ *Md St*. Two elements are exposed, the agent and the second post-verbal element. The exposed agent is shown to be such by the occurrence of the determinative particle *jy*. The exposed directive is shown to be such by the occurrence of the directive particle *yu*. Exposure is demarked by the occurrence of *yee*. In the sentence proper the second post-verbal element is replaced by anaphoric *yan*. By restoring the exposed elements to their customary position in the sentence, the sentence is then stated in non-emphatic form, viz. 寡人盡心於國 ($\alpha\, \beta\, \gamma^1\, \gamma^2$). Something of the nature of the rhetorical effect achieved by emphatic exposure here might be conveyed by translating respectively as (with emphatic exposure): "I can say this as far as the State and I are concerned, I do give my whole mind to it," and (without emphatic exposure) "I give my whole mind to the State."

EXAMPLES

(1) With exposure of the agent[71]

---

[71] The exposure of the agent, and its replacement by *chyi*, together with the occurrence of *hu* in the sentential modal position, frequently occurs in sentences in the injunctive or subjunctive mood. This has led to commentators glossing *chyi* by *jiang* (potential) and *dang* (injunctive) and to the appearance of a "modal *chyi*" in grammatical works. In the first example cited above the mood is made explicit by *wu*. In the examples which follow modal *jiang* and *dang* are in *contrastive* distribution with agential *chyi*. *Jin chyu-yuh lai chaur, chyi jiang jyi hu!* (今鸜鵒來巢其將及乎) "Now that the mynahs have come to nest, might not the ominous thing overtake us!" (*Tso* 415.12). *Wu-tzyy, chyi buh kee yii bwu jieh* (吾子其不可以不戒) "Master! you must be warned" (*Tso* 339.5) (*buh kee yii bu* "you cannot but" is injunctive in sense of *dang*). Clearly *chyi* is not, in these examples, substituting for, or interchangeable with *jiang* or *dang*.

Wu-tzyy, chyi wu fey Shian-jiun jy gong (吾子其無廢先君之功) "You should not dissipate the achievements of your Royal Ancestors "(*Tso* 8.14).
Jiun chyi hoei shyh tzai (君其悔是哉) "Would that my Lord repented of this" (*Tso* 107.10).
Song chyi shing hu (宋其興乎) "Surely Sung will flourish again?" (*Tso* 59.2).
Ji, chyi dann wey ren yonq hu (雞其憚爲人用乎) /cock/it/fears/on behalf of/man/use/mood/ "The cockerel fears that men will use it [for sacrifice]" (*Tso* 407.15).

Chyi is sometimes omitted:

Shyh neau yee, hae yunn tzer jiang shii yu Nan Ming (是鳥也海運則將徙於南冥) "This bird, when the sea is turbulent, is about to go to the Southern Darkness" (*Chuang* 1.2) (observe order: exposure/time indication/sentence).
Fwu shyh yee, yih wu wang minq erl sy show jy yu tzyy (夫士也亦無王命而私受之於子) "The knight, too, without Royal Authority for doing so, privately gave it to his son" (*Mencius* 2b.8.2).

(2) With exposure of post-verbal elements[72]

First post-verbal element:

Farn ju-hour sheau gwo Jinn Chuu suoo yii bing uei jy . . . (凡諸侯小國晉楚所以兵威之) "the reason why Tsin and Ch'u intimidate the petty states of the Feudatories is . . ." (*Tso* 318.10).
Bing chyi shao mii yii (兵其少弭矣) "warfare might gradually be brought to an end" (*Tso* 306.16).
Wuu muu jy jair, shuh jy yii sang (五畝之宅樹之以桑) "the five-mu homesteads being planted with mulberry trees" (*Mencius* 1a.5.4).

Second post-verbal element:

Jinn gwo, tian-shiah moh chyang yan (晉國天下莫強焉) /state of Tsin/of the world's states/none/ was stronger/than it/ "No state in the world was stronger than Tsin" (*Mencius* 1a.5.1).
Wann cheu chian yan (萬取千焉) /ten thousand/take/one thousand/from it/ "subtract a thousand from ten thousand" (*Mencius* 1a.1.4).
Yii u-daw bih Ju-hour, tzuey moh dah yan (以誣道弊諸侯罪莫大焉) /with/pernicious/doctrine/to deceive/the Feudal Lords/of crimes/none/is greater/than that/ "no crime is graver than that of corrupting the Feudal Lords with pernicious doctrine" (*Tso* 318.14).

(2a) With exposure of post-verbal elements and directive particle

Yu Chyi-gwo jy shyh, wu bih yii Jong-tzyy wei jiuh-poh yan (於齊國之士吾必以仲子爲巨擘焉) "Among the gentlemen of Ch'i, I would have to regard Chung Tzu as chief, but . . ." (*Mencius* 3b.10.2).
Yu Ji-shinq, woo wei bor (於姬姓我爲伯) "But, in the Chi clan, it is we who would be senior" (*Tso* 486.10).

[72]The occurrence of *jy* and *yu* together in this form of distribution does not occur in the allegro form *ju*.

(3) With exposure of other elements or groups of elements

(a) *Agent and verb*

Yih jy shing yee, chyi yu jong-guu (易之興也其於中古) /Changes/det. part./ rise-up//it/dir. part. middle-antiquity/ "The book of Changes originated in Middle Antiquity" (*Li Chi, Hsi Tz'u*).

(b) *Agent and* γ²

See 3.11.1 Note.

(c) *Agent and determinant of first post-verbal element*

Jiun-tzyy jy yu chyn show yee jiann chyi sheng buh reen jiann chyi syy (君子之於禽獸也見其生不忍見其死) /Gentleman/det. part./dir. part./animal//see/ its/life/not/bear/see/its/death/ "A gentleman having seen an animal alive cannot bear to see it killed" (*Mencius* 1a.7.11).

(4) With exposure of the elements of a syntagma

Wann cherng jy gwo, shyh chyi jiun jee . . . (萬乘之國弒其君者) /ten-thousand/ chariot/det. part./state//kill/its [i.e., ten-thousand chariot state's] ruler/that person . . ./ "He who kills the ruler of a large state, [one capable in feudal duty of mobilizing a thousand chariots] . . ." (*Mencius* 1a.1.3).

Bae muu jy tyan, wuh dwo chyi shyr (百畝之田勿奪其時) "You should not deprive the hundred acre farms of their labour in the farming seasons" (*Mencius* 1a.7.44).

3.11.2. Proper Names and Pronouns in Emphatic Exposure

When the agent is a proper name, it is commonly exposed (i.e., as PN *yee*).[73] *Yee* (也) does not however always occur. If the agent is a personal non-status pronoun, the pregnant form occurs when in emphatic exposure.

3.12. Accentuation

A class of signs occur in LAC texts, with the class-meaning of "imposing a stress in the environment in which they occur."[74] These

---

[73]Karlgren (4) makes the observation that *yee* occurring after proper names in LAC occurs exclusively in *oratio recta*, which adds confirmation to the view expressed in 3.12 that the function of *yee* is prosodic. It is difficult not to believe that the exposure of the proper name has not to do with the all-pervasive ritualistic milieu in which LAC texts are written, and which they describe.

[74]In an analytical system such as this, which proceeds independently of phonological data (in this case without information about the prosodic features of the language), it is difficult to account for the class of "particle" represented by *fwu* and by *yee* and *yii*, other than by supposing it to be a prosodic marker of some kind. *Fwu* (夫) *piwo is clearly cognate with the demonstrative *bii* (彼) *pia and occurs, for example, in *Ch'u tz'u* as the deictic demonstrative. In LAC, however, *fwu* is not in complementary distribution with *bii* (but, see 6.2.1, where both *fwu*

and *bii* occur as a quasi-pronoun). It occurs (*a*) in introducing an exposed element (see 3.11), and (*b*) in random distribution before what seems clearly to be words that are stressed. *Yee* and *yii* occur finally in the sentence (*yee* occurring with the highest rate of frequency of any word except *jy*, see Kennedy (1), p. 3). But *yee* and *yii* are not in complementary distribution with the other class of particles occurring finally (*hu tzai* etc., see 3.9), since they also occur demarking an exposed element. An important observation here is that of Karlgren (see 3.11.2 footnote 73), who notes that *yee* occurs after proper names only in *oratio recta*. In referring *fwu*, *yee* and *yii* to the prosodic system, one has only to quote the observation of Firth (1), p. 130, in another connection, that "there is scientific convenience in regarding 'h' and the glottal stop in certain languages, as belonging to the prosodic rather than to the sound system." Robins (1), p. 140, speaking of the glottal stop in Sundanese as "functioning as a prosodic mark of word and morpheme boundaries in many contexts" goes on to say "if it were considered desirable to indicate the actualization of the potential half-stress on a prefixial morpheme, with the concomitant glottal stop after the vowel, this could be achieved by means of *the half-stress mark*."

It is true (as a correspondent points out) that an earlier generation of sinologists dismissed all "particles" that they could not otherwise account for as "emphatic, euphonic or exclamatory," but this should not obscure the fact that some codification of accentuation may very well be included in the orthographic system of LAC or that a morpheme may occur whose "linguistic meaning" is realized only as a stress in the environment in which it occurs.

I have not been persuaded by attempts, such as that of Simon (in a paper read to the XXI° Congrés International des Orientalists in Paris (see Simon (8)) to find in *yee* a "pronoun" or by parallels drawn between *yii* and *liao* in modern vernaculars whereby *yii* is explained as "aspectual." A recent attempt to get away from treating *yee* and *yii* as meaningful dictionary entries is that of Shadick and Wu (1), p. 100, who speak of "the declarative particles *yee* and *yii* (and *yan*)" as "comparable in their functions to commas, semi-colons, and periods" (? as juncture-phonemes?). More recently still, Kennedy (1), p. 30, speaks of *yee* as "the mark of emphatic pause" observing that in a modern *Wu* dialect "it is evident that every sizable segment of speech ends in a particle of expression intonation" and he continues "the relation of such particles to a tonal language is most intriguing, since it is clear that their function in European languages is taken care of largely by tonal inflection of the final word." In other words in a language in which the pitch and contour of words is part of their intrinsic phonetic shape, pitch and contour ("intonation") if used as an emphatic or modal device, cannot be imposed upon the word itself, but is, as in this case, imposed upon a class of morpheme in its environment, existing specifically for that purpose. If this be so, we have an explanation here for the particles of sentential mood (see 3.9). But, if modern dialectology is to be adduced in evidence, to pitch and contour must be added force and length of utterance as a meaningful and contrastive factor. (E.g., *ting*! "listen," *ting* "I am listening.") It is this factor (stress) that seems to me to account most plausibly for the occurrence of a morpheme of such high frequency as *yee*.

are *fwu* (夫) *piwo imposing the stress *fwu*/x́; *yee* (也) *dia imposing the stress x́/*yee*; and *yii* (矣) *ziəg imposing the stress x́ y/*yii* or zéro y/*yii*.

EXAMPLES

Fwu shwei yeu wang dyi (夫誰與王敵) /St→/who/and/king/oppose/ "Who would oppose the King?" (*Mencius* 1a.5.6).

Wang jy fwu miau hu (王知夫苗乎) "Does the King know about *seedlings*?" (*Mencius* 1a.6.3).

Ruoh fwu cherng-gong tzer tian yee (若夫成功則天也) "If it is a matter of *results*, then that lies with Heaven" (*Mencius* 1b.14.3).

... *erl gwo wei yii* (而國危矣) "it is *the state* that will be endangered" (*Mencius* 1a.1.3).

... *buh wei buh duo yii* (不為不多矣) "that would be *not* a little" (*Mencius* 1a.1.4).

Jin ryh binq yii, yu juh miau jaang yii ... *miau tzer gao yii* ... (今日病矣予助苗長矣 ... 苗則槁矣) "It has been a busy day *today*, I have been helping the young *shoots* to grow ... but the seedlings *by that time* had withered" (*Mencius* 2a.2.19).

Swei yeu jy jiu shyue, fwu ruoh jy yii (雖與之俱學弗若之矣) "Though he took his studies at the same time as the other did, he did *not compare* with him" (*Mencius* 6a.9.5).

Wen ju i-fu Jow yii, wey wen shyh jiun yee (聞誅一夫紂矣未聞弒君也) "I have heard of the punishment of *that fellow* Chou but I have not heard of the assassination of a *Prince*" (*Mencius* 1b.8.2).

3.12.1. Stress and Meaning

Certain roles played by stress in syntax can be observed from the distribution of the particles of accentuation.

(*a*) A stressed form, occurring initially in the verbal sentence is in absolute relation to the main verb. (See 3.11.)

(*b*) The stressed term in the determinative sentence, is the determinant term. (See 4.2.)

(*c*) A stressed verb, in situations where polarity (negative/reflex-positive) is present, subsumes its object.[75]

(*d*) If *hu* (乎) were classified in the definite/indefinite polar system (see 6.5.2 footnote 12), the stressed verb (*verb/yee*) would be the definite-reflex form of the indefinite *verb/hu*.

(*e*) In a series of verbal sentences in narrative sequence, penultimate stress (*yii*) (矣) marks "narrative incomplete" while ultimate stress (*yee*) (也) marks "narrative complete."[76]

---

[75] See 3.3.1.1 footnote 6. In antithetical statements, for example, *yaw tsyy* (樂此) ... *bwu yaw yee* (不樂也) "enjoys this ..." "does not enjoy this," the affirmative form is stated as β γ¹ and the negative form is stated as Md β St.

[76] Cf. also 3.6.3.

3.13. The Verbal Sentence in Summary

The verbal sentence is in minimal form a verb, and at maximal form a verb modified as to agency and to instrumentation (or other antecedent considerations), to scope and to direction. These four modifications comprise the principal subordinate elements of the sentence. The verb itself is "built up" in the verbal syntagma (though with no prescriptive rules to do so of necessity), by material qualifications, by qualifications of mood, of aspect, and of manner. The verbal syntagma also includes indications of the state of agency. The verb or verbal syntagma is further determined pre-positionally by agency and instrumentation. Agency is governed (largely as to number) in the agential syntagma, and its nature imposed by the voice of the verb. The scope and direction of the verb are indicated post-positionally, and the disposition of these elements governs the voice of the verb. Time and place treated as temporal and spatial settings, occur as over-all determinations of the verbal sentence, and are placed before it. The verbal sentence is terminated with a class of morphemes indicating "intonation."

The order of distribution of the elements of the sentence is fixed and rigid. Emphasis upon individual elements of the sentence (other than the verb) is effected by stating them absolutely, and replacing them in the sentence proper by anaphoric pronouns. Emphasis upon individual words is indicated by the use of emphatic particles. As an element in a piece, the verbal sentence can be shown to be "incomplete" by stress patterns, and by the resultative use of the particles *yii* and *erl*. It can be shown to be complete by a contrastive stress pattern.

IV. The Determinative Sentence

4.1. Definition and Description

The determinative sentence has as its irreducibly minimal form two terms, the grammatical value of which is nominal. These two terms stand in a relationship to each other analogous to that of the determinant word and the determined word in syntagma (see 2.6.1 and hence the term "determinative sentence"). In syntagma the process of determination might be thought of as morphological since it provides for the qualification of a word, resulting in a more precise or specific term. At the sentential level, determination makes such qualifications matters of assertion or declaration. Such declarations may be of fact, opinion or judgment. Determination, therefore, at this level might be thought of as modal (see 4.7).

4.2. Syntax

The two elements of the determinative sentence are distributed as "determined term/determinant term" (with which compare the order of syntagmatic distribution, "determinant word/determined word"). The determinant term is stressed and is typically followed by the particle of accentuation *yee* (也) (see 3.12). The substitution of *yii* (矣) for *yee* creates a continuative form. The addition of the particles of sentential mood (e.g., *hu* 乎 and *tzai* 哉) adds to the mode of judgment an "intonation" of surprise or tentativeness. *Yee hu* (也乎) is realized in an allegro form in *yu* or *ye* (與邪) (see 3.9).

The determinative sentence is a form used for categorical assertion. Where the assertion is unqualified or unemphatic, the simple apposition of the two terms serves to mark the relationship between them, but when qualifications (mood), emphasis (in antithetical forms), and so on are introduced, copulae[1] occur between the two terms.

[1] The term "copula" in this description is used for any word occurring *between* the two terms. The term "determinative particle" would have done as well, except that the term is pre-empted already, for the particle of syntagmatic determination. The term "copula" as used here is used for a purely formal observation, and has nothing to do with the etymology or "meaning" of any word occurring in this form of distribution; it is nothing more than, and by definition, it is simply a word occurring between the two terms, and not forming an element in either.

Since the determinative sentence form is categorical, the second term designating a category in which the first term is said to partake, the two terms (however constituted) are nominal, since their function is to identify class and member.

4.3. The Properties of the Two Terms

4.3.1. The Determinant Term

The determinant term designates a category in which the determined term is said to partake either wholly or in part. Within this general description, four classes of determinant term occur. These are:

(a) An attribute[2] in which the determined term is said to share.

EXAMPLES

Jinn Chuu jy fuh, buh kee jyi yee (晉楚之富不可及也) "such wealth as Tsin and Ch'u possess is [for us] unattainable" (*Mencius* 2b.2.11).

Shyng ren jenq erl wang, moh jy neng yuh yee (行仁政而王莫之能禦也) "to rule as a true King practising humane government, is irresistible" (*Mencius* 2a.1.15).

Deeng bae shyh jy wang, moh jy neng wei yee (等百世之王莫之能違也) "One hundred generations of Kings hence [the dynasty] would still be unassailable" (*Mencius* 2a.2.36).

Lii yu? iue lii yee (禮與曰禮也) "Is this in accord with the laws of propriety? It is" (i.e., it is "comme il faut") (*Mencius* 4a.18.1).

Shyh-shoou yee, fei shen jy suoo neng wei yee (世守也非身之所能爲也) "[The throne] is hereditary, it is not something that one personally can contrive" (*Mencius* 1b.15.5).

Ren ren yee, buh kee shy yee (仁人也不可失也) "He is a benevolent man, he is indispensable" (*Mencius* 1b.15.5).

(b) A species-class to which the determined term is said to pertain.

---

[2] As in syntagma, attributive determination is a property of an element in distribution, and not of a class of words. Attribute is the property of the term, and not of the class of words occurring as the term. With certain attributes the term may consist of one word, with others by constructions formed upon the analogy of verbal sentences, but however constituted the term is attributive and its value nominal. Cf. for example, the attributive terms formed with *buh kee*:

buh kee jyi (不可及) /not/can/reach/ "unattainable";

buh kee shy (不可失) /not/can/lose/ "indispensable";

buh kee yonq (不可用) /not/can/use/ "unusable, impracticable"; and those formed with the agential distributive *moh*:

Moh jy neng yuh (莫之能禦) "that which no one is able to oppose," "unassailable";

moh jy neng wei (莫之能違) "that which no one is able to disobey," "irresistible."

EXAMPLES

Jinn Chuu Chyi Chyn, pii yee (晉楚齊秦匹也) "The States of Tsin, Ch'u, Ch'i, and Ch'in are co-equals" (*Tso* 316.21).
Woo, lieh gwo yee (我列國也) "We [i.e., the State of Lu] are a ranking state" (a state ranking as an independent Feudatory) (*Tso* 317.12).
Terng, sheau gwo yee (滕小國也) "The State of T'eng is a minor state" (*Mencius* 1b.13.1).
Bii janq-fu yee, woo janq-fu yee (彼丈夫也我丈夫也) "He is a man, I [too] am a man" (*Mencius* 3a.1.2).
Jou-gong dih yee, Goan-shwu shiong yee (周公弟也管叔兄也) "The Duke of Chou was a younger brother, Kuan-shu an older brother" (*Mencius* 2b.9.5).

(*c*) A class of acts, states or processes, of which the act, state or process of the determined term is said to be an instance.

EXAMPLES

Jin fwu jeue jee, chiu jee, shyh chih yee (今夫蹶者趨者是氣也) "Jumping and running are actions of the physical self" (*Mencius* 2a.2.14).
Shyue bwu yann, jyh yee; jiaw bwu jiuann, ren yee (學不厭智也教不倦仁也) "To study without becoming bored is to be wise, to teach without tiring is to be humane" (*Mencius* 2a.2.26).

(*d*) An attribute of the act, state or process, in which the act, state or process of the determined term is said to share. (This type of determined term is the corollary on the sentence level, of the determinations of intensity and quality, and determinations of manner, in the verbal complex [at the syntagmatic level].)

EXAMPLES

Fu-tzyy guoh Menq Pen, yeuan yii (夫子過孟賁遠矣) "You, Sir, surpass Meng P'en by a wide margin" (lit: the surpassing of Meng P'en by you, Sir, was a distant [surpassing]) (*Mencius* 2a.2.2).
Tian-shiah guei In, jeou yii (天下歸殷久矣) "The government of the world has been in the hands of Yin for long" (lit: the world's being in the hands of Yin, is long) (*Mencius* 2a.1.9).
Tian-shiah jy bwu juh miau jaang jee, goa yii (天下之不助苗長者寡矣) "It is rarely that men do not try to help the seedlings grow" (*Mencius* 2a.2.20).
Yii tian-shiah yeu ren, yih; wey tian-shiah der ren, nan (以天下與人易爲天下得人難) /taking/world/giving to/man/is easily [taken and given]/for/the world/to obtain/a man/is difficult/[to obtain]/ "To place the world in the hands of a man is simple, to get a man into whose hands it can be placed is difficult" (*Mencius* 3a.4.25).
Yi-tzyy tzanq chyi chin, how (夷子葬其親厚) "Yi-tzu buried his relatives lavishly" (i.e., gave them funerals on a lavish scale) (*Mencius* 3a.5.4).

4.3.2. The Determinant Term in Summary

The common defining characteristic of the determinant term is that it designates a category, whether of attribute or of class, whether of spatial concepts (objects) or of temporal concepts (acts).[3] Such categories may be summarized as: of an object, an attribute it possesses; of an object, a class to which it belongs; of an act, a class of acts to which it belongs; and of an act, an attribute it possesses.

4.4. Qualifications of the Predication

The predication of the determinative sentence is categorical. In simple apposition the predication is unqualified and unemphatic. Certain qualifications and emphases are imposed upon the predication by the use of copulae occurring between the two terms.[4]

4.4.1. Negation of the Unqualified Categorical

The unqualified categorical predication states that A (the determined term) is of the class B (the determinant term). A simple negation of this statement (A is not of the class B) is made with the use of the copula *Fei* (非) *piwər. The positive-reflex form, where the predication is contrastive with the negative, is made with the antonym of *fei*, *shyh* (是) *dieg. Thus in A / B / *yee*, polarity is not present, but in A *shyh* B *yee*, polarity is present.

EXAMPLES

Fei: *Tzyy fei woo* (子非我) "You, Sir, are not me" (*Chuang* 45.89); *Shyng-jyy fei ren suoo neng yee* (行止非人所能也) "Preferment in office is not within the ability of the individual [to determine]" (*Mencius* 1b.16.8); *Wu shiou wuh jy shin, fei ren yee* (無羞惡之心非人也) "To lack feelings of shame and disgust is not an attribute of human beings" (*Mencius* 2a.6.5).

Shyh: *Wu chuh erl kuey jy, shyh huoh jy yee* (無處而餽之是貨之也) "To give a man gifts when there is no occasion to do so, *is* to bribe him" (*Mencius* 2b.3.5); *Moh jy yu erl buh ren, shyh bwu jyh yee* (莫之禦而不仁是不智也) "Benevolence being irresistible, not to practise it is folly" (*Mencius* 2a.7.3); *Jy erl shyy jy*,

---

[3] No formal or objective criteria (other than apposition and stress by which the sentential form is distinguished) is present in the material to make these distinctions among the categories. The analogy of the form with that of determination in syntagma is, I think, both apt and useful. A division is formally observable in syntagma between attribute and class (see 2.6.2). Thereafter I see no formal procedure by which to account for the variety here distinguished, except that in the fourth class *yii* (矣) is the preferred stress particle. In the event I have been guided by the usefulness of the observation, as an expository device, in introducing it here.

[4] See 4.2 footnote 1.

shyh buh ren yee, buh jy erl shyy jy, shyh bwu jyh yee (知而使之是不仁也不知而使之昰不智也) "To appoint him to office, knowing [that he would start a rebellion] was inhumane, to appoint him, not knowing that he would start a rebellion, was folly" (*Mencius* 2b.9.2); *Guh wang jy bwu wanq, fei jia Tay-Shan yii chau Beei-hae jy ley yee, wang jy bwu wanq, shyh jer jy jy ley yee* (故王之不王非挾太山以超北海之類也王之不王是折枝之類也) "Therefore, the King's failing to be a true King, is not in the 'lifting Mount T'ai, and leaping over the North Sea with it' category of things [i.e., impossible things], the King's failing to be a true King is in the 'cracking rheumy joints' category of things [i.e., things that are in one's power to do if one is willing]" (*Mencius* 1a.7.19).

4.4.2. Emphasis or Restriction upon the Unqualified Categorical

A rhetorical rather than material quality is given to the predication (which remains unqualified and categorical) by the use of *cherng* (誠) *dieng "true, sincere" (A is indeed, in truth, of the class B), and *bih* (必) *piet "must" (A must be B). *Cherng* and *bih* are not restricted in this usage. Restricted are *nae* (乃) *nəg, and *jyi* (即) *tsiet which are emphatic or insistent forms of the copula of unqualified predication. The conjunction of sequential connection, *tzer* (則) *tsək, occurring as a copula, is both contrastive and restrictive, "A rather than, or in contrast to B, is of the class C."

EXAMPLES
Cherng: *Tzyy cherng Chyi-ren yee* (子誠齊人也) "You, Sir, are indeed a man of Ch'i" (*Mencius* 2a.1.1); *Shyh cherng sheau ren yee* (士誠小人也) "I, Shyh, am indeed a petty person" (*Mencius* 2b.12.8). (Note that Legge's "a true man of Ch'i" for the first example, though plausible in English is impossible in Chinese.)
Bih: *Woo bih buh ren yee, bih wu lii yee* (我必不仁也必無禮也) "I must certainly be inhumane, must certainly be lacking in courtesy" (*Mencius* 4b.28.3); *Shenq-ren fuh chii, bih tsorng wu yan yii* (聖人復起必從吾言矣) "In the event of a sage arising again, it certainly will be in accordance with my words" (*Mencius* 2a.2.23).
Nae: *Shyh nae ren shuh* (是乃仁術) "This [act] really was a humane device" (*Mencius* 1a.7.11); *Fwu woo nae shyng jy* (夫我乃行之) "I myself really did do that" (*Mencius* 1a.7.12).
Jyi: *Jyi buh reen chyi hwu-suh* (即不忍其觳觫) "[The reason] was in fact that I could not bear its shuddering" (*Mencius* 1a.7.8).
Tzer: *Terng jiun tzer cherng shyan jiun yee* (滕君則誠賢君也) "As far as the Lord of T'eng is concerned, he is indeed a worthy prince" (*Mencius* 3a.4.5); *Wu jin tzer kee yii jiann yii* (吾今則可以見矣) "As far as my circumstances today are concerned [in contrast to those of yesterday] I could see him," (lit: my-today-copula-could see him) (*Mencius* 3a.5.2); *Jin shyr tzer yih ran yee* (今時則易然也) "At the present time, it would be simple" (*Mencius* 2a.1.13); *Woo yu tsyr minq tzer buh neng yee* (我於辭命則不能也) "As far as formal speeches are concerned [in contrast to other abilities] I am incompetent" (lit: I/directive particle/speeches/copula/incompetent/stress particle/) (*Mencius* 2a.2.24).

THE DETERMINATIVE SENTENCE

A restriction upon the predication is imposed by the use of *Jyr* (直) *d'iek and *Wei* (惟) *diwər. The predication is then "A is of the class B but nothing more," or "A is 'nothing but' of the class B."

EXAMPLES

Jyr: *Shen jyr yanq jee yee, an neng wei shiaw?* (參直養者也安能爲孝) "I, Shen, am merely one of those who feed their parents, in what respect may I be called 'filial'" (*Li Chi Jih-yih* (ii)); *Goa-ren fei neng haw Shian-wang jy yueh yee, jyr haw shyh-swu jy yueh eel* (寡人非能好先王之樂也直好世俗之樂耳) "I am not one who can appreciate the music of the former Kings, I am merely one who likes the popular music of today" (*Mencius* 1b.1.3).

Wei: *Tsyy wei jiow syy erl koong bwu shann* (此惟救死而恐不贍) /this/is merely/ rescuing/from death/to fear/not/to get enough to eat/ "This is merely subsistence living" (i.e., being kept from actually starving to death, only to live in fear of starving) (*Mencius* 1a.7.42); *Wen Wang shuay In jy pann gwo, yii shyh Jow, wei jy shyr yee* (文王師殷之叛國以事紂惟知時也) "The taking the lead of the revolting states of Yin by King Wen, by which he rendered a service to Chou, was merely a matter of recognizing the signs of the times" (*Tso* 257.8).

4.4.3. Qualified Categorical

If the types of predication already described are thought to be indicative (judgments alleged to be factual or having to do with actual situations), predications in which the copulae *wei* (爲) *gwia "to become" and *buh wei* (不爲)[5] "not to become" occur might be thought of as subjunctive (judgments which are only potentially, or hypothetically true).

EXAMPLES

Tsyr shyr-wann erl show wann, shyh wei yuh fuh hu (辭十萬而受萬是爲欲富乎) "Having declined a hundred thousand, and accepted ten thousand, would this be lusting for riches!" (*Mencius* 2b.10.5).
Yii suh yih shieh chih jee, buh wei lih taur jyh (以粟易械器者不爲厲陶冶) "Procuring tools and utensils by bartering grain would not be oppressing the potter and caster" (*Mencius* 3a.4.9).
Taur jyh yih yii chyi shieh chih yih suh jee chii wei lih nong-fu tzai (陶冶亦以其械器易粟者豈爲厲農夫哉) "and the potters and casters by bartering their wares for grain would surely not be oppressing the farmer!" (*Mencius* 3a.4.10).
Tzyy shyh jy shyue, yih wei bwu shann biann yii (子是之學亦爲不善變矣) "Your studying this, would after all, not be a change for the better" (*Mencius* 3a.4.35).

---

[5]Yang Bor-jiunn (8.15) observing that *fei* and *buh wei* are not interchangeable in Archaic Chinese translates them into Modern Standard Chinese as *bwu-shyh* (不是) "is not" and *bwu suann* (不算) "is not thought of as or reckoned to be."

4.5. The Properties of the Two Terms (cont'd)

1. *The Determined Term*

The determined term, in the classes summarized in 4.3.2 was, by definition, "a specimen or an instance" of a class. A further variety is introduced when the determined term denotes a class. The predication then is "The class designated by the determined term, is a minor class within the major class designated by determinant term." It is a sub-class.

EXAMPLES

Shiuh jiun jee, haw jiun yee (畜君者好君也) "He who restrains his prince, loves his prince" (*Mencius* 1b.4.12).

Chu hu eel jee, faan hu eel jee yee (出乎爾者反乎爾者也) "That which emanates from you will return to you" (*Mencius* 1b.12.4).

Fwu ming-tarng jee, wang jee jy tarng yee (夫明堂者王者之堂也) "Spirit Halls are Halls pertaining to Kingship" (*Mencius* 1b.5.1).

Fwu wuh jy buh chyi, wuh jy chyng yee (夫物之不齊物之情也) "Inequality among living things is of the nature of living things" (*Mencius* 3a.4.37).

4.6. Total Inclusion of Terms and Common Inclusion in a Third Term

A characteristic that all types of predication described so far share is the total inclusion of term A within term B. There is no sense in which term B is contained within term A.[6]

A further type of predication (distinguished by special copulae) is that in which both term A and term B are included within an unspecified third term C. Term A is then stated to be of a common though unspecified kind with term B, or to have been enacted in a common though unspecified manner with term B.[7]

---

[6] For this reason, such terms as "equational sentences" and "equivalent sentences" which have crept into usage in this connection, are singularly inappropriate.

[7] The types distinguished in the sets of examples i and ii, may be formally distinguished. In type ii the second term may be concluded with *ran* (然) "thus," "in this manner."

EXAMPLES

Ren jy shyh jii ru jiann chyi fey-gan ran (人之視己如見其肺肝然) "Others see [through] him, just as though they gazed upon his very lungs and liver" (*Great Learning* 6.2).

Wu ruoh Sonq-ren ran (無若宋人然) "You should not [behave] as the man of Sung [behaved]" (*Mencius* 2a.2.18).

Yu chii ruoh shyh sheau janq-fu ran tzai (予豈若是小丈夫然哉) "I surely do not behave as this petty person behaves" (*Mencius* 2b.12.7).

THE DETERMINATIVE SENTENCE

The copulae so used are *You* (猶) *ziôg, *You* (由) *diôg, *Ruoh* (若) *ńiak, and *Ru* (如) *ńio.[8]

EXAMPLES

(i) Both terms designate entities which partake in a common attribute (A is like B):

Jin jy yueh you guu jy yueh yee (今之樂猶古之樂也) "The music of today is like the music of antiquity [in this respect]" (*Mencius* 1b.1.4).

Shyh jy shy wey yee, you Ju-hour jy shy gwo-jia (士之失位也猶諸侯之失國家) "The loss of preferment to a gentleman, is the same as the loss of his Feudal holding to a Feudal Lord" (*Mencius* 3b.3.3).

Ruoh wu-tzuey erl jiow syy dih (若無罪而就死地) "[The sacrificial ox] is like one who being innocent, goes to the execution yard" (*Mencius* 1a.7.5).

You yuan muh erl chyou yu yee (猶緣木而求魚也) "[Seeking such objects] is like climbing a tree to catch fish" (*Mencius* 1a.7.30).

(ii) Both terms designate actions performed in a common manner:

Min wanq jy ruoh dah hann jy wanq yun ni yee (民望之若大旱之望雲霓也) "The people look [expectantly] to him, just as, in a drought, they look [expectantly] for clouds and rainbows" (*Mencius* 1b.11.3).

Yii Chyi wanq, you faan shoou yee (以齊王由反手也) "To make of Ch'i an ideal kingdom is [as simple] as turning the hand" (*Mencius* 2a.1.6).

Wuu-ding chaur Ju-hour, yeou tian-shiah, you yunn jy jaang yee (武丁朝諸侯有天下猶運之掌也) "Wu Ting exercised his sovereignty over the Feudal Lords, and retained possession of the world, as though he turned them round in the palm of his hand" (i.e., easily) (*Mencius* 2a.1.9).

---

[8]*Ru* occurs in a set formula *ru . . . moh ru . . .* in the sense of "rather than . . . it were better to. . . ."

EXAMPLES

Ru wuh jy, moh ru guey der erl tzuen shyh (如惡之莫如貴德而尊士) "Rather than despise these things, it were better to enoble the virtuous, and render honour to gentlemen" (*Mencius* 2a.4.1).

Ru chyy jy, moh ru wei ren (如恥之莫如爲仁) "Rather than be ashamed of these things, it were better to become humane" (*Mencius* 2a.7.4). The origin of the form *moh ru* "of the agent, none compares > nothing is comparable to > it is better to" is seen in *Chyi-ren moh ru woo jing wang* (齊人莫如我敬王) "Of the men of Ch'i, none compares favourably with me in respecting the King" (*Mencius* 2b.2.9). *Buh ru* and *bwu ruoh* (不如, 不若) occur as the negation of "A is like B," that is, "A is not like B," for example, in *Menq Shy-sheh jy shoou chih yow buh ru Tzeng-tzyy jy shoou iue yee* (孟施舍之守氣又不如曾子之守約也) "Meng Shih-she's guarding his physical self, was not like Tseng Tzu's guarding his principles" (*Mencius* 2a.2.9); but also, as above in the sense "it were better to," for example, in *Jinn shinn shu, tzer buh ru wu shu* (盡信書則不如無書) "If we are to believe all that is written in the Book (of History), then it were better that there was no Book of History" (*Mencius* 7b.3.1).

Shyh bwu shenq you shenq yee (視不勝猶勝也) "I look upon a defeat just as I would look upon a victory" (i.e., indifferently) (*Mencius* 2a.2.5).

Modal qualifications of this type of predication are as follows:

Shyh-you (是猶) "is like"; *Wei-ruoh* (爲若) "would be like."

EXAMPLES

Fwu Yih-tzyy, shinn yii-wei ren jy chin chyi shiong jy tzyy, wei-ruoh chin chyi lin jy chyh-tzyy hu (夫夷子信以爲人之親其兄之子爲若親其鄰之赤子乎) "Does Yi Tzu really think that the love of a man for the child of his own brother would be like his love for a neighbour's child?" (*Mencius* 3a.5.6).

Wuh ruu erl jiu buh ren shyh-you wuh shy erh jiu shiah yee (惡辱而居不仁是猶惡濕而居下也) "To hate disgrace, yet associate with inhumane people, is like hating the damp, yet living in low-lying places" (*Mencius* 2a.4.1).

4.6.1. Common and Total Inclusion

Common and total inclusion within classes might be illustrated as follows:

Total inclusion: (i) of an object A in a generic class B; (ii) of an object A in an attributive class B; (iii) of an act A in a generic class B; (iv) of an act A in an attributive class B; (v) of a sub-species A within a species B.

Common inclusion: (i) entities A and B share a common attribute C; (ii) actions A and B are performed in a common manner C.

4.7. Modal Use of the Determinative Sentence Form

The determinative sentence is in essence a categorical judgment. It makes statements about values, rather than happenings or events. Its mode might be thought of as judgmental. Something of this mode can be imparted to a statement made in verbal sentence form by recasting the elements of the verbal sentence into the determinative form.[9]

[9] The verbal sentence recast in the determinative sentence form, and the verbal sentence which has elements exposed for emphasis (see 3.11) are seemingly similar, but differ in that the former has to do with *mood* and the latter with *emphasis*. Formally, the defining characteristics which are contrastive are as follows.

For emphatic exposure: (i) use of the anaphoric pronouns *jy* and *chyi*; (ii) use of the particles of accentuation placing the stress upon the exposed element.

For determinative mood: (i) the use of the copulae; (ii) the use of the particles of accentuation placing the stress upon the determinant term.

THE DETERMINATIVE SENTENCE

A sentence so recast has its elements redistributed into two sets. A number of varieties of such rearrangements occur, but common to all is the two-term form and the distinctive stress pattern of the determinative sentence. Diagnostic of such redistribution is the reversal of the elements "verb/post-verbal elements" viz. "post-verbal elements/verb" and the occurrence of the particle of determination, between post-verbal elements and verb.[10]

Type 1. (α) (γ(之)β)

EXAMPLES

Fwu jyh, chih jy shuay yee; chih, tii jy chong yee (夫志氣之帥也氣體之充也) "The will is the governor of the physical nature, the physical nature is the permeator of the physical frame" (in the verbal sentence form: *jyh shuay chih chih chong tii* /the will/governs/the physical nature/the physical nature/fills/the body/ (*Mencius* 2a.2.12).

Jeng shang, tzyh tsyy jiann janq-fu shyy yii (征商自此賤丈夫始矣) "The taxing of merchants was something which began with this petty man" (in verbal form: *jeng shang shyy yu tsyy jiann jang-fu* "the taxing of merchants began with this petty man") (*Mencius* 2b.10.8).

Fwu ren jenq bih tzyh jing-jieh shyy (夫仁政必自經界始) "Humane government is something that must be initiated by boundary settlements" (i.e., "humane government must begin with boundary settlements") (*Mencius* 3a.3.14).

Type 2. (γ) (α β)

EXAMPLES

Guu, buh kee sheng shyr yee (穀不可勝食也) "Grain would be more than enough to eat" (in verbal form: /could not/successfully/eat/grain/) (*Mencius* 1a.3.5).

Jeou yu Chyi, fei woo jyh yee (久於齊非我志也) "To stay long in Ch'i was not my intention" (in verbal form: "I did not intend to stay long in Ch'i) (*Mencius* 2b.14.2).

Chern Liang Chuu chaan yee (陳良楚產也) "Ch'en Liang was a product of Ch'u" (in verbal form: /Ch'u /produced/Ch'en Liang/) (*Mencius* 3a.4.27).

Type 3. (α) (β γ^2)[11]

EXAMPLES

Woo, fei ay chyi tsair erl yih jy yii yang yee (我非愛其財而易之以羊也) "I am not one who would grudge its worth, and so substitute for it a sheep" (*Mencius* 1a.7.10).

---

[10] In effect, verb/affectee is re-rendered in nominal form, nominal being the value of either term of the determinative sentence.

[11] Here the verbal sentence order is preserved, but diagnostic is (i) the use of the negative copula *fei*, and (ii) the use of the particle of accentuation. The difference between verbal and determinative form is not unlike the English "I do not grudge" and "I am not one who grudges."

Goa-ren fei neng haw Shian-wang jy yueh yee (寡人非能好先王之樂也) "I am not one who can appreciate the music of the Former Kings" (*Mencius* 1b.1.3).
Woo shyue bwu yann erl jiaw bwu jiuann yee (我學不厭而教不倦也) "I am one who studies without becoming bored, and teaches without tiring" (*Mencius* 2a.1.26).

Type 4. $(\alpha\ \gamma)\ (\beta)$

EXAMPLES

Fenq-hwang jy yu neau, ley yee (鳳凰之於鳥類也) "The phoenix is supreme among birds." This is a transposal of the verbal form $\alpha\ \beta\ \gamma^2$ where β is an attribute (here *ley* "similar," "to be of a kind") and where the γ^2 is the object of comparison, thus "the phoenix is of a superlative comparative degree of 'like category' with other birds," that is, "it is the best of the birds." (*Mencius* 2a.2.37). (For degree of comparison see 3.4.6.)
Woo yu tsyr-minq tzer buh neng yee (我於辭命則不能也) "As far as formal speeches are concerned I am incompetent" (*Mencius* 2a.2.24).

Type 5. $(\alpha\ \beta)\ (\gamma)$

EXAMPLE

Choou jiann, Wang jy jinq Tzyy yee, wey jiann, suoo yii jinq wang yee (丑見王之敬子也未見所以敬王也) "What I, Chou, observed, was the King's respectful treatment of you, Sir, what I did not observe, was any way in which you behaved respectfully towards the King!" (*Mencius* 2b.2.7).

Summary of structural types of permutations of the elements of the verbal sentence, to create a determinative form:

No.	Determined term	Determinant term
1	α	$\gamma^1\ \beta$
2	γ	$\alpha\ \beta$
3	α	$\beta\ \gamma$
4	$\alpha\ \gamma$	β
5	$\alpha\ \beta$	γ

4.8. Occurrence or Presence

Yeou (有) *giug and its negation *Wu* (無) *miwo "to possess" and "not to possess" occur as both determined and determinant terms in the determinative sentence[12] in the sense of "There occurs or is

[12] *Yeou* (有) and *wu* (無), *shyh* (是) and *fei* (非) require special statements, since, while they are here placed in the determinative class, there are formal particulars in which they are not typical of the class, and others in which they approximate more closely to the verbal sentence. *Yeou* cannot be agentially determined, but its indications of place precede it, *Paur yeou fei row* (庖有肥肉) "In your kitchens, there is fat meat" (*Mencius* 1a.4.2), or occur at γ^2 as in the verbal sentence. For

present B" and "A occurs or is present." These are best described separately.

4.8.1. *Yeou* and *Wu* as Determined Terms

As determined terms, *yeou* and *wu* (有) (無) "there is/was... *yee*" "there is not/was not... *yee*," may be determined in a variety of ways. The modal determinations are indicative when *yeou* is negated with *wey* (未) (*wey-yeou* is the universal negation,[13] *wu* the particular negation), and subjunctive when determined by *you*, *you-yeou* (猶有) "there would be...." The interrogative substitute *ian* determining *yeou* (焉有) asks "When or where is or has there been...," and *chii*, *chii-yeou* (豈有) "Surely it is not so that there is...."

EXAMPLES

Yeou yii yih hu, wu yii yih yee (有以異乎無以異也) "Is there a way of differentiating between them? There is no way of differentiating between them!" (*Mencius* 1a.4.2).

Yeou yuh wey Wang liou shyng jee (有欲為王留行者) "There was one who wished to detain him on the King's behalf" (*Mencius* 2b.11.1).

Wey yeou ren erl yi chyi chin jee yee (未有仁而遺其親者也) "There has never been one who being humane, neglected his own kin" (*Mencius* 1a.1.5).

Wang jee jy bwu tzuoh, wey yeou su yu tsyy shyr jee yee (王者之不作未有疏於此時者也) "There has been no time in our history when so long a time has elapsed after a failure to put into effect true Kingship has occurred, than the present time" (*Mencius* 2a.1.10).

Jin fwu tian-shiah jy ren-muh, wey yeou bwu shyh sha-ren jee yee (今夫天下之人牧未有不嗜殺人者也) "At present, among the rulers of men, there is nowhere one who has not a predilection for killing people" (*Mencius* 1a.6.4).

4.8.2. *Yeou* as the Determinant Term

The determinant term is the stressed term, and with *yeou* (有) as determinant term a categorical stress falls upon the fact of occurrence

---

example, *Yeou yu yan* (有魚焉) "There is a fish in it [the sea]" (*Chuang* 1.14); *Yeou jiann janq-fu yan* (有賤丈夫焉) "[If] there was a petty man among them" (*Mencius* 2b.10.7). *Yeou* never takes a copula. On the other hand, the two forms of distribution of *Yeou* (i.e., *Yeou* ... *yee* and ... *yeou yee*) are structurally more akin to the determinative sentence.

[13]The universality of the negation of *wey* (未) (see 3.3.1.1) is often a universal negation in time (hence such explanations of *wey* as "not yet"). It is, however, sometimes a denial in space, as "there nowhere exists ..." as, for example, in *Wey yeou bwu shyh sha-ren jee* (未有不嗜殺人者) "There is nowhere a ruler who has not a predilection for killing people."

or presence. This form is used when occurrence or presence is emphatically denied or questioned (i.e., when negative or indefinite polarity is present—see 3.4.8). The interrogative substitutes are then made determinative of *yeou* with the particle of determination *jy* (之). In this form *jy* occurs between the negative *wey* (未) and *yeou*.

EXAMPLES

Ran erl bwu wanq jee, wey jy yeou yee (然而不王者未之有也) "The circumstances being such as I have described, but the ruler failing to practise true kingship [is a circumstance] which has simply never existed!" (*Mencius* 1a.7.46).

Jyh cherng erl bwu donq jee wey jy yeou yee (至誠而不動者未之有也) "The person who is perfectly sincere yet fails to move others is simply non-existent" (*Mencius* 4a.13.4).

Kow-chour her fwu jy yeou (寇讎何服之有) "What mourning can there be for an outlaw!" (*Mencius* 4b.3.6).

Her wang gwo bay jia jy yeou (何亡國敗家之有) "[Under those circumstances] would such things as lost states and ruined families be?" (*Mencius* 4a.9.2).

Guh bwu-shiaw buh-tsyr wu-yeou, you-yeou daw tzeir hu (故不孝不慈亡有猶有盜賊乎) "Therefore, with unfilial and unparental behaviour non-existent, would there still be theft and robbery?" (*Micius* 22.14).

4.9. The Use of *Shyh* and *Fei*

The use of *Shyh* (是) and *fei* (非) as copulae has been described (see 4.4.1). *Shyh* and *fei* have other usages.

4.9.1. *Shyh* and *Fei* as Determined Terms

Shyh and *fei* occur substituting for the determined term, comprising then both anaphoric demonstrative and copula.

EXAMPLE

Bii jaang erl woo jaang jy, fei, yeou jaang yu woo yee (彼長而我長之非有長於我也) "Being older than I, I treat him as an elder should be treated, but *this is not* because there is in me some innate sense of treating elders as they should be treated" (*Mencius* 6a.4.2).

In the example cited, *fei* comprises an anaphoric factor (substituting here as "this," i.e., the entire happening previously described) and copula. *Fei* and *shyh* also occur where no anaphora is involved, but where the demonstrative factor serves for impersonal reference much as "it" is used in English.

EXAMPLES

Fei yu jyue jy erl shwei yee (非予覺之而誰也) "If it is not I that teach them, then who will?" (*Mencius* 5a.7.8).

Cherng fei buh gau yee, chyr fei buh shen yee, bing-ger fei buh jian lih yee, mii-suh fei buh duo yee, woei erl chiuh jy. (城非不高也池非不深也兵戈非不堅利也米粟非不多也委而去之) "It was not that the city walls were not high, or that the moat was not deep, or that arms and armour were not strong and sharp, or that food supplies were not in abundance, yet the city was overcome and taken" (*Mencius* 2b.1.1).

Fei tzer erl cheu jy, buh der yii yee (非擇而取之不得已也) "It was not that he took [the location] of choice, he had no other alternative" (*Mencius* 1b.14.2).

4.9.2. *Shyh* and *Fei* as Determinant Terms

Shyh (是) and *fei* (非) occur as determinant terms, in the sense "right" and "wrong."[14]

EXAMPLES

Buh der erl fei chyi shanq jee, fei yee (不得而非其上者非也) "having failed to obtain it, to condemn one's superiors, is wrong" (*Mencius* 1b.4.1).

Chyan-ryh jy bwu show, shyh yee, tzer jin-ryh jy show, fei yee (前日之不受是也則今日之受非也) "If your not accepting it yesterday was right, then your accepting it today is wrong" (*Mencius* 2b.3.2).

4.9.3. *Shyh* and *Fei* in Plerematic Usage

An attributive use of *shyh* and *fei* has been described in 4.9.2. *Shyh* and *fei* follow the normal pattern of attributive verbal usage (see 3.4.6), thus, "to make right or wrong," "to impute right or wrong to" etc. "to approve, to regard as right," "to disapprove, to regard as wrong, to condemn," "to reject."

EXAMPLES

Jih yii fei jy, her yii yih jy (既以非之何以易之) "Since you have thereby rejected it [the proposition previously argued] with what are you to replace it?" (*Micius* 23.10).

Swei woo yih jiang fei jy (雖我亦將非之) "Even I would condemn that" (*Micius* 25.22).

---

[14] It is not difficult to see in *shyh* and *fei*, intensions and extensions of meaning, from a simple gesture of pointing:

(1) demonstrative "this..." and "not this" (for "not this" see examples in 4.9.1 and cf. similarity of phonological shape of *fei* (非) *piwər with the far demonstrative *bii* (彼) *pia) to

(2) copulae *"this is this"* (a gesture of identification) *"this not this"* (a gesture denying identification), and finally to

(3) plerematic usages "right and wrong" (subjective identification with, or rejection of) and "to approve, to applaud" and "to disapprove, to condemn."

Compare here also the use of *fei* in the formation of privatives in the sense "what is contrary to" (see 2.6.4.3) and the following occurrence in syntagma of *fei*: *Her shyh fei jiun* (何事非君) /How/serve/ disapproved/ruler/ "How could he serve a ruler of whom he disapproved?" (*Mencius* 2a.2.30).

In substantival usage *shyh* and *fei* are used in sense of "the right" and "the wrong."

EXAMPLE

Shyh fei jy shin (是非之心) "A mind distinguishing right from wrong" (*Mencius* 2a.6.5).

4.10. The Properties of the Two Terms (cont'd)

4.10.1. Grammaticized Determinant Terms

As has already been pointed out, the determinative sentence is simply a realization at the sentential level of the principles and purposes of determination described at the syntagma level. To the classes of categorical determinant terms already described must now be added further classes (also parallel to those of syntagma)—the pronouns, the demonstratives, number, and distributives.

4.10.2. The Non-status Personal Pronouns

When for either of the terms of a determinative sentence the non-status personal pronouns are used, the pregnant form occurs.

4.10.3. The Demonstratives and Anaphora in the Determinative Sentence

Where either of the terms of a determinative sentence is replaced by anaphoric substitutes, the deictic demonstratives are used. The anaphoric pronouns of the verbal sentence, *jy* (之) and *chyi* (其), never occur as substitutes for either term. The pregnant form of the demonstrative *tsyy* (此) occurs in this usage.

EXAMPLES

Tsyy, Wen Wang jy yeong yee (此文王之勇也) "This [i.e., the incident previously described] is an instance of the bravery of King Wen" (*Mencius* 1b.3.6).

Tsyy, shuay show erl shyr ren yee (此率獸而食人也) "This [the policy previously described] is a policy of 'governing animals and eating men'" (*Mencius* 3b.9.14).

But the preponderating usage is of the determinant form *shyh* (是) and its negated counterpart *fei* (非).

THE DETERMINATIVE SENTENCE

EXAMPLES

Shyh: *Shyh, donq tian-shiah jy bing* (是動天下之兵) "This [i.e., the action previously described] is of the kind likely to arouse the world to arms" (*Mencius* 1b.11.7); *Shyh, wey san jiun jee yee* (是畏三軍者也) "This [to act in the way previously described] is to show fear for the enemy's forces" (*Mencius* 2a.2.6); *Shyh, luann tian-shiah yee* (是亂天下也) "This will upset the whole world" (*Mencius* 3a.4.38).

Fei: *Shyh, jyi yih suoo sheng jee yee, fei, yih shyi erl cheu jy yee* (是集義所生者也非義襲而取之也) "It [the physical nature] is that which is produced by the accumulation of right deeds; it is not that which is derived from a single right deed" (*Mencius* 2a.2.17); *Fei tsyy jy wey yee* (非此之謂也) "It is not that, that this describes" (*Mencius* 2b.2.9).

4.10.4. Number as the Determinant Term

Number and units of measure occur as the determinant term in statements of quantitative judgment.[15]

EXAMPLES

You Jou erl lai, chi-bae you yu suey yii (由周而來七百有餘歲矣) "From the time of Chou down to the present time, is some seven hundred years ..." (*Mencius* 2b.13.2).

Guei-tian wuu-shyr muu (圭田五十畝) "The Holy Field was fifty Chinese acres" (*Mencius* 3a.3.18).

Shiong-nian ji-suey, Tzyy jy min, lao lei, juann yu gou-huoh, juang jee, sann erl jy syh fang jee, jii chian ren yii (凶年饑歲子之民老羸轉於溝壑壯者散而之四方者幾千人矣) "When the harvest fails, those of your subjects who are old and feeble, roll dying into the gutters, those who are able-bodied disperse to the four quarters. [These subjects number] some several thousand men" (*Mencius* 2b.4.2).

---

[15]*Jiang* (將) and *chiee* (且) (potential aspect, see 3.3.2.1) occur before the term of quantity, for example, in *Jin Terng, jyue charng buu doan, jiang wuu-shyr lii yee* (今滕絕長補短將五十里也) "The State of T'eng, is fifty miles square" (*Mencius* 3a.1.4); *Cheu chyi dih chiee tian-shiah jy bann* (取其地且天下之半) "and took their lands, which would be half of the known world" (*Chan Kuo Ts'e*). *Jiang* above is glossed as *jii* (幾) "approximately" and *chiee* and *jiang* occurring before round numbers is common in Han usage in this sense. However, it is not difficult to see in the above examples, a meaning more closely akin semantically to the potential quality of *jiang* and *chiee*, since the first example is, lit: Now/T'eng/cut off/long-side/add-on/short-side/would be/50/miles. Here, "cut off long side, add on short side" simply means "to square off land," to assess its acreage. Thus "if T'eng were squared [which it is not] it would then be fifty miles square."

4.11. The Instrumental and the Determinative Sentence

Statements of cause and consequence are made in the determinative sentence form.[16] The instrumental *yii* (以) then occurs as the copula between the two terms.[17]

Yii (and *yii* with distinguishing modifications) is used both ingressively and resultatively. Used ingressively the determinant term then states the cause of which the determined term is said to be the consequence. Used resultatively the determinant term then states the consequence, of which the determined term is said to be the cause. (That is, "A happened because of B" [*yii* ingressive], "Because of A, B happened" [*yii* resultative].)

In ingressive usage, *yii* occurs between the two terms as *yii* (以), *yii-wey* (以爲), *wey* (爲),[18] and negated as *fei-wey* (非爲) and *fei* (非), and also with the two instrumental particles *yonq* (用) and *yii* (以) realized in an allegro form *In* (因) *.ien. In resultative usage, *yii* occurs with *shyh* in *shyh-yii* (是以) or is replaced by *guh* (故)[19] which occurs also as *shyh-guh* (是故). In summary, therefore, cause and consequence forms, occur as:

Term of cause	Copula	Term of consequence	yee
	是以 故		
	是 故		也
	"therefore"		

---

[16]See 3.6.2 footnote 51 where attention is drawn to the use of the instrumental clause for the occasioning of an act, that is, where cause is treated as instrument. There is an intimate connection between instrumentation and cause in LAC. It is not difficult to see the evolution of the one from the other. The change of mode from indicative narration to judgments of value that takes place when verbal sentences are transposed into the determinative form, may well account for the transference of instrument > cause. It is thanks to the peculiar nature of the material (its script system) which preserves in the sign *yii* the essential link, that this connection is observable, and is, linguistically speaking, a phenomenon of extraordinary interest.

[17]The agent, particularly a proper name or personal pronoun, occurs before the copulae (as in emphatic exposure, see 3.11) in such instances as *Jiun, shyh-yii, buh guoo lai yee* (君是以不果來也) "Therefore the King did not in fact come" (*Mencius* 1b.16.7), and *Woo guh iue "Gaw-tzyy wey-charng jy yih"* (我故曰告子未嘗知義) "Therefore I say 'Master Kao will never understand righteousness'" (*Mencius* 2a.2.17).

[18]A tone change in Modern Standard Chinese marks the specialization of usage of *wei* in these contexts. Dr. Hawkes informs me that *yonq-fwu* (用夫) or *yonq-erl* (用而) occur in similar sense in *Li Sao*. This is an important observation, since the use of both *yonq* (用) "to use" and *yii* (以) "to use" in instrument and cause reduces the possibility that the connection between the two uses is purely fortuitous.

[19]See commentary on 8.6.25.

THE DETERMINATIVE SENTENCE

Term of consequence	Copula	Term of cause	yee
	以		
	以爲	爲	
	非爲	非	也
	因	用以	
		"because"	

The causal copulae, in common with all copulae, may be modally determined, restricted, made interrogative (see 6.5.3.6) etc. Cf., for example, *fei jyr-wey* (非直爲) "not merely because," *chii-wey* (豈爲) "surely not because," *fei-twu* (非徒) "not only because of," etc.[20]

EXAMPLES

(1) Cause as the determined term

Menq-tzyy jy how sang yu chyan sang, shyh-yii buh woang jiann yee (孟子之後喪踰前喪是以不往見也) /Mencius'/latter/mourning/exceeded/former/mourning/therefore/not go/to see/ "The funeral which Mencius gave on the latter occasion [for his mother] was much more lavish than the funeral he gave on the former occasion [for his father], therefore I did not go to see him" (*Mencius* 1b.16.4).

... *Wen chyi sheng buh reen shyr chyi row shyh-yii jiun-tzyy yeuan paur-chwu yee* (聞其聲不忍食其肉是以君子遠庖廚也) "Hearing the death cry of an animal [the gentleman] cannot bear to eat its flesh, therefore gentlemen keep their kitchens at a distance" (*Mencius* 1a.7.12).

Ruoh wu-tzuey erl jiow syy dih, guh yii yang yih jy (若無罪而就死地故以羊易之) "[The ox] was like a person being innocent, going to the place of execution, therefore I substituted for it a sheep" (*Mencius* 1a.7.8).

Shyy-ren wei koong buh shang ren, harn-ren wei koong shang ren, u jianq yih ran, guh, shuh, buh kee bwu shenn yee (矢人惟恐不傷人函人惟恐傷人巫匠亦然故術不可不慎也)/arrow/maker/only/fear/not injure/man/armourer/only/fear/injure/man/shaman/coffin maker/also/like this/therefore/profession/cannot/not/be careful/ "The arrow-maker's concern is that his arrows should injure human beings, the armourer's concern is that human beings should not be injured; the shaman and the coffin maker have similar opposing interests [the shaman in an ill man recovering, and the undertaker in his death], therefore in the matter of the choice of a profession, one cannot be too careful" (*Mencius* 2a.7.1).

---

[20] The operation of the rule of economy in this form, is found not only in the copulae (e.g., *fei-wey* occurring as *fei*), but also in the omission of the copulae, for example, *Jiann niou, wey jiann yang yee* (見牛未見羊也) "It was because you had seen an ox, but had not seen a sheep [in such a predicament]" (*Mencius* 1a.7.11); or in *Chii yeou tuo (ta) tzai, bih shoci huoo yee* (豈有他哉避水火也) "It can surely be for no other [reason] [it was because they wished] to escape from flood and fire" (*Mencius* 1b.10.4).

Bor-yi fei chyi jiun bwu shyh ... shyh-guh Ju-hour swei yeou shann chyi tsyr-minq erl jyh jee, bwu show yee (伯夷非其君不事是故諸侯雖有善其辭命而至者不受也) "Po-I would not serve a ruler of whom he disapproved, etc., ... therefore even if a Feudal Lord sending him elegant invitations [pressed] him to come, he would not receive [such invitations]" (*Mencius* 2a.9.1).

... shyh-guh, shyan jiun bih gong jean lii shiah, cheu yu min yeou jyh (...是故賢君必恭儉禮下取於民有制) "...therefore the worthy ruler must be polite and restrained, courteous to inferiors, and, in his exactions from the people, keeping within due bounds" (*Mencius* 3a.3.4).

In cf. *Wu herng chaan erl yeou herng shin* (無恆產而有恆心) "to possess a constant mind while lacking a constant means of livelihood" (*Mencius* 1a.7.37) and *Wu herng chaan in wu herng shin* (無恆產因無恆心) "they have no constant livelihood, therefore they lack a constant mind" (*Mencius* 1a.7.38).

(2) Cause as the determinant term

Gaw-tzyy wey charng jy yih, yii chyi way jy yee (告子未嘗知義以其外之也) "Master Kao will never understand righteousness because he regards it as something external!" (*Mencius* 2a.2.18).

Chyi-ren wu yii ren yih yeu wang yan jee, chii yii ren yih wei buh meei yee (齊人無以仁義與王言者豈以仁義為不美也) "Among the men of the State of Ch'i there are none who speak to the King about humanity and justice; surely this is not because they think these things inelegant?" (*Mencius* 2b.2.7).

Tzyy jy tsyr Ling-Chiou erl chiing shyh-shy syh yee; wey chyi kee yii yan yee (子之辭靈丘而請士師似也為其可以言也) "the reasons why, you Sir, declined the [governorship of] Ling Ch'iu, and asked for the office of Leader of the Knights, were identical, it was because of the opportunities either office offered of speaking your mind" (*Mencius* 2b.5.1).

I yeu jy buh jeu, wey bwu yonq lih yan (一羽之不舉為不用力焉) "If a feather were not lifted, it would be because one did not use one's strength to lift it" (*Mencius* 1a.7.16).

Tzyh Tian-tzyy dar yu shuh-ren, fei jyr wey guan-meei yee ran-how jinn yu ren shin (自天子達於庶人非直為觀美也然後盡於人心) "[The funeral observances were followed by all] from the Son of Heaven down to the commoners, not merely because of a desire to impress, but because having done so, it met a response in their hearts" (*Mencius* 2b.7.3).

Guh wang jy bwu wang, buh wei yee, fei buh neng yee (故王之不王不為也非不能也) "Therefore, the King's failure to practise true kingship is because he does not, not because he cannot practise it" (*Mencius* 1a.7.17).

4.12. Distributives and the Determined Term

The occurrence of the distributive *jie* (皆) at the end of the determined term states that "all members named, pertain to the class...."

EXAMPLES

Wei Tzyy, Wei-jonq Wang-tzyy Bih-gan, Ji-tzyy, Jiau-ger jie shyan ren yee (微子微仲王子比干箕子膠鬲皆賢人也) "The Lord of Wei, his second son the

Prince Pi-kan the Lord of Chi, and Chiao-ke were all worthy men" (*Mencius* 2a.1.10).

... *jie guu shenq-ren yee* (皆古聖人也) "[Those mentioned in the previous context] all were Sages of Antiquity" (*Mencius* 2a.2.31).

4.13. The Determinative Sentence in Summary

The determinative sentence is in minimal form two terms, both nominal in value, in simple apposition in the order, given/new.[21] The relationships of *given* to *new*, when analysed present a paradigm, complementary to that of the *new/given* in syntagmatic determination. The prosodic features of the determinative sentence are pause between the two terms, and stress upon the "new" term. The stress particle *yee* is indicative, but not symptomatic of the form. The determinative sentence is in essence a categorical statement. The categorical "mood" may be conditioned by the use of copulae. This "mood" of judgment, rather than of simple assertion or narration, may be imparted to the verbal sentence, by recasting it in the determinative form. Cause and consequence are so stated. Peculiar to the form, is its distinctive negative, *fei*, and the use of the demonstratives, rather than the anaphoric pronouns, as anaphoric substitutes for its two terms.

[21] To use Dr. Halliday's term (see Halliday (1)).

V. Sentences in Distribution

5. Introduction

No attempt has been made in this analysis to account exhaustively for the distribution of the elements in the "piece."[1] No element, however, other than the conjunctions to be described hereafter, occurs in the piece that cannot be accounted for by one of the two sentential types described in chapters III and IV. The interrelationships of the elements of the "piece" may assume great complexity. Certain relationships are explicitly marked (e.g., by conjunctions, by marked stress patterns, and by anaphoric substitution) but these devices are subject to the rule of economy, and must sometimes be inferred (e.g., a "reluctance to repeat" is a marked feature of LAC, and, though the resources for anaphoric substitution are adequate, their use is not obligatory, and repetition is often avoided by simple silence).

The elements in the piece stand in one of two broad classes of relationships, that of co-ordination and subordination. A general observation is that the dominant or major consideration is stated as the last element in the piece.

In the following paragraphs, the formal devices for marking a relationship only are described.

5.1. Co-ordinate Sentences in Sequence

The conjunction *Yow* (又) *giug "also, too" indicates that the consideration of the second sentence is a further consideration, additional to that of the first.[2] The conjunction *yih* (亦) *ziak "in the light of the foregoing, after all" indicates that the consideration of the second sentence is in some way contingent upon that of the first. The conjunction *chiee* (且) *ts'iă "moreover" indicates that the consideration of the second sentence is unrelated to that of the first, though both are relevant to the general consideration of the discourse.[3]

[1] See 3 footnote 1.

[2] *Yow*, incorporated in the verbal syntagma, however, is aspectual, "once again, to repeat, for a second time ... " (see 3.3.2.8).

[3] *Chiee* also occurs as a link between two verbs having a common agent.
EXAMPLES
Ren chiee jyh (仁且智) "is both humane and wise" (*Mencius* 2b.9.1).

SENTENCES IN DISTRIBUTION

Yow and *Yih* occur between agent and verb of the second sentence. *Chiee* between the two sentences.

EXAMPLES

Yow: Chyi dih torng, shuh jy shyr yow torng ... (其地同樹之時又同) "If the soil" for it [the barley] is comparable, and the time of planting it also comparable, then ... (*Mencius* 6a.7.2); *Chiuh, tzer jiun shyy ren dao jy chu jiang, yow·shian yu chyi suoo woang.* (去則君使人導之出疆又先於所往) "When he leaves, the Prince sends a man to escort him beyond the frontier, he also notifies the place to which he is going" (*Mencius* 4b.3.3); *Buh der yii yanq chyi fuh-muu, yow cheng day erl yih jy* (不得以養其父母又稱貸而益之) "They have not only no means of nurturing their parents, but too, they must borrow to supplement their livelihood"[4] (*Mencius* 3a.3.8).

Yih: Wang her bih iue lih, yih yeou ren yih erl-yii yii. (王何必曰利亦有仁義而已矣) "Why must the King speak about profit, there is, after all, only humanity and justice [worth speaking about]" (*Mencius* 1a.1.2); *Wang yih iue ren yih erl-yii yii* (王亦曰仁義而已矣) "The King should, in the light of what has been said, speak only of justice and humanity" (*Mencius* 1a.1.5).

Chiee: Show shiang chyr, chiee ren wuh jy (獸相食且人惡之) "Beasts eat their own kind, and further, men despise them for doing so" (*Mencius* 1a.4.3); *Ru woang daw erl tsorng bii, her yee. Chiee, Tzyy guoh yii, woang jii jee wey yeou neng jyr ren jee yee.* (如枉道而從彼何也且子過矣枉己者未有能直人者也) "If I were to pervert my doctrine and follow those people, what would be said of me? Furthermore, You, Sir are in error, for among those who have perverted themselves, there will never be one who could put others straight" (*Mencius* 3b.1.9).

5.2. Subordinate Sentences in Sequence

The particle of subordination *erl* occurring as a conjunction of subordination has been described (3.7.2). The use of the ingressive instrument as a subordinating device has been described (3.6.3). In narrative sequence, the stress particles *yee* (也) and *yii* (矣) occur with the meaning: *yii* "sentence formally complete but narrative not concluded," and *yee* "narrative concluded." The stress pattern is *yii* penultimate stress (suspensive—more to come), and *yee* ultimate stress (conclusive—end of narration).

Bae gong jy shyh, guh buh kee geng chiee wei yee (百工之事固不可耕且為也) "One assuredly cannot both engage in agriculture, and undertake the myriad tasks of the artisan" (*Mencius* 3a.4.11).

[4]The last example "not only to... but also to..." also occurs in the form "*Jih ... yow ...*"; *Jih buh neng linq, yow buh neng minq* (既不能令又不能命) "Not only to be unable to give orders, but also to be unable to take orders" (*Mencius* 4a.8.1). Cf. also "*Jih iue ... yow iue ...*" (既曰...又曰...) "not only did you say... but too you said..." (*Mencius* 2a.2.13).

5.3. Conditioned Sequence

The conditioning of one statement by another is indicated typically by the conjunction of condition *tzer* (則) *tsək. *Sy* (斯) *sieg (e.g., in *Mencius*) and *Jyi* (卽) *tsiet (e.g., in *Micius*) also occur.

The conjunction of condition occurs in both fulfilled and unfulfilled conditional statements. The fulfilled form occurs in narrative, for example, *Gong shyy Yang-chu Fuh juei jy, Jyi ju Her, tzer tzay jou jong yii* (公使陽處父追之及諸河則在舟中矣) "The Duke sent Yang-ch'u Fu in pursuit of him, but by the time he had caught up with him at the Yellow River, he was already in a boat" (lit: [when] catch-up/him-at/river/then/placed/boat/middle/stress) (*Tso* 142.23). But it occurs most frequently in its metaphorical and extended sense "at such time as ... then ... " in statements of hypothesis in reasoning.[5] In the unfulfilled conditional, the verb is modally determined, and is subjunctive (potential) (see 3.3.1.3).[6] The condition is sometimes shown to be fulfilled by the occurrence of *Jih* (旣) (perfective aspect) in the protasis "having already ... ," "since. ..."

5.3.1. Fulfilled Condition

EXAMPLES

Jih yii fei jy, her yii yih jy (旣以非之何以易之) "Since you have thereby rejected it [i.e., that argument] then with what are you to replace it?" (*Micius* 23.10.)

Wu yii tzer wang hu (無以則王乎) "Since I lack the means [to discuss the question you raise] then [shall I discuss] true Kingship?" (*Mencius* 1a.7.2).

Chi ba yueh jy jian, hann, tzer miau gao yii (七八月之間旱則苗槁矣) "During the seventh and eighth month, at such times as a drought occurs, then the sprouts wither" (*Mencius* 1a.6.3).

Ren syy tzer iue fei woo yee, suey yee (人死則曰非我也歲也) "When people die then you say 'the blame does not lie with me, it lies with the harvest' " (*Mencius* 1a.3.11).

NOTE 1. *Ran-tzer* (然則) substituting for the protasis in an extended passage of reasoning indicates "since that is so, then ...."

EXAMPLES

Ran-tzer sheau guh buh kee yii dyi dah (然則小固不可以敵大) "Since that is so, then the smaller certainly cannot oppose the greater" (*Mencius* 1a.7.32).

---

[5] Hence the occurrence of *Jin* (今) "now" and *dang* (當) "when" introducing the protasis of conditional statements in the sense of "if" (see 5.3.2 Note 2).

[6] Observe that it is the verb and not the clause that is determined by *ru* (如) and *ruoh* (若). A form occurs in Micius where the protasis is introduced by *ruoh-shyy* (若使) "should you cause," which then becomes an introductory conjunction "if" (see 8.6.20).

Ran-tzer i yeu jy buh jeu wey bwu yonq lih yan (然則一羽之不擧爲不用力焉) "Since that is so, then a feather's not being lifted would be because the physical strength was not used to lift it" (*Mencius* 1a.7.16).

Ran-tzer fey shinn jonq yu (然則廢毀鐘與) "Since that is so, then we dispense with the ceremony of dedicating the bell, do we not?" (*Mencius* 1a.7.5).

NOTE 2. With *tzer* (則) replaced by *ran-how* (然後) the condition is made exclusive, that is, "when ... then only...."

EXAMPLES

Jiann buh kee yan, ran-how chiuh jy (見不可焉然後去之) "It is only when you see something remiss in him that you should reject him" (*Mencius* 1b.7.5).

Ru tsyy, ran-how kee yii wei min fuh-muu (如此然後可以爲民父母) "It is only when these [conditions have been fulfilled] that then you could become the father and mother of the people" (*Mencius* 1b.7.7).

5.3.2. Unfulfilled Condition

EXAMPLES

Wang ru shy ren jenq yu min ... juanq jee yii shya-ryh shiou chyi shiaw-tih jong shinn (王如施仁政於民壯者以暇日修其孝悌忠信) "If the King were to show to the people humane governmental policies ... then the able-bodied, taking advantage of the leisure [that relief from exorbitant forced labour would provide] could cultivate their brotherly duties, their loyalty and sincerity" (*Mencius* 1a.5.3).

Wang ru shann jy tzer her wey bwu shinq (王如善之則何爲不行) "If the King approves of my teaching, then why does he not put it into effect?" (*Mencius* 1b.5.6).

Wang wu tzuey suey, sy tian-shiah jy min jyh yan (王無罪歲斯天下之民至焉) "If the King would not blame the harvest, then the people of the world would come to him" (*Mencius* 1a.3.12).

Wang jy haw yueh sheen, tzer Chyi-gwo chyi shuh-ji hu (王之好樂甚則齊國其庶幾乎) "If the King's love of music were serious, then would not the State of Ch'i be near [the classical ideal]" (*Mencius* 1b.1.2).

Cheu jy erl Ian min yaw tzer cheu jy, cheu jy erl Ian min bwu yaw tzer wuh cheu (取之而燕民悅則取之取之而燕民不悅則勿取) "If, in taking Yen its people would be pleased, then take it, but if in taking Yen its people would not be pleased, then you should not take it" (*Mencius* 1b.10.2).

Wang suh chu linq, faan chyi maw-ni, jyy chyi jonq chih, mou yeu Ian jonq, jyh jiun erl-how chiuh jy, tzer you kee jyi jyy yee (王速出令反其旄倪止其重器謀與燕衆置君而後去之則猶可及止也) "If the King were quickly to issue orders ordering the return of their young people and the cessation of the removal of their treasures, talk things over with the people of Yen, set up a King for them and then vacate their territory, then he might achieve a cessation [of the threat of a punitive expedition by Yen's allies]" (*Mencius* 1b.11.8).

NOTE 1. Use of *goou* (苟) (*ku) and *cherng* (誠) (*dieng). When the protasis is introduced by *goou* or *cherng* "sincere, true," then the condition is further determined, viz: "if indeed, if in fact."

EXAMPLES

Goou wei how yih erl shian lih (苟爲後義而先利) "If in fact you were to put profit first, relegating justice to a secondary place, then . . ." (*Mencius* 1a.1.4).

Cherng ru shyh yee min guei jy you shoei jy jiow shiah (誠如是也民歸之猶水之就下) "If indeed things were like this, then the people would return to him as water flows downwards" (*Mencius* 1a.6.5).

NOTE 2. *jin* (今) (*kiəm) "present, now" or *dang* (當) (*tâng) "at such time as, when" also introduces the protasis of a conditioned sequence.

EXAMPLES

Jin Wang yeu bae-shing torng yaw tzer wanq yii (今王與百姓同樂則王矣) "If your Majesty shared his pleasures with the populace, then [he would be behaving as a] true King" (*Mencius* 1b.1.13).

Jin en tzwu yii jyi chyn-show erl gong bwu jyh yu bae-shing jee dwu her yeu (今恩足以及禽獸而功不至於百姓者獨何與) "If your kindness is sufficient to reach to your animals, but its efficacy does not get as far as your people, how can you allow that?" (*Mencius* 1a.7.15).

Dang shyy-ruoh ell shyh jee, yan bih shinn, shing bih guoo (當使若二士者言必信行必果) "If we imagine there to be two gentlemen, whose words can be relied upon, and whose conduct befits their pretensions . . ." (*Micius* 25.29).

NOTE 3. *Uei* (微) *miwər "small, minute, subtle" occurs in the protasis of conditioned sequences in the sense of "If it were not for . . ." As a grammatical word it is peculiar to this usage.

EXAMPLES

Uei Yeu, wu chyi yu hu (微禹吾其魚乎) "Were it not for Yü, would we not [by now] all be fish?" (*Tso* 341.10).

Uei Tzyy, tzer buh jyi tsyy (微子則不及此) "If it had not been for you Sir, I would never have reached my present position" (*Tso* 103.22).

Uei Jiun jy huey, Chuu shy chyi you tzay bih yih jy cherng shiah (微君之惠楚師其猶在敝邑之城) "If it were not for the kindness of My Lord, the armies of Ch'u would still be at the walls of our city" (*Tso* 311.3).

5.4. Concession

The concessive conjunction is *swei* (雖) *siwər "although, though."

5.4.1. Simple Concession

Where the concessive clause and the main clause share a common agent, the concessive clause occurs between agent and verb of main clause, and is introduced by *swei*.

EXAMPLES

Buh shyan jee swei yeou tsyy bwu yaw yee (不賢者雖有此不樂也) "One who is not worthy, though he possesses these things does not enjoy them" (*Mencius* 1a.2.2).

Woo swei buh miin chiing charng-shyh jy (我雖不敏請嘗試之) "Though I am not clever, I beg you to try it [explaining it to me]" (*Mencius* 1a.7.37).

Where the concessive clause and the main clause have different agents, the concessive clause is stated first, the concessive conjunction occurring between agent and verb of the concessive clause.

EXAMPLES

Ju-hour swei yeou shann chyi tsyr-minq erl jyh jee, bwu show yee (諸侯雖有善其辭命而至者不受也) "Although there were those among the Feudal Lords who, having sent elegant invitations, summoned him to come, he would not receive them" (i.e., gifts and invitations) (*Mencius* 2a.9.3).

Chyi-gwo swei bean sheau wu her ay i niou (齊國雖褊小吾何愛一牛) "Though the State of Ch'i is small and narrow, how could I grudge a single ox?" (*Mencius* 1a.7.7). (Note: "small and narrow" is a conventional deprecatory epithet, here suggesting "not a rich state" although Ch'i was, in fact, quite wealthy.)

A concessive clause may be stated, and then related to the main clause, by the use of the anaphoric *ran* (然) "thus." The concessive conjunction then occurs before *ran*. (Concession/*swei-ran*/main clause.) *Swei-ran* (雖然) (lit: *swei ru tsyy* (雖如此) "though like this") "even so, nevertheless, however," etc.[7]

EXAMPLES

Terng Jiun tzer cherng shyan jiun yee, swei-ran wey wen daw yee (滕君則誠賢君也雖然未聞道也) "As far as the Lord of T'eng is concerned, he is indeed a worthy Prince but despite this he has never heard of the Way" (*Mencius* 3a.4.5).

Woo buh reen yii fu-tzyy jy daw faan hay fu-tzyy, swei-ran, jin ryh jy shyh jiun shyh yee (我不忍以夫子之道反害夫子雖然今日之事君事也) "I cannot bear to use the skill you have taught me against you to your detriment, but nevertheless this present business is the King's business [and I have no choice]" (*Mencius* 4b.24.8).

Swei also occurs as a determinant word in syntagma, in the sense of "an extreme case of something more generally implied," "even a," etc.

EXAMPLES

Swei dah gwo bih wey jy (雖大國必畏之) "Even a great state would certainly fear him" (*Mencius* 2a.4.2).

---

[7]Sometimes occurring as *swei* (雖), but still retrospective. For example, see 8.6.14.

Yonq erl buh kee, swei woo, yih jiang fei jy (用而不可雖我亦將非之) "[A policy] which in practice is impractical, even I, after all, would condemn" (*Micius* 25.22).

5.4.2. Conditioned Concession (i)

A protasis, when concessive, may be introduced by *swei* (雖) "even if ... even though...."

EXAMPLES

Yuan muh chyou yu, swei buh der yu, wu how tzai (緣木求魚雖不得魚無後災) "When climbing a tree to catch fish, even though one may catch no fish there would be no subsequent harm" (*Mencius* 1a.7.30).

Swei yeou jyh-huey buh ru cherng shyh (雖有智慧不如乘勢) "Even though one may be very wise, it is preferable to [proceed on the principle of] exploiting the situation as it is" (*Mencius* 2a.1.12).

A protasis, introduced by *tzonq* (縱) *tsiung is both concessive and conditional. (*Tzonq* in contrast to *swei* occurs before the agent of the concessive clause.)

EXAMPLES

Tzonq Tzyy wanq jy, shan-chuan goei-shern chyi wanq ju hu (縱子忘之山川鬼神其忘諸乎) "Even if you, Sir, forget it, will the spirits of the hills and the streams forget it?" (*Tso* 437.6).

Tzonq yeou gong chyi way moh gong chyi ney, chern chiing woang yee (縱有共其外莫共其內臣請往也) "Even if there are those who supply his external needs, there are none to supply his inner needs. I beg leave to depart" (*Tso* 311.22).

Tzonq wu-tzyy wei jenq erl kee, how jy ren, ruoh shuu yeou jiang charng jy yan, bih yih huoh lih erl Feng shyh show chyi dah tao (縱吾子爲政而可後之人若屬有疆場之言敝邑獲戾而豐氏受其大討) "Even though, while you, Sir, are on the Throne, he might do so, under your successor suppose we become involved in a border dispute, our city would be culpable, and the Feng family would receive the full weight of their [i.e., Tsins'] displeasure" (*Tso* 365.1).

5.4.3. Conditioned Concession (ii)

You (猶) *ziôg, *shanq* (尚) *diang, and *you-shanq* (猶尚) occurring between two sentences make the first concessive, in the sense of "contrary to expectation, despite that, even so, nevertheless."

EXAMPLES

Iue "her guh sha jiun" you lih Wen Gong erl hwan (曰何故弒君猶立文公而還) "[The delegation] said 'Why did you assassinate your Prince?' but even so they concurred in the enthronement of Duke Wen, and returned home" (*Tso* 173.15).

Terng jyue charng buu doan, jiang wuu-shyr lii yee, you kee yii wei shann gwo (滕絕長補短將五十里也猶可以爲善國) "If the territory of the State of Teng were squared it would be only fifty miles on each side but even so it could become an excellent State" (*Mencius* 3a.1.4).

Jang-tih yeou jyh, chyi you tzay jiun-tzyy jy how hu (張豴有知其猶在君子之後乎) "Chang T'i has wisdom, but even so does he not fall short of being a true gentleman?" (*Tso* 348.5).

Bair guei jy diann shanq kee mo yee (白圭之玷尚可磨也) "The flaws in a piece of white jade might nevertheless be ground out" (*Tso* 101.20).

Chin, yii choong, bi, you-shanq hay jy (親以寵偪猶尚害之) "The near relatives [of the House of Tsin], because of their favoured positions, could bring their influence to bear on Tsin, but even so Tsin killed them" (*Tso* 96.13).

VI. Substitution

6.1. Substitution

Substitution occurs at all levels of distribution in LAC. Within the general class "substitute words" the following are distinguished.

(1) Personal pronouns, substituting for and replacing proper names.

(2) Anaphoric pronouns, substituting for and replacing sentential and other elements, to avoid repetition.

(3) Demonstratives, substituting a "gesture" (that of pointing) for the thing named.

(4) Interrogative substitutes, substituting in a question, for the element unknown, and extending, as it were, an invitation to the person addressed, to supply it, by way of an answer.

(5) Indefinite substitutes, substituting for an element known, but held in suspense. In subclasses (1), (2), and (3), and also between (4) and (5), there is occasional overlapping of function.

6.2. The Personal Pronouns

In forms of address in LAC a status-relationship is involved. When the personal pronouns are used, the status-relationship is one of equality (hence the term "non-status personal pronouns") and the form of address is direct. The direct form of address, however, implies an absence of formality. Formality requires an indirect form of address, and this can be of two kinds: (*a*) that in which proper names, titles and ranks are used as forms of address (and degrees of formality are here made possible by the use of titles, ranks, and family names [more formal] and by personal and familiar names [less formal]), and (*b*) that in which status-pronouns which establish the relative status of speaker and person addressed, are substituted for such names or titles.

It must be remembered that LAC texts are written in a milieu where ritualistic courtesy is all-pervasive. The direct form of address is therefore of infrequent occurrence.

The use of the status pronouns may be realistic, that is, indicative of actual status, or conventional, conveying an assumed status (honorific or depreciatory) other than real status.

6.2.1. The Non-status Personal Pronouns

Two persons are distinguished among the non-status personal pronouns: the person or persons speaking, and the person or persons addressed. Number is not distinguished. The non-status personal pronouns are, (i) person speaking *Woo* (我) *ngâ, and (ii) person addressed *Ruu* (汝女) *ńio and *Ruoh* (若) *ńiak.[1] (For the determinant forms of these pronouns see 2.6.4.1.)

EXAMPLES

Woo (first person): *Bii u gaan dang woo tzai* (彼惡敢當我哉) "How dare he oppose me" (*Mencius* 1b.3.5); *Ren jie wey woo hoei Ming-tarng* (人皆謂我毀明堂) "Everyone tells me to destroy the Hall of Immanences" (*Mencius* 1b.5.1); *Jou Gong chii chi woo tzai* (周公豈欺我哉) "The Duke of Chou would surely not deceive me" (*Mencius* 3a.1.4); *Wey woo tzuoh jiun chern shiang yueh jy yueh* (為我作君臣相說之樂) "Compose for me some music [typifying] the pleasure which rulers and subjects take in each other" (*Mencius* 1b.4.12); *Tzyy-aur yii woo wei jean* (子敖以我為簡) "Tzu Ao thinks I was slighting him" (*Mencius* 4b.27.4); *Woo yih yuh jeng ren shin* (我亦欲正人心) "I, after all, wish to rectify men's hearts" (*Mencius* 3b.9.19); *Woo, janq-fu yee* (我丈夫也) "I am a man" (*Mencius* 3a.1.3).

Ruu and *Ruoh* (second person): *Ruu jeau jiun-wey, erl tzuey san yee* (女矯君位而罪三也) "You have arrogated to yourself the princely authority, that is the third of your offences" (*Tso* 347.7); *Jiang jau-shih tsorng ruu* (將朝夕從女) "[He] will pursue you day and night" (*Tso* 347.10); *Ruu buu lai jyi hu* (女卜來吉乎) "Did you consult the oracle to see if your coming was auspicious?" (*Tso* 359.22); *Ruu-fu yee bih wang, ruu sanq erl tzong-shyh* (女夫也必亡女喪而宗室) "You, Sir, will come to a bad end, you have [already] ruined your own House" (*Tso* 361.15); *Jye, wu yii ruu wei fu-ren* (捷吾以女為婦人) "If this thing succeeds, I will make you my wife" (*Tso* 54.23).

NOTE 1. *Other usages of Woo*

(a) *Woo* occurs in the sense "themselves, ourselves, us."

Farn yeou syh duan yu woo jee, jy jie kuoh erl chong jy yii. (凡有四端於我者知皆擴而充之矣). "All those who have these four principles within themselves should know that they are all to be developed and fulfilled." (*Mencius* 2a.6.8).

Wann-wuh jie bey yu woo yii (萬物皆備於我矣) "All things are complete in us" (*Mencius* 7a.5.1).

Yang-tzyy cheu wey woo (楊子取為我) /Yang-tzu/took/on behalf of/ himself/ "Yang-tzu sought his own interests" (*Mencius* 7a.26.1).

(b) *Woo* occurs when the speaker identifies himself with the state to which he belongs, in sense of "us, our state."

---

[1] See Appendix 3 for a note on *Ruu* and *Ruoh* as pregnant forms.

Tian tzann woo yee (天贊我也) "Heaven is assisting us [the armies of Sung]" (*Tso* 120.2).

Chyi-hour fa woo beei bii (齊侯伐我北鄙) "The State of Ch'i attacked our [i.e., the State of Lu's] northern frontier" (*Tso* 173.22).

(c) Both *woo* and *wu* (determinant form) occur in compounded forms of address, for example, *wu-tzyy* (吾子) "My master" with much the same nuance as "monsieur" or "my dear Sir," and *Woo Lao Perng* (我老彭) "our Lao P'eng" (in referring to Lao P'eng, the Nestor of Chinese Antiquity).

NOTE 2. The first person non-status pronouns *Yu* (予) *dio and *Yu* (余) *dio of EAC occur in LAC as archaisms,[2] usually, though not invariably, in citations from older works. They survive from a period in the language in which pregnant and determinant forms were not distinguished. Both were comprised indifferently in a single form of the pronoun.

EXAMPLES

Yu jih peng erl shyr jy (予既烹而食之) "I have already cooked and eaten it" (*Mencius* 5a.2.10).

Yu erl suoo jiah fuh-ren jy fuh yee (余而所嫁婦人之父也) "I am the father of the woman for whom you provided a husband" (*Tso* 204.18).

Yu yan ruu yu Jiun (余言女於君) "I shall report you to our Prince" (*Tso* 406.4).

Gong-ruoh yuh shyy yu, yu buh kee erl chyh yu (公若欲使余余不可而抶余) "Kung Jo wanted to seduce me, and when I would not allow him he beat me" (*Tso* 416.23).

NOTE 3. The usages of the pregnant and determinant forms of the personal non-status pronouns might be summarized as follows:

The pregnant forms of the pronouns (*Woo* and *Ruu*) occur in the verbal sentence (i) in the post-verbal positions; (ii) after *wey* (delegated agency), and *yeu* (two agents), and after *yii* (instrumental); (iii) whenever an element is in emphatic exposure.

The determinant forms of the pronouns (*Wu* and *Eel, erl, nae*) occur (i) as a determinant word in syntagma, and (ii) as the agent of a verbal sentence (except where the agent is in emphatic exposure). Pronouns are never determined terms in syntagma. (See 2.6.4.1; 3.5.2; 3.5.4; 3.5.5; 3.11.1 and Appendix 3.)

The two forms in contrastive distribution occur in the following:

Fa woo, wu chyou jiow yu Tsay erl fa jy (伐我吾求救於蔡而伐之) "If they attack us, I shall seek help from Ts'ai and attack them" (*Tso* 58.10).

[2]The tendency to retain archaistic forms of pronouns is a feature also of modern Chinese vernaculars. See Demiéville (2).

Jin jee wu sanq woo (今者吾喪我) "Today I lost myself" (*Chuang* 3.3).

Woo, shann yeang wu haw ran jy chih (我善養吾浩然之氣) "I am an adept at cultivating my deep breathing" (*Mencius* 2a.2.15).

See examples in Appendix 3 of *Ruu/eel*.

There is no special form of personal pronominal substitute for a person other than the person speaking or the person addressed.[3] A reference by substitution to a third person may be made by the use of the far demonstrative *bii* (彼) (see 6.3).

EXAMPLES

Bii dwo chyi min shyr (彼奪其民時) "They [the States of Ch'u and Tsin] exact corvée labour during the agricultural seasons [so depriving their peasants of a time to sow and reap their own grain]" (*Mencius* 1a.5.5).

Bii u jy jy (彼惡知之) "How could they know?" (*Mencius* 1a.7.9).

Bii ru iue "shwu kee yii fa jy" tzer jiang yinq jy iue (彼如曰孰可以伐之則將應之曰) "Were he to ask me which state might attack them, then I would answer him..." (*Mencius* 2b.8.4).

Bii janq-fu yee, woo janq-fu yee, wu her wey bii tzai (彼丈夫也我丈夫也吾何畏彼哉) "He is a man, I too am a man, why should I be afraid of him?" (*Mencius* 3a.1.2).

For *bii* (*pia) in this usage, *fwu* (*piwo) occasionally substitutes.

EXAMPLES

Shyy fwu woang erl shyue yan, fwu yih yuh jy jyh yii (使夫往而學焉夫亦愈知治矣) "If we let him go and learn about it, he, after all, will then the better know how to govern" (*Tso* 336.17).

Woo jie yeou lii, fwu you bih woo (我皆有禮夫猶鄙我) "Though all of us should observe the rituals, they will still think us uncouth" (*Tso* 390.12).

Fwu also occurs determining *ren* (person) in similar sense.

EXAMPLES

Uei fwu ren jy lih, buh jyi tsyy (微夫人之力不及此) "But for his [lit: that-person's] assistance I should not have attained my present state" (*Tso* 138.11).

... tzer fwu ell ren jee, Luu-gwo sheh-jih jy chern yee (則夫二人者魯國社稷之臣也) "... in that case, they [lit: those two men] are ministers upon whom the State of Lu's altars depend" (*Tso* 245.12).

6.2.2. Status Pronouns

Status pronouns derive from ranks and titles, from kinship terms and from laudatory or deprecatory determinant words, but are

---

[3]See Wang (1), 4.7, and Yang Bor-jiunn 5.4.

characterized as status pronouns when, by convention and usage, they become customary forms of address.[4]

The following illustrate the principle, but are far from exhausting the repertory of status pronouns in LAC.

EXAMPLES

Person speaking of himself

Goa-ren (寡人) (lit: "lonely one") used by Princes and Kings of themselves, "I".[5]
i ren (一人) "single man" is similarly used.
Gu (孤) (lit: "orphan, lonely") used similarly to *goa-ren*.
Buh-der (不德) (lit: "not-virtuous") used by rulers of themselves "I."
Pii-fu (匹夫) "I" used by a commoner (this is pejorative if used of another person).
Bey-tzyy (婢子) "I" used by servant girls.
Sheau-ren (小人) (lit: "petty person") "I" used when speaking to a superior.
Lao-ren, Lao-chern (老人;老臣) used by old men, old retainers, when speaking of themselves.
Chern (臣) common form for any but equals speaking to a ruler, of themselves, "I."

Person addressed

Wang (王) "king" as a form of address to kings, "Your Majesty."
Jiun-tzyy (君子) or *Jiun* (君) (from *Jiun* "a ruler" and *tzyy* "a son" thus "a prince," but, in depreciated sense, used to any gentleman).
Tzyy (子) a title of nobility, "baronet" but used as form of address among gentlemen, and particularly by disciples to a master.
Fu-tzyy (夫子) as previously.
Soou (叟) as form of address to elderly men.
Shwu-fuh (叔父) (*shwu*—"father's younger brother," *fuh*—"father") used by kings to other kings of same surname, and to grandees.
Shwu-shyh (叔氏) (*shwu* as previously, *shyh*—family name) used by kings to princes.

NOTE. When addressing more than one person, the status pronoun is sometimes prefixed by numerals, for example,

i-ell fuh-shiong (一二父兄) "you, my uncles and cousins" (lit: one-two-father-older brother);
i-ell chin-nih (一二親昵) "you, Princes of my own surname" (lit: one-two-relative-intimate);
Ell-san jiun-tzyy (二三君子) "You gentlemen." The "one-two" and "two-three" are used in an imprecise sense for "a few, more than one," etc.

[4]Compare here the remarks of Emeneau (1), p. 117, "It must be emphasized that, though these [i.e., Vietnamese] status pronouns are translated by English and French personal pronouns, they have as their class meaning only 'substitution' and 'status' in the main either with a real kinship system or a fictitious extension of this."
[5]See Waley (1), p. 251 (XVI.14) for the significance of *goa-ren*.

In 8.3.3 an example is given of the establishment of status by the use of the status pronouns, and the establishment thereof described.

6.3. The Demonstratives

The demonstrative is deictic in type and does not distinguish number. In distinguishing between two objects, *tsyy* (此)·*tsiar identifies the object nearer to the speaker, "this," and *bii* (彼) *pia the object more remote, "that." When there is no necessity for such distinctions, *tsyy* is used.[6]

EXAMPLES

Bii i shyr tsyy i shyr (彼一時此一時) "That was one time, this is another" (*Mencius* 2b.13.2).

Twu cheu ju bii yii yeu tsyy (徒取諸彼以與此) "If it were merely a matter of taking it from that and giving it to this, then ..." (*Mencius* 6b.8.6).

Chuen-chiu wu yih jann, bii shann yu tsyy, tzer yeou jy (春秋無義戰彼善於此則有之) "The Spring and Autumn Annals have no [records of] just wars. But if it is a question of that [war] being more commendable than this [war], then there are such cases" (*Mencius* 7b.2.1).

By contrast with *bii* and *tsyy*, the word *ta* (他) *t'â occurs in LAC in the sense of "other than the thing indicated or pointed at."[7] It occurs in syntagma as a determinant word, for example, *ta ryh* (他日) "on another day" (contrary to the one under discussion), (cf. *sy ryh* (斯日) "this day"), *ta ren* (他人) "other men" (contrary to those under discussion), but also in sense of "something else" *Wang guh tzuoo-yow erl yan ta* (王顧左右而言他) "The King turned to his courtiers, and spoke of something else" (i.e., he "changed the subject") (*Mencius* 1b.6.3).

6.4. Anaphoric Pronouns

The anaphoric pronouns have been described in the forms of distribution in which they occur. For *jy* and *chyi* in the verbal sentence see 3.8, for *chyi* in syntagma see 2.6.4.1, and for anaphora in the determinative sentence see 4.10.3.

6.5. The Interrogative Substitute

Questioning takes two forms in LAC. The first, a question inviting assent or dissent, is indicated by the use of the particles of sentential mood (see 3.9). The formal structure of the statement differs in no way from that of simple assertion, except that *hu* or *yu* (乎 or 與)

---

[6] See 4.10.3 for anaphoric use of demonstratives.
[7] Cf. also use of *Yih* (8.6.18).

in final position replace any other particle indicating "tone of voice." The answer given when assent is indicated, is a simple reiteration of the question, for example, *Yeou ju (jy hu)* (有諸(之乎)) "There is such a thing?" *Yeou jy* (有之) "There is such a thing!" (i.e., "Was that so? Yes!") (*Mencius* 1a.7.6). When dissent is indicated, the assertion is negated; *Yeou yii yih hu?* (有以異乎) "There is a way of differentiating between them?" *Wu yii yih yee* (無以異也) "There is no way of differentiating between them!" (*Mencius* 1a.4.1).[8]

The second form of questioning invites a material answer (rather than a formal indication of assent or dissent) and the structure of the statement is conditioned accordingly. The assertion is made, substituting for the material but unknown element an interrogative substitute. The answer is a reiteration of the assertion substituting for the interrogative substitute, the material answer.

Interrogative substitution occurs at all levels of distribution. The interrogative or indefinite is the third of a three term polar system (see 3.4.8). Elements which, when polarity is neutral, occur in the post-verbal positions in the verbal sentence, occur, as with negation, before the verb when the mood is indefinite.[9] Further, when interrogative substitutes occur together with the particle peculiar to the position in which they occur, the interrogative is placed *before* the particle, and not after it as is the element for which it substitutes in neutral mood.

The interrogative particle *her* (何) *g'â is of unrestricted distribution, substituting for all elements at all levels. Other interrogative substitutes are restricted, specialized to certain elements in distribution. Others are allegro forms, incorporating *her* and the particles of the position.

In the following description, interrogative substitution is described according to level and type of distribution.

The interrogative mood is used without formal distinction in questions which range from simple enquiry (inviting an answer) to rhetorical questions, better rendered in English by some form of heightened positive assertion.

There is an overlapping of function between the interrogative substitutes and indefinite substitutes, for example, *shwei* (誰) "who?" "whom?" and *shwei* "anyone"; *her* (何) "what?" and *her* "whatever";

---

[8] Assent is also indicated by *Ran (ru tsyy)* (然(如此)) (lit: like/this), that is, "It is as you say," "yes," or, even more simply, *Nuoh!* (諾) "I concur," "I concur with that statement," "yes," or *Foou* (否) "I do not concur," "no!"

[9] The formal distinction made between "neutral," "negative," and "interrogative mood" in the polar system, is the placing of elements represented by substitutes (pronouns and interrogatives) before the verb, in the negative and interrogative, and after the verb, in the neutral mood (see 3.4.8).

jii (幾) "how many?" and *jii* "a few" (an indefinite number).¹⁰ (See 6.8.)

6.5.1. Interrogative Substitution in Syntagma

In syntagma, interrogative substitution occurs in the parataxical syntagma (in simple connection with *yeu* (與)) and in the hypotaxical syntagma (in the determinative syntagma).

Interrogatives occurring in this form of distribution are *Her* (何); *Shwei* (誰) *diwər "substitute for personal names"; and *jii* (幾) *kiər "substitute for small numbers, a few, how many?"¹¹

	Parataxis	Hypotaxis
Simple Assertion (polarity neutral)	α(A 與 B)	A → B
Interr. (polarity interr.)	(1) α(誰 與 B) α(A 誰 與)	(2) 何 B (3) A 何 (4) 幾 B (5) 誰 B

(1) asks "with whom? speak, contend" etc.
(2) asks "of what species? possessing what attribute?" "what kind of."
(3) asks "what is determined by A?" (see below).

---

¹⁰There might be a better case for regarding the terms of the polar system as *neutral*, *negative*, and *indefinite*. There would then be neutral (a-polar), negative (polarity between negative and positive), and indefinite (polarity between known or definite and unknown or indefinite). In such a system, the emphasis placed (as in the description here) upon *interrogation* would be lessened, and more attention directed to the "unknown" versus the "known." It would, I think, be nearer to the genius of the language, but poses problems in statement (see Introduction iv.a footnote 10).

¹¹*Jii* (interrogative) is also used for indefinite reference "a few," for example, *Yeou jii* (有幾) "There are a few" (*Tso* 120.24). In this sense it occurs determining *her*, viz. *jii her* (幾何) "a few what, days? months? years?" and is used for "how long?" but also for "a few what?"

Shyh meng yee, chyi yeu jii-her? (是盟也其與幾何) /this/treaty/(st)/it/adhered to/a few/what?/ "How long will such a treaty be observed?" (*Tso* 328.15).

Ren-sheng jii-her (人生幾何) /man/life/few/what?/ "How brief is man's span of life!" (*Tso* 333.13).

Suoo huoo jii-her (所獲幾何) /that which/gain/few/what?/ "What have you gained?" (*Tso* 129.21).

(4) asks "what number of? how many?"
(5) asks "what proper name would substitute as the determinant term?" (see below).

EXAMPLES

(1)

Fwu shwei yeu wang dyi (夫誰與王敵) /st/who?/and/king/oppose each other/ "Who would oppose the King?" (*Mencius* 1a.5.6).
Wang shwei yeu wei shann (王誰與爲善) "With whom would the King do good?" (*Mencius* 3b.6.5).
Jiun shwei yeu shoou (君誰與守) "With whom would the King guard the State?" (*Mencius* 4b.31.5).

(2)

U shyh her yan yee (惡是何言也) "Oh! What kind of talk is this?" (*Mencius* 2a.2.25).
Jou Gong her ren yee (周公何人也) "What kind of man was the Duke of Chou?" (*Mencius* 2b.9.4).
Shyh her ru-jyh yee (是何濡滯也) "How dilatory this was!" (used here rhetorically) (*Mencius* 2b.12.2).
Jiau jih her shin yee (交際何心也) /exchange/gifts/what kind of/thoughts?/ "What kind of thoughts lie behind the giving of gifts?" Answer: *gong yee* (恭也) "thoughts of respect" (*Mencius* 5b.4.1).
Wang her ching jy wenn yee (王何卿之問也) "What kind of minister is your Majesty asking about?" (*Mencius* 5b.9.1).

(3)

For examples see 6.5.1 footnote 11, *jii her*.

(4)

Tzyy lai jii ryh yii (子來幾日矣) "How many days have you been here?" (*Mencius* 4a.24.2).

(5)

Buh jy chyi shwei shyh jy tzyy (不知其誰氏之子) /not/know/of what/family/(det. part.)/son/ "I do not know whose son he is" (the answer here would be to supply before the word *shyh* [clan] the name of the clan) (*Chuang* 74.19).

6.5.2. Interrogative Substitution in the Verbal Sentence

Interrogative substitution occurs in the verbal sentence for each of its elements, except for the elements occurring in final position (sentential mood, and stress).[12] Elements which, when polarity is neutral occur after the verb, are placed before the verb when inter-

---

[12] In this description *hu* (乎) is classified with the particles of sentential mood on the formal basis of similarity of distribution and interchangeability (see 3.9) and is thus excluded here. An alternative descriptive solution would be to include *hu* in the range of indefinite substitutes on the basis of its polarity indefinite/definite, that is, $\alpha \beta \gamma hu/\alpha \beta \gamma yee$, thus including *hu* in the class of indefinite substitutes.

rogative. In the following schema the range and variety of substitution occurring in the verbal sentence is set out. The elements are arranged as in neutral mood, the transpositions made in interrogative mood being shown by the use of arrows. The elements are numbered to facilitate reference, and are discussed in detail *seriatim*.

Interrogative Substitution in the Verbal Sentence

1	2	3	4	5	6	7 and 7a	8	9	10
		Agent		Instrumental /Subordinate Clause		Verb			Post-verbal position
Time	Place	α	Dist.			Det.	β	γ¹	γ²
		誰	孰	何		←			何自
		何		何用 何以 奚	奚而 何而	←			何由
						←			惡
						←			惡乎
焉 →						←			安
幾 →						←			奚
曷 →						←			焉
					何				
						←		何	
						←		誰	

6.5.2.1. Substitution in the Time Position (column 1)

Ian (焉) substituting in the time position, asks such questions as "when?" "at what time?" "what time for?" etc. Used in rhetorical sense (with, e.g., *tzai* as sentential mood), it implies an emphatic "no!" as answer, and is better rendered in English as "Never!..."[13]

Jii (幾) *kiər in time position asks "how many times?" "on how many occasions?" etc.

Her (曷) *g'ât in time position asks "when?"[14]

---

[13]*Ian* (焉) *.ian and *Yan* (焉) *gian (yu-jy) are clearly cognate (see, e.g., Simon (3), p. 122). Is the difference in initial *.-and *g-really phonemic? Or is the glottalized onset non-phonemic—a prosodic feature, contrastive only when *ian* occurs in initial rather than in final position?

[14]*Her* (曷) occurs once in *Tso* (as above), twice in *Chuang* (once before *charng* (嘗), experiential aspect, and once before *charng* (常) "always"), for example, as in *her charng buh faa Shenq-ren tzai!* (曷嘗不法聖人哉) in which *her-charng* is the indefinite form of the negative form *wey-charng* (未嘗) "Did they ever not pattern themselves on the Sages!" (that is, they always did!) (*Chuang* 10.5). It occurs

EXAMPLES

Ian der jyh (焉得智) "When did he become wise!" (*Mencius* 2a.7.2).
Ian der ren-ren erl jih jy (焉得人人而濟之) "What time has he to ferry any and everyone across the river?" (*Mencius* 4b.2.2).
Shyh, ian der wei dah janq-fu hu (是焉得為大丈夫乎) "When did these people become great men!" (*Mencius* 3b.2.2).
Ren, ian sou tzai! (人焉廋哉) "A man can never conceal his true character!" (*Mencius* 4a.16.2).
Eel ian neng meei woo tzai (爾焉能浼我哉) "You could never defile me!" (*Mencius* 5b.1.9).
Jii, chian ren erl gwo buh wang (幾千人而國不亡) "How many times can you use a thousand men [for the purposes previously described] before the State is ruined!" (*Tso* 373.3).
Jii ru shyh erl buh jyi Ying (幾如是而不及郢) "How often can you behave in this way before calamity falls upon the city of Ying!" (*Tso* 413.19).
Wu tzyy chyi her guei (吾子其曷歸) "When Sir are you returning to your native state?" (*Tso* 342.19).

6.5.2.2. Substitution in the Place Position (column 2) and in the Second Post-verbal Position (column 10)

In Interrogative substitution, place indications (locality at which) and directives are treated indifferently, both occurring before the verb.

Ian (焉) asks "to what place? whither? at what place? where?" etc.
An (安) asks "to what place? at which place? in what respect?"
When the lexical directives occur (see 3.4.5.1), they are preceded by *her*, thus: *her-you* (何由)   *her-tzyh* (何自).
U (惡) and *U-hu* (惡乎) substitute for the second post-verbal element and incorporate the directive particle. Since, in the passive voice, the directive is the causal agent, *U* and *U-hu* in addition to asking

---

once only in *Mencius* (in citation), and does not occur in *Micius*. It is common in *Kung Yang*, particularly in composition *her-wey* (曷為) "why?" Dr. Graham, in a private communication, points out that in *Hsun-tzu*, *her* occurs seemingly interchangeable with *her* (何), while in *The Book of Songs* (EAC), it is used in sense of "when" (see Ding (2)). Miller (1) suggests that *her* is an allegro form of *her-yueh* (何曰). Peir Shyue-hae (1), connecting *her* with *her* (盍) suggests an allegro form of *her-fwu* (何不). It would be surprising if *her* plus some element of time were not realized as an allegro form (e.g., ?何時) providing for the lexicon a "when?" The etymology, however, remains, to me at least, unclear, and in recording LAC usage one must observe that, in view of the evidence of *Hsun-tzu* and the *Kung Yang chuan*, blunting in the use of *her*, however precise its earlier meaning and usage, seems to have taken place already before Han times.

"to what place, at which place?" etc. also ask "by whom? by what?"[15] *Shi* (奚) *gieg occurs in complementary distribution with *U* and *U-hu*, asking such questions as "to what place? whither?" etc.[16]

EXAMPLES

Tian-shiah jy fuh guei jy, chyi tzyy ian woang? (天下之父歸之其子焉往) "When the world's fathers return in allegiance to him, to whom could their children go?" (*Mencius* 4a.14.3).

Gong ian tzay . . . iue. Wu gong tzay huoh-guu (公焉在曰吾公在壑谷) "Where is the Duke?" "The Duke is in the valley!" (*Tso* 331.1).

You ian yi jy (又焉移之) "Further, upon whom is it to be transferred?" (cf. *Yi jy yu Linq-yiin, Sy-maa* (移之於令尹司馬) ("Transfer it to the Premier, or to the Master of the Horse") (*Tso* 474.14).

Pyi jy buh tswen, mau jiang an fuh (皮之不存毛將安傅) "When the skin is dead, to what can you attach the hair?" (*Tso* 107.7).

Jiun syy, an guei (君死安歸) "Our ruler is dead, to where should I return?" (*Tso* 305.7).

Tzyy an der jy (子安得之) "On what grounds Sir should *you* get it!" (*Tso* 232.3).

Woo an der jyi yan (我安得吉焉) "From whence is good fortune to be got for us from this?" *Tso* 480.9).

Jiang an yonq jy (將安用之) "Where could we use it!" (i.e., "it is useless") (*Tso* 248.25). *An yonq* and *ian yonq* occur commonly in this sense.

[15] The "meanings" of these interrogative substitutes given here should not mislead. All substitutes substituting for the directive have the class-meaning of "substituting for the element which appears at γ^2 when polarity is neutral." This element may be location, goal, causal agent, etc. (see 3.4 ff.), and however the form of the question is realized in English translation (of which the above "meanings" are examples), the interrogatives in LAC have only the class-meaning "directive substitute" and do not *mean* "whither," etc.

[16] *Shi* occurs in complementary distribution with other substitutes for the second post-verbal position, and also substitutes for the instrumental position. It seems clearly to be an allegro form of *her* plus *?yii* or *?yu* or of either, depending on the environmental conditions in which it occurs, for *shi* clearly distinguishes between *her yii* (何以) "by what means? how? why?" and *何於 "to what place? whither?" In EAC *yu-her* (于何) occurs, for example, in *The Book of Songs*, a distribution which is the reverse of the distribution of the lexical directives (*her-tzyh* and *her-you*).

Her does not, however, occur with the directive particle in LAC, and *yii* does occur introducing second post-verbal elements. The conclusion to be drawn, therefore, would be that *shi*=(*her-yii*).

Yang Shuh-dar (Yang (3), 3.134), citing glosses of the *Han* scholars *Jenq Shyuan* (鄭玄) and *Her Shiou* (何休) understands *u-hu* as *yu-her* (於何), noting that the occurrence of the interrogative before the directive particle (as in *u-hu*) is "regular." Yang Bor-jiunn (5.36) concurs.

Her-you jy wu kee yee (何由知吾可也) "From what do you deduce the notion that I could" (i.e., be a true king) (lit: from where/know/I/could) (*Mencius* 1a.7.3).

Her-tzyh chii (何自起) "From whence does it arise?" (Answer: "*Chii buh shiang-ay*" [起不相愛] "It arises from a failure to practise mutual love") (*Micius* 21.4).

Tian-shiah u-hu dinq. . . . Dinq yu i (天下惡乎定定于一) /world/by what/made settled?/settled/by/unification/ "What will settle the world? [It will be] settled by unification" (*Mencius* 1a.6.1).

U der wu-tzuey (惡得無罪) "In what respect could he be innocent?" (cf. previous context *wu-tzuey yan* (無罪焉) "innocent in this respect") (*Mencius* 4b.24.2).

Fu-tzyy u-hu jaang (夫子惡乎長) "In what respect Master are you superior?" (Answer: *jaang hu jy yàn* (長乎知言) "I am superior in respect of my knowledge of words") (*Mencius* 2a.1.14).

Jiun-tzyy bwu lianq u-hu jyr (君子不亮惡乎執) "If a gentleman believes nothing, by what will he be held fast?" (*Mencius* 6b.12.1).

U yonq shyh woo-woo jee wei tzai (惡用是鶃鶃者為哉) /what/use/this/goose/ cause to become/mode/ "What could I do with this goose?" that is, "take this goose and make it what?" (*Mencius* 3b.10.8).

Bii u jy jy (彼惡知之) "How could they know?" (*Mencius* 1a.7.9).

Bii chiee shi shyh yee (彼且奚適也) "Where is that [bird] going to?" (*Chuang* 1.15).

Tzyy jiang shi jy? Jiang jy dah-huoh (子將奚之將之大壑) "Where are you going? I am going to the Sea" (*Chuang* 31.70).

6.5.2.3. Interrogative Substitution in the Agential Position.
1. The Agent (column 3)

Substitution in the agential position asks "what agent?" Substitutes occurring in this form of distribution are *shwei* (誰) *diwər substituting for personal names, persons, etc., and *her* (何) substituting usually for non-personal agents.[17]

EXAMPLES

Shwei neng yuh jy (誰能禦之) "Who can resist him?" (*Mencius* 1a.6.6).
Shwei gaan wuu jy (誰敢侮之) "Who dare insult him?" (*Mencius* 2a.4.4).
Shwei neng jyr reh (誰能執熱) "Who can hold a heated thing?" (*Mencius* 4a.8.6).
Her cheu yu shoei yee (何取於水也) "What was deduced from water?" (*Mencius* 4b.18.1).
Her wey jy yan (何謂知言) "What is meant by 'knowing words'?" (*Mencius* 2a.2.21).

---

[17] For substitution in the agential position where two agents are connected by *yeu*, see 6.5.1.

6.5.2.4. Substitution in the Agential Position. 2. Agential Distributives (column 4)

Shwu (孰) *diôk is restricted to the agential distributive position, and asks "of the agents [named or unnamed] what one? which of them?" etc.[18]

EXAMPLES

Wang yii-wei shwu shenq (王以爲孰勝) "Which of the two does Your Majesty think would win?" (*Mencius* 1a.7.32).
Shwu yaw (孰樂) "Which of these [two] is the more pleasurable?" (*Mencius* 1b.1.5).
Wu-tzyy yeu Tzyy-luh shwu shyan (吾子與子路孰賢) "Which is the more worthy, You, Sir, or Tzu-lu?" (*Mencius* 2a.1.2).
Bii ru iue shwu kee yii fa jy tzer jiang yinq iue (彼如曰孰可以伐之則將應曰) "Had he asked me which state might attack them, then I would have answered ..." (*Mencius* 2b.8.4).

6.5.2.5. Substitution in the Instrumental Position (column 5)

Substitution in the instrumental position asks "what instrument?" (for instrument see 3.6 ff.). Where the instrumental particles occur, the interrogative substitute precedes them. Interrogative substitutes that occur in this position are *her* (何), *her-yii* (何以), *shi* (奚),[19] and *her-yonq* (何用). They ask such questions as "by what means? how? use what? for what purpose?" etc.[20]

EXAMPLES

Her-yii lih wu gwo (何以利吾國) "How can I benefit my State?" (*Mencius* 1a.1.2).
Her-yii day jy (何以待之) "How shall I deal with them?" (*Mencius* 1b.11.1).
Her-yii wei Koong-tzyy (何以爲孔子) "How could he [otherwise] have been Confucius?" (*Mencius* 5a.8.7).
Jau yu-ren, her yii? Yii pyi guan (招虞人何以以皮冠) "When summoning the huntsmen, what should one use? Use your fur cap [and not the flags of rank, by which gentlemen are summoned]" (*Mencius* 5b.7.10).
Shi guan? guan suh! (奚冠冠素) /how/hat [himself]—hat[himself]/[with] plain stuff/ "What hat should he wear? A hat made of plain stuff" (*Mencius* 3a.4.7).
Koong-tzyy shi cheu yan (孔子奚取焉) /Confucius/took what/deduce/from that/ "What did Confucius deduce from that?" (*Mencius* 3b.1.3).

---

[18]For *her-dwu*, *shi-dwu* and *chii-dwu*, see 8.6.8 Commentary.
[19]See 6.5.2.2 footnote 16.
[20]The substitution illustrated is one of the ingressive instrument. The resultative instrument can be similarly substituted. *Shi yeou yu shyh?* (奚有於是) /What? thereby/exists/in/this/ "What has that to do with it?" (*Mencius* 6b.2.2).

Shi kee-yii yeu woo yeou (奚可以與我友) "How could he be on friendly terms with me?" (*Mencius* 5b.7.8).
Shi kee tzai? (奚可哉) "How could you!" (*Mencius* 7a.34.2).
Her-yonq sheng tzai (何用生哉) "How is it produced?" (*Micius* 22.4).

6.5.2.6. Substitution for the Subordinate Clause (column 6)

Substitution in the position of the subordinate clause asks for an answer of the kind for which the clause in *erl* (see 3.7) is used. It asks, for example, "Having done what? then ...."

EXAMPLES

Shi erl buh jy yee (奚而不知也) /because of having done what?/erl/not know/ "What has happened that he does not know?" (*Mencius* 5a.2.7). (Cf. here *jiann erl jy jy.... Wen erl jy jy* (見而知之.... 聞而知之) "Having seen [the Sages] they knew about it, having heard [of the Sages] they knew about it" (*Mencius* 7b.38.1).) The question therefore is something like "Is it because he has not been told, or heard of it, or seen it, that he does not know?"

6.5.2.7. Substitution in the Verbal Syntagma (column 7). 1. Determinations of Manner

The interrogative substitute *her* (何), substituting in the verbal syntagma, may ask "in what manner? in what way? how?"

EXAMPLES

Shyh her yih yu tsyh ren erl sha jy (是何異於刺人而殺之) "In what way is this different from killing a man by stabbing him?" (*Mencius* 1a.3.12).
Shyh her tzwu yeu yan ren yih yee (是何足與言仁義也) "This man is in what way adequate to be spoken to about justice and humanity?" (*Mencius* 2b.2.8).
Tzyy jiun yee, woo chern yee, her gaan yeu jiun yeou yee (子君也我臣也何敢與君友也) "You, Sir, are a Prince, I, a mere subject, How dare I presume to be on friendly [i.e., familiar] terms with you?" (*Mencius* 5b.7.7).

NOTE. *Her* in *her-yii* (何以) (see 6.5.2.5) occasionally substitutes for determinations of *yii* (cf., e.g., *gaan-yii, tzwu-yii* (敢以)足以) etc. see 3.3.3.2 footnote 24) in addition to asking for the instrument.

EXAMPLES

Shi shya jyh lii yih tzai (奚暇治禮義哉) /what-way-use/leisure/cultivate/courtesy /justice/mode/ "How can they use their leisure to cultivate courtesy and justice?" (*Mencius* 1a.7.42).
Shyh, shi tzwu tzai (是奚足哉) "How is this enough?" (*Mencius* 7b.22.1).

6.5.2.8. Substitution in the First Post-verbal Position

Elements which in neutral polar mood, occur in the first post-verbal position, are placed before the verb, in the interrogative mood. The

SUBSTITUTION

substitutes that occur in this position are *her* (impersonal affectees) and *shwei* (personal affectees).

EXAMPLES

Wu her shiou erl kee yii bii yu Shian-wang guan yee (吾何修而可以比於先王觀也) "What should I cultivate in order to make my state-visits comparable with those of the Former Kings?" (*Mencius* 1b.4.5).
Her jia yan (何加焉) /what/add/to him/ "What advantage is it to him?" (*Mencius* 6a.10.9).
Woo her yii Tang jy pinn-bih wei tzai? (我何以湯之聘幣爲哉) /I/what/take /T'ang/'s/send-with-invitation/silk/make it/mode/ "What shall I do with this gift of silk sent to me by T'ang?" (*Mencius* 5a.7.4) (see 3.6.1 footnote 52).
Shwei jinq (誰敬) *Jinq shiong* (敬兄) "To whom should you show [the greater] respect?" "Show it to your elder brother" (*Mencius* 6a.5.2).
Jwo tzer shwei shian? Shian jwo shiang-ren (酌則誰先先酌鄉人) "If I offer wine, to whom should I first offer it?" "Offer it first to the villager" (*Mencius* 6a.5.2).

6.5.3. Interrogative Substitution in the Determinative Sentence

Interrogative substitution occurs in the Determinative Sentence for either of the two terms, in total and partial inclusion (see 4.5), in the usages of *yeou* (有) (see 4.8 ff.), and for the determinative use of the instrumental in cause and consequence sequences (see 4.11).

The types of substitution are summarized as follows:

	Type	Determined term	Copulae	Determinant term
1	Total inclusion	何		何也
2	Partial inclusion		何如	
3	Predication of presence or occurrence	焉有 奚有 豈有		何…之有也
4	Reality	豈		
5	Cause and consequence	何	何以 何爲 奚爲 何 蓋(何不)豈爲 何故 胡	何

6.5.3.1. Total Inclusion of the Terms (line 1)

Her (何) substitutes for either term, and asks such questions as "what can be said determinatively of A?" (A, *her yee*), "of what is B determinative?" (*her* B *yee*). Substitution occurs for all the types of determined and determinant terms described in detail in 4.3.2, 4.5, etc.

EXAMPLES

Her, Sheu-tzyy jy bwu dann farn (何許子之不憚煩) "What can be said of Hsu-tzu's going to so much trouble?" (*Mencius* 3a.4.11).

Ru woang daw erl tsorng bii, her yee (如枉道而從彼何也) "Were I to pervert my principles and conform with those people, what would be said of me?" (*Mencius* 3b.1.9).

Jiun-tzyy jy nan shyh, her yee (君子之難仕何也) /Gentlemen/det. part./make difficult [go to great pains about]/taking office/what?/ "What can be said about the fact that a gentleman is exacting in the terms upon which he will be employed?" (*Mencius* 3b.3.7).

6.5.3.2. Partial Inclusion (line 2)

Her-ru (何如) substitutes in the sense of "thing given, is like what?" that is, "has common affinities with, or shares a common attribute with, what?" *Her-ru* is used in a very general sense from "to what would you liken" > "what can be said about?"

EXAMPLES

Haw yueh, her-ru (好樂何如) "What can be said about fondness for music?" (*Mencius* 1b.1.1).

Buh cheu, bih yeou tian iang, cheu jy her-ru (不取必有天殃取之何如) "If I do not annex it [Yen] certainly there will be Heaven's disapproval to face, but if I do, what would you say about that?" (*Mencius* 1b.10.2).

Bor-yi, I-yiin, her-ru (伯夷伊尹何如) "What would you say about such people as Po Yi and Yi Yin?" (*Mencius* 2a.2.28).

Yii wuu-shyr buh shiaw bae buh tzer her-ru (以五十步笑百步則何如) "If because they had fled only fifty paces, they laughed at those who had fled a hundred paces, then what would you say to that?" (*Mencius* 1a.3.4).

6.5.3.3. Occurrence and Presence

Interrogative substitution occurs with *yeou* both when *yeou* occurs as the determinant term and in the determined term. *Ian-yeou* (焉有) asking "when or where is there/has there been," *chii-yeou* (豈有) "Surely there is not . . . ?"[21] while *her-yeou* (何有) or *her x jy yeou* (何 . . . 之有) occurring in the determinant term, asks either "what exists?" (in a rhetorical sense, "how can it be!") or "what . . . x . . . exists," for example, in *her nan jy yeou* (何難之有) "What difficulty is there?"

[21] *Chii* corresponds in interrogative polar mood to *shyh* and *fei* in negative polar mood (as in 4.9) when used in the sense "it is so, it is not so!" and thus *Chii* means "Surely it is not so?" For *Ian-yeou* see 6.5.2.1. Again, *Ian-yeou* is better rendered in English as an emphatic assertion "There never has been," although in LAC it is interrogative "When or where has there been!"

SUBSTITUTION

EXAMPLES

Ian-yeou jiun-tzyy erl kee yii huoh cheu hu! (焉有君子而可以貨取乎) "There has never been a gentleman who could be procured with a bribe!" (*Mencius* 2b.3.5).

Ian-yeou ren ren tzay wey, woang min erl kee wei! (焉有仁人在位罔民而可為) "When has there been a humane ruler who could pursue a policy of laying traps for his people!" (*Mencius* 3a.3.3).

Ian-yeou buh ren jee hu (焉有不仁者乎) "[Under such circumstances] there would never be an inhumane person!" (*Mencius* 7a.23.3).

Chii-yeou tuo [i.e., *ta*] *tzai* (豈有它哉) "Surely there is no other reason?" (*Mencius* 1b.10.4).

Yu wang, her yeou? (於王何有) "What is there to concern the King in this?" (*Mencius* 1b.5.11).

Yu dar shyh yee, her yeou (於答事也何有) "What difficulty is there in answering this?" (*Mencius* 6b.1.3).

Buh chyy bwu ruoh ren, her ruoh ren yeou (不恥不若人何若人有) /not/feel shame/ not/like/others/what/like/others/exists?/ "If one differs from normal men in feeling no shame, in what will one be like normal men?" (*Mencius* 7a.7.1).

Kow-chour her fwu jy yeou (寇讎服何之有) "What mourning can there be for an outlaw?" (*Mencius* 4b.3.6).

Her wang gwo bay jia jy yeou (何亡國敗家之有) "Would there be such things as lost states and ruined families?" (*Mencius* 4a.9.2).

6.5.3.4. Substitution for *Fei* and *Shyh* (line 4)

Where *fei* and *shyh* occur as the determined term (see 4.9) in the sense "it is so, it is not so . . ." the substitution of *chii* (豈) *k'iər combines both negative and interrogative moods, in sense of "It surely is not so that . . ." "It surely is not true that . . ." etc.

EXAMPLES

Chii neng dwu yaw tzai (豈能獨樂哉) "He surely cannot take his pleasures by himself?" (*Mencius* 1a.2.6).

Koong-tzyy chii buh yuh jonq-daw tzai (孔子豈不欲中道哉) "It is surely not true to say that Confucius did not want the Middle Way!" (*Mencius* 7b.37.3).

Chii nan jy tzai (豈難知哉) "This surely is not difficult to understand?" (*Mencius* 6b.2.8).

Shyh chii shoei jy shinq tzai (是豈水之性哉) "This is surely not an intrinsic property of water?" (*Mencius* 6a.2.4).

6.5.3.5. Substitution in Cause and Consequence Sequences (line 5, columns 1 and 3)

Her (何) substitutes for either of the principal terms in cause and consequence sequences. (*Her . . . yee*) asks "what consequence results from..?" and (... *her yee*) "this consequence results from what? why?"

EXAMPLES

Her chyi shyy sy min ji erl syy yee (何其使斯民飢而死也) "What will happen to the person who causes the people to starve to death?" (*Mencius* 1a.4.5).

Shuenn jy bwu gaw erl cheu, her yee (舜之不告而娶何也) "Why did Shun marry without informing his parents?" (*Mencius* 5a.2.1).

Jiun-tzyy bwu jiaw tzyy, her yee (君子不教子何也) "A gentleman does not tutor his own son, why is this?" (*Mencius* 4a.19.1).

Iue chyr chyi jyh wu baw chyi chih jee, her yee (曰持其志無暴其氣者何也) "You say 'one should be firm of purpose, and never allow the passions to offend.' Why do you say that?" (*Mencius* 2a.2.13).

6.5.3.6. Substitution in Cause and Consequence Sequences (cont'd) (line 5, column 2)

Her occurring with the copulae of the cause and consequence sequence, (see 4.11) (*her-yii* (何以), *her-wey* (何爲), *her* (何)) asks "why?" *Shi* occurs in a similar sense, (*shi* (奚), *shi-wey* (奚爲)).[22] *Her* occurring with *bu* is realized in an allegro form *her* (盍) *g'âp (lit: "why/not") but is used in a rhetorical sense "surely not because," "surely one should...," etc. *Chii* (see 6.5.3.4) also occurs in sense "surely it is not because...". *Her guh* (何故) "for what reason" is also realized in an allegro form *hwu* (胡) *g'o "for what reason" but also in a rhetorical sense "What possible reason could there be for...."

Occurrences are as follows:

	Question	Answer	
1.	何以...	以...	
2.	何爲...	爲...	
3.	奚爲...	爲...	
4.	何...	} Rhetorical	
5.	盍(何不)蓋...		
6.	豈...		
7.	何故...	以...	...之故也
8.	胡...	以...	...之故也

EXAMPLES

Line 1:

Her-yii "for what reason? Why?" *Her-yii wey yih ney yee* (何以謂義內也) "Why do you describe justice as an internal thing?" (*Mencius* 6a.5.1).

---

[22] *her-yii wey* see 6.5.2.2 footnote 16.

SUBSTITUTION

Line 2:

Her-wey "for what reason? Why?" *Her-wey buh shyng* (何爲不行) "Why do you not put it into practice?" (*Mencius* 1b.5.6); *Yu her-wey bwu show* (予何爲不受) "Why should I not accept it?" (*Mencius* 2b.3.4); *Her-wey chiuann jy tzai* (何爲勸之哉) "Why should I have urged this?" (*Mencius* 2b.8.7); *Wu her-wey dwu buh ran* (吾何爲獨不然) "Why should I be any exception?" (*Mencius* 2b.7.4).

Line 3:

Shi-wey "for what reason?" "Why?" *Jiun shi-wey bwu jiann Menq-ke?* (君奚爲不見孟軻) "Why, Sir, did you not go to see Mencius?" (*Mencius* 1b.16.4); *Sheu-tzyy shi-wey bwu tzyh jy* (許子奚爲不自織) "Why does not Hsü-tzu weave for himself?" (*Mencius* 3a.4.8); *Shi-wey shii erl bwu mey* (奚爲喜而不寐) "Why were you so happy that you could not sleep?" (*Mencius* 6b.13.2); *Shi bwu chiuh yee* (奚不去也) "Why did he not leave?" (*Mencius* 5b.4.12).

Line 4:

Her in rhetorical use. *Her shyy woo jyh yu tsyy jyi yee* (何使我至於此極也) "Why has he reduced us to these extremities?" (*Mencius* 1b.1.8); *Yu her yan tzai* (予何言哉) "Why should I speak?" (*Mencius* 2b.6.3); *Her dai lai nian* (何待來年) "Why wait until next year?" (*Mencius* 3b.8.3); *Chyi Chuu swei dah, her wey yan* (齊楚雖大何畏焉) "Though Ch'i and Ch'u are powerful, why be afraid of them?" (*Mencius* 3b.5.13).

Line 5:

Her (allegro form of *her-bu*) and *Gay* (same as *Her* (*her-bu*)). *Wey charng buh bao, gay buh gaan buh bao* (未嘗不飽蓋不敢不飽) "He never failed to eat to repletion, but this surely was because he would hardly presume to do otherwise?" (*Mencius* 5b.3.7); *Her faan chyi been yii?* (盍反其本矣) "Why not go back to the root of the matter?" (*Mencius* 1a.7.43); *Gay yih faan chyi been yii* (蓋亦反其本矣) "Why not, after all, go back to the root of the matter?" (*Mencius* 1a.7.34).

Line 6:

Chii in combination with *wey* "surely it is not because of...." *Chii-wey shyh tzai!* (豈爲是哉) "Surely it is not because of this" (*Mencius* 1a.7.28).

Line 7:

Her-guh "for what reason?" *Her-guh fey hu* (何故廢乎) "Why should you be set aside!" (*Tso* 84.13); *Her-guh shyh jiun* (何故弒君) "Why did you assassinate the Prince?" (*Tso* 173.15); *Her-guh buh kee* (何故不可) "Why cannot you?" (*Tso* 293.4); *Her-guh bwu jiuh* (何故不懼) "Why should I not be afraid?" (*Tso* 297.10); *Her-guh chin sheau* (何故侵小) "Why do you attack the small states?" (*Tso* 307.6); *Her-guh wu jy* (何故無之) "Why [do you say] there is no such thing?" (*Tso* 499.3).

LINE 8:

Hwu (allegro form of *her-guh*). *Hwu tzay buh mou* (胡再不謀) "Why did you twice act without consulting [me]?" (*Tso* 303.12); *Tzyy-woei chi Jinn, Jinn hwu show jy* (子尾欺晉晉胡受之) "Tzu-wei deceived Tsin, so why should Tsin accept her?" (*Tso* 350.11); *Ruu hwu jyr ren yu wang-gong* (女胡執人於王宮) "Why did you arrest a man within the Palace precincts?" (*Tso* 363.4).

Hwu is also used rhetorically "what possible reason could you give for?" *Hwu kee bii yee* (胡可比也) "How can you compare them!" (*Tso* 42.6); *Hwu kee shyh yee* (胡可恃也) "How can one depend on them?" (*Tso* 84.19); *Yu hwu fwu jy* (余胡弗知) "How should I not know [i.e., of course I know!]" (*Tso* 312.4).

6.5.4. Interrogative Substitution in Conditioned Sequences

Her substitutes for either protasis or apodosis but also substitutes for elements of the protasis or apodosis, following the patterns already described. In the following, examples are shown in distribution, to illustrate the contrasting levels at which substitution occurs in conditioned sequences.

		Protasis		Conj.	Apodosis			
		Mode	Verb					
1			何 her	則 tzer	可 kee			*Mencius* 1b.14.1
2	娶妻// cheu chi	如 ru	之 jy		何 her			*Mencius* 5a.2.1
3			何如 her-ru	則 tzer	可 kee	爲 wey	服 fwu	矣 yii	*Mencius* 4b.3.2
4		如 ru	何 her	斯 sy	可 kee	謂 wey	養 yanq	矣 yii	*Mencius* 5b.6.8
5				則 tzer	何 her	如 ru			*Mencius* 1b.9.3
6	舍我 shee woo			其 chyi	誰 shwei	也 yee			*Mencius* 2b.13.4

EXAMPLES

(1) (above) invites the protasis, thus "If I do what? Then such would be possible?" That is, "What should I do, so that then, this would be possible?"

(2) invites the apodosis, thus "Were I to marry a wife, then what should I do?"

(3) *Her-ru* in the protasis asks "To what should I be compared?" That is, "What sort of a person should I be, so that then my ministers would for me wear such mourning?"

(4) *Ru-her* in the protasis asks for a verb modally determined by *ru*, thus "If I did what? then it would be called 'true nurturing of parents.'" That is, "What should I do so that my care for my parents would be called 'true nurturing.'"

(5) ... *tzer her ru*, asks "If I did so and so, then what would you say to that?"

(6) invites the verb and affectee of the apodosis, "If [Heaven] sets me aside, then Heaven [*chyi*] will appoint whom?"

6.6. The Indefinite Substitute

The indefinite substitute *suoo* (所) *sio occurs in various types of distribution, and at various levels of distribution. It has the meaning "substituting for an unidentified or undefined person(s), place(s) or object(s)."

6.6.1. Types of Occurrence
6.6.1.1. Substitution for Post-verbal Elements

The indefinite substitute *suoo* occurs in distribution before transitive and intransitive verbs, and substitutes for elements which, where mood is neutral (rather than indefinite) occur defined in the post-verbal positions. It substitutes for the affectee (γ^1) (e.g., in the sense of "that which is...," "he who is..."), for the directive (γ^2) of a verb in active voice (e.g., in the sense of "the place to which..."), and for the directive of a verb in passive voice (e.g., in the sense of "he by whom, that by which"). When substituting for the directive, the lexical directives *tzyh* and *you* may occur as *suoo-tzyh* (所自) and *suoo-you* (所由). In the paradigm which follows, these distributions are illustrated, and the indefinite modal forms contrasted with the neutral modal forms.

		Neutral	Indefinite
1.	去之	"rejects it"	所去 "that which [agent] rejects"
2.	非之	"condemns it"	所非 "that which [agent] thinks wrong"
3.	生之	"begets it"	所生 "that which [agent] begets"

Active

4.	起不相愛	"arises from a failure in mutual love"	所自起 "that from which [agent] arises"
5.	從外來	"came from outside"	所由來 "the place from which [agent] comes"
6.	受業於門	"to receive instruction at your Gate"	所受之 "those from whom [agents] received this"

Passive

| 7. | 生於慮 | "begotten by careful thought" | 所由(自)生(所生) "that by which [agent] is begotten" |

The examples of the paradigm are from:
(1) *Shuh-min chiuh jy* (庶民去之) "The masses reject it" (*Mencius* 4b.19); *Jonq suoo torng chiuh yee* (衆所同去也) "[Your teaching is] that which the commonalty unanimously rejects" (*Chuang* 3.44).
(2) *Jih yii fei jy, her yii yih jy* (既以非之何以易之) "Since you have thereby condemned it, with what are you to replace it?" (*Micius* 23.10); *Yii shyh, chyi*

suoo fei (以是其所非) "[Confucians] think right, that which they [Mohists] think wrong" (*Chuang* 4.26).

(3) *Chyi dih sheng Juo-tzyy* (其娣生卓子) "Her younger sister gave birth to Cho-tzu" (*Tso* 74.12); *Shyh jyi yih suoo sheng jee* (是集義所生者) "It is that to which the accumulation of right deeds gives birth" (*Mencius* 2a.2.8).

(4) *Dang char luann her-tzyh chii, chii buh shiang-ay* (當察亂何自起起不相愛) "When we examine from whence disorder arises, [we find] it arises from a failure to practise mutual love" (*Micius* 21.4). *Bih jy luann jy suoo-tzyh chii, ian neng jyh jy* (必知亂之所自起焉能治之) "We must know that from which disorder arises, then we can control it" (*Micius* 21.3).

(5) *Shyy-shyy tsorng way lai* (施施從外來) "Jauntily he came in from outside" (*Mencius* 4b.33.6); *Wu jy chyi suoo you lai yii* (吾知其所由來矣) "I know from whence it [peace with Ch'i] will come!" (*Tso* 97.17).

(6) *Yuann liou erl show yeh yu men* (願留而受業於門) "I would like to stay here and receive instruction at your Gate" (*Mencius* 6b.2.7); *Wu yeou suoo show jy yee* (吾有所受之也) "We have those from whom we have received it" (*Mencius* 3a.2.7).²³

(7) *Lih ay sheng yu liuh* (利愛生於慮) "[Mutual] benefit, and [reciprocal] love, are begotten of deep thought" (*Micius* 76.41); *Bii sheen hu jinn guoh erl buh jy guoh jy suoo you sheng* (彼審乎禁過而不知過之所由生) "He is well-versed in the forbidding of error, but does not know that by which error is begotten" (*Chuang* 29.23). *Tsyy jee* (suppress *teh*) *shiong yan jy suoo tzyh sheng* (此者(持)凶言之所自生) "It is this by which evil doctrine is begotten" (*Micius* 58.35).²⁴

6.6.1.2. Substitution for the Agent

Suoo occurs in distribution before the class of verbs capable of factitive and putative usage (attributive verbs), and substitutes as

---

²³Line 6. Another example of *suoo* substituting for the directive, when the affectee is present, is "*Yau Shuenn jy jyh tian-shiah, chii wu suoo yonq chyi shin tzai!*" (堯舜之治天下豈無所用其心哉) "It surely cannot be that in ruling the world, Yao and Shun had nothing about which to exercise their minds!" (*Mencius* 3a.4.26). An example of statement with great economy is *Gaan wenn suoo an* (敢問所安) "Might I presume to ask wherein you place yourself?" (*Mencius* 2a.2.28).

²⁴Line 7. Cf. line 3. In these examples *suoo* is shown to be substituting in the second post-verbal position by the use of *you* and *tzyh*. Yang Bor-jiunn (1), p. 224, cites *Songs* 196 "*Wu tean eel suoo sheng*" (無忝爾所生) "Do not disgrace those who gave you birth," and points out that this is not "Do not disgrace those to whom you give birth." The distinction is important, for *suoo* may substitute for both post-verbal positions (not only for the affectee, but for the directive which, when the verb is passive is the causal agent). The same feature is observed in *An suoo kuenn-kuu tzai* (安所困苦哉) "What is there to make it suffer?" but literally /Where? /that by which/ [agent]/made to suffer/ (*Chuang* 3.47).

an indefinite agent, for what, in neutral mood, would be the agent of realization.

EXAMPLES

Suoo buh tzwu (所不足) "that which is insufficient" (cf. *Ryh yih buh tzwu yii* [日亦不足矣] "The days after all are insufficient" (*Mencius* 4b.2.3).) as in *Sha suoo buh tzwu erl jeng suoo you yu* (殺所不足而爭所有餘) "[Fighting against Sung] is killing off that which is insufficient [i.e., population] and contending over, that which is in surplus supply [i.e., natural resources]" (*Micius* 93.4).

Suoo nan (所難) "that which is difficult" as in *Wei chyi suoo nan jee, bih der chyi suoo yuh yan* (爲其所難者必得其所欲焉) "He who does that which to him is difficult, will always get what he wants out of it" (*Micius* 1.6).

6.6.1.3. Substitution for the Instrument

Suoo also occurs in distribution before the instrumental particle *yii*, substituting as an undefined instrument for what, in neutral mood, would be a defined instrument introduced by *yii*. *Suoo-yii* occurs as "the means by which" and also "the reason for which." *Suoo-wey* occurs also in the sense "the reason for which."[25]

EXAMPLES

Jiun-tzyy suoo-yii yih yu ren jee, yii chyi tswen shin yee (君子所以異於人者以其存心也) "That by which a gentleman differs from others, is by that which he keeps in his mind" (*tswen shin* must be understood here as *suoo tswen yu shin*, for the next line is "*Jiun-tzyy yii ren tswen shin*" (君子以仁存心) "The gentleman keeps humanity in his mind" (*Mencius* 4b.28.1; and see Legge's note loc. cit.)).

Wey jiann suoo-yii jinq wang yee (未見所以敬王也) /not/see/that by which/revere/King/ "I did not notice any way in which you showed respect to the King" (*Mencius* 2b.2.7).

Tsyy shin jy suoo-yii her yu wang jee, her yee? (此心之所以合於王者何也) "In what way is this mind of mine compatible with true Kingship?" (lit: this/mind/'s /that-by-which/conforms/with/true kingship/syn./is-what-"that-by-which"/st.) (*Mencius* 1a.7.14).

Fei suoo-yii nah jiau yu ru-tzyy jy fuh-muu yee (非所以內交於孺子之父母也) "This is not something by means of which they can gain the favour of the little child's parents" (*Mencius* 2a.6.3).

Suoo-yii wey ren jie yeou buh reen ren jy shin jee ... (所以謂人皆有不忍人之心者...) "The reason why I say that all men have a mind which cannot bear others [to suffer] [might be illustrated as follows]" (*Mencius* 2a.6.2).

---

[25]Not to be confused with *suoo wei* "that which [agent] does"; for example, in *Shann tuei chyi suoo wei erl yii yii* (善推其所爲而已矣) "It was simply that they were good at putting to good effect that which they could do" (*Mencius* 1a.7.23).

Shyh-guh, farn dah gwo jy suoo yii buh gong sheau gwo jee, ji wey duo, cherng gwo shiou, shanq-shiah tyau-her, shyh-guh dah gwo buh jyy gong jy. (是故凡大國⊙ 所以不攻小國者積委多城郭修上下調和是故大國不眘攻之) "Therefore, the reason why great states would not attack small ones, would be because the small ones have many public granaries, keep their walls in good repair, and because their people high and low maintain amiable relations with one another. It is for these reasons, that a great state would not care to attack a small one" (*Micius* 38.46).

Jiun suoo-wey ching shen yii shian yu pii-fu jee, yii-wei shyan hu (君所爲輕身以先於匹夫者以爲賢乎) "Is the reason why My Lord demeans himself by giving precedence to a commoner, because he things the commoner a worthy?" (*Mencius* 1b.16.2).

6.6.1.4. Substitution in the Agential Syntagma

Suoo also occurs before *yeu* (與) (particle of simple connection in syntagma) in constructions where, in neutral mood, *yeu* occurs between two agents. *Suoo-yeu* (所與) is used in sense of "the undefined person with whom."

EXAMPLE

Chyi chi wenn suoo-yeu yiin-shyr jee tzer jinn fuh guey yee (其妻問所與飮食者則盡富貴也) "Whenever his wife asked him about those with whom he had been eating and drinking, they all proved to be either rich or noble" (*Mencius* 4b.33.1).

6.7. Levels of Distribution

6.7.1. In Syntagma

(*a*) A verb preceded by *suoo* may occur as the determinant word in a determinative syntagma. Its value is then nominal.

EXAMPLES

Suoo jiu jy shyh (所居之室) "the house that he lives in" (*Mencius* 3b.10.4).
Suoo shyr jy suh (所食之粟) "the food that he eats" (*Mencius* 3b.10.5).

(*b*) A verb preceded by *suoo* may occur as the determined word in a determinative syntagma. Its value is nominal.

EXAMPLES

Bor-yi jy suoo jwu (伯夷之所築) "built by Po Yi" (*Mencius* 3b.10.4).
Bor-yi jy suoo shuh (伯夷之所樹) "sown by Po Yi" (*Mencius* 3b.10.5).
   Cf. English "hand-made," "jerry-built."

(*c*) A verb preceded by *suoo* may occur as a syntagma, and as such occur as a single element in a sentence.

SUBSTITUTION

EXAMPLES

Yu cheu suoo chyou yan (余取所求焉) "I take *what I want* in these things" (*Tso* 321.13).

Guei suoo cheu yan (歸所取焉) "[He required the people] to return *what they had taken* to him" (*Tso* 294.22).

Bwu jiann suoo uei yan (不見所畏焉) "I did not see *anything to respect* in him" (*Mencius* 1a.6.1).

Shee ruu suoo shyue erl tsorng woo (舍女所學而從我) "Abandon *what you have learned* hitherto and follow me" (*Mencius* 1b.9.4).

6.7.2. In the Verbal Sentence

Syntagmas formed in *suoo* occur in the verbal sentence (see 6.7.1 (*c*)). A common occurrence as a single element is a syntagma formed from a verbal sentence (α 之所 β), the value of which is nominal.

EXAMPLES

Tzyy jy tzyy jy suoo buh jy ye (子知子之所不知邪) "Do you Sir know what you do not know?" (*Chuang* 6.65).

Chyou wu suoo dah yeu yee (求吾所大欲也) "I seek that which I greatly desire" *Mencius* 1a.7.26).

Shann tuei chyi suoo wei erl yii yii (善推其所為而已矣) "It was simply that they were good at putting to good effect that which they could do" (*Mencius* 1a.7.23).

6.7.3. *Suoo* in the Determinative Sentence

Suoo occurs in the determinative sentence, substituting for an element of one term (an indefinite reference) which occurs (as a definite reference) in the other term. In this form, a simple assertion (e.g., *wu jy jy* (吾知之) "I know this") is stated in a type of suspensive form *Tsyy, wu suoo jy yee* (此吾所知也) "This is something I know," or *Suoo jy jee, tsyy yee* (所知者此也) "what I *do* know, is this" providing an emphasis and nuance to an element, which in simple assertion, is unemphasized.

Elements in the terms of a determinative sentence for which *suoo* substitutes are as follows:

Type	Determined term	Determinant term
1a	γ^1	α 之 [γ^1] β 也
1b	α 之 [γ^1] β	γ^1 也
2	[γ^1] β	γ^1 也
3	β	α [β] SA 也
4a	Ins.	α [Ins.] β γ^2 也
4b	α [Ins.] β γ	Ins. 也

Square brackets enclose the element for which *suoo* occurs as substitute.

EXAMPLES

Type 1a

Ling-yiin jy bwu-shinn, Ju-hour jy suoo wen yee (令尹之不信諸侯之所聞也) "The lack of integrity of the Premier is something of which the Feudal Lords are well aware" (cf. *Ju-hour wen linq-yiin jy bwu-shinn* ("The Feudal Lords are aware of the lack of integrity of the Premier") (*Tso* 339.1).

Goan-jonq, Tzeng-shi jy suoo buh wei yee (管仲曾西之所不爲也) "A Kuan-chung is the sort of person Tseng-hsi would never become" (*Mencius* 2a.1.5).

... soou jy suoo jy yee (... 叟之所知也) "... is something you, Sir, know" (*Mencius* 1a.5.1).

Type 1b

Dyi-ren jy suoo yuh jee, wu tuu-dih yee (狄人之所欲者吾土地也) "What the Ti tribesmen want, is our territory" (*Mencius* 1b.15.3).

Wang jy suoo dah yuh kee jy yii (王之所大欲可知已) "Now I understand what it is that the King wants so badly, it is to..." (*Mencius* 1a.7.29).

Type 2

Nae suoo yuann, tzer shyue Koong-tzyy yee (乃所願則學孔子也) "If there is any question of what I would wish for, then it would be to have studied with Confucius" (*Mencius* 2a.2.31).

Type 3

Shyng-jyy fei ren suoo neng yee (行止非人所能也) "It is not within a man to ordain whether he will advance or be hindered in his official career" (*Mencius* 1b.16.8).

Type 4a

Shyh, Chuu suoo yii jiah yu Jinn yee (是楚所以駕於晉也) "It was for this reason that Ch'u behaved so arrogantly towards Tsin" (*Tso* 339.6).

Yii shyh Dah-gwo, suoo yii tswen yee (以事大國所以存也) "Serving great states, is the way we survive" (*Tso* 318.11).

Type 4b

Meng-shy Sheh jy suoo yeang yeong yee, iue "shyh bwu shenq you shenq" yee (孟施舍之所養勇也曰視不勝猶勝也) "The way in which Meng-shih She cultivated his ability to engage in feats of strength was, [as he said] by looking upon a loss [in a contest of strength] as a win" (*Mencius* 2a.2.5).

6.7.4. *Suoo* and *Her* in Complementary Distribution

Suoo also occurs in the determinative sentence, where the element for which it substitutes is, in the other term, replaced by *her* (何). *Her* then asks "for what is *suoo* the substitute?"

EXAMPLES

Tsyy shin jy suoo yii her yu wanq jee, her yee (此心之所以合於王者何也) /this/heart/'s/that-by-which/compatible/with/true-kingship/syn./what-that-by-which?/ "In what way is this heart of mine compatible with true kingship?" (*Mencius* 1a.7.14).

Shin jy suoo torng ran jee her yee (心之所同然者何也) "What is it that unanimously meets with approval in men's hearts?" (Answer: *Lii yee, yih yee* [禮也義也] "It is courtesy, it is justice") (*Mencius* 6a.7.10).

6.8. Interrogative and Indefinite

There is an alternation among substitutes between interrogative and indefinite usage. *Jii* "a few" (undefined number), and *jii* "what undefined number?" "how many?" has already been discussed (6.5.1 footnote 11). *Her* also occurs as both "what?" and "whatsoever."[26]

EXAMPLES

Tian-shiah her shyh, jie tsorng Yih-ya jy yu wey yee (天下何嗜皆從易牙之於味也) "Whatever mankind likes to taste, each and every flavour derives from the work on flavourings of Yi ya" (*Yi ya* was the Escoffier of Ancient China, the author of sauces and flavourings) (*Mencius* 6a.7.6).

Her bwu shuh jy yu wu her yeou jy shiang (何不樹之於无何有之鄉) "Why not plant it in the Land of Nothing Whatever?" (*Chuang* 3.46).

Ian "at what time or place" also occurs as "at whatsoever time, at such time, then, then only."

EXAMPLES

Ian neng jyh jy (焉能治之) "At such time only can he govern it" (*Micius* 21.3).
Bih jy jyi jy suoo-tzyh chii, ian neng gong jy (必知疾之所自起焉能攻之) "[The physician] must know from whence the illness comes, at such time as he knows he can cure it" (*Micius* 21.2).

---

[26]*Shwei* "who?" in Modern Standard Chinese has a similar ambivalence. (*Sheir dou jy-daw* [誰都知道] "anybody knows"; *Sheir dou neng* [誰都能] "anybody can." But *sheir?* (誰) "who?" See Chao (2), p. 185 and p. 52.)

VII. Miscellaneous

7.1. Degrees of Comparison

There is nothing in LAC comparable to a series of degrees of comparison. But comparison in a greater, or in the superlative degree can be expressed by periphrastic means.[1]

A word determined by *Jia* (加) *ka or *Yih* (益) *iek "to add to, to increase" forms a comparative.

EXAMPLES

Min buh jia shao (民不加少) "His population gets no smaller" (*Mencius* 1a.3.2).
Buh jia chiuann . . . buh jia tzuu (不加勸 . . . 不加沮) "He was no more encouraged [than he was before]; he was no more discouraged [then he was before]" (*Chuang* 2.18).
Ru shoei yih shen, ru huoo yih reh (如水益深如火益熱) "Deeper than water, hotter than fire" (*Mencius* 1b.10.5).

A word determined by *Jyh* (至) *tied "to arrive at, or reach, the peak or acme, the furthest point," forms a superlative degree.[2]

EXAMPLES

Jyh dah jyh gang (至大至剛) "the greatest, the toughest" (*Mencius* 2a.2.16).

A word made determinative of *shenn* (甚) *diəm or *you* (尤) *giug "in a superlative degree," forms a superlative degree.[3]

[1] Apart, of course, from the feature described in 3.4.6 where "greater degree" is imposed upon the verb, by its post-verbal elements. Examples occur, however, where "greater degree" is implicit, though not stated formally. For example, *Jianqren jwo erl sheau jy* (匠人斲而小之) "The carpenter, having trimmed the lumber, cut it smaller than he should have done" (*Mencius* 1b.9.2) where *sheau jy* (小之) is simply "smalled it." Or again, in *Bii jaang erl woo jaang jy* (彼長而我長之) "He being older than I am, I will treat him as an elder should be treated" (*Mencius* 6a.4.2).

[2] Cf. also 8.9.15 *fei jy jyh* (飛之至) "flying at its best," and *Dah jy jyh!* (大之至) "the greatest of the great" (*Tso* 327.3).

[3] *Shenn* is also used as a determinant word in sense of "superlatively," "very," for example, in *Chern jy tzucy shenn duo* (臣之罪甚多) "My crimes have been very many" (*Tso* 122.18). *Jiuh jee, shenn jonq yii* (懼者甚眾矣) "Very many people are fearful" (*Tso* 123.11).

EXAMPLES

Wu yann jy shenn yee (無厭之甚也) /There is not/of despicable things/the more so/ "It is most despicable" (*Tso* 318.14).

Bwu shinn jy you (不信之尤) "The acme of bad faith" (*Tso* 339.2).

Wuh jie ran, shin wei shenn (物皆然心爲甚) "This is true of all things but most true in things of the heart" (*Mencius* 1a.7.24).

Kuanq (況兄) *xiwang occurs in sense both of "more so" and in interrogative "how much more so?"

EXAMPLES

Wang kuanq tzyh tzonq yee (王兄自縱也) "The King behaved in an even more dissolute fashion" (*Micius* 33.44).

I-fu buh kee nuoo, kwanq gwo hu (一夫不可狃況國乎) "The individual must not be perverted, how much more so the State?" (*Tso* 109.15).

7.2. Status

The influence upon the language of status (i.e., the respective social or hierarchical standing of the speaker and the person addressed) has been touched upon in the description. Considerations of status govern the use, or otherwise, of the personal pronouns (see 6.2). Considerations of status give rise to a class of honorific and depreciatory determinants in syntagma (see 2.6.4.1 and 2.6.4.5 footnote 23). Status has other influences upon usage.

When a verb is determined by *chieh* (竊) *ts'iat "to steal, stealthily," a statement which otherwise would be a plain assertion, is given a deferential tone.[4] It is used under circumstances where, because of the status of the user, plain statement might seem brash, and deference is called for.[5]

EXAMPLES

Shyi jee, chieh wen jy (昔者竊聞之) "Formerly, though I say so myself, I have heard about this" (*Mencius* 2a.2.26).

---

[4]*Chieh* appears in some dictionaries as the pronoun "I." In the examples quoted above, *chieh* occurs with a PN in the distribution PN/*chieh*. Pronouns do not occur in this distribution in LAC. Legge (1), commenting on the use in *Mencius* of *chieh*, observes, correctly, "*chieh* is used with other words to give a deferential tone to what they say." (*Mencius* Part 1, ii.20, Note).

[5]Yang Bor-jiunn cites occurrences of *chiing* (請) "to beg"; *shinq* (幸) "good fortune, [to have the good fortune to]"; *jinq* (敬) "to respect, [respectfully]"; *gaan* (敢) "to presume to"; *huey* (惠) "kindness [have the kindness to]"; *fwu* (伏) "to prostrate"; *tean* (忝) "ashamed"; *woei* (猥) "humble"; in which he says they have "no substantial meaning, but merely indicate the status of the persons speaking" (Yang Bor-jiunn 8.23).

Jin yuann chieh yeou chiing yee (今願竊有請也) "Now I wish, with all deference, to make a request" (*Mencius* 2b.7.2).

Chyi yih tzer Chiou chieh cheu jy yii (其義則丘竊取之矣) "If it is a question of the justice of these decisions then I, Ch'iu, with all due respect, decided that myself" (*Mencius* 4b.21.2).

Considerations of status are in evidence in the vocabulary of LAC, thus, *shyh* (弒) "to murder a superior"; *beng* (崩) "to die" (used of sovereigns only); *hong* (薨) "the death of a prince"; *fenq* (奉) "to receive from a superior," "to offer to an inferior"; *tsyh* (賜) "to give to an inferior," "to receive from a superior."[6]

7.3. The Use of *Meei* and *Shi*

Meei (每) *mwəg "each, every" is used as a distributive determinant in syntagma, for example, *meei yeh* (每夜) "each evening," *meei sheh* (每舍) "at each staging point," *meei ryh* (每日) "every day," *meei suey* (每歲) "every year." When *meei* occurs in the verbal syntagma, it is used in sense of "on each occasion that, each time . . ." (see 3.3.2.8). When an element which otherwise occurs after the verb is determined by *meei*, that element and *meei* are placed before the verb.

EXAMPLES

Meei ren erl yueh jy (每人而悅之) /each/person/sub/please/them/ "to please everyone" (*Mencius* 4b.2.3).

Meei shyh wenn (每事問) "He asked about each and every affair" (*Analects* 3.15).

In 3.5.3 footnote 45, collectives determining the instrument are shown to occur before the instrumental particle *yii* (以). *Shi* (悉) (like *meei*) is peculiar in that when *shi* determines the instrument, both *shi and* the instrument occur before the instrumental particle.

EXAMPLES

Ju-hour shi shy yii fuh fa Jenq (諸侯悉師以復伐鄭) "The Feudal powers, with all their armies, again attacked Cheng" (*Tso* 274.15).

Jiang shi bih fuh yii dai yu Yu (將悉敝賦以待於鯈) "We will, with all our levies, await you at Yü" (*Tso* 174.12).

Woo shi fang cherng way yii hoei chyi jou (我悉方城外以毀其舟) "We will, with all [our troops] outside the defensive wall, destroy their boats" (*Tso* 444.20).

---

[6]These definitions are taken from Fraser and Lockhart (1), s.v.; under the entry *duey* (對) they observe "to reply (usually of an inferior)."

7.4. Inversions of Word Order

Examples occur sporadically where word order is simply irregular.[7] The examples are idiosyncratic and it is not possible to establish series. Textual critics and editors usually treat such occurrences as aberrations and restore the text to conventional word order.

EXAMPLES

Yee yu yiin shyr (野於飲食) (γ^2/directive part/drink/eat). That is, *yiin shyr yu yee* "drinking and eating in the countryside" (*Micius* 56.47).

Yann suoo wey "*Shyh yu nuh, shyh yu seh jee*" (諺所謂室於怒市於色者) that is, *nuh yu shyh, seh yu shyh* "As the proverb says, 'He who is angry in private, will betray the fact in public'" (*Tso* 398.7).

Erl how nae jin (而後乃今) cf. the conventional *Erl jin yii how* (而今以後) "from henceforth..." (*Chuang* 1.7).

7.5. The Allegro Form

The principle of the allegro form has long been recognized. *Wang Yiin-jy* (王引之) (1766-1834), for example, defined *ju* (諸) as *jyi yan jy iue "ju" shyu yan jy iue "jy hu"* (急言之曰諸徐言之曰之乎) "rapidly enunciated it is 'ju,' slowly enunciated it is 'jy hu'" (see Wang, 2, s.v.). The table on the following page is a conspectus of allegro forms mentioned in the course of this book.

NOTE. *Erl* (而), the determinant form of the non-status second-person pronoun, may well be an allegro form of *ruu-jy* (汝之) (see 2.6.4.1 footnote 16). Jou Faa-gau also proposes Eastern Chou bronze form of the determinative pronoun *yi* (台) *diəg = *yu jy* (余之), and *chyi* (其) as an allegro form of *g-+jy* (*g+之) (see *Jou* (4), p. 249). *Mieh* (蔑) perhaps *wu yeou* (無有) despite the occurrence of *mieh yeou* in *Tso*, where *yeou* may be modal "would not have." *Iong* (庸) occurs in *Tso* as (?)indefinite form of *yonq* (用) but may be an allegro form of *her-yonq* (何用). *Shwu* (孰), in view of its unique distributional class, might be suspected of being an allegro form of an agent + agential distributive (perhaps *shwei-dwu* (誰獨)).

---

[7] The word "inversion" has crept into usage in speaking of Chinese grammar in a much wider and looser sense. For example, the distribution of the substitutes in the negative and indefinite moods is described as "inversion" whereas it is the distribution proper to the mood. There is no scientific basis for regarding neutral polar mood as "normal" and other moods as "inversions." All have their distinctive distributional patterns, and one is no more "normal" than the other. Here "inversion" is used strictly, in the sense that "reversion" is required to render the passage intelligible.

Sign	GR	Hypothetical value in LAC as given by Karlgren	Allegro form of a		b		c		References	
爾	EEL	*ńiar	而	*niəg	已	*ziəg			3.9	
耳	EEL	*ńiəg	而	*niəg	已	*ziəg			3.9	
夫	FWU	*piwo	否	*piug	乎	*g'o			3.9	
盍 蓋	HER (gay)	*g'âp (*g'âp > *kâb)	何	*g'â	不	*pwət			6.5.3.6	
曷	HER	*g'ât	何	*g'â	?時	*diəg			6.5.2.1	
胡	HWU	*g'o	何	*g'â	故	*ko			6.5.3.6	
焉	IAN	*.ian	於	*.io	kk	*tiəg			3.8	
	YAN	*gian							6.5.2.1	6.5.2.2
因	IN	*.ien	用	*diung	以	*ziəg			4.11	
旃	JAN	*tian	之	*tiəg	於	*.io	之	tiəg	3.8	
諸	JU	*tio	之	*tiəg	於 乎	*.io *g'o			3.8	
乃	NAE	*nəg	如	*ńio	之	*tiəg			3.3.3.1	footnote 22
然	RAN	*ńian	如	*ńio	此	*ts'iar			6.5 3.3.3.1	footnote 8
奚	SHI	*g'ieg	何	*g'â	以	*ziəg			6.5.2.2	footnote 16
惡	U	*.ak	何	*g'â	於	*.io			6.5.2.2	
與歟	YU	*zio	也	*dia	乎	*g'o			3.9	
邪耶	YE	*ziâ	也	*dia	乎	*g'o			3.9	

7.6. Number

The formal basis of the number system employed in LAC is decimal. The terms of counting are the numbers from one to ten, *I* (一) "one"; *ell* (二) "two"[8] *san* (三) "three"; *syh* (四) "four"; *wuu* (五) "five"; *liow* (六) "six"; *chi* (七) "seven"; *ba* (八) "eight"; *jeou* (九) "nine"; *shyr* (十) "ten," and the multiples of ten, viz. 10×10 *bae* (百) "hundred," 10×10×10 *chian* (千) "thousand," and 10×10×10×10 *wann* (萬) "ten thousand."

The numbers intermediate between ten and its multiples are made by determining ten or its multiples, for the multiples of ten, hundred, thousand and ten thousand (e.g., *syh-shyr* [四十] is 4×10, i.e. 40); and, by co-ordination, for numbers from one to nine between multiples (e.g., *ell-shyr-san* [二十三] is 2×10+3, i.e., 23).[9] Determination is

---

[8] When numerals are used to determine the verb in sense of "once, twice, thrice," etc., *ell* (二) is replaced by *tzay* (再). (See 3.3.2.8).

[9] Numbers also occur in co-ordinate connection unmarked, which are in sequence; for example, *ell-san* (二三) "two or three," *chi ba yueh* (七八月) "seventh or eighth month," but this only occurs in consecutive sequence. (See Kennedy (1), p. 18.)

unmarked, but co-ordination may be indicated by the particle *you* (有) thus *shyr-you-i-yueh* (十有一月) /ten/plus/one/month/ "the eleventh month."[10]

No distinction is made in LAC between cardinals and ordinals. *San yueh* (三月) thus, may be either "three months" or "the third month."

Fractions are compound forms.[11] The terms are distributed as follows: Denominator/*fen* (分) "divide"/["thing divided"]/determinative particle *jy* (之)/numerator; for example, in *ba-shyr-i fen ryh jy syh* (八十一分日之四) /eighty-one/divide/day/of it/four [parts]/ "4/81 of a day" (*Shih Chi*). Fractions are, however, stated with considerable economy. With the above as the maximal paradigm (which does not occur in LAC in its maximal form)[12] the following will indicate the degrees of economy employed.

1	八十一	分	日	之	四	"4/81st of a day" (*Shih Chi*)
2	三	分	□	之	一	"a third" (*Tso* 479.9)
3	叁[13]	□	國	之	一	"A third of the size of the Capital" (*Tso* 2.24)
4	五	□	□	之	一	"a fifth" (*Tso* 2.24)
5	九	□	□	□	一	"a ninth" (*Mencius* 1b.5)

---

[10] *You* (有) is also used in *you-yu* (有餘), which is added to numerals in sense of "plus a few more"; for example, *Chi-bae you yu suey* (七百有餘歲) "A little more than seven hundred years" (*Mencius* 2b.13).

[11] With the exception of "a half," which is *bann* (半).

[12] Compare, however, *San fen gong shyh erl geh yeou chyi i* (三分公室而各有其一) "They divided the Ducal establishment's prerogatives into three each taking one part" (*Tso* 273.1).

[13] In fractions and multiples, the signs 叁 for 三, 什 for 十, are sometimes used for the denominator or multiple. (See Yang Bor-jiunn 7.10.)

VIII. Texts from LAC Authors

8.1. Introduction

The texts which follow are taken from typical LAC authors. The analysis and commentary which accompany them are designed to supplement, by way of illustration, the grammatical description of chapters Two to Seven. The Chinese text is unpunctuated and appears in the form preserved in the standard editions. Each excerpt has been analysed sentence by sentence, and a commentary gives references to the appropriate sections of the grammar. The conventional signs used in analysis, and which occur throughout the grammar, are summarized below.

8.2. List of Conventional Signs and Abbreviations

Derivation
A A   Reduplication, whether in geminative or dissimilated form.
A+B   Co-ordinate connection (simple).
A/B   Co-ordinate connection (alternative).
A=A   Hendiadys.
A→B   Determinative.
A←B   Directive.

Syntagma
( )   Parentheses enclose a syntagma. Where the internal analysis of a syntagma is pursued further, parentheses within parentheses are used. For example, *shian wang jy daw* (A(A→B)→B) indicates that *daw* is determined by *shian wang*, and *shian wang* is itself formed by determination, since *shian* determines *wang*.
Syn.   Used for the particle of syntagma *jee*.
A+B   Co-ordinate connection, whether the particle of co-ordination is used or not.
→   Determination.
←   Direction.

Verbal Sentence
β   Verb.
Md β   Modal determination of the verb.
As β   Aspectual determination of the verb.

Man β	Determinations of the verb of manner.
SA	State of the agent.
γ^1	First post-verbal position.
γ^2	Second post-verbal position.
Dir.	Directive particle.
α	The agent.
α/Dist.	Distributives of the agent.
Rec.	Reciprocity in the agents.
Refl.	Reflexive particle.
Del.	Particle of delegated agency.
[ ]	Brackets enclose the instrumental or subordinate clause.
[In ...]	Ingressive instrument.
Res. Ins.	Resultative instrument.
[Con ...]	Continuative use of the instrument.
[... erl]	Integral subordinate clause with *erl*.
Md.	(At end of sentence) sentential mood.
...||...	A double line marks the point between exposed elements and the sentence proper.
Time||	Time indication.
Place||	Place indication.
St.	Particle of stress.

The Determinative Sentence

DT( )	The words within the parentheses constitute the determined term.
Dt ( )	The words between the parentheses constitute the determinant term.
Cop.	Copulae.

Complexities of Sentence Structure

Conj.	Conjunction.
Conc.	Concession.
Prot.	Protasis.
Apod.	Apodosis.

Substitution

□	An interrogative or indefinite substitute.

Miscellaneous

⟨ ⟩	Matter within broken brackets is not in text but provided by author.
>	Meaning evolving into.
<	Meaning evolving from.
°	Full point.
,	Approximately as in English usage.
/ / /	Words between soliduses indicate "literal" translation.

8.3. "On Justice and Humanity" (*Mencius*)

	11	10	9	8	7	6	5	4	3	2	1
a	曰	後	不	焉	其	國	利	國	曰	亦	孟
b	利	其	屨	不	君	弒	吾	大	利	將	子
c		君	未	為	者	其	亦	夫	亦	有	見
d		者	有	不	必	君	有	曰	有	以	梁
e		也	仁	多	百	者	曰	何	仁	利	惠
f		王	而	矣	乘	必	何	以	義	吾	王
g		亦	遺	苟	之	百	以	利	而	國	王
h		曰	其	為	家	乘	利	吾	已	乎	曰
i		仁	親	後	萬	之	吾	家	矣	孟	叟
j		義	者	義	取	家	國	士	王	子	不
l		而	也	而	千	千	危	庶	曰	對	遠
m		已	未	先	焉	乘	矣	人	何	曰	千
n		矣	有	利	千	之	萬	曰	以	王	里
o		何	義	不	取	家	乘	何	利	何	而
p		必	而	奪	百	弒	之	以	吾	必	來

Free Translation

Mencius went to see King Hui of Liang. The King said "Sir, since you did not think a journey of a thousand miles too long to come to see me, you no doubt know some way by which I might profit my State?" Mencius replied "Why must the King use that word 'profit'? There are after all only two things worth speaking about—'justice' and 'humanity.' When the King asks about ways to profit the state, the nobles will ask about ways to profit their estates, and gentlemen and commoners about ways to profit themselves. With everyone high and low competing for profits, Your Majesty's state will be endangered. For the profit accruing to the murderer of the ruler of a major state* must be at least an estate of a thousand chariots, and for that of a minor state a feudal estate of a hundred chariots. That is a profit of a thousand in ten thousand, a hundred in a thousand—no small profit. If you were in fact to give precedence to profits at the expense of justice, then no one will be happy unless they are perpetually seizing something. On the other hand, when humanity prevails, no one ever forswears his kin and when justice prevails no one turns upon his ruler. It were better if Your Majesty spoke only of 'justice' and 'humanity.' Why must you use that word profit?" (*Mencius* 1a.1.1–6.)

*Or, as the text says, "a state capable in feudal duty of mobilizing ten thousand war chariots." A minor state would be capable of mobilizing a thousand chariots.

8.3.1. Sentence 1a-1f

Menq-tzyy jiann Liang Huey wang. α (A→B) $\beta \gamma^1$(A→B(A→B)). Mencius/see/Liang/Huey/King.

Commentary. A verbal sentence ($\alpha \beta \gamma$). Note that the verb is uncommitted to mood and aspect and has no tense (see 3.1). The tense and aspect indicated in the free translation are not present in the Chinese. *Jiann* is transitive. The active voice is imposed upon it by the presence of the affectee at γ^1 (see 3.4.1). The proper names *Mencius* (a latinized transcription of the Chinese *Menq-tzyy*) and *King Huey of Liang* are both formed by syntagma (see 2.6.3.2).

8.3.2. Sentence 1g-1h

Wang iue "...." The King/said/"...."

Commentary. *Iue* is most commonly used to introduce reported speech. For a further note on *iue* see sentence 8.3.6. The use of "say" and "said" in translation should be understood accordingly.

8.3.3. Sentence 1i-1p

Soou buh yeuan chian lii erl lai. α [Md $\beta \gamma^1$(A→B) erl] β. Old man/not/thinking distant/thousand/mile/(subordinate)/come.

Commentary. A verbal sentence with the subordinate clause in *erl* (see 3.7). The main verb *lai* is uncommitted to mood, voice, and aspect. The verb in the subordinate clause (*yeuan*) is used putatively (see 3.4.6). Determined by *buh* it is indicative, "not thinking" (see 3.3.1.1). The verb in the subordinate clause may indicate either concomitant or sequential action in relation to the main verb (see 3.7). Here it is sequential "not having thought distant, you have come." The affectee of *yeuan* is formed by syntagma (see 2.6.4.4). Note the indirect form of address used and the status relationship established. Mencius in addressing the king uses the title "King," establishing the relationship of subject to ruler. The king addresses Mencius as *soou* "an old man," "a father," establishing the respectful relationship of a younger to an older man (see 6.2).

8.3.4. Sentence 2a-2h

Yih jiang yeou yii lih wu gwo hu. Conj. As β Res.Ins. $\beta \gamma^1$(A→B) Md. In the light of the foregoing/⟨you⟩ may/have/⟨something⟩ by means of which/to profit/my/state/(mood).

Commentary. A verbal sentence with resultative instrumental clause (β Res.Ins. $\beta \gamma$) (see 3.6.2). The verb of the instrumental clause is determined as to aspect (here *jiang*—potential (see 3.3.2.1)). The affectee of the main verb is formed in syntagma (see 2.6.4.1). The final modal particle indicates the tentativeness felt by the speaker in making the assertion (see 3.9). The conjunction *yih* connects two co-ordinate sentences, indicating that the subject matter of the second sentence is contingent upon that of the first, thus, "in the light of what has been said, after all," etc. (see 5.1). The force of *yih* here would best be brought out by paraphrasing (see free translation).

8.3.5. Sentence 2i-2m

Menq-tzyy duey iue. α (A→B) β "..... Mencius/replied/"....

8.3.6. Sentence 2n-3b

Wang her bih iue lih α. || DT (□) Dt (β→β γ¹). King/why/must/use-word/profit.

Commentary. A determinative sentence of cause and consequence (see 4.11) in which the interrogative substitute *her* invites the supplying of the cause (see 6.5.3.5). For the positioning of the agent of the causal term before the copula of cause (see 4.11 footnote 17), *bih* "must" is a verb determining the verb *iue*. The use of *iue* is unusual and provokes comment by glossarists since *iue* is usually simply a sign of reported speech. It is variously explained as meaning "a word, a term, an idea expressed in words" but it is here used verbally, and means "to-use-the word or saying."

8.3.7. Sentence 3c-3i

Yih yeou ren yih erl-yii yii. Conj. DT ( ) Dt (A+B) Md. St. After-all/there is/humanity/justice/(mood)/(stress).

Commentary. A determinative sentence of the type described in 4.8. The determinant term is formed in syntagma (simple connection —no particle (see 2.5)). *Erl-yii* particle of sentential mood, imparts to the declaration the feeling of finality, that the speaker feels in making it. "That, nothing more and nothing less," "final!" "finish!" "period!" The grammaticization of *erl-yii* (and consequently its loss of stress) is attested by the fact that wherever it is used, the particle of accentuation *yii* (imposing the penultimate stress) occurs, thus throwing the determinative stress upon *ren yih*. *Erl-yii* never occurs with the particle of accentuation *yee*. Its grammaticization is further attested by the evolution of an allegro form *eel* (see 3.9).

8.3.8. Sentence 3j-4a

Wang iue her-yii lih wu gwo. ⟨Prot.⟩ α (β) γ¹ (□ β γ¹(A→B)). King/use-phrase/what-whereby/profit/my/state.

Commentary. A verbal sentence, the γ¹ of which is itself a verbal sentence. The interrogative substitute *her* is in position before the particle of the resultative instrument and substitutes therefore for a verbal clause, thus "do what, whereby . . ." that is, "What should I do in order to . . . ." With this compare sentence 8.3.6. Sentence 8.3.8 therefore asks "how?" Sentence 8.3.6 asks "why?" This sentence is in conditioned sequence with sentences 8.3.9 and 8.3.10. No conjunction marks this connection (see 5.3). The practised reader, however, would suspect the sequence from the rhythm and the parallelism of the three sentences, *wang*, *dahfu*, and *shyh*, *shuhren*; and *gwo*, *jia*, and *shen* being in parallel.

8.3.9. Sentence 4b-4i

Dah-fu iue her-yii lih wu jia. ⟨Apod.⟩ α (A→B) (β) γ¹ (□ β γ¹(A→B)). Nobles/use phrase/what-whereby/profit/our/estates.

Commentary. See sentence 8.3.8. Note that *dah-fu* is a derivative compound, lit. "great-man," but specialized as a term for "a class of aristocrat" (see 1.2). Note that the pronouns do not distinguish number (see 6.2).

8.3.10. Sentence 4j-5c

Shyh shuh-ren iue her-yii lih wu shen. ⟨Apod.⟩ α (A+B(A→B)) (β) γ¹ (□ β γ¹ (A→B)). Gentlemen/commoners/use phrase/what-whereby/profit/our/persons.

Commentary. See sentence 8.3.8. The two agents, here in simple connection with no syntagmatic conjunction (2.5; 3.5.4), *shuh-ren* is a derivative compound. Lit. "many men," it is specialized as "the masses," "the commonalty."

8.3.11. Sentence 5d-5m

Shanq shiah jiau jeng lih erl gwo wei yii. α (A+B) Rec. β γ Conj. α β St. Superiors/inferiors/(rec.)/contending/profit/(subordinate)/state/endangered/(stress).

Commentary. An example of the feature described in 3.7.2 where the subordinate clause has an agent other than the agent of the main verb, and *erl* is used conjunctively. For reciprocity in the agent and the use of *jiau* see 3.5.4. *Shianq shiah* are in simple connection but no conjunction is used (see 2.5). Note that *shanq shiah* is the acting agent, while *gwo* is the agent of realization (see 3.5.1). The particle of accentuation *yii* throws a stress on *gwo*, "It is [your] *state* that is endangered" (see 3.12).

8.3.12. Sentence 5n-6j

Wann cherng jy gwo shyh chyi jiun jee bih chian cherng jy jia. DT (γ^1 (A(A→B)→B) || β γ^1 (A→B) Syn.) Cop. D+(A(A→B)→B). Ten thousand/chariot/(determinative)/state/kill/that state's/ruler/(syn) /must be/thousand/chariot/(determinative)/estate.

Commentary. A determinative sentence, with copula *bih* "must be" (see 4.4.2). The determined term is formed from a verbal sentence reduced to syntagma by *jee* (see 2.7.1), thus "One who . . . ." The verbal sentence itself has the determinant of the γ^1 exposed, and this is resumed in the sentence itself by the anaphoric *chyi*. Lit. "[A state capable of mobilizing] ten thousand chariots/slay/that state's/ruler/ he who/," that is, "He who slays the ruler of a large state" (see 3.11). This sentence is intelligible only if we remember that the subject of the entire speech is "profit" and "gain." No grammatical prescriptive necessity makes essential the naming of the "subject." Therefore we understand this sentence as "He who [for profit] . . . must be [the profiter by] . . ." Note the use of the particle of determination in the syntagma *wann cherng jy gwo* (see 2.6.2).

8.3.13. Sentence 6k-7h

(Essentially a repetition of sentence 8.3.12 reading *chian* for *wann*, and *bae* for *chian*.)

Commentary. Note how emphatic exposure in 8.3.12 and 8.3.13 enables the writer to contrast strongly, "a large state" and "a small state."

8.3.14. Sentence 7i-8f

Wann cheu chian yan chian cheu bae yan buh-wei buh duo yii. DT (γ^2 || β γ^1 γ^2, γ^2 || β γ^1 γ^2) Cop. Dt (A→B) St. Ten thousand/subtract /thousand/from it/thousand/subtract/hundred/from it/would not be /*not*/much/(stress).

Commentary. A determinative sentence (A would not be B). The copula *wei* is subjunctive and is negated (see 4.4.3). The determinant term is formed in syntagma (determining with privative *buh*) (see 2.6.4.3). Note the use of the particle of accentuation, *yii*, imposing a penultimate stress (*buh/duo*) (see 3.12). The determined term is composed of two syntagmas in simple connection reduced from verbal sentences. In these verbal sentences the γ^2 is exposed, thus $(\gamma^2 \parallel \beta\ \gamma^1\ \gamma^2)$ and is resumed with the anaphoric *gan* (allegro form of *yu-jy* (see 3.8.)) (see 3.11.1). These verbal sentences are in reality forms of numeration "a thousand in ten thousand," that is, one tenth, thus "A tenth, whether in a large state or a small one, would not be an insignificant profit."

8.3.15. Sentence 8g-9b

Goou wei how yih erl shian lih buh dwo buh yan. Prot. [Md $\beta\ \gamma^1$ erl] β $\gamma^1\langle$Apod.$\rangle$ $\langle$Apod.$\rangle$ Md β $\langle$Prot.$\rangle$ Md β. If indeed/were to/having put last/justice/(subordinate)/put first/profit/⟨then⟩ ⟨when⟩ not/grasping/⟨then⟩ not/satisfied.

Commentary. Verbal sentences in conditioned sequence (see 5.3). The protasis is introduced by *goou* "if indeed" (see 5.3.2 Note 1). The apodosis is unmarked. The apodosis is itself two verbal sentences in conditioned sequence (fulfilled), that is, *if* (A) *then* (when A then B) .... Note the use of *wei* modally determining *how* "If you were to put last" (see 3.3.1.2). *How* and *shian* "last" and "first" are used transitively and factatively, that is, "make first, make last" or "accord first or last place to" etc. (see 3.4.6). Note also the use of *erl* in the integral subordinated clause "Having accorded last place to justice, accord first place to profit" (see 3.7).

8.3.16. Sentence 9c-9k

Wey-yeou ren erl yi chyi chin jee yee. DT (A→B) Dt ([β erl] $\beta\ \gamma^1$ (A→B) Syn.) St. No time existent/being humane/(subordinate)/abandon/his/kin/(syn)/(stress).

Commentary. An example of the type of sentence described in 4.8.1. The determined term is negated with *wey* (see 3.3.1.1), that is, "At no time, has there, does there, or will there exist . . . ." Note the integral subordinate clause in *erl*; such clauses are by definition verbal (see 3.7). Here, it is a single word *ren* "humanity," which becomes, therefore, "being humane." The determined term is reduced by *jee* to syntagma form, thus, "One who being . . ." (see 2.7.1). For the use of *yee* see 3.12.

8.3.17. Sentence 9m-10e

Essentially a repetition of 8.3.16, substituting *yih* for *ren* and *jiun* for *chin*.

8.3.18. Sentence 10f-10n

Wang yih iue ren yih erl-yii yii α. || Conj. (β) γ (A+B) Md. St. King /in light of foregoing/use-phrase/humanity/justice/(mood)/(stress).

Commentary. For the use of *yih* cf. sentences 8.3.4 and 8.3.7. Note that dictionary definitions notwithstanding, *yih* rarely means "also, in addition" in LAC.

8.3.19. Sentence 11p-11b

Her bih iue lih. DT (□) Dt (β→β γ¹). Why/must/use-the-word/ profit.

Commentary. This sentence is essentially the same as sentence 8.3.6 q.v.

8.4. "The Pleasures of Kings" (*Mencius*)

7	6	5	4	3	2	1	
雖	鹿	其	文	後	鹿	孟	a
有	魚	臺	王	樂	曰	子	b
臺	鼈	曰	以	此	賢	見	c
池	古	靈	民	不	者	梁	d
鳥	之	臺	力	賢	亦	惠	e
獸	人	謂	為	者	樂	王	f
豈	與	其	臺	雖	此	王	g
能	民	沼	為	有	乎	立	h
獨	偕	曰	沼	此	孟	於	i
樂	樂	靈	而	不	子	沼	j
哉	故	沼	民	樂	對	上	k
	能	樂	歡	也	曰	顧	m
	樂	其	樂	詩	賢	鴻	n
	其	有	之	云	者	鴈	p
	有	麋	謂	⋮	而	麋	q

Free Translation

Mencius went to see King Hui of Liang. The King was standing by a fish-pool [in his hunting preserve]. Looking around at the wildfowl and small game, the King said, "Yes, but do 'worthies' enjoy these things?" Mencius replied: "It is only 'worthies' who really do enjoy them, for those who are not 'worthies' may possess these things

but they do not enjoy them." As it says in *The Book of Songs* ...*
King Wen built a pleasure tower and a fishing pool with his subjects' labour, and his subjects enjoyed them both. They called the tower "The Divine Tower," and the fish-pool "The Divine Pool." They were pleased that he kept game and fish. In those days, gentlemen and their labourers shared their pleasures, and so they could really enjoy them. One might well have pleasure-towers, fish-pools and animals of the chase, but how can one take pleasure in them when they are kept for oneself alone? (*Mencius* 1a.2.1–6.)

8.4.1. Sentence 1a-1f

See sentence 8.3.1.

8.4.2. Sentence 1g-1k

Wang lih yu jao shanq. $\alpha \beta$ Dir. γ^2 (A→B). King/stand/(directive)/pool/top.

Commentary. A verbal sentence. *Lih* "to stand up" is intransitive. In the second post-verbal position *jao shanq* is directive, and is an example of spatial relationships treated substantivally (see 2.6.3.3).

8.4.3. Sentence 1m-2a

Guh horng-yann mi-luh. $\beta \gamma^1$ (A(A+B)+B(A+B)). Look around at/wild-fowl/deer.

Commentary. *Horng-yann* and *mi-luh* are derivative compounds formed in simple connection. Here, two given species named create a generic term, that is, the genera of which these two are representative species (see 1.2.3.1).

8.4.4. Sentence 2b-2h

Iue "shyan jee yih yaw tsyy hu." (β) α (β Syn.) Conj. $\beta \gamma^1$ Md. ⟨The King⟩ said/worthy/who are/after all/enjoy/this/(mood).

Commentary. The conjunction *yih* shows that we are introduced by the author to a remark made in the course of a conversation in progress, the effect of which might be represented as, "In the light of what you have been saying about 'worthies,' do 'worthies' enjoy such things as these?" (See 5.1.) *Shyan jee* (reduction to syntagma form of a verbal clause (see 2.7.1)) is *shyan* "to be worthy" and thus "Those who are worthy." Note the demonstrative (see 6.3). The mood of the speaker is one of incredulity and doubt (see 3.9).

*Quotation omitted.

8.4.5. Sentence 2i-3c

Menq-tzyy duey iue "shyan jee erl-how yaw tsyy." α (A→B) β (β) [β Syn. erl-how] β γ¹. Mencius/replied/say/be worthy/that person/ then only/enjoys this.

Commentary. The subordinate clause with *erl-how* is specifically sequential action in relation to the main verb. With *erl* alone it is either concomitant or sequential action (see 3.7).

8.4.6. Sentence 3d-3m

Buh shyan jee swei yeou tsyy bwu yaw yee. α (Md β Syn.), Conc. β γ¹, Md β St. Not/worthy/that person/although/possess/these/not/enjoy/ (stress).

Commentary. The particle of accentuation *yee* indicates a verb subsuming its affectee, *yaw tsyy* and *bwu yaw yee* being positive-reflex and negative of the negative polar mood (see 3.4.8). For concessive *swei* see 5.4.1.

8.4.7. Sentence 3n-3p

Shy yun ". . . ." Book of songs/says/(quote) ". . . ."

Commentary. The deleted portion here is a set of verses from the Book of Songs (EAC). Note the use of *yun* to introduce a quotation from written works, and the use of *iue* in previous examples for quotation from reported speech.

8.4.8. Sentence 4a-4p

Wen wang yii min lih wei tair wei jao erl min huan-yaw jy. α (A→B) [In. A→B] β γ¹, β γ¹ Conj. α β (β=β) γ¹. When/King/by means of/ people's/strength/made/tower/made/pool/(subordinate)/people/enjoy/them.

Commentary. Two verbal sentences in subordinate narrative sequence with the conjunction *erl* (see 3.7.2). In the subordinated sentence *yii . . . wei* are used factatively (see 3.6.2 footnote 52 for the idiomatic use of *yii wei*). Note the possessive *min lih*, effected by position alone (see 2.6.3). *Huan-yaw*, an example of hendiadys, should be noted (1.2.3.3). (Both *huan* and *yaw* are also used as free forms.) The anaphoric *jy* distinguishes no number (see 3.8).

8.4.9. Sentence 4q-5k

Wey chyi tair iue "ling-tair" wey chyi jao iue "ling-jao." β γ¹ ((A→B) (A→B)), β γ¹ ((A→B) (A→B)). Called/his/tower/say/"the spirit-fraught"/tower/called/his/pool/say/"spirit-fraught"/pool.

Commentary. Wey means "to describe, to speak." (See 3.4.7. paragraph 3, fourth variant.) Note determinant form of anaphoric pronoun *chyi* (possessive at syntagma level—agential at sentence level) (see 2.6.4.1). Note that *ling-tair* is determination by attribute "spirit-fraught," "magic" not "Tower of the Spirits" (see 2.6.2).

8.4.10. Sentence 5m-6c

Yaw chyi yeou mi-luh yu-bie. $\beta \gamma^1 (\alpha \beta \gamma^1 ((A+B)+(A+B)))$. Took pleasure in/his/possessing/deer/⟨and⟩ fish.

Commentary. Verbal sentence with affectee a verbal sentence. Note use of *chyi* for agent in anaphora (see previous sentence). *Yu-bie* (lit: fish and turtles) is generic term for fish and pond life (cf. sentence 8.4.3 and see 1.2.3.1).

8.4.11. Sentence 6d-6j

Guu jy ren yeu min jie yaw. α (A[A→B]+B) Dist. β. Antiquity/(determinative)/men/together with/people/both/enjoy.

Commentary. A verbal sentence. The two agents *ren* and *min* are joined with the syntagmatic particle of simple connection *yeu* (see 2.5.) *Ren* is determined by *guu*, thus "men of old" using the particle of determination *jy*. For the use of the distributive see 3.5.3.

8.4.12. Sentence 6k-6p

Guh neng yaw yee. Cop. Dt (SA β) St. ⟨They⟩ therefore/⟨were⟩ able/ to enjoy ⟨these⟩/(stress).

Commentary. A determinative sentence. For *neng* see 3.3.3.2. For *guh* see 4.11.

8.4.13. Sentence 7a-7k

Swei yeou tair chyr neau show. Chii neng dwu yaw tzai. Conc. $\beta \gamma$ (A+B+C+D) DT (□) Dt (SA Man β) Md. Though/⟨one⟩ possesses /towers/pools/birds/animals/surely it cannot be that/able to/in solitude/enjoy/mood.

Commentary. For the use of *chii* see 6.5.3.4. In *neng dwu yaw*, *dwu* determines the verb "in solitude," "by oneself"; care should be taken to distinguish the use of *dwu* as an agential restrictive, as in (*dwu neng*) "only the agent can" (see 3.5.3). *Tzai* indicates a mood of indignation on the part of the speaker (see 3.9). Note the position of the concession (see 5.4). In the concessive clause the first postverbal position is occupied by four words in co-ordinate relationship. No particle is used (see 2.5).

8.5. "Half-measures in Government" (*Mencius*)

	10	9	8	7	6	5	4	3	2	1	
a	多	耳	十	或	喻	不	之	內	河	梁	
b	於	是	步	百	填	加	用	河	內	惠	
c	鄰	亦	笑	步	然	多	心	東	凶	王	
d	國	走	百	而	鼓	何	者	凶	則	曰	
e	也	也	步	後	之	也	鄰	亦	移	寡	
f		曰	則	止	兵	孟	國	然	其	人	
g		王	何	或	刃	子	之	察	民	之	
h		如	如	五	既	對	民	鄰	於	於	
i		知	曰	十	接	曰	不	國	河	國	
j		此	不	步	棄	王	加	之	東	也	
k		則	可	而	甲	好	少	政	移	盡	
m		無	直	後	曳	戰	寡	無	其	心	
n		望	不	止	兵	請	人	如	粟	焉	
p		民	百	以	而	以	之	寡	於	耳	
q		之	步	五	走	戰	民	人	河	矣	

Free Translation

King Hui of Liang said "I devote my entire mind to thinking about my state. For example, when there is a famine in the Ho-nui district I move my stricken people to Ho-tung, and send supplies of my grain as relief to Ho-nui. When Ho-tung is stricken I do the same for them. But if you were to look at the governments of our neighbouring states you would not find one comparable to mine in such devotion. Yet their populations do not decrease, and mine does not increase. Why is this?" Mencius replied "Since the King is fond of war, let me answer him with an illustration drawn from war. Suppose there is a battle, the war drums have sounded, and the troops have been drummed into action. But, the moment blade met blade they ran away, throwing away their coats of mail and trailing their weapons after them. Now, what would you think if, of the soldiers who ran away, those who ran only fifty yards jeered at those who ran a hundred yards?" The King said "They should not do so, for they too ran away. They merely did not run so far." Mencius said "If the King understood the import of this, he would not expect his population to grow larger than that of his neighbour." (*Mencius* 1a.3.1–5.)

8.5.1. Sentence 1a-1d

Liang huey wang iue. A→B (A→B) (β). Liang(PN)/Huey/King/say.

8.5.2. Sentence 1e-1q

Goa-ren jy yu gwo yee jinn shin yan eel yii. α (A→B)→ Dir. γ^2 St. $\parallel$ $\beta \gamma^1 \gamma^2$ Md. St. I/(determinative)/(directive)/state/(stress)/exert/mind /in it/(mood of finality)/(stress).

Commentary. A verbal sentence with agent and directive ($\alpha\gamma^2$) exposed. ($\alpha \gamma^2 \parallel \langle\alpha\rangle \beta \gamma^1 \gamma^2$). In the exposed element, *goa ren* is shown to be agential by the use of the determinative particle *jy*, *gwo* is shown to be directive by the use of the directive particle *yu*. (Usually when *jy* and *yu* are juxtaposed, the allegro form *ju* is used (see 3.8), but here the missing verb between them imposes a slight pause between *jy* and *yu*, and the allegro form cannot be used.) *Yu gwo* is substituted in the main sentence by anaphoric *yan* (see 3.8). *Eel* is the allegro form of *erl yii* (see 3.9). *Goa-ren* (lit: "lonely one") is a status pronoun used by kings of themselves (see 6.2). Without the emphatic exposure, the sentence would read: *goa-ren jinn shin yu chyi gwo* "I exert my mind in state affairs."

8.5.3. Sentence 2a-3a

Her-ney shiong tzer yi chyi min yu her-dong, yi chyi suh yu her-ney. $\langle$Prot.$\rangle$ α (A→B) β Apod. $\beta \gamma^1$ (A→B) Dir. γ^2 (A→B), $\beta \gamma^1$ (A→B) Dir. γ^2 (A→B). $\langle$When$\rangle$ Ho-nui (place name)/distressed/then/transfer/my /people/to/Ho-tung (place name)/. Transfer/my/food-supplies/to/ Ho-nui.

Commentary. Verbal sentences in conditioned sequence (fulfilled). For *tzer* conjunction of sequence (see 5.3). The anaphoric *chyi* refers to the speaker (*goa-ren* in sentence 8.5.2). *Her-ney* is the agent of realization (see 3.5). Note that in the composition of the two place names, the principles explained in 2.6.3.3 are applied thus: of *her* (the Yellow River), *ney* the inner part, and of *her* (the Yellow River) *dong* (the eastern part), that is, "within the bend of the Yellow River" and "East of the Yellow River."

8.5.4. Sentence 3b-3f

Her-dong shiong yih ran. $\langle$Prot.$\rangle$ α (A→B) β $\langle$Apod.$\rangle$ Conj. ($\beta \gamma^1$). $\langle$When$\rangle$ Ho-t'ung/distressed/$\langle$then$\rangle$ as foregoing/act—like-that.

Commentary. See sentence 8.5.3. *Ran* is an allegro form of *ru-tsyy*. Lit: "like this." (See 3.3.3.1.)

8.5.5. Sentence 3g-4d

Char lin gwo jy jenq wu ru goa-ren jy yong shin jee. $\langle$Prot.$\rangle$ $\beta \gamma^1$ (A (A→B)→B) $\langle$Apod.$\rangle$ Md. $\beta \gamma^1$ (α(A→B)→B γ^1 Syn.). $\langle$If$\rangle$ examine/

neighbour/states/(determination)/governments/⟨then⟩ would not/be like/I/(determination)/use/mind/(syn).

Commentary. Two verbal sentences in conditioned sequence (unfulfilled) (see 5.3.2). Though no conjunctions mark the sequence, the modal determination of the verb in the apodosis (*wu ru* "would not compare" cf. *bu ru* "does not compare") indicates that the condition is unfulfilled (see 3.3.1.3). The affectee of *ru* is a verbal sentence reduced to syntagma form by *jee* (and the particle of determination between agent and verb underlines this) (see 2.7.1 and 2.7.2).

8.5.6. Sentence 4e-5c

Lin gwo jy min buh jia shao, goa-ren jy min buh jia dwo. α (A(A→B)→B) Md. Man β α (A(A→B)→B) Md. Man β. Neighbour/states/(determination)/people/not/increasingly/become-few/I/(determination)/people/not/increasingly/become many.

Commentary. Two verbal sentences in parallel. The agent is the agent of realization (see 3.5.1). The verbs *shao* and *duo* "to be few," "to be many" are determined as to manner by *jia* "to add to," "to increase." This is one of several devices for creating degrees of comparison (see 7.1).

8.5.7. Sentence 5d-5c

Her yee. Dt (□) St. Why/(stress).

Commentary. See 6.5.3.1.

8.5.8. Sentence 5f-5i

Menq-tzyy duey iue. α (A→B) β. "...." Mencius/replied/(quote)"...."

8.5.9. Sentence 5j-6a

Wang haw jann. Chiing yii jann yuh. α β γ¹, β γ¹ ([In A] β). King/enjoys/warfare./ Request/by/warfare illustrate.

Commentary. Simple verbal sentences in co-ordinate sequence. The verb *haw* (from *hao* "good, excellent" [attribute]) is putative "to think good, approve, like." (See 3.4.6.) Though all attributes can be used verbally in this way, *hao* as a verb has come to be specialized, and this specialization has gained recognition by a phonological differentiation, *hao* > *haw*. This tonic shift is, however, idiosyncratic and no series can be established (see Appendix I).

8.5.10. Sentence 6b-6i

Tyan-ran guu jy bing renn jih jie. Man $\beta \gamma^1$, α (A→B) As β. "Dong"-like-that/drummed/them/weapon/blades/already/clashed.

Commentary. *Tyan* (*d'ien) is onomatopoeic, the sound of the drum beat. *Guu* "a drum" is here verbal "to drum" (see 3.2). (the drum was the signal for advance in battle). For *jih* perfective aspect (see 3.3.2.5).

8.5.11. Sentence 6j-6q

Chih jea yih bing erl tzoou. [$\beta \gamma^1 \beta \gamma^1$ erl] β. ⟨Soldiers⟩ discarding/armour/trailing/weapons/⟨subordinate⟩/fled.

Commentary. Verbal sentence with integral subordinated clause in *erl*. (See 3.7.) Note the omission of the agent which is "soldiers," though it is nowhere mentioned. Note, too, the co-ordination within the subordinated clause of ($\beta \gamma \beta \gamma$)—no conjunction.

8.5.12. Sentence 7a-7n

Huoh bae buh erl-how jyy, huoh wuu-shyr buh erl-how jyy. ⟨α⟩ Dist. [β (A→B) *erl-how*] β ⟨α⟩ Dist. [β (A(A→B)→B) *erl-how*] β. ⟨Of soldiers⟩/some/⟨having fled⟩ hundred/paces/then-after/stopped/some/⟨having fled⟩ fifty/paces/then-after/stopped.

Commentary. Two verbal sentences in parallel. The agent is omitted, the distributive *huoh* "some" indicating the omission (see 3.5.3.1). Note that the subordinated clauses "hundred paces," "fifty paces" are verbal (see 3.7) and, with *erl-how*, in sequential relation to main verb, thus "having fled hundred paces, stopped" etc.

8.5.13. Sentence 7p-8h

Yii wuu-shyr buh shiaw bae buh tzer her-ru. ⟨Prot.⟩ [Ins. (A(A→B) →B)] $\beta \gamma$ (A→B) Apod. □. ⟨If⟩ by/fifty/paces/mock/hundred/paces,/then/what-like.

Commentary. Note the economy in expressing the instrumental *wuu-shyr buh* lit: "fifty paces," but *yii wuu-shyr buh* "by virtue of their having run fifty paces"; similarly, the affectee of the verb "mock" is "those who had run fifty paces." However truncated these elements become, their position in the sentence imposes these grammatical qualities upon them.

8.5.14. Sentence 8i-9a

Iue "buh kee, jyr buh bae buh eel." (β) Md β, ⟨DT⟩ Cop. Dt (Md β (A→B)) Md. ⟨King⟩ said,/"not/permissible/⟨They⟩ merely/did not/⟨flee⟩ hundred/paces"/(mood).

Commentary. Buh kee refers to *shiaw* in sentence 8.5.13., that is, *buh kee shiaw* "not permissible to mock." The determined term "they" is omitted. For use here of *jyr* see 4.4.2.

8.5.15. Sentence 9b–9e

Shyh yih tzoou yee. DT ( ) Conj. Dt ( ) St. This is/after all/fleeing/(stress).

Commentary. A determinative sentence, the determined term (*shyh*—anaphoric demonstrative plus copula) refers to the content of the previous sentence. For use of *shyh* here see 4.9.1.

8.5.16. Sentence 9f–10e

Iue "wang ru jy tsyy tzer wu wanq min jy duo yu lin gwo yee." (β) ⟨Prot.⟩ ($\alpha \parallel$ Md β γ^1) Apod. (Md β γ^1 ($\alpha \rightarrow \beta$ Dir. γ^2 (A→B))) St. ⟨Mencius⟩ said ⟨if⟩/King/were to/understand/this,/then/⟨he⟩ would not/expect/people/(determination)/become larger/(directive)/neighbouring states/(stress).

Commentary. Two sentences in conditioned sequence. The condition is unfulfilled. In both protasis and apodosis, the modal determinations of verbs *jy* and *wanq* are subjunctive. In the apodosis the extended affectee has as its main verb *duo* "much" with γ^2 as object of comparison (see 3.4.6).

8.6. "The Love that Embraces All Things" (*Micius*)

12	11	10	9	8	7	6	5	4	3	2	1	
故	亦	之	故	之	所	人	起	疾	能	自	聖	a
虧	天	不	虧	不	以	以	則	之	治	起	人	b
子	下	慈	父	孝	自	治	弗	所	嘗	焉	以	c
而	之	子	而	君	起	天	能	自	之	能	治	d
自	所	兄	自	父	當	下	攻	起	如	治	天	e
利	謂	之	利	所	察	為	治	焉	醫	之	下	f
⋮	亂	不	⋮	謂	亂	事	亂	能	之	不	為	g
⋮	也	慈	⋮	亂	何	者	者	攻	攻	知	事	h
是	父	⋮	此	也	自	也	何	人	人	亂	者	i
何	弟	君	所	子	起	不	獨	之	之	之	也	j
也	自	之	謂	自	不	可	不	疾	疾	所	必	k
皆	愛	不	亂	愛	相	不	然	者	者	自	知	m
起	也	慈	也	也	愛	察	⋮	之	然	起	亂	n
不	不	臣	雖	父	不	⋮	⋮	所	必	則	之	p
相	愛	此	父	子	愛	聖	聖	自	知	不	所	q

	24	23	22	21	20	19	18	17	16	15	14	13
a	愛	交	得	則	亂	下	孝	兄	愛	此	室	愛
b	人	相	不	天	盜	象	不	與	愛	何	不	雖
c	者	惡	禁	下	賊	不	慈	君	人	也	愛	至
d	此	則	惡	治	無	相	亡	若	若	皆	異	天
e	也	亂	而	故	有	愛	有	愛	愛	起	室	下
f		故	勸	聖	君	國	猶	其	其	不	故	之
g		子	愛	人	臣	與	有	身	身	相	竊	為
h		墨	故	以	父	國	盜	惡	猶	愛	異	盜
i		子	天	治	子	不	賊	施	有	⋮	室	賊
j		曰	下	天	皆	相	⋮	不	不	若	以	者
k		不	象	下	能	攻	⋮	孝	孝	使	利	亦
m		可	相	象	孝	家	若	⋮	者	天	其	然
n		以	愛	相	慈	與	使	⋮	乎	下	室	盜
p		不	則	愛	若	家	天	故	視	象	⋮	愛
q		勸	治	則	此	不	不	父	相	⋮		其

Free Translation

The man of sagacity, concerned with the creation of a well-ordered society, must know the causes of society's disorders, for it is only then that he can bring about a well-ordered society. Without such knowledge he cannot do so. It is like a doctor treating an illness. The doctor must know the cause of the illness before he attempts to cure it. If he does not, he cannot do so. Is the creation of order out of disorder any exception? No, the sagacious man, concerned with the creation of a well-ordered society, must enquire into the causes of society's disorders.

Upon enquiring, he will find that all disorders come from a failure to practise reciprocal love. All would concede that a failure in filial piety on the part of a son to his father, or upon the part of a subject to his sovereign would be disorderly conduct, since the son, loving himself would fail to love his father, so that he would deprive his father only in order to enrich himself, etc. Such things are rightly called "disorderly conduct." But, too, we must concede that a failure in affection on the part of a father to his son, or of an older brother to his younger brother, or of a sovereign to his subjects, would be disorderly conduct, since the father, loving himself would fail to love his son, so that he would deprive his son in order to enrich himself, etc.

Where do these two forms of disorder come from? They come from a failure to practise reciprocal love. And this holds good too, even in the case of such disorders as theft and robbery. For the thief, caring only about his own house, cares nothing about the house of a stranger so that he will steal from a stranger's house in order to enrich his own house. The robber, caring only about his own person, cares nothing about the person of a stranger, so that he will rob a stranger in order to enrich himself. Where do disorders of this kind come from? They come from a failure to practise reciprocal love.

Suppose that men everywhere were to practise this all-embracing, fully reciprocated love, and suppose that all men were to love each other as they loved themselves, would such a thing as unfilial conduct exist? If all concerned were to look upon their sons, their younger brothers, and their subjects, as they look upon themselves, where would unfilial conduct manifest itself? Therefore, if unfilial conduct and lack of affection become non-existent, would such things as theft and robbery continue to exist?

Suppose, too that with men everywhere practising this all-embracing, fully reciprocated love, with no attack by one state upon another, with no despoiling of one feudal household by another, with theft and robbery non-existent, then everyone could practise the virtues of filial piety and parental affection. Under such conditions we would have a well-ordered society, because the practice of such love produces a well-ordered society, while the practice of mutual hatred produces a disordered society. Our master, Micius had this in mind when he said, "We cannot but preach the doctrine of love for others." (*Micius* 21.1–19.)

8.6.1. Sentence 1a-2b

Shenq-ren yii jyh tian-shiah, wei shyh jee yee, bih jy luann jy suoo-tzyh chii. α (α(A→B) [In. (β γ¹ (A→B)] β γ¹ Syn.) St. || β (β→β) γ¹ (α→□ Dir. β). Sage / takes / govern / world / cause-to-become / affair / (syn) / (stress)/must/know/disorder/(determination)/that from which/arises.

Commentary. Basically a verbal sentence (α β γ). The agent is a verbal sentence reduced to a syntagma in *jee* (see 2.7), (α (A→B) [Ing—] β γ) becoming "The Sage who makes governing the world his business." The agent is in rhetorical exposure (note *yee*) (see 3.11). The affectee (γ¹) of *jy* is the reduction of a verbal sentence to substantival status by placing the particle of determination between agent and verb, and making the directive determinative of the verb. Thus α *jy* γ² β. The γ² is represented by the indefinite substitute *suoo*, and is shown to be directive by the use of the lexical directive *tzyh* (see 3.4.5.1 and 6.6.1.1). Thus, "that from which." *Suoo-tzyh* cf. *her-tzyh* (6.5.2.2).

8.6.2. Sentence 2c-2f

Ian neng jyh jy. Time || SA β γ. At such time as this/able/govern/it.

Commentary. Ian (allegro form of *yu-jy*) here in the time position, is the use for indefinite reference of interrogative substitutes, that is, "at what time," "at such time" (see 6.8).

8.6.3. Sentence 2g-3b

Buh jy luann jy suoo-tyzh chii tzer buh neng jyh. ⟨When⟩ Md β γ^1 ($\alpha \to \square$ Dir. β) then Md. SA β. When not/know/disorder/(determination)/that from whence/arises/then/not/able/govern.

Commentary. Sentences 8.6.1 and 8.6.2 are discrete sentences, two positive assertions. Sentence 8.6.3 is the negative corollary of the argument of sentences 8.6.1 and 8.6.2 and is stated as a conditioned sequence.

8.6.4. Sentence 3c-3m

Pih jy ru i jy gong ren jy jyi jee. ⟨When⟩ β γ ⟨then⟩ ⟨DT ( )⟩ Cop. Dt ($\alpha \to \beta$ γ^1 (A→B) Syn.). ⟨When⟩ illustrate/this/⟨then⟩ ⟨it⟩ resembles /a doctor/(determination)/curing/man/(determination)/illness/(syn).

Commentary. Note particles of determination between agent and verb in forming the determinant term (see 2.7 and 4.7).

8.6.5. Sentence 3n-4e

Ran bih jy jyi jy suoo-tzyh chii. (β γ), β (β β) γ^1 ($\alpha \to \gamma^2$ ($\square$ Dir.) β). That being so/must/know/illness/(determination)/that from which/ arises.

Commentary. For use of *ran*, see 5.3.1 Note 1.

8.6.6. Sentence 4f-4j

Ian neng gong jy. Time || SA β γ^1. At such time as this/able/to cure /it.

Commentary. Compare sentence 8.6.2.

8.6.7. Sentence 4j-5e

Buh jy jyi jy suoo-tzyh chii tzer fwu neng gong. ⟨When⟩ || Md β γ^1 ($\alpha \to \gamma^1$ ($\square$ Dir.) β) ⟨then⟩ Md. SA. β. ⟨When⟩ not/know/illness/(determination)/that from which/arises/then/not/able/to effect a cure.

Commentary. Compare sentence 8.6.3. Note that the negation of *gong* (in 8.6.3 it is the unstressed form) is in the stressed form *fwu* (see 3.3.1.1).

8.6.8. Sentence 5f-5m

Jyh luann jee her-dwu buh ran. α (β γ^1 Syn.) $\Box$ Md β (β γ). The putting into order/of disorder/(syn)/why this alone/not/like this.

Commentary. Her-dwu (cf. also *shi-dwu* and *chii-dwu*) is the interrogative form of the distributive *dwu* "the agent to the exclusion of all others" and thus "Is the agent, to the exclusion of all others ... ," "is the agent any exception in ...."

8.6.9. Sentence 5q-7c

Shenq-ren yii jyh tian-shiah wei shyh jee yee. α (α (A→B) [In. (β γ^1 (A→B))] β γ^1 Syn.) St. *buh kee buh char luann jy suoo-tzyh chii.* Md. SA Md β γ^1 (α→γ^1 ($\Box$ Dir.) β). Sage/take/good-order/world/to become/affair/(syn)/(stress)/not/can/not/examine/disorder/(determination)/that from which/arises.

Commentary. Essentially the same as sentence 8.6.1 but note that for *bih* "must" is substituted *buh kee buh* "cannot not", a circumlocution for "must." (See 3.11. 1 footnote 71.)

8.6.10. Sentence 7d-7n

Dang char luann her-tzyh chii, chii buh shiang ay. Time $||$ β γ^1 (α γ^2 ($\Box$ Dir.) β), β γ^1 (Md β (A→B)). When/examine/disorder/from what place?/arises,/⟨then we find it⟩ arises/⟨from⟩ a failure to practise/mutual/love.

Commentary. Cf. this sentence with 8.6.1 where the indefinite *suoo* substitutes for *her*.

8.6.11. Sentence 7p-8j

Chern tzyy jy bwu shiaw jiun fuh suoo wey luann yee. DT (α (A/B)) →Md β γ^1 (A/B) Dt ($\Box$ β γ^2) St. Subject/son/(determination)/not/behaving-filially to/ruler/father/⟨is⟩ something/we call/disorder/(stress).

Commentary. A determinative sentence. The determined term (reduction of a verbal sentence to syntagma form with *jy*; see 2.7) is a telescoping of two sentences. The agents, "subjects," "son" have as their affectees "rulers" and "fathers," respectively. For *wey*, see 3.4.7.

8.6.12. Sentence 8j-9f

Tzyy tzyh ay buh ay fuh guh kuei fuh erl tzyh lih. DT (α Refl. β, Md β γ^1) Cop. Dt ([β γ^1 erl] Refl. β). Son/self/loves/does not/love/father,/therefore/depriving/father/⟨subordination⟩/himself/profits.

Commentary. For use of *tzyh* see 3.5.4.1.

NOTE. The deletions from text here are a series of repetitions grammatically parallel with the above.

8.6.13. Sentence 9i-9n

Tsyy suoo wey luan yee. DT ( ) Dt (□ β γ^2) St. These things/⟨are⟩ those things which/are called/"disorderly"/⟨stress⟩.

Commentary. See sentence 8.6.11. *Tsyy* "these things" is anaphoric for the determined term of sentence 8.6.11.

8.6.14. Sentence 9p-11h

Swei fuh jy buh tsyr tzyy, shiong jy buh tsyr dih, jiun jy buh tsyr chern, tzyy, yih tian-shian jy suoo wey luann yee. Conc. DT (α→Md β γ^1), (α→Md β γ^1), (α→Md β γ^1), DT ( ) Dt (Conj. α (A→B)→γ^1 □ β γ^2) St. Nevertheless / a father / ⟨determinative⟩ / not / practise-affection/⟨to his⟩ son,/an older brother/⟨determinative⟩/not/practise-affection/⟨to his⟩ younger brother,/a sovereign/⟨determinative⟩/not/practise-affection/⟨to his⟩ subjects,/these things/⟨are⟩ after all/of the world/⟨determinative⟩/that which/is called/disorderly/⟨stress⟩.

Commentary. In this determinative sentence, the determined term (a series of syntagmas) is resumed in anaphora by the demonstrative *tsyy* (see 4.10.3). Note that the concessive *swei* is here retrospective (see 5.4.1).

8.6.15. Sentence 11i-12f

Fuh tzyh ay yee bwu ay tzyy guh kuei tzyy erl tzyh lih. DT (α Refl. β St. Md β γ) Cop. Dt ([β γ^1 erl] Refl. β). Father/self/loves/⟨stress⟩/does not/love/⟨his⟩ son/therefore/⟨while⟩ depriving/⟨his⟩ son/⟨subordinate⟩/self/profits.

Commentary. Essentially the same as sentence 8.6.12 q.v.

8.6.16. Sentence 12j-12a

Shyh her yee jie chii buh shiang ay. DT ( ) Dt (□) St. ⟨DT ( )⟩ Dt (Dist. β γ^2 (Md β (A→B)). These/⟨are⟩ what?/⟨stress⟩/⟨these are⟩ all/⟨things which⟩ arise/⟨from⟩ not practise/mutual/love.

Commentary. Note the use of the distributive in the determinative sentence (see 4.12). Cf. also 8.6.19 where *tsyy* replaces *shyh*, and see 4.10.3.

8.6.17. Sentence 13b-13m

Swei jyh tian-shiah jy wei daw tzer jee yih ran. ⟨Prot.⟩ Conc. β γ¹ (α (A→B)→β γ¹ (A+B) Syn.) ⟨Apod.⟩ Conj. (β γ¹). Even ⟨if⟩/go to /of the world/(determinative)/⟨who⟩ have become/thieves/⟨and⟩ robbers/(syn)/⟨then⟩ in the light of the foregoing/it would be like this.

8.6.18. Sentence 13n-14n

Daw ay chyi shyh, bwu ay yih shyh, guh chieh yih shyh yii lih chyi shyh. DT (α β γ¹ (A→B), Md β γ¹ (A→B)) Cop. Dt (β γ¹ (A→B) Res. In. β γ¹ (A→B)). Thief/loves/his/house/does not/love/stranger /house/therefore/burgles/stranger/house/in order to/profit/⟨his⟩ own /house.

Commentary. Note use here of *yih* "strange, stranger, different" > (putative) "think strange, marvel at" (factitive) "make different, differentiate" here used in apposition to *chyi* "his own," and thus, "that of the other, the different." Cf. use of *ta* 6.3.

8.6.19. Sentence 15a-15h

Repetition of sentence 8.6.16 with *tsyy* replacing *shyh*.

8.6.20. Sentence 15j-16n

Ruoh-shyy tian-shiah jian shiang ay, ay ren ruoh ay chyi shen, you-yeou bwu shiaw jee hu. Prot. α (A→B) β (A→B(A→B)), DT (β γ) Cop. Dt (β γ¹ (A→B)) ⟨Apod.⟩ DT (Md β) Dt (Md β Syn.) St. Suppose/the world/practises all-embracing/mutual/love/⟨suppose they⟩/ loved/others/as they/love/their own/selves/⟨then⟩ would there be/ not/filial/(syn)/(mood).

Commentary. The determination of the verb *ay*, by *jian* (all embracing, comprehensive, universal) and *shiang* (mutual), becomes in Mician philosophy a technical term "love which is fully reciprocated [*shiang*] and indiscriminate, or comprehensive [*jian*]." Here a verb, but in English perhaps "to practise universal mutual love." Note that the protasis is introduced by *ruoh-shyh* "as though cause"— creating a hypothetical "if" (see 5.3 footnote 6). Note also the determination of *yeou* "there is" by the subjunctive *you* "there would be"; with the modal *hu* this becomes "would there be?"

8.6.21. Sentence 16p-17j

Shyh tzyy dih yeu chern ruoh chyi shen u shy bwu shiaw. ⟨Prot.⟩ DT (β γ¹ (A+B+C)) Cop. Dt (⟨β⟩ γ¹ (A→B)) ⟨Apod.⟩ γ² □ β γ (Md β). ⟨If⟩ looks upon/⟨one's⟩ sons/⟨and⟩ younger brothers/and/subjects/just as/⟨one looks upon⟩ his own/person/⟨then⟩ where/⟨would be⟩ displayed/not/practise filial piety.

Commentary. Note the use of the syntagmatic conjunction *yeu* (see 2.5). *U* the substitute interrogative for the second post-verbal elements asks "to what," "at what place," "where" (see 6.5.2.2).

NOTE. Deleted passage in text is reiteration.

8.6.22. Sentence 17p-18j

Guh bwu-shiaw buh-tsyr wu yeou, you-yeou daw tzer hu. Cop. Dt (⟨Prot.⟩ DT ((A→B)+(A→B)) Dt (Md β) ⟨Apod.⟩ DT (Md β) Dt (A+B) Md. Therefore/⟨if⟩unfilial behaviour/and a lack of parental affection/would not/exist/⟨then⟩ would there be/thieves/⟨and⟩ robbers/⟨mood⟩.

Commentary. On this sentence see 4.8.2. Note the determinations of *yeou*, viz. *wu-yeou* "would not exist," *you yeou* "would exist." The sign *wu* here (18d) is interchangeable with *wu* in 20d.

8.6.23. Sentence 18n-20n

Ruoh-shyy tian-shiah jian shiang ay, gwo yeu gwo buh shiang gong, jia yeu jia buh shiang luann, daw tzer wu yeou, jiun chern fuh tzyy jie neng shiaw tsyr. Prot. α (A→B) β (A→B(A→B)), ⟨Prot.⟩ α (A+B) Md Recip. β, ⟨Prot.⟩ α (A+B) Md Recip. β, DT (A+B) Dt (Md β), ⟨Apod.⟩ α (A+B+C+D)/Dist. SA β (β+β). Suppose/the world/⟨practised⟩ all-embracing/mutual/love/⟨suppose⟩ state/together with /state/did not/each other/attack/⟨suppose⟩ household/together with /household/did not/each other/despoil/⟨suppose⟩ thieves/robbers/ were not existing ⟨then⟩/ruler/subject/father/son/all/able/practise filial piety/practise parental love.

Commentary. Note that the agential particle of reciprocation can be negated. It is for this reason that reciprocity (*shiang*) and the reflexive (*tzyh*) have been treated as part of the verbal complex and not of the agential complex (see 3.5.4.1 and 3.5.4.2).

8.6.24. Sentence 20p-21d

Ruoh tsyy, tzer tian-shiah jyh. ⟨Prot.⟩ β γ Apod. α (A→B) β. ⟨When⟩ like/this/then/the world/is-well-ordered.

8.6.25. Sentence 21e-22g

Guh sheng-ren yii jyh tian-shiah wei shyh jee, u der bwu jinn wuh erl chiuann ay. Cop. Dt α (α (A→B) [In. β γ¹ (A→B)] β γ¹ Syn.) γ² □ Md. Md [β γ¹ erl] β γ¹. It is for those reasons/the sage/⟨who⟩ takes/governing/the world/to become/his affair/(syn)/how/must/not/⟨while⟩ prohibiting/hatred/(subordination)/exhort/love.

Commentary. U der "must." *U* is the interrogative substitute for second post-verbal elements (see 6.5.2.2), in this case, for the causal agent. Determining *der* (which is injunctive, see 3.3.1.2) asks, in effect, "by what would he be compelled?" When negated and used rhetorically it means "by what would he be compelled not to," that is, "he must." In treating *guh* grammatically as a causal link (see 4.11) the etymology of *guh* should not be forgotten. It is cognate with *guu* "ancient" and thus derives the meanings "old—of long-standing, firm, secure, established, true" (cf. here the modal use of *guh* "in reality") and thus *guh* "proven," "it is established or true that," "therefore." My feeling here is that *guh* is nearer "I have firmly established that" rather than "it is for this reason, therefore."

8.6.26. Sentence 22h-23e

Guh tian-shiah jian shiang ay tzer jyh, jiau-shiang wuh tzer luann. Cop. Dt (⟨Prot.⟩ α (A→B) β (A→B(A→B)) Apod. β, ⟨Prot. α⟩ Recip. β Apod. β). It is for this reason/⟨if⟩ all the world/⟨practises⟩ all-embracing/mutual/love/then/⟨it would be⟩ well governed/⟨if the world⟩ reciprocally/practises hatred/then/⟨it will be⟩ disordered.

Commentary. See sentence 8.6.25 on *guh*.

8.6.27. Sentence 23f-24e

Guh Tzyy Moh-tzyy iue "buh kee bwu chiuann ay ren" jee tsyy yee. ⟨DT⟩ Cop. Dt ((α (A→B(A→B)) β γ¹ (Md SA Md β γ¹ (β γ¹))) syn. Dt ( )) St. It is for this reason/⟨when⟩ our master/Micius/said/Not /could/not/preach/love/others/(syn)/⟨what he was saying was⟩ this/ (stress).

Commentary. See notes on 8.6.25 for *guh*. This determinative sentence says in effect "what I am saying is only what Micius said." The determined term, the quotation from Micius, is reduced to syntagma by *jee* (see 2.7.1 for *jee* used with quotations). The determined term *tsyy* refers anaphorically to the entire argument of the preceding context.

8.7. "The Perennial Philosophy" (*Chuang Tzu*)

	8	7	6	5	4	3	2	1	
a	无	逍	何	今	大	不	大	惠
b	所	遙	有	子	而	中	本	子
c	可	乎	之	有	无	規	擁	謂
d	用	寢	鄉	大	用	矩	腫	莊
e	安	臥	廣	樹	眾	立	而	子
f	所	其	莫	患	所	之	不	曰
g	困	下	之	其	同	塗	中	吾
h	苦	不	野	无	去	匠	繩	有
i	哉	夭	彷	用	也	者	墨	大
j		斤	徨	何	莊	不	其	樹
k		斧	乎	不	子	顧	小	人
m		物	无	樹	曰	今	枝	謂
n		无	爲	之	:	子	卷	之
p		害	其	於	:	之	曲	樗
q		者	側	无	:	言	而	其

Free Translation

Hui Tzu said to Chuang Tzu "I had an enormous tree, the tree which men call the chu-tree. Its great trunk was knotted and gnarled and not true to the carpenter's line. Its branches were bent and twisted, and were not true to the carpenter's rule. I left it by the side of the road but the carpenters would not give it a glance. Now Sir! Your sayings, like my tree, are 'great' but useless. The common man unanimously rejects them, much as the carpenters rejected my tree." Chuang Tzu said, "You, Sir, have a great tree and complain of its uselessness. Why did you not plant it in the Land-of-Nothing-at-all, in the Country-of-Deserts? Go into trance, and practise actionless-activity by its side. Journey into ecstasy while sleeping beneath its shade. The tree which escapes the axe, the tree left unharmed by its fellow-creatures, is the useless tree. Nothing causes it pain." (*Chuang-tzu* 3.42–47.)

NOTE. "Great, large" and "small" are terms used esoterically in Chuang-tzu. They refer respectively to the transcendental knowledge of the mystic, and to the everyday knowledge of the uninitiate.

8.7.1. Sentence 1a-1f

Huey-tzyy wey Juang-tzyy iue. α (A→B) β γ² (A→B) "...." Hui-tzu /said to/Chuang-tzu/(quote) "...."

8.7.2. Sentence 1g-1p

Wu yeou dah shuh, ren wey jy shu. $\alpha\beta\gamma^1$ (A→B) $\alpha\beta\gamma^1\gamma^2$. I/possess/⟨a⟩ large tree/men/call/it/"the chu-tree."

Commentary. For *wey* see 3.4.7 paragraph 3 (fourth variant).

8.7.3. Sentence 1q-2i

Chyi dah been iong-joong erl bwu jonq sherng moh. α (A→B(A→B)) [β (AA) erl] Md $\beta\gamma^1$ (A+B). Its/great/trunk/⟨being⟩ gnarled/⟨subordinate⟩/⟨it⟩ does not/square/⟨with the⟩ string/⟨and⟩ ink.

Commentary. For *iong-joong* (a dissimilated reduplicative) see 1.2.2.5. *Sherng-moh*, lit: "string and ink" is a carpenter's instrument, used for drawing straight lines, by stretching a string soaked in ink and then plucking it, leaving a straight ink line. *Jonq* is "to hit a target," thus, "to square with, conform to," etc.

8.7.4. Sentence 2j-3d

Chyi sheau jy jeuan-chiu erl bwu jonq guei-jeu. α (A→B(A→B)) [β (A=B) erl] Md $\beta\gamma^1$ (A+B). Its/small/branches/being twisted ⟨and⟩ bent/⟨subordinate⟩/⟨it⟩ does not/square ⟨with⟩/arcs-squares.

Commentary. For *jeuan-chiu* lit: "curled up, bent," see morphological hendiadys 1.2.3.4. *Guei-jeu* "arcs and squares," but here clearly has nothing to do with arcs. It is an example of the generic term derived from the naming of two species and thus "measuring instruments in general" (see 1.2.3.1).

8.7.5. Sentence 3e-3k

Lih jy twu, jianq jee bwu guh. $\beta\gamma^1\gamma^2, \alpha$ ( ) Syn. Md β. Set/it/⟨by the⟩ road/carpenters/(syn)/did not/turn head to look.

Commentary. In *lih jy twu* note omission of directive particle.

8.7.6. Sentence 3m-4o

Jin tzyy jy yan dah erl wu-yonq. Time || DT (A→B) Dt ([β erl] β (A→B)). Now/your/(determinative)/sayings/being great/(subordinate)/are useless.

Commentary. The determinant term is formed on the analogy of a verbal sentence by subordinating *dah* in *erl* thus creating a sort of adversative, "are great but useless." The adversative as a lexicized form does not appear until Han times. (See 3.7 footnote 55.)

8.7.7. Sentence 4e-4i

Jonq suoo torng chiuh yee. ⟨DT⟩ Dt ($\alpha \gamma^1$ (□) As β) St. ⟨Your sayings are⟩ commonality/that which/unanimously/rejects/(stress).

Commentary. The determinant term is formed in syntagma, by the reduction of a verbal sentence "multitude reject them" ($\alpha \beta \gamma$) with the indefinite substitute in γ^1 position. *Chiuh* "to go out" provided with an affectee (here *suoo*) is therefore causative "to cause to go out," "to reject" (see 6.6.1.1).

8.7.8. Sentence 4j-5i

Juang-tzyy iue jin tzyy yeou dah shuh, huann chyi wu-yonq. α (A→B) (β) Time $\parallel \alpha \beta \gamma^1$ (A→B) $\beta \gamma^1$ (A→B(A→B)). Chuang-tzu/said/now/you sir/have/large/tree/⟨and⟩ complain/its/uselessness.

Commentary. Huann "suffering," "grief" is here used putatively and transitively, that is, "to regard as grievous," "complain about."

8.7.9. Sentence 5j-6h

Her bwu shuh jy yu wu-her-yeou-jy-shiang, goang-moh jy yee. DT (□) Dt (Md $\beta \gamma^1$ Dir. γ^2 (A (DT ( ) Dt ( ))→B), γ^2 (A(A→B)→B). Why/not/plant/it/in/not have/whatever/exists/(determinative)/and/⟨in the⟩/desert/(determinative)/country.

Commentary. The second post-verbal position after *shuh* "to plant" is occupied by a syntagma, *wu-her-yeou-jy-shiang. Wu her yeou* is the determinant term. In *wu her yeou, her* is an example of the indefinite use of the interrogative substitute (see 6.8). *Wu her yeou* is a determinative sentence, that is, (determined term) *wu* "there is not" (determinant term) "something which exists" and thus: "Where there is nothing whatever." *Goang-moh-jy-yee* is taken by *Cherng Shyuan-ying* (成玄英) literally, *moh* being equated with *wu* and thus "of width, none, that land" which he says means "solitary and silent, cut off, the land of wu-wei." This, though attractive in this context, is not without its difficulties. Professor Demiéville (in a private letter) cites the variants (嘆漠) and (壙窦) and refers to *Tso* 74.14 where *dyi jy goang-moh* is certainly "the deserts of the Ti tribes."

8.7.10. Sentence 6i-7g

Parng-hwang hu, wu-wei chyi jai, shiau-yau hu chiin-woh chyi shiah.
β (AA) Md β (Md β) γ² (A→B), β (AA) Md, β (A=A) γ² (A→B). Go into trance /(mood),/ practise *wu-wei* / ⟨by⟩ its/side/, journey into ecstasy/(mood),/sleeping/⟨beneath⟩ its /underneath.

Commentary. Wu-wei, a technical term among the Mystics, is composed of the modal *wu* "should not" and *wei* "to cause to come into being." Here it is used verbally, "practise *wu-wei*." *Daw*, the mystical principle, causes things to come into being. Human activity is contrary to *daw* and interferes with things coming into being as they should. Therefore, the initiate should not "cause things to come into being," and should cultivate the art of "not causing things to come into being," by going into trance by the side of the mystical tree, and not by feckless activity in the world of men.

Note here these examples of derivation. *Parng-hwang* and *shiau-yau*, reduplication with dissimilation, and *chiin-woh*, morphological hendiadys. (See 1.2.2 and 1.2.3.4.)

8.7.11. Sentence 7h-8d

Buh yeau jin-fuu, wuh wu hay jee, wu suoo kee yonq. DT (Md β [Con.] α Md β Syn.) Dt (α γ¹ □ SA β). Not/being cut down ⟨by⟩/the axe,/living-things/would not/harm/(syn)/⟨is the kind of tree⟩/no one/that which/can/use.

Commentary. A determinative sentence, the determined term is formed in syntagma with *jee*, which governs both *bu yeau jin-fuu* "not cut down by the axe," and *wuh wu hay* "living things would not harm," and thus "the tree which is not cut down by the axe and which living things would not harm."

8.7.12. Sentence 8e-8i

An suoo kuenn-kuu tzai. γ² □ γ² □ β (A+B) Md. Where/by whom /suffers/(mood).

Commentary. An interrogative substitute for place "where?"; *Suoo* substitutes for second post-verbal position (here causal agent) thus, "by whom." *Kuenn-kuu* is passive. Thus, "where is there anything to make it suffer?" (See 6.6.1.1.)

8.8. "Chapped Hands" (*Chuang Tzu*)

	8	7	6	5	4	3	2	1	
a								莊	
b	或	人	難	技	世	客	為	子	
c	不	裂	吳	百	世	聞	不	曰	
d	免	地	王	金	為	之	龜	夫	
e	於	而	使	請	洴	請	手	子	
f	洴	封	之	與	澼	買	之	固	
g	澼	之	將	之	絖	其	藥	拙	
h	絖	能	多	客	不	方	者	於	
i	則	不	與	得	過	百	世	用	
j	所	龜	越	之	數	金	世	大	
k	用	手	人	以	金	聚	以	矣	
m	之	一	水	說	今	族	洴	宋	
n	異	也	戰	吳	一	而	澼	人	
p	也	或	大	王	朝	謀	絖	有	
q		以	敗	越	而	曰	為	善	
		封	越	有	鬻	我	事		

Free Translation

Chuang Tzu said, "Sir, you are certainly inept in the way you use the 'great.' There was a man of Sung whose family for years had been bleachers of silk-floss and who knew a way to prevent chapped hands. A traveller hearing of this, begged him to sell the secret, offering him a hundred pieces of money. The man called his family together to discuss it. He said, 'We have been bleachers of silk-floss for years, but have never earned more than a few pieces of money in one year. Now, in a single day, we can get a hundred pieces of money. I beg you to agree to this offer.' The traveller obtained the formula. He told the King of Wu about it. At that time, Wu was having trouble with Yueh. The King of Wu appointed the traveller to a command in his navy. When winter came, the Wu fleet fought a naval battle with Yueh and routed them. The King of Wu divided up the captured territory and granted a fief to the traveller.

Both the traveller and the man of Sung knew the secret of preventing chapped hands, but the one used his knowledge to gain a fief, while the other used it merely to remain at his trade. The difference lies in the use to which they put their knowledge." (*Chuang* 2.27–41.)

8.8.1. Sentence 1a-1k

Juang-tzyy iue "Fu-tzyy guh jwo yu yonq dah yii". α (A→B) (β) α (A→B) Md β Dir. γ² (A→B) St. Chuang Tzu/said/master/truly/inept/in/the use of/great/(stress).

8.8.2. Sentence 1m-2g

Song-ren yeou shann-wei-buh-jiun-shoou jy yaw jee. α (A→B) β γ¹ (A(A→B) (A→B)))→B Syn.). A man of Sung/had/⟨an⟩ effective/cause to become/not/chapped/the hands/(determinative)/medicine/(syn).

Commentary. The affectee of *yeou* "to possess" is a determinative syntagma (see 2.6.1).

8.8.3. Sentence 2h-2q

Shyh-shyh yii pyng-pih kuanq wei shyh. Time || [In. A(A→B)→B] β γ¹. Year by year/by means of/bleaching/silk-floss caused to become/business.

Commentary. For *yii ... wei shyh* see sentence 8.6.1. The distributive "year by year" is formed by gemination (see 1.2.2.1).

8.8.4. Sentence 3a-3i

Keh wen jy chiing mae chyi fang bae jin. α β γ¹, β γ¹ (β γ¹ (A→B) γ² (A→B)). A traveller/heard of/it/⟨and⟩ requested/to buy/his/prescription/⟨for⟩ one hundred/coins.

Commentary. For the γ² here, see 3.4.7 paragraph 2.

8.8.5. Sentence 3j-3p

Jiuh tzwu erl mou iue. [β γ¹ erl] β "...." Gathering/clan/(subordinate)/discussed/(said) "...."

8.8.6. Sentence 3q-4j

Woo shyh-shyh wei pyng-pih kuanq bwu guoh shuh jin. α || Time || β' γ¹ (A(A→B)→B), Md β γ¹ (A→B). We/year by year/practise/bleaching/silk-floss/not/exceed/few/coins.

Commentary. Note that when the agent is exposed the pregnant form of the pronoun is used (see 3.11.2).

8.8.7. Sentence 4k-5f

Jin i jau erl yuh jih bae jin. chiing yeu jy. Time || [A→B⟨β⟩ erl] β γ¹ (A→B(A→B)) β γ¹ (β γ¹). Now/in a single/morning/(elapsing)/sell/ ⟨our⟩ skill/⟨for⟩ one hundred/pieces of money/request/⟨we⟩ grant/it.

Commentary. For this use of the subordinate clause in *erl* see 3.7 Note. For the γ elements of *yuh* see 3.4.7 paragraph 2.

8.8.8. Sentence 5g-5n

Keh der jy yii shuo Wu-wang. α β γ¹, γ¹ β γ² (A→B). ⟨The⟩ traveller /obtained/it/of it/told/King Wu.

Commentary. For *yii* here see 3.4.7 paragraph 3 (second variant).

8.8.9. Sentence 5p-6b

Yueh yeou nan. Place || DT ( ) Dt ( ). In Yueh/there were/ troubles.

8.8.10. Sentence 6c-6f

Wu-wang shyy jy jianq. α (A→B) β γ¹ γ². King Wu/appointed/him /an admiral.

Commentary. Shyy "to order" takes as post-verbal elements (1) person ordered and (2) the order (see 3.4.7 paragraph 4) and here (1) person ordered or deputed (2) rank or duties ordered or deputed.

8.8.11. Sentence 6g-6m

Dong yeu Yueh-ren shoei-jann. Time || α (⟨A⟩+B(A→B) β (A→B)). In winter/⟨Wu⟩ with/the men of Yueh/fought a naval engagement.

8.8.12. Sentence 6n-7f

Dah-bay Yueh-ren lieh dih erl feng jy. β (A→B) γ¹ (A→B), [β γ¹ erl] β γ¹. Routed/the men of Yueh/splitting up/⟨their⟩ territories/⟨subordinate⟩/enfeoffed/him.

8.8.13. Sentence 7g-7m

Neng buh jiun shoou i yee. DT (SA Md β γ¹) Dt ( ) St. Ability/not /to get chapped/hands/was identical/(stress).

8.8.14. Sentence 7n-8g

Huoh yii feng huoh buh mean yu pyng-pih kuang. ⟨α⟩ Dist. Res. In. β, ⟨α⟩ ⟨Dist.⟩ Md β Dir. γ² (β (A+B) γ¹). ⟨If⟩ some/thereby/are enfeoffed/⟨and⟩ some/do not/escape/from/bleaching/silk-floss.

8.8.15. Sentence 8h-8n

Tzer suoo yonq jy yih. Apod. ⟨DT⟩ Dt (DT (Res. In. □ β γ¹) Dt (   )). Then/⟨it is⟩/that for which/use/it/is/different.

Commentary. The apodosis is a determinative sentence but the determined term is omitted, thus "then [that is a difference in the use to which it was put]." In *suoo yonq jy*, *suoo* is substituting for the resultative instrument (as, e.g., in *yonq jy yii feng* "using it to gain a fief").

8.9. "The Mystical Journey" (*Chuang Tzu*)

	8	7	6	5	4	3	2	1
a	而	仞	之	負	雲	鳥	廣	窮
b	彼	而	曰	青	搏	焉	數	髮
c	且	下	彼	天	扶	其	千	之
d	奚	翶	且	然	搖	名	里	北
e	適	翔	奚	後	羊	爲	未	有
f	也	蓬	適	圖	角	鵬	有	冥
g	此	蒿	也	南	而	背	知	海
h	小	之	我	且	上	若	其	者
i	大	閒	騰	適	者	泰	脩	天
j	之	此	躍	南	九	山	者	池
k	辯	亦	而	冥	萬	翼	其	也
m	也	飛	上	也	里	若	名	有
n		之	不	斥	絕	垂	爲	魚
p		至	過	鴳	雲	天	鯤	焉
q		也	數	笑	氣	之	有	其

Free |Translation

To the north of the barren tundra, there is the Dark Sea. It is the fish-pool of the Heavens. There is a fish in that sea which is several miles in girth, and no one knows how long it is. It is called the Kun. There is a bird there which is called the P'eng.* The body of the bird

*In another version of this story, the *Kun* metamorphoses and becomes a *P'eng*.

is as large as Mount T'ai, its wings in the sky look like a huge hanging cloud. Flapping its great wings for support, and circling upon the thermal currents it rises to a height of ninety thousand miles. At this height it intersects the blue sky and the clouds, and with the clouds below and the blue sky above, it sets its face to the south. It is going to the Southern Darkness. The Quail, on hearing about this, laughed, saying, "It is going where? For I, too, go hop-hop, rise into the air, and after a dozen yards I alight, fluttering in the artemisia bushes. This, after all, is flying at its best. Where is *that* bird going!" This illustrates the difference between "great" (i.e., mystical knowledge) and "small" (i.e., common knowledge). (*Chuang-tzu* 1.13–17.)

8.9.1. Sentence 1a–1k

Chyong faa jy beei yeou Ming Hae jee. Tian chyr yee. Place (A (β γ^1) →B) || DT ( ) Dt (A→B) Syn. ⟨DT⟩ Dt (A→B) St. Denuded/-hair /(determinative)/north of/there is/⟨the so-called⟩ Dark/Sea/(syn)/ ⟨it is⟩ heavens/pool/(stress).

Commentary. Ming Hae is a proper name. *Jee* here is used in sense described in 2.7.1 (last paragraph). For *place* before *yeou* see 4.8 footnote 12.

8.9.2. Sentence 1m–1p

Yeou yu yan. DT ( ) Dt (γ^1 γ^2). There is/a fish/in it.

Commentary. See notes on this sentence in 4.8 footnote 12.

8.9.3. Sentence 1q–2d

Chyi goang shuh chian lii. Wey-yeou jy chyi shiou jee. DT (A→B) DT (Md β) Dt (β γ^1 (A→B) Syn.) Dt (A(A→B)→B). Its/breadth/ several/thousand/miles./There has never been/knew/its/length/(that person).

Commentary. For number as the determinant term in a determinative sentence see 4.10.4.

8.9.4. Sentence 2k–2p

Chyi ming wei Kuen. α β γ^1 (⟨A⟩ part. B). It (the bird)/named/ (particle)/K'un.

Commentary. For the distribution of the post-verbal elements of *ming* see 3.4.7 paragraph 3 (fourth variant). Observe how the flow of direction alters the voice of the verb. Active = *ming jy yueh yih-duo*

$\beta\ \gamma^1$ part. γ^2 "[we] call that 'excessive,'" but with the affectee > agent of realization ($jy > chyi$) (i.e., flow of action reversed), the verb is passive.

8.9.5. Sentence 2q-3f

Yeou neau yan, chyi ming wei Perng. DT ( ) Dt ($\beta^1\ \gamma^2$), $\alpha\ \beta\ \gamma$ (⟨A⟩ part. B). There is/a bird/in it/it/is named/P'eng.

8.9.6. Sentence 3g-4a

Bey ruoh Tay-Shan, Yih ruoh chwei tian jy yun. DT ( ) Cop. Dt (A→B), DT ( ) Cop. Dt (A ($\beta\ \gamma^1$)→B). ⟨Its⟩ back / is like / T'ai Mountain/⟨its⟩ wings/are like/suspend/in sky/(determination)/clouds.

Commentary. On *ruoh* as copula see 4.6.

8.9.7. Sentence 4b-4m

Bor fwu yau yang-jeau erl shanq jee, jeou wann lii. DT ([β ⟨Res.⟩ β, $\beta\ \gamma^1$ (A→B) erl] β Syn.) Dt (A(A→B)→B). Beat ⟨wings⟩/⟨thereby⟩ supports / ⟨itself⟩ flaps / ⟨upon⟩ spirals (thermals) / (subordinate) / ascends/(syn)/nine/ten-thousand/miles.

Commentary. Note here that the first two verbs *bor* and *fwu* are in the relationship of two verbs with resultative instrument "strikes, thereby support" (see 3.6.2 footnote 54). *Yang-jeau* (lit: "ram's horns") is a derivative compound, specialized "spiral." In another version of this story it is made clear that such spirals cause the dust-whorls on the dry North China plain, hence it is used here for "thermals," that is, hot currents of air rising. Note too that the determined term is reduced to syntagma by *jee*.

8.9.8. Sentence 4n-5g

Jyue yun-chih fuh ching tian ran-how twu nan. ⟨When⟩ $\beta\ \gamma^1$ (A→B), $\beta\ \gamma^1$ (A→B) then $\beta\ \gamma^2$. ⟨When⟩ Cleave/cloud-mist/support/blue/sky/then-only/set its face/⟨to the⟩ south.

Commentary. For sentence type see 5.3.1 Note 2.

8.9.9. Sentence 5h-5m

Chiee shyh Nan Ming yee. As. $\beta\ \gamma^2$ (A→B) St. About to/journey/Southern/Darkness/(stress).

Commentary. For *chiee* (aspect) see 3.3.2.1.

8.9.10. Sentence 5n-6b

Chyh-yen shiaw jy iue. α (A→B) β γ² "...." Saltings-quail/ridicules/it/(saying) "...."

8.9.11. Sentence 6c-6g

Bii chiee shi shyh yee. α As. γ² □ β St. That ⟨i.e., the P'eng⟩/about to/where/go/(stress).

8.9.12. Sentence 6h-6m

Woo terng-yueh erl shanq. α || [β (A+B) erl] β. I/rise-jump/(subordinate)/ascend.

Commentary. That is, "I, having taken a few hops, rise in the air." Cf. the description in sentence 8.9.7, of how the P'eng becomes airborne.

8.9.13. Sentence 6n-7c

Bwu guoh shuh renn erl shiah. [Md β γ¹ (A→B) erl] β. Not/going past /few/fathoms/(subordinate)/alight.

8.9.14. Sentence 7d-7i

Ao-shyang perng-hau jy jian. β (A+B) γ² (A(A+B)→B). Fluttering /artemisia bushes/(determinative)/in between space.

Commentary. That is, "among the bushes" (see 2.6.3.3).

8.9.15. Sentence 7j-8f

Tsyy yih fei jy jyh erl bii chiee shi shyh yee. DT ( ) Conj. Dt (A→B) Conj. α Md γ² □ β St. This/after-all/flying/(determinative)/ perfection/(subordinate)/that (i.e., the P'eng)/about to/what-place/ go/(stress).

Commentary. For *fei jy jyh*, see parallels in 7.1.

8.9.16. Sentence 8g-8m

Tsyy sheau dah jy biann. DT ( ) Dt (A(A/B)→B). This/⟨is⟩ small /great/(determinative)/difference.

8.10. "The Feudal States Abolish the Resort to Arms" (*Tso Chuan*)

	15	14	13	12	11	10	9	8	7	6	5	4	3	2	1
a	小	之	弭	陳	人	將	將	兵	晉	令	可	若	新	⋯	趙
b	國	齊	兵	文	許	許	或	民	告	尹	以	敬	得	⋯	文
c	為	人	而	子	之	之	弭	之	趙	子	弭	行	政	曰	子
d	會	許	我	曰	如	以	之	殘	孟	木	⋯	其	將	自	為
e	於	之	弗	如	楚	召	雖	也	趙	欲	宋	禮	求	今	政
f	宋	告	許	楚	亦	諸	曰	財	孟	弭	向	道	善	以	令
g		於	則	許	許	侯	不	用	謀	諸	戌	之	於	往	薄
h		秦	固	之	之	則	可	之	諸	侯	善	以	諸	兵	諸
i		秦	攜	我	如	我	必	蠹	大	之	於	文	侯	其	侯
j		亦	吾	焉	齊	失	將	小	夫	兵	趙	辭	以	少	之
k		許	民	得	人	為	許	國	韓	以	文	以	武	弭	幣
m		之	矣	已	難	盟	之	之	宣	為	子	靖	也	矣	而
n		皆	將	且	之	主	弗	大	子	名	又	諸	知	齊	重
p		告	焉	人		矣	許	菑	曰	⋯	善	侯	楚	崔	其
q		於	用	曰		晉	楚	也		如	於	兵	令尹	慶	禮

Free Translation

(546 B.C.)

Chao Wu, the reigning politician in the State of Tsin, gave orders to lessen the contributions made by the feudal states to Tsin as Presiding Power of the Feudal League, and to increase the ceremonials accorded to them. He said, "From now on, the resort to arms might gradually be brought to an end. The government of the State of Ch'i has recently fallen into the hands of Ts'ui Chu and Ch'ing Feng and those gentlemen will seek for good relations with the feudal states. I know the Premier of the State of Ch'u personally, and if we are scrupulously courteous to him, and are careful to address him in polite language, we might as a result reduce tension among the feudal powers, and gradually bring about the abolition of the resort to arms."

(544 B.C.)

Hsiang Hsu, the Master of the Left in the State of Sung, was on excellent terms with both Chao Wu of Tsin and with Tzu Mu, the Premier of Ch'u, and seeing an opportunity to make a name for himself proposed to bring about the abolition of the resort to arms among the feudal powers. He now came to Tsin and apprised Chao Wu of his scheme. Chao Wu discussed the matter with the court advisers of Tsin. One of them, Han Hsuan-tzu, said "The resort to arms means destruction for the common people, is a parasite upon our natural resources, and a major catastrophe for the minor powers. Whether we are to abolish war or not is one thing, but though we may say among ourselves that such a thing is impossible, we should have to agree to any proposal to do so, for if we did not, then our most serious rival Ch'u would at once agree, and use the occasion to convene the feudal powers. We might thus lose our position as Presiding Power." Tsin decided to support the proposal. Hsiang Hsu then went to Ch'u and Ch'u also agreed. Hsiang Hsu then went to Ch'i, but there objections were raised. Chen Hsiu-wu (one of the court advisers of Ch'i) however, argued, "What alternative have we but to agree if Tsin and Ch'u have already done so? For if there is any serious advocacy of the abolition of arms and we appear to be against it, we should then be forced to drag our people into battle, and what could we do with unwilling troops?" Ch'i decided to agree. Hsiang Hsu notified Ch'in and Ch'in agreed. The minor powers were then informed by the major powers that a meeting would be convened in the State of Sung to ratify an agreement to abolish the resort to arms. (*Tso* 306, 15-17; 316, 11-16.)

8.10.1. Sentence 1a-1e

Jaw Wen-tzyy wei-jenq. α (A→B(A→B)) β (β γ^1). Chao/Wen-tzu/controlled government.

Commentary. Wei-jenq is a customary compound "to govern."

8.10.2. Sentence 1f-1q

Linq baur ju-hour jy bih erl chorng chyi lii. β γ^1 ([β γ^1 (A(A)→B)→B) erl] β γ^1 (A→B). Ordered/⟨while⟩ lightening/feudatories/(determinative)/contributions/(subordinate)/to increase/their/ceremonials.

Commentary. Baur "thin" and *chorng* > *jonq* "heavy" are used factitively "to make light," "to make heavy" (see 3.4.6). *Chyi lii* "their ceremonies," that is, the "protocol accorded to them." Note that the verb of the subordinated clause and the verb of the main clause are concomitant action (see 3.7.1).

8.10.3. Sentence 2c-2m

Tzyh-jin-yii-woang bing chyii shao mii yii. Time || γ^1 || α As β St. Henceforward/warfare/they/gradually/bring to an end/(stress).

Commentary. Tzyh-jin-yii-woang (or *tzyh-jin-yii-how*) is a cutsomary syntagma in the time position, lit: from/now/thereby/forward, that is, henceforward, henceforth, etc. (see 3.10). *Chyi* is an anaphoric reference to the agent (the feudatories previously mentioned), and *bing* the element of the first post-verbal position in emphatic exposure. For *shao* "a little" and in aspectual position "little by little" see 3.3.2.8.

8.10.4. Sentence 2n-3i

Chyi Tsuei Chinq shin der jenq, jiang chyou shann yu ju-hour. α (A→B (A+B)) As β γ¹, As β γ¹ Dir. γ² (A→B). Ch'i State/Tsuei ⟨Juh⟩/⟨and⟩ Chinq ⟨Feng⟩/newly/obtained/the government/⟨they⟩ will/seek/to be on good terms with/⟨directive⟩/the feudatories/.

Commentary. Note the telescoping in the agent, "of Ch'i, both Tsuei (Juh) and Chinq (Feng)." *Shann* "good, effective," is here putative "to think good," and with the causal agent in the second post-verbal position "to be thought well of by," that is, "to be on good terms with."

8.10.5. Sentence 3j-3q

Wuu yee jy Chuu Linq-yiin. α St. || β γ¹ (A→B(A→B)). (I) Wu/ (stress)/know/Ch'u/premier.

Commentary. Linq-yiin is a derivative compound. Note the exposure of the agent and the use of the personal name, establishing status (the Prime Minister of Tsin is speaking to a noble of the State of Lu). (See 6.2.)

8.10.6. Sentence 4a-5c

Ruoh jinq shyng chyi lii, dau jy yii wen-tsyr, yii jinq ju-hour bing kee yii mii. ⟨Prot.⟩ Md Man β γ¹ (A→B), β γ¹ [Con. A→B], Res. In. β γ¹ (A→B) ⟨Apod.⟩ γ¹ || SA Res. In. β. ⟨If⟩ ⟨we⟩ were to/reverently/ conduct/his/ceremonials/ speak to /him / using / court language / we would thereby / reassure / the feudatories / ⟨then⟩ / warfare / could be / thereby/brought to an end.

Commentary. Two verbal sentences in conditioned sequence (unfulfilled). *Shyng* "to walk," "to proceed" (causative), "to cause to walk," "cause to proceed" and thus, "put into practice." Note the continuative form created by the ingressive instrument in post-verbal position (see 3.6.3). *Wen-tsyr* (lit: "patterned speech") refers to the formal form of speech used at court. *Jinq* is "calm, placid" and thus "make calm, pacify, reassure."

8.10.7. Sentence 5e-6d

Sonq Shianq Shiu shann yu Jaw Wen-tzyy Yow shann yu Linq-yiin Tzyy-muh. α (A→B(A→B)) β Dir. γ² (A→B(A→B)), Conj. β Dir. γ² (A(A→B)→B(A→B)). State of Sung / Hsiang / Hsu / ⟨was⟩ thought well of / by / Chao / Wen-tzu / and also / thought well of / by / Premier / Tzyymuh.

Commentary. For the use of *shann* see sentence 8.10.4. For the determining sequence of names and titles see 2.6.3.2 footnote 12.

8.10.8. Sentence 6e-6n

Yuh mii ju-hour jy bing yii wei ming. β γ¹ (β γ (A(A→B)→B)) Res. In. β γ¹. Wished / to cause to stop / the feudal lords / (determinative) / wars / ⟨and⟩ thereby / make / a name / ⟨for himself⟩.

Commentary. Wei ming (from *wei* "to become," used transitively "to cause to become, to make, to create," and *ming* "a name, fame"). Thus, "to become famous, to make a name for himself."

8.10.9. Sentence 6q-7d

Ru Jinn gaw Jaw Menq. β γ², β γ¹ (A→B). He went to / State of Tsin / and informed / Chao / Meng.

Commentary. The use of *ru* for "to go to" seems to be peculiar to the Tso Chuan.

8.10.10. Sentence 7a-7k

Jaw Menq mou yu ju dah-fu. α (A→B) β Dir. γ² (A→B(A→B)). Chao / Meng / discussed / ⟨this⟩ among / the various / nobles.

Commentary. Ju determinative collective "many varieties conceived of as one," "various," is restricted to determining such terms as "feudal lords, nobles, ministers," etc., and as such has a status quality (see 2.6.4.5 footnote 23).

8.10.11. Sentence 7m-7q

Harn Shiuan-tzyy/iue. α (A→B(A→B)) " . . . ." Han / Hsuan-tzu / ⟨said⟩ ". . . ."

8.10.12. Sentence 8a-8q

Bing min jy tsarn yee, tsair-yonq jy duh sheau gwo jy dah tzai yee. DT ( ) Dt (A→B) St., A(A+B)→B, A(A→B)→B(A→B) St. Warfare/⟨is a⟩/common people/(determinative)/destroyer/(stress)/commodities/(determinative)/parasite/small/state/(determinative/disaster/(stress).

Commentary. A series of determinative sentences in parallel, the determinant terms sharing a common determined term (warfare). Note how the syntactical position invests words with grammatical quality. As determined terms, the following are substantival: *tsarn* "to destroy" and *yonq* "to use." *Duh* "an insect, a grub in the wood" is also used elsewhere as "to act as a grub in wood, to bore into."

8.10.13. Sentence 9a-9m

Jiang huoh mii jy swei iue buh-kee bih jiang sheu jy. As Md $\beta \gamma^1$, Conc. (β) "Md β," $\beta \gamma^1$ (As $\beta \gamma^1$). Going to/or not/stop/it ⟨war⟩/though/⟨we say⟩/impossible/⟨we⟩ must/be going to/accede to/it (i.e., a request to do so).

Commentary. Note the use of *huoh* for "whether we are going to stop it or not." *Huoh*, most frequently encountered in LAC as the agential distributive (of the agent, some . . .) is here in the modal position (see 3.3.1.4). From the construction "huoh . . . huoh . . ." "some do this, some do that" there develops the usage "either do this, or do that," and *huoh* eventually becomes the conjunction of alternative connection "or," but it is not found as such in LAC. Here in the modal position determining verb, *huoh* is "whether to . . . or not."

This sentence paraphrased is: "We might say among ourselves that to stop war is impossible, but whether war is to be stopped or not, we shall have to agree to any proposal to stop it, for if we do not, then Ch'u will, and will take it as an opportunity for summoning the Feudal League, in which case we shall jeopardize our position as Presidents of the League."

8.10.14. Sentence 9n-10p

Fwu sheu Chuu jiang sheu jy, yii jaw ju-hour tzer woo shy wei meng juu. ⟨Prot.⟩ (⟨Prot.⟩ Md β ⟨Apod.⟩ α As $\beta \gamma^1$ Res. In. $\beta \gamma^1$ (A→B)) Apod. ($\alpha \parallel \beta \gamma^1$ ($\beta \gamma^1$ (A→B))). ⟨If we⟩ do *not*/accede/⟨then⟩ Ch'u/will/accede to/it/⟨and⟩ thereby/summon/the Feudatory/⟨and⟩ then/we/lose/acting as/the League/Lords.

Commentary. Note the use of the pregnant or emphatic form of the negative *bu*. Note the use of *wei* "to act as."

8.10.15. Sentence 10q-11c

Jinn-ren sheu jy. α (A→B) $\beta \gamma^1$. Tsin-people/agreed to/it.

8.10.16. Sentence 11d-11i

Ru Chuu, Chuu yih sheu jy. $\beta \gamma^2$, α Conj. $\beta \gamma^1$. Went to/Chu/Chu/too/agreed to/it.

8.10.17. Sentence 11j-11q

Ru Chyi Chyi-ren nann jy. $\beta \gamma^2$, α (A→B) $\beta \gamma^1$. Went to/Ch'i/Ch'i-people/raised objections to/it.

Commentary. *Nan* "difficult" is here used putatively "to impute difficulty to" thus "to raise objections to," and modernly read *nann.*

8.10.18. Sentence 12a-12m

Chern Wen-tzyy iue "Jinn Chuu sheu jy, woo ian der yii." α (A→B (A→B)) (β) "α (A+B) $\beta \gamma^1$, $\alpha \,||\, \square$ As β." Ch'en/Wen-tzu/(said)/⟨since both⟩ Tsin/⟨and⟩ Ch'u/have agreed to/it/we/what time/successfully/complete/(stress).

Commentary. For the idiom *der yii* see 3.3.2.6 footnote 20.

8.10.19. Sentence 12n-13m

Chiee ren iue mii bing erl woo fwu sheu tzer guh shi wu min yii. Conj. ⟨Prot.⟩ α (β) "$\beta \gamma$," Conj. $\alpha \,||\,$ Md β, Apod. Md $\beta \gamma^1$ (A→B) St. Moreover/⟨if⟩ others/are saying/abolish/war/(subordination)/⟨while⟩/we/do *not*/agree to/⟨do so⟩ then/⟨we⟩ in fact/⟨will have to⟩ drag/our/people ⟨to the battlefield⟩ (stress).

Commentary. Note the stress particle *yii* imposing penultimate stress "*drag* our people" (see 3.12).

8.10.20. Sentence 13n-14j

Jiang ian-yonq jy. As $\square$ $\beta \gamma^1$. Might/where/use/them.

Commentary. *Ian-yonq* and *an-yonq* "where use?" > "nowhere use," occur commonly in rhetorical sense for "useless!"

8.10.21. Sentence 14b-14e

Chyi-ren sheu jy. α (A→B) $\beta \gamma^1$. Ch'i/agreed to/it.

8.10.22. Sentence 14f-14m

Gaw yu Chyn, Chyn yih sheu jy. β Dir. γ^2 α Conj. $\beta \gamma$. ⟨It⟩ was announced/⟨to⟩/Ch'in/Ch'in/too/agreed to/it.

Commentary. Notice that *gaw* in previous contexts has been used transitively "to announce to." Here the affectee is shifted to the second post-verbal position, becoming causative, "caused to be announced to." The agent (Shianq Shiu) himself informed Chao Meng (sentence 8.10.9) and went personally to Ch'u and Ch'i but "had it announced to Ch'in."

8.10.23. Sentence 14f-15f

Jie gaw yu sheau gwo wei huey yu Sonq. ⟨α⟩ Dist. β Dir. γ² (A→B), Md β Dir. γ². Each State/⟨Tsin, Chu, Ch'i and Ch'in⟩/had it announced to/⟨their⟩ satellite/States/⟨that they⟩ would/convene a meeting/in/Sung.

Commentary. Note that the agential distributive *jie* refers to all four of the states consulted, though no agent is mentioned. *Wei* makes *huey* "to meet" subjunctive "would convene a meeting" (see 3.3.1.3).

8.11. "The Politician's Reward" (*Tso Chuan*)

	12	11	10	9	8	7	6	5	4	3	2	1
a	師	討	誣	昏	文	能	亡	也	而	楚	六	宋
b	辭	而	乎	明	德	去	也	無	後	所	十	左
c	邑	又	以	之	也	兵	天	威	能	以	以	師
d		求	誣	術	聖	兵	生	則	安	兵	示	請
e		賞	道	皆	人	之	五	驕	靖	威	子	賞
f		無	蔽	兵	以	設	材	驕	其	之	罕	曰
g		厭	諸	之	與	久	民	則	國	畏	子	請
h		之	侯	由	人	矣	並	亂	家	而	罕	免
i		甚	罪	也	以	所	用	生	以	後	曰	死
j		也	莫	而	廢	以	之	亂	事	上	凡	之
k		削	大	子	廢	威	廢	生	大	下	諸	邑
m		而	焉	求	與	不	一	必	國	慈	侯	公
n		投	縱	之	存	軌	不	滅	所	和	小	與
p		之	無	不	亡	而	可	所	以		慈	之
q		左	大	亦		昭	誰	以	存		和	邑

Free Translation

Shiang Hsu, the Master of the Left in Sung, (having brought to fruition [see previous passage] his scheme to abolish the resort to arms) asked his Duke for a reward. He requested some cities to be held in fief which were to be the "Cities of Death Averted." The Duke granted him a fief of sixty cities. He showed the patent of his fief to Tzu-han. Tzu-han, on reading it, observed "Tsin and Ch'u, the two greatest powers, intimidate the lesser powers by the force of their arms, and they do this because, being intimidated, the lesser powers are compliant, and they, the major powers, can then be beneficent. With compliance on the one hand, and beneficence on the other, both major and minor states can live in peace and amity. It is by such compliance that we in Sung survive. If we were not afraid of the major powers we would become arrogant, and with arrogance there would come disorder, and with disorder we would be heavily suppressed. In such suppression, we as a minor power would perish. The five basic materials* are sent to us by Providence. The common people use each equally. To deprive them of one of them would be quite wrong. Will anyone deprive them of arms? Arms are a commodity of establishing standing. They are the means of terrorizing the lawless, and shedding lustre upon the virtues of civilization. Wise men are thereby assured of ascendency, and evil men cast down. Weapons originated precisely in order to provide the means of casting down evil, of promoting the good, of preserving the orderly state, and of destroying the disorderly state. They provide for the separation of confusion from enlightenment. That is why arms exist. Yet, you Sir, have deigned to propose their abolition. This is heterodoxy! There is no crime greater than that of misleading the feudal powers with pernicious doctrine. And not only have you not been severely punished for this, but you seek to be rewarded for it! Nothing could be more grave!" Taking the patent he scratched out the writing upon it, and threw it away. The Master of the Left politely declined the grant of the cities. (*Tso* 318.9–15.)

8.11.1. Sentence 1a-1k

Sonq tzuoo-shy chiing shaang iue "Chiing mean syy jy yih." α (A→B (A→B)) β γ, (β), β γ¹ (A(β γ)→B). Sung/Master of the Left/⟨in⟩ requesting/to be rewarded/(said) ⟨I⟩ request/averting/death/(determination)/cities.

Commentary. Mean syy from *mean* "to avoid" (intransitive, see sentence 8.8.14) here used transitively > causative, thus, "to avert." "Avert-death cities"—cities given as a reward for advocating abolishing warfare, and therefore of "averting death." *Mean syy* A (β γ) as a determinant > A in (A→B), that is, it is nominal.

*That is, wood, metal, water, fire, and earth.

214   LATE ARCHAIC CHINESE

8.11.2. Sentence 1m-2b

Gong yeu jy yih liow-shyr. α β γ¹ γ² (A→B(A→B)). Duke/granted/him/sixty/cities.

Commentary. Note the determination of number here (see 2.6.4.4). For *yeu* see 3.4.7 paragraph 1.

8.11.3. Sentence 2c-2i

Yii shyh Tzyy-haan, Tzyy-haan iue. Res. In. β γ² (A→B), α (A→B) (β). As a result/⟨he⟩ showed/⟨the grant⟩ to Tzu Han/Tzu Han/said.

Commentary. The resultative instrument *yii* refers back to the grant made to him by the Duke. From sentence 8.11.20 it is clear that he showed Tzu Han the title to his grant.

8.11.4. Sentence 2j-3f

Farn ju-hour sheau gwo Jinn Chuu suoo-yii bing uei jy. γ¹ (A→B (A(A→B)→B(A→B)))|| α (A+B) Res. Ins. □ [Ins.] β γ¹. All/Feudal Lord/minor/states/Tsin/⟨and⟩ Ch'u/that by which/by arms/makes-fear/them.

Commentary. The affectee of the verb *uei* "put fear into" is exposed and replaced by *jy*. The exposed element has the determinant collective *farn* (see 2.6.4.5) and *ju-hour* is determining *sheau gwo*. The indefinite substitute *suoo yii* is in the instrumental resultative position "that by virtue of which," that is, "the reason why." The sentence then is incomplete (see next sentence).

8.11.5. Sentence 3g-3n

Wey erl-how shanq shiah tsyr her. [β erl-how] α (A/B) β (β/β). ⟨Is because⟩ being intimidated/(subordination)/the major powers/the minor powers/practise paternalism/practise compliance.

Commentary. Shanq shiah tsyr her (α (A/B) β (β/β)) is an example of chiambus, the first and second agent determining the first and second verb respectively. Thus "the major powers practise paternalism, the minor powers practise compliance."

8.11.6. Sentence 3p-4h

Tsyr her erl-how neng an-jinq chyi gwo-jia. [β (β/β) erl-how] SA β (A=A) γ¹ (A→B(A+B)). ⟨And⟩ practising paternalism/⟨and⟩ compliance/⟨major and minor rulers⟩ can/pacify/their/states.

Commentary. Both *an* and *jinq* mean "calm, placid," and "to make calm, to pacify." *An-jinq* is an example of hendiadys *metri causa*. *Gwo-jia* "states and estates" is a specialized term meaning simply "states." A *gwo* is a city held in fief. *Jia* are family estates held in fief (see sentence 8.3.9 ff.) but *jia* in this context becomes virtually devoid of meaning, while *gwo* "city," with the growth of feudalism, had become "a state."

8.11.7. Sentence 4h-5a

Yii shyh dah gwo suoo-yii tswen yee. DT ([Md β γ^1 (A→B)] Dt (In. □ β) St. By/serving/great/states/⟨is⟩ the means by which/⟨we⟩ survive/(stress) (i.e., we survive by serving great states).

Commentary. A verbal sentence recast as a determinative sentence. As a verbal sentence "serve" (β) "great states" (γ^1) thereby (Res. Ins.) "survive" (β). Recast it becomes "by (Ins.) serving (β) great states (γ^1) (that is the) that by which (Ins. □) survive β," that is, "service to great states is the means of survival." (See 6.7.3.)

8.11.8. Sentence 5b-5n

Wu uei tzer jiau, jiau tzer luann sheng, luann sheng bih mieh. ⟨Prot.⟩ Md β Apod. β, ⟨Prot.⟩ β Apod. α β, ⟨Prot.⟩, α β ⟨Apod.⟩ β (β→β). (If) were not/intimidated/then/would be arrogant/⟨if⟩ arrogant/then/ disorder/would be engendered/⟨if⟩ disorder/is engendered/⟨then we⟩ inevitably would be/wiped out.

Commentary. A series of conditioned sequences (unfulfilled). Note the use of the modal *wu* (see 3.3.1.3).

8.11.9. Sentence 5p-6b

Suoo-yii wang yee. ⟨DT⟩ Dt (Ins. □ β) St. ⟨That is⟩ the reason why/ ⟨we⟩ perish/(stress).

Commentary. The determined term is the topic of the preceding sentence.

8.11.10. Sentence 6c-6p

Tian sheng wuu tsair. Min binq yong jy. Fey i buh kee. α β γ^1 (A→B), α As β γ^1, DT ($\beta\gamma$) Dt (Md β). Heaven/begat/the Five/⟨basic⟩ Materials/, the common people/each and every one equally/use/them,/ set aside/one/⟨is⟩ not/permissible.

Commentary. Fey i buh kee is a recasting of a verbal sentence as a determinative sentence. *Buh kee fey i* "[one] cannot neglect one," *fey i buh kee* "to neglect one, is a cannot do [thing]."

8.11.11. Sentence 6q-7c

Shwei neng chiuh bing. α □ SA β γ¹. Who/can/do away with/arms.

Commentary. For *shwei*, interrogative substitute, see 6.5.2.3. *Chiuh* "to go out" is thus transitive and causative (by providing affectee) "to cause to go out, expel, banish, do away with."

8.11.12. Sentence 7d-7h

Bing jy sheh jeou yii. DT (A→B) Dt ( ) St. Arms/(determination)/establish/⟨is⟩/of long-standing/(stress).

Commentary. For this type of determinative sentence see 4.3 (type 4).

8.11.13. Sentence 7i-8c

Suoo-yii uei buh-goei erl jau wen der yee. Dt (Res. Ins. □ [β γ¹ (A→B) erl] β γ¹ (A→B)) St. ⟨Arms are⟩ those things whereby/⟨while⟩ terrorizing/the lawless/(subordinate)⟨we⟩/illuminate/the virtue/of culture/(stress).

Commentary. The determined term, though omitted, is inferred from previous context. The verbs of the subordinate clause and of the main sentence are concomitant action "while terrorizing . . . illuminate. . . ." *Jau* "bright, shining" used transitively > causative "to make shine," "to illuminate." *Buh-goei* from *goei* "a cart track, a rut, an accustomed path, the right and proper path, a guide, criterion, precept, law," and with privative *bu* *buh-goei* "lawless."

8.11.14. Sentence 8d-8k

Shenq-ren yii shing, luann-ren yii fey. α (A→B) Res. Ins. β, α (A→B) Res. Ins. β. Sages/thereby/made to flourish/disorderly men/thereby/are set aside.

Commentary. The agent here is the agent of realization.

8.11.15. Sentence 8m-9i

Fey shing tswen wang huen ming jy shuh jie bing jy you yee. DT (A (A/B)+(A/B)+(A/B)→B) Dist. Dt (A→B) St. ⟨The art of⟩/setting aside ⟨the bad⟩/⟨or⟩ promoting ⟨the good⟩/of preserving ⟨the orderly⟩/⟨or⟩ destroying ⟨the disorderly⟩/of obscuring ⟨the lawless⟩/⟨or⟩ highlighting ⟨the virtuous⟩/all these arts/⟨are⟩ arms/(determination)/ *raison d'être*/(stress).

Commentary. You is both "origin" and "cause" and thus *raison d'être*. Note the use of *jie* (agential distributive) as distributive for the determined term (see 4.12).

8.11.16. Sentence 9j-10b

Erl Tzyy chyou jy. Bwu yih u hu. Conj. $\alpha \beta \gamma^1$, ⟨DT⟩ Dt (Md. Conj. β) Md. ⟨That being so⟩/you Sir/sought/this (i.e., the abolition of arms)/⟨is this⟩ not/after all/perverse.

Commentary. Erl here used conjunctively shows the subordination of the previous sentence (see 3.7.2). The determined term is omitted, as is often the case when the entire previous context constitutes its subject matter.

8.11.17. Sentence 10c-10m

Yii u daw bih ju-hour tzuey moh dah yan. γ^2 ([Ing A(A→B)] $\beta \gamma^1$ (A→B) || α Dist. $\beta\gamma^2$). With/pernicious/teaching/deceive/Feudatories/, ⟨of⟩ crimes/none/greater/than-that.

Commentary. The elements of the second post-verbal position are exposed, and replaced by the anaphoric *yan*. The agent has the agential distributive *moh* (see 3.5.3.1) *dah* "to be great," but "to be greater," with the object of comparison in γ^2 (see 3.4.6). *Bih* "a screen" is here "to draw a screen around, to hide something from, to mislead, deceive."

8.11.18. Sentence 10n-11e

Tzonq wu dah tao erl yow chyou shaang. [Conc. Md β (A→B) erl] Conc. $\beta \gamma^1$. Even though/⟨you⟩ were not/heavily/punished/(subordinate)/even so/seek/reward.

8.11.19. Sentence 11f-11j

Wu yann jy shenn yee. DT ( ) Dt (A→B) St. There is not/of grave matters/the more so.

Commentary. Yann "grave, serious" is, as a determined term, substantival, that is, "grave matters." *Shenn* "very, extreme" is one of the ways of forming degrees of comparison (see 7.1).

To bring out the full force of the text one would have to paraphrase "despite the fact that you were not punished, and that you have exacerbated your guilt by asking for a reward—your crime is very grave."

8.11.20. Sentence 11k-11p

Shiau erl tour jy. [β erl] β γ¹. Scraping/(subordinate)/threw away/it.

Commentary. What *Shiang Shiu* showed to *Tzu Han*, was a bamboo slip on which the patent for his grant of cities was written (see sentence 8.11.3). After delivering a homily on the evils of abolishing war, Tzu Han took the bamboo slip, scraped off (*shiau*) the writing thereon with a knife, and threw the bamboo slip to the floor.

8.11.21. Sentence 11q-12c

Tzuoo-shy tsyr yih. α (A→B) β γ¹. The Master of the Left/politely declined/the Cities.

APPENDIXES

Appendix 1

ORTHOGRAPHY

Although Chinese and its cognate languages have been written in a number of writing systems, the system native to China, which was used exclusively in the Late Archaic Period, is of especial importance from a linguistic point of view, since it is a source of linguistic evidence of a peculiar kind.

It is a very complicated system and an adequate description of it would range far beyond the useful purposes of this work.[1] But since its evidential value has been utilized in arriving at grammatical solutions, some description of the script is essential, if such solutions are to be understood properly.

(a) Phonological-morphemic Basis of the Script

Essentially, the system seeks to provide a unique sign for each lexic. Each sign gives both morphological and phonological indications about the lexic it represents. What those indications are depends, in each case, on the history of the formation of the given sign. This is further complicated by the fact that the period of orthographic formation extends from an unknown date prior to the sixteenth century B.C. until the Late Archaic Period.[2]

The phonological indications are, unfortunately, from the linguist's point of view, not those which a writing system based on spelling provides. It is the phonology of the lexic as a whole which is symbolized, and not that of its segmental phonemes. The sign reveals to what homophonous group a lexic belongs (or quasi-homophonous, for the authors of orthographic formation were not scientific phoneticians) without indicating the values of its segmental phonemes.

---

[1] A scholarly and modern treatment is that of Tarng Lan, *Jong-gwo Wen-tzyh Shyue* (Shanghai, 1949).

[2] New formations do not stop, of course, with the Late Archaic Period. New signs are currently being created in China for new lexics. But the main period of formation came to its close especially after political action taken in the First Emperor's time and in the Han Dynasty to standardize the script (*jeng wen* (正文) that is, to use one form exclusively for one lexic). Neologisms thenceforward were created principally by morphological derivation, which did not require the creation of new written forms.

The system is not even like a syllabary since all homophonous units are not comprised (in their phonological indication) under one sign. A further complication is that, although the phonological value of the lexic may evolve and change, its written sign remains constant and unchanged. Its homophonous *congéres* therefore, are those lexics with which it was homophonous at the time of orthographic formation. The script gives no indications of later divergences subsequent to the time of formation. Its morphological indications again, depend on the process of formation used in the creation of any given sign. If the sign attempts directly to symbolize its meaning, we have indications of one kind, but if its sign symbolizes it only indirectly, we have indications of another and different kind.

(b) Processes of Formation

No examples of the script survive from the earliest period of formation. There is, however, reason to believe that the earliest signs were directly pictured representations of the lexic for which they substitute in writing. Such signs depict some aspect of the meaning of the lexic they represent, for example, the signs for "horse," "elephant," "deer," "pig," and "tiger" are linear or solid pictures of those animals.[1] From thence it may be supposed abstractions were evolved whereby, for instance, a picture of a human form with long hair becomes the sign for the lexic *lao* (老) "old age"; a human form with a large head *tzyy* (子) "child"; a human form with the abdomen exaggerated, *shen* (身) "pregnant," "body," "self," and so forth. A number of further stages stemming from these two processes are recognizable, for example, the compounding of elements, whereby a human form with a spear becomes *fa* (伐) "to attack," a child (left) in a basket, *chih* (棄) "to desert," a human figure holding a bow and arrow *sheh* (射) "archery, to shoot," two hands holding a ritual vessel over a fire *juh* (鑄) "casting, to cast," or the duplication of elements, whereby three "stars" (叒) represent "the constellation Orion," "grass" doubled (竹) *tsao* "grass," and tripled *huey* (卉) "plants, herbs," two trees for *lin* (林) "forest," three trees for *sen* (森) "dense forest."

Such signs are symbols for morphemes. The script preserves some thousand or more of them. Because the morpheme is coextensive with the phonological unit, it was possible to use a number of morphemic signs as phonetic signs, using them to symbolize only the sound of the lexic. The sign then represented, not one lexic, but the phonetic value of a group of homophonous lexics.

The phoneticized sign was used commonly for a group of homo-

---

[1] See *Grammata Serica* sub *Maa* (K.40), *Shiang* (K.728), *Luh* (K.1209), *Shyy* (K. 1238 f and i), *hu* (K. 57).

phones. Individual lexics in a homophonous group were then differentiated by the addition of a morphemic sign. Thus, a unique sign was evolved for each lexic in a homophonous group. Already in the sixteenth century B.C. this process was in use. By the eleventh century B.C. it was the principal process of orthographic formation.

EXAMPLES

The modern sign 羊 is a conventionalization of a picture of a ram's head. It is the sign for *ziang (yang) "sheep." The sign divorced from its parent lexic then becomes the phonological value *ziang, (yang)—a value shared in common by a number of lexics. Among them are lexics meaning "name of a river," "name of a tribe," "name of an insect," "an auspicious omen," and "happiness." The written form of these lexics then becomes 羊 indicating the phonetic value *ziang, (yang) with the morphemic character of the new sign restored by compounding with it (氵) "running water"—thus *ziang 洋 "name of a river" and thence by extension, "ocean"; with "woman," thus *ziang 姜 "name of a tribe" (a reflection of the matriarchal system in vogue at the time of orthographic formation); with 虫 "insect" and thus *ziang 蛘 "name of an insect"; with 示 "a sign in divination" and thus *ziang 祥 "an auspicious omen"; and with 忄 "the heart, the emotions," and thus 恙 "happiness, felicity."

A parallel development with the above was the grouping of synonyms under a common morphemic element and differentiating that element with a phoneticized sign, for example, li (黧) "black"; hei (黑) "black"; chyan (黔) "black." The conventions became so fixed and the period of formation extended over so long a period of time, that often the origins of signs were forgotten, so that, for instance, (樂) leh, which, as a sign, is a picture of an oak with acorns, became the sign for "ritual dancing and music" (rites at one time associated with oaks?) later broadening into "pleasure," but the origins of the graph were forgotten, for the lexic for "oak tree" was later rediffertentiated with (木) "tree," to become lih (櫟) "an oak tree." Similarly, the graph for "scorpion" was originally 禸, but 萬 becoming phoneticized, and used for wann "ten thousand," the lexic for scorpion was later rediffertentiated by the addition of "insect" as 蠆. The graph for "silkworm" was a picture of a silkworm producing a silk thread from its mouth thus 弓. Later it was differentiated with 虫 "insect" thus 蜀 and then rediffertentiated with a further 虫 to become 蠋 "silkworm."

(c) Graphic Variants

In principal, therefore, the Chinese script provides a unique sign for each lexic, a sign which at once provides phonological and morphemic indications. But a system of formation so complex, and a period of formation so extended gave rise to a number of aberrations from this principle.

In the script as used in LAC (and indeed as it has survived to this day) there are variant forms of the sign for a single lexic which might properly be called purely orthographic variants—relics from a period of freer formation, and of local differences—which survived political attempts at standardization. Certain of these are only partial variants, for example, 欣 (in *Tso*); 忺 (in *Micius*); 訢 (in *Mencius*). Here the variation is one of the differencing sign, a notoriously infirm element. Others are material differences, for instance, *dier* "to tarry" has both (遲) and (遅), *sier* "to roost" has both (栖) and (棲), *dier* "to sow late" has both (稚) and (穉).

(d) Morphological Variants

But there are other variants, which are morphological in character. During the period of orthographic formation lexics developed extensions and intensions of meaning, and when such developments reached a point where one meaning was sufficiently specialized, the specialization might gain recognition as a separate lexic. Such specializations occur very early in the language, but they proliferated in the Late Archaic Period. The derived lexic (when recognition was accorded it) began life anew as a separate lexic. Such recognition might be marked either with some phonological change (revealed in the modern phonology by differences of tone, of segmental phonemes, or both), or with simply a graphic change, with no phonological change, or with both.

EXAMPLES

(巨) *jiuh* is "a carpenter's square," and the sign depicts the square. "Troops drawn up in a square formation" becomes specialized as (拒) *jiuh* and thence develops the meaning "to defend," "to ward off." (正) *jenq* is "correct, to correct," but when used in the military vocabulary of LAC for "a campaign of correction" (a punitive expedition) it is differentiated as (征) *jeng*. (正) became a tabu word in the First Emperor's time, and (征) was substituted for it so that even after the separation, we may suppose both lexics had the same phonological value. Later they developed tonic differences. (糴) is "grain" (ap. *Shuo-wen*), but with the differentiating signs (入) *ru* "enter" and *chuh* "go out" (出), "grain" becomes (糴) **diok/dyi* "to buy grain" and (糶) **tiog/tiaw* "to sell grain." Here *diok and *tiog are differentiated both graphically and phonologically—although the orthography reveals that both are bifurcations from a common parent form.

(e) Lexic and Semanteme

In the above examples, the affinities of cognate lexics are clearly revealed by the orthographic formation of their written signs. This is not always the case, as, for example, in the following:

*tieng (正)	straight	correct	regulate (keep straight)	just
*dieng (亭)			regulate	precisely
*tieng (征)			regulate	
*tieng (政)			regulate, govern	
*dieng (窺)	look straight		govern	
*tieng (鼎)				just, precisely
*tieng (貞)	straight	correct proper		
*tieng (廷)			palace, courtyard	
*tieng (庭)	straight		palace, courtyard	
*dieng (挺)	straight			

In this series, even allowing for orthographic variants, and for the loan use of the sign of one lexic for a homophonous lexic, there is a recognizable phonological and semantic affinity. Meaning here ranges from the physical property of "straightness," to its metaphorical use, "straight, upright, correct," and from "to make straight, to straighten, to rectify, to put in proper order, to govern," and grammaticized, "precisely, exactly, just," etc. The matrix of such a series might be called the semanteme. Each instance of derivation from the semanteme is, however, peculiar to itself. There is no discoverable *regular* process of derivation by which, for instance, on the basis of one derivative a series of comparable derivatives can be projected from other semantemes. No constant semantic values have as yet been correlated with phonological mutations. The processes are idiosyncratic. They are not predictable. A meaning once specialized from a common stock may go unmarked but it also may acquire sufficient recognition as a "specialization of sense" that a new written form is given it, or a change in phonology marks it. But these changes (orthographic or phonological) are not made by common processes, so that, for example, derivatives with a common class-meaning are not marked with common phonological changes, or common orthographic changes. Each instance is peculiar to itself. Derivation from the semanteme has to do with specialization of sense and not with restriction of usage, so that the derivative is no more restricted in usage or invested with special grammatical quality, than is the parent semanteme.

NOTE. The word "semanteme" as used here differs from the use of the term, for example, in speaking of French (e.g., *don* the "meaning core" of *donner, donation, donatur*) in that in French formal and regular change produces a regular process of derivation.

Lexics may therefore derive from a semanteme, but all lexics are not so derived. The undifferentiated lexic may itself preserve all its intensions and extensions of meaning. There are, therefore, two processes of word derivation (i) the process by which new words are derived from a semanteme, and (ii) the process by which compound words derive from the single lexic. The grammarian is concerned only with (ii), since all derivatives of (i) appear in the material as lexics. Their prior history is a matter of etymology and not of grammar.

While the movement to standardize the script cannot be said to have arrested the process of creating new lexics by specializations of meaning from the semanteme, it did come at a time when the process was nearing the end of its development. Thenceforward, compounding became not only the common means for creating neologisms, but also the compound word largely usurped the role of the single lexic in common usage.

(f) Orthography and Linguistic Evidence

As a source of linguistic evidence, the Chinese script is unique. It permits a classification of homonyms or near homonyms so that a great deal is known about the phonological affinities of lexics although the precise value of their segmental phonemes may not be known. It provides valuable etymological evidence, preserving evidence of affinities among lexics which might otherwise have been irrecoverable or become a matter of conjecture. This is not only of value in lexicography, but is also of particular importance in a study of the "grammaticized" lexics, which, through phonetic attrition, might well have become unrecognizable as stemming from a fully meaningful parent form.

Although it remains true in principle that each lexic has a unique sign, some provision must be made for graphic varieties and for specializations of meaning within the lexic, whereby certain lexics which once enjoyed a wide range of meaning reference were subsequently narrowed by custom and usage, and then specialized as derivative lexics.

Appendix II

PHONOLOGICAL AFFINITIES AMONG CENEMATIC LEXICS

Phonological affinities, perhaps "word families," among groups of grammaticized lexics, are suggested by the following:

	Gutteral initials	Supradental initial	Labial initial
Pronouns	我 *ngâ 吾 *ngo	汝 *ńio 若 *ńiak 爾 *ńiar 而 *ńiəg 乃 *nəg	
Demonstratives		此 *ts'iar 是 *dieg 斯 *sieg 之 *tiəg (cf. 邇 *ńiar "near")	彼 *pia 匪 *piwər
Anaphora	其 *kiəg	之 *tiəg	
Copulae		是 *dieg	非 *piwər
Particle of acc.			夫 *piwo

With 而 *ńiəg "whiskers" cf. 髭 *tsiar "whiskers."

NOTE. The reconstructed phonetic values are those of Karlgren. For a comparison of Karlgren's reconstruction of the pronouns and that of Tung T'ung-ho see Bodman (1), p. 342 and his remarks thereon.

In the supradental initial series, the phonemes *d-, *s-, *t-, distinguished by Karlgren, may in fact be phones of a common phoneme articulated supradentally with grading (i.e., with voicing and fricative as infirm elements). Among the pronouns, the first person distinguishes pregnant and determinant forms by vowel change. Might not the whole pronominal series be accounted for by vowel grading? Might not there be also some supra-segmental phonemic factor such as length or force of utterance, to account for the difference between pregnant and determinant forms? That some such factor is present is attested by early sources. The *Shuo Wen* (first century A.D.) sub *nae* (乃) says 乃曳詞之難 "*nae* is the stressed form of the 'trailing particle.'" The "trailing particle" is *erl* (i.e., "trailing" after the subordinate clause). The distinction between *nae* and *erl* is explained in *Gong Yang* 公羊傳注 as 言乃者內而深言而者外而淺 "in reading *nae* the reading being 'internal' [i.e., intrinsic to the metre] it is deep [ly articulated], in reading *erl* the reading is 'external' [i.e., extrinsic to the metre] and is shallow [ly articulated]." *Nae* is thus a stressed form, and included in the reckoning of metre, *erl* is an unstressed form and is elided in the reckoning of metre.

A series is suggested by the negatives:[4]

Labial plosives	Labials with nasalization
不 *pwət	
	無 *miwo
	未 *miwəd
	勿 *miwət
弗 *piwət	毋 *miwo
非 *piwər	
否 *piug	
	莫 *mâk

NOTE. *miwo (無) and *miwo (毋) distinguish contrastive moods, and the distinction can hardly be merely one of orthography. Some extra segmental phonemic factor must be present to distinguish them although the script affords no evidence of what it might be. Again, is the difference between the stressed and unstressed forms of the modal negatives really, as Karlgren suggests, *piwət and *pwət; *miwət and *miwo; and *piwər and *piug, or is it not in fact attributable to vowel grade and length and force of utterance?

[4]See Gau p. 539 who points to phonological similarities between the Chinese negatives and those of Tibetan and Tai.

Appendix III

THE SECOND PERSON PRONOUNS *RUU* (女汝), *RUOH* (若), AND *EEL* (爾), *ERL* (而), *NAE* (乃)

A great deal has been written about the two forms of the personal pronouns in LAC. The following three theories predominate. (1) The difference in form is not material and can be accounted for by differences of periodical or regional orthographic conventions. (2) The difference is material and represents the vestigial remains of a case system. The determinant form (of my own description) is thought to be a nominative and genitive and the pregnant form (of my description) the accusative. (3) The difference is material and represents a phonetic alternance depending upon whether the pronoun is in a determining position or otherwise.

My own analysis of LAC material confirms the correctness of the third view. A possible explanation for this would be that under the influence of the force of utterance (strong for the pregnant form and weaker for the determinant form), and the relative openness or closeness of juncture, vowel grading has taken place and has resulted in a specialization of sense from a common semanteme (i.e., the undifferentiated pronoun of Early Archaic Chinese).

In most of the literature it seems to be accepted that the second person, *ruu, ruoh* is the determinant (or nominative and genitive) form, and *erl, eel, nae* the pregnant (or accusative) form. Though it has been observed that in *Chuang tzu* the roles are "reversed," my own findings show that *ruu, ruoh* are the pregnant forms and *eel, erl, nae* are the determinant forms consistently in LAC. For example, in *Tso Chuan*, a text in which there is a sufficient number of occurrences to make statistical treatment useful, I find the following:

	Syntactical distribution	汝	爾	而	乃
	Agent/verb/*affectee*	32	—	?1	—
	In syntagma A 與 B	4			
Pregnant Form Usages	以 □ 爲 ...	1			
	□ 何故 ...	5			
	□ 爲 B (delegated agency)	24			
	In determinative sentence as determined term □ B 也	4	2		
Determinant Form Usages	In syntagma □ → B	1	18	35	10
	A 所 β 也		3		
	As agent		14	21	13

As the affectee of a verb, the figures for *ruu* are decisive. In syntagma as the determinant term, the figures for *erl, eel, nae* are decisive. The admixture lies in the use of the pronoun in the agential position. This is fully accountable in my view, by the exposure or non-exposure of the agent. Where the agent is exposed the pregnant form is used; where the agent is not exposed the determinant form is used. The exposure of the agent where it follows the normal syntactical rule, that is, by resumption with an anaphoric pronoun, invariably uses the pregnant form. (E.g., *ruu chyi shyng hu?* 汝其行乎 /You!/that person/go/?/"had you not better go" (*Tso* 123.3).) I take it that other occurrences of the pregnant form in the agent are similarly exposed. It is observable that, in most contexts, the use of *ruu* in the agent occurs when superiors are talking to inferiors or the subject matter is one of scolding, or admonition. An exposed pronoun might then be a type of vocative You! That there is an element of status in the usage of the second person pronoun is attested by *Mencius*. *Ren neng chong wu show eel ruu jy shyh, wu suoo woang erl buh wei yih yee* (人能充無受爾汝之實無所往而不為義也) "If a man can fully exploit his reluctance to give and receive the niceties of the salutation *ruu* and *eel*, then wherever he goes he will act justly" (*Mencius* 7b.31.3). The question is settled definitively, in my view, by the sentences in which the two pronouns occur simultaneously in a single piece, and are contrastive in usage.

EXAMPLES

Bwu gaw ruu, iong wei jyr hu jiang yii sha eel fuh (不告女庸為直乎將以殺爾父) "If I did not tell *you*, how could I be honest? I am going to kill *your* father" (*Tso* 493.17).

Eel wu yeu yan, yeu, jiang jyr ruu (爾無與焉與將執女) "*You* may not take part in it [i.e., the meeting], if you do, then I will arrest *you*" (*Tso* 278.7).

Shanq-dih lin ruu, wu ell eel shin (上帝臨女無貳爾心) "God looks down with favour upon *you*, do not let doubts arise in *your* mind" (*Tso* 302.10).

Ruu jeau jiun wey erl tzuey san yee (女矯君位而罪三也) "*You* arrogated [to yourself] the rights of the Throne, this is the third of *your* offences" (*Tso* 347.7).

Ruu tzer chih jy, suh jyi eel shyng (女則棄之速即爾刑) "It is *you* [rather than me] who have abandoned it [i.e., good faith] [may you] go quickly to *your* punishment!" (*Tso* 203.13).

Yu buh ruu reen sha, yow ruu yii yeuan, mean suh shyng hu, wu chorng erl tzuey (余不女忍殺宥女以遠勉速行乎無重而罪) "I cannot bear to kill *you*, I will treat *you* leniently by exiling you, exert yourself and depart quickly, and do not repeat *your* offence" (*Tso* 342.7).

LIST OF WORKS MENTIONED

Abbreviations

AL	Acta Linguistica (Copenhagen)
AM	Asia Major (New Series) (London)
AO	Archiv Orientální. (Prague)
AS	Bulletin of the Institute of History and Philology (Academia Sinica) (Peiping and Taiwan)
BMFEA	Bulletin of the Museum of Far Eastern Antiquities (Stockholm)
BSOAS	Bulletin of the School of Oriental and African Studies (London)
DLTJ	Dah-luh Tzar-jyh (大陸雜誌) (Taiwan)
GHÅ	Göteborgs Högskolas Årsskrift (Göteborg)
HH	Han Hiue (Peking)
HJAS	Harvard Journal of Asiatic Studies (Cambridge)
JAOS	Journal of the American Oriental Society (Baltimore)
Lang.	Language. Journal of the Linguistic Society of America (Baltimore)
MS	Monumenta Serica (Peking)
SSJK	Shyue-shuh Jih-kan (學術季刊) (Taiwan)
TP	T'oung Pao (Leiden)
TPS	Transactions of the Philological Society (London)
YWSS	Yeu-wen Shyue-shyi (語文學習) (Peking)
WT	Wennti (New Haven)

Allen, W. S. Relationship in Comparative Linguistics, TPS (1953), 52–108.

Bacot, Jacques, *Grammaire du Tibetain Litteraire* (Paris, 1946).

Bloch, Bernhard and G. L. Trager, *Outlines of Linguistic Analysis* (Baltimore, 1942).

Bodman, N. (1), Review *The Chinese Language* (Karlgren), Lang. 26 (1950), 339–45.

——— (2), The Function of 厥 in the Shang Shu, JAOS 68 (1948), 52–60.

Chao, Yuen Ren, and Lien Sheng Yang (1), *Concise Dictionary of Spoken Chinese* (Cambridge, 1947). (Referred to in text as Chao (1).)

Chao, Yuen Ren (2), *Mandarin Primer*, 2 vols. (Cambridge, 1948). (Referred to in text as Chao (2).)

Demiéville, Paul (1), *Le Chinois* (Paris, 1948).

―― (2), Archaïsmes de Prononciation en Chinois Vulgaire, TP40. (1952), 1-59.

Ding Sheng-shuh (丁聲樹) (1), Shyh foou-dinq tsyr "fwu" "bu", (釋否定詞弗不) A.S. (Suppl.) (1935), 967-96.

―― (2), Luenn Shy-jing jong de Her, Her, Hwu, 論詩經中的何曷胡 A.S.10 (1948), 349-70.

Emeneau, M. B., *Studies in Vietnamese (Annamese) Grammar* (Berkeley, 1951).

Firth, J. R. (1), Sounds and Prosodies, TPS (1948), 127-52.

―― (2), Philology in the Philological Society, TPS (1956), 1-25.

―― (3), General Linguistics TPS (1951), 69-87.

Fraser, Sir Everard, and Sir James Lockhart, *Index to the Tso Chuan* (Oxford, 1930).

Frei, Henry, Un système Chinois des Aspects, AL II (1941), 137-50.

Gabelentz, G. v.d., *Chinesische Grammatik* (Leipzig, 1881).

Gau Ming-kae (高名凱), *Hann-yeu Yeu-faa Luenn* (漢語語法論) (Shanghai, 1948).

Graham, A. C. (1), A probable fusion word 勿 wuh = 毋 wu + 之 jy, BSOAS 14 (1952), 139-48.

―― (2), The relation between the final particles yu 與 and yee 也, BSOAS 19 (1957), 105-23.

―― (3), The final particle fwu 夫, BSOAS 17 (1955), 120-32.

Halliday, M. A. K. Grammatical Categories in Modern Chinese, TPS (1956), 157-224.

Hjelmslev, L., La Comparaison en Linguistique Structurale, AL IV (1944), 144-7.

Hockett, C. F. (1), Peiping Morphophonemics, Lang. 26 (1950), 63-85.

―― (2), Peiping Phonology, JAOS 67 (1947), 253-67.

Jenq Chyuan-jong (鄭權中), Guu Hann-yeu de Foou-dinq-jiuh shyh (古漢語的否定句式), YWSS 42 (1955), 43.

Jou Faa-gau (周法高) (1), "Jy" "jyue" "chyi" yonq-faa jy yean-biann (之厥其用法之演變), SSJK (1956), 4.4.1–7.

——— (2), Shanq-guu Yeu-faa Jar-jih (上古語法札記), AS 22 (1950), 171–207.

——— (3), *Jong-gwo Yeu-wen Yan-jiou* (中國語文研究) (Taipeh, 1955).

——— (4), Pyng Gao-been-hann "Yuan-shyy jong-gwo yeu wei biann-huah yeu shuo" (評高本漢原始中國語為變化語說), *DLTJ* (Special Issue No. 1) (1952), 241–53.

Karlgren, Bernhard (1), On the Authenticity and Nature of the Tso Chuan, GHÅ XXXII (1926), 3–65.

——— (2), Word Families in Chinese, BMFEA 5 (1933), 9–120.

——— (3), Grammata Serica, BMFEA 12 (1940), 1–472.

——— (4), Excursions in Chinese Grammar, BMFEA 23 (1951), 107.

——— (5), The Pronoun Küe in the Shu King, GHÅ XXXIX (1933), 35.

Kennedy, George A. (1), Word-classes in Classical Chinese, WT 9 (1956), 1–68.

——— (2), A Study of the Particle Yen, JAOS 60 (1940), 1–22.193–207.

——— (3), Another Note on Yen, HJAS 16 (1953), 226–36.

——— (4), Negatives in Classical Chinese, WT.1 (1952), 1–16.

Kin P'eng (金鵬), Etude sur le Jyarung, HH 3 (1949), 271.

Legge, James, *The Chinese Classics*, 5 vols. (Oxford, 1893).

Leu Shwu-shiang (呂叔相) (1), *Hann-yeu yeu-faa Luenn-wen Jyi* (漢語語法論文集) (Peking, 1955).

——— (2), *Tsorng jwu-yeu bin-yeu de fen-bye tarn Gwo-yeu jiuh-tzyy de fen-shi* (從主語賓語的分別談國語句子的分析) in *Kai-ming Shu-diann ell-shyr jou-nian jih-niann wen-jyi* (開明書店二十周年紀念文集) (Shanghai, 1947).

Lo Ch'ang-p'ei, A Preliminary Study of the Trung Language of Kung Shan, HJAS 8 (1945), 343–50.

Maspero, Henri (1), *La Langue Chinoise* (Conférences de l'Institut de Linguistique de l'Université de Paris 1933) (Paris, 1934).

―――― (2), *Les Langues d'extrême-orient*, in *Encyclopédie française* (Paris, 1937).

Martin, Samuel E., The Phonemes of Ancient Chinese, JAOS, Suppl. 16 (1953).

Mathews, R. H., *Chinese-English Dictionary* (Revised American Edition) (Cambridge, 1950).

Miller, Roy Andrew, Another Chinese Interrogative, Lang. 26 (1950), 282–4.

Mullie, Joseph (1), Le Mot-particule 之 tche, TP XXXVI 3–5 (1942), 1–237.

―――― (2), Review *Structural Analysis of Chinese* (Shadick and Wu), HJAS 15 (1952), 213–43.

Mundy, C. S., Turkish Syntax as a System of Qualification, BSOAS 17 (1955), 279–305.

Peir Shyue-hae (裴學海) (1), *Guu-shu Shiu-tzyh Jyi Shyh* (古書虛字集釋) (Shanghai, 1934).

Peir Shyue-hae (裴學海) and Wang Yinn-nong (王蔭濃) (2), Jii-geh wen-yan shiu-tsyr de yonq-faa (幾個文言虛字的用法), YWSS 42 (1955), 45. (Referred to in text as Peir (2).)

Průšek, J., Quelques remarques sur les aspects en Chinois, AO XVIII (1950), 408–30.

Robins, R. H., Formal Divisions in Sundanese, TPS (1953), 109–42.

Shadick, H. E. and Hsin-min Wu, *Structural Analysis of Literary Chinese* (preliminary edition) (Ithaca, 1950).

Schafer, E. H., The Camel in China down to the Mongol Dynasty, Sinologica 2 (1949), 165.

Simon, Walter (1), *Chinese-English Dictionary* (London, 1947).

―――― (2), Der Erl Jiann and Der Jiann in Luenyeu VII 25, AM (NS) 2 (1951), 46–67.

―――― (3), Functions and Meanings of Erl (I), AM (NS) 2 (1952), 179–202.

―――― (4), Functions and Meanings of Erl (II), AM (NS) 3 (1952), 7–18.

―――― (5), Functions and Meanings of Erl (III), AM (NS) 3 (1953), 117–31.

―――― (6), Functions and Meanings of Erl (IV), AM (NS) 4 (1954), 20–35.

―――― (7), "Bih (比) = Wey" (爲)?, BSOAS 12 (1948), 789–802.

―――― (8), *The Pronominal Nature of the so-called Final Particle Yee*, in *Actes du XXIᵉ Congrès International des Orientalistes* (Paris, 1949), 258.

Solomon, Bernard, One is no number in East and West, HJAS 17 (1954), 253–60.

Tarng Lan (唐蘭), *Jong-gwo Wen-tzyh Shyue* (國中文字學) (Shanghai, 1949).

Waley, Arthur, *The Analects of Confucius* (London, 1938).

Yang Bor-jiunn (楊伯峻), *Wen-yan Yeu-faa* (文言語法) (Peking, 1955).

Yang Shuh-dar (楊樹達) (1), *Tsyr Chyuan* (詞詮) (Shanghai, 1928). (Referred to in text as Yang (1).)

―――― (2), Inversion in Classical Chinese (Trans. Achilles Fang), MS 7 (1942) 267–84. (Referred to in text as Yang (2).)

―――― (3), *Gau-deeng Gwo-wen-faa* (高等國文法) (Shanghai, 1930). (Referred to in text as Yang (3).)

Yang Lien-sheng (1), The concept of "free" and "bound" in spoken Chinese, HJAS 12 (1949), 462–9.

―――― (2), Review *Jong-gwo Yeu-faa Lii-luenn* (中國語法理論) (Wang Lih), HJAS 10 (1947), 62–75; 12 (1949), 245–52.

Wang Lih (王力) (1), *Jong-gwo Yeu-faa Lii-luenn* (中國語法理論) 2 vols. (Shanghai, 1944–5). (Referred to in text as Wang (1).)

Wang Yiin-jy (王引之) (2), *Jing-juann shyh-tsyr* (經傳釋詞) (first pub. 1819) (reprint, Shanghai, 1932). (Referred to in text as Wang (2).)

LEXICON AND INDEX OF WORDS TREATED AT SOME LENGTH

NOTE. Arrangement is alphabetical, by the G.R. system. A starred entry is the hypothetical reconstruction of the phonology given in Karlgren (3), whose typography has been modified. A number preceded by K is the paragraph reference to *Grammata Serica* (see Karlgren (3)). A number preceded by YST, is the page and section reference to the Particle Lexicon (*Tsyr Chyuan*) of Yang Shuh-dar (Yang (1)). The six-figure reference is to the classification number under which the entry will be found in the Harvard-Yenching Index Series. Finally, (pl.) is plerematic usage and (gr.) is grammaticized usage.

An (安): *.ân (refs. K146; YST.10.2; 3.02340)
 (pl.) peace, pacify, tranquil, secure.
 (gr.) in, from, or to what place? in what respect? see (*a*).
  (*a*) Interrogative substitute, substituting for place and for second post-verbal elements. 6.5.2.2.
Biann (徧): see *Piann*
Bih (畢): *piet (refs. K407; YST.1.11; 1.88508)
 (pl.) a small fowler's net (of which the sign is a picture); to finish, to complete.
 (gr.) all; see (*a*).
  (*a*) Agential distributive, collective. 3.5.3.
Bih (俾): *pieg (refs. K874; YST.1.7; 5.90234)
 (pl). to cause.
 (gr.) make; see (*a*).
  (*a*) Used for periphrastic treatment of voice. 3.4.5.
Bih (敝): *b'iad (refs. K.341; 5.62940)
 (pl.) tattered, in shreds, worn out, cast aside.
 (gr.) my, our; see (*a*).
  (*a*) Status pronominal determinant. 2.6.4.1.
Bih (必): *piet (refs. K405; YST.1.10; 1.03010)
 (pl.) must
 (gr.) must be; see (*a*).
  (*a*) Copula of unqualified categorical predication, emphatic. 4.4.2.
Bih (*Bii*) (比): *piər (refs. K566; YST.1.8; 5.71710)
 (pl.) read *Bii* to come together (sign depicts two human figures standing side by side, and thus) to unite, to side with; from place together > to compare, comparable, similar, equal.
 (gr.) read *Bih* by the time that, until; see (*a*).
  (*a*) In time phrases. 3.10 Note.
Bii (彼): *pia (refs. K25; YST.1.5; 5. 29340)
 (gr.) far demonstrative "that" in contrast to *tsyy* (q.v.) "this." 6.3. Used as determinant demonstrative 2.6.4.2. Used as third person pronoun 6.2.1.
Binq (並): *b'ieng (refs. K840; YST.

1.14; 3.91270)

(pl.) side by side (original sign depicted two men standing side by side).

(gr.) together, unanimously, simultaneously, indiscriminately; see (a).

(a) Aspectual determinant of the verb. 3.3.2.9.

Bu (不): *pwət (refs. K999; YST.1.16; 1.70600)

(read *buh* before first, second, and third tone words, and *bwu* before fourth tone)

(gr.) not; see (a); un-a-; see (b).

(a) In verbal syntagma, formal indicative negative, particular negation (in contrast to *wey* universal negation); unstressed form (in contrast to *fwu* emphatic form). 3.3.1.1.

(b) In syntagma—forms privatives. 2.6.4.3.

Buh (不): see *Bu*

Bwu (不): see *Bu*

Charng (嘗): *diang (refs. K725; YST. 5.42; 3.60083)

(pl.) to taste (physically, and thus metaphorically), to experience.

(gr.) see (a).

(a) Aspectual determinant of the verb, customary aspect. 3.3.2.7.

Chern (臣) *dien (refs. K377; 2.81223)

(pl.) slave, servant, public servant (sign depicts an eye in profile averted, as seen when the head is bowed).

(gr.) I, we; see (a).

(a) Status pronoun used by subjects addressing a ruler. 6.2.2.

Cherng (誠): *dieng (refs. K818; YST. 5.45; 5.08510)

(pl.) sincerity, sincere.

(gr.) If indeed ...; see (a); "A is indeed of the class B"; see (b).

(a) In conditioned sequences, introduces the protasis. 5.3.2 Note 1.

(b) Copula of unqualified categorical, emphatic. 4.4.2.

Chian (僉): ? *k'siam (refs. K613; YST.6.68; 5.99992)

(gr.) all; see (a).

(a) Agential distributive, collective. 3.5.3.

Chiee (且): *ts'iă (refs. K.46; YST.6.55 and 6.60; 2.87113)

(gr.) going to; about to, would, might; see (a); and, moreover, furthermore; see (b); approximately, roughly; see (c).

(a) In verbal complex, aspectual determinant of the verb, potential aspect. 3.3.2.1.

(b) Placed between two verbal sentences or between two verbal predicates, co-ordinate conjunction. 5.1 footnote 3.

(c) Determinant of number. 4.10.4 footnote 15.

Chieh (竊): *ts'iat (refs. K.309; 3.02933)

(pl.) to steal, stealthily.

(gr.) with all deference; see (a).

(a) Determinant of verb indicating deference. 7.2.

Chih (取): see *Jyi*

Chii (豈): *k'iər (refs. K548; YST.4.46; 3.28111)

(pl.) read *k'ər* joyous, happy (sign is drawing of a drum. Cf. **k'ər* "triumphal music" and **k'ər* "pleasant").

(gr.) "it surely is not true that ...," see (a).

(a) Interrogative substitute. 6.5. 3.3 footnote 21; 6.5.3.4; 6.5.3.6.

(b) Used in *chii-yeou* 4.8.1; 6.5.3; *chii-wey* 6.5.3; *chii-dwu* 6.5.2.4.

Chorng (重): see *Jonq*.

Chow (驟): see *Tzow*

Chu (初): *ts'io (refs. K87; YST.5.48;

5.09720)
(pl.) first, firstly.
(gr.) for the first time; see (a). Prior to this; see (b).
  (a) In verbal complex, aspectual determinant of the verb. 3.3.2.8 (a).
  (b) In the time position. 3.10 Note. (See also 3.3.2.10. Note 3).

Chyi (其) 7: *kiəg (refs. K952; YST. 4.38; 3.37903)
(sign is a drawing of a basket cf. 箕 *kiəg "basket")
(gr.) determinant form of the anaphoric pronoun Jy (q.v.)
  (a) In syntagma, forms possessives. 2.6.4.1.
  (b) In the verbal sentence is the form proper to the agential position. 3.5.2. (See also 3.8; 3.11.1 3.11.1 footnote 71; and 6.4.)

Chyun (群): *g'iwən (refs. K459; YST. 4.51; 4.85853)
(pl.) a flock, a herd.
(gr.) various; see (a).
  (a) In syntagma, collective determinant, "in all their variety, as a totality," involves status. 2.6.4.5.

Dah (大): *d'âd (refs. K317; YST.2.1; 1.30900)
(pl.) large, great (sign depicts frontal view of a man, "a great person"); (think great), admire; (make great), enlarge.
(gr.) your; see (a); overwhelmingly; see (b).
  (a) Status pronominal determinant. 2.6.4.1.
  (b) Determinant of the verb of quality or intensity. 3.3.

Dan (單): *tân (cf. 但寶) (refs. K147; YST.2.10; 3.88856)
(pl.) single.
(gr.) only, merely; see (a).
  (a) Aspectual determinant of the verb, restrictive. 3.3.2.9. paragraph 2.

Dang (當): *tâng (refs. K725; YST.2.12; 3.60085)
(pl.) to match, be comparable to, stand up to, be equal to (in sense of both "of a rank with" and "equal to a task"), meet with, to happen upon.
(gr.) ought, should, must; see (a); when, during, at, in; see (b); "when ... (then) ..."; (see c).
  (a) Modal determinant of the verb, injunctive. 3.3.1.2. and 3.11.1 footnote 71.
  (b) In time phrases. 3.10.
  (c) In conditioned sequences, introduces the protasis. 5.3.2 Note 2.

Day (代): *d'əg (refs. K.918; YST.2.8; 5.90300)
(pl.) succeed, a generation, dynasty; take place of, supersede, substitute for, act on behalf of.
(gr.) for, on behalf of; see (a).
  (a) Particle occurring between agent and delegating agent. 3.5.5.

Der (得): *tək (refs. K905; YST.2.4; 5.29832)
(pl.) to obtain, to get. (Sign originally depicted "hand" and "cowrie shell" [i.e., money].)
(gr.) should, ought; see (a); managed to, succeeded in; see (b).
  (a) Modal determinant of the verb, injunctive. 3.3.1.2.
  (b) Aspectual determinant of the verb, resultative aspect. 3.3.2.6.
Used in *buh-der-yii* and *der-jyh*. See 3.3.2.6 footnote 20.

Duo (多): *tâ (refs. K3; YST.2.2; 4.82220)
(pl.) many, much (to regard as much), to think much of, admire (to make many), to increase.
(gr.) most or many; see (a); many;

see (*b*); frequently, often, constantly; see (*c*).

(*a*) Agential distributive, "of the agents, most." 3.5.3.1.

(*b*) Determinant (via the verb) of post-verbal elements. 3.5.3.1 footnote 47; 3.5.3 Note.

(*c*) Aspectual determinant of the verb. 3.3.2.8 paragraph (*b*). See also 3.3.2.10 Note 3.

Dwu (獨): *d'uk (refs. K1224; YST.2.21; 5.42825)

(pl.) privacy.

(gr.) only; see (*a*); alone; see (*b*); only; see (*c*).

(*a*) Agential distributive, restrictive. 3.5.3.

(*b*) In verbal syntagma, aspectual determinant of the verb. 3.3.2.9 paragraph 3; 3.5.3 Note.

(*c*) Restrictive determinant (via the verb) of post-verbal elements. 3.5.3 Note.

Dye (迭): *d'iet (refs. K402; YST.2.19; 2.09290)

(pl.) to alternate.

(gr.) alternately; see (*a*).

(*a*) Aspectual determinant of the verb. 3.3.2.8 paragraph (*a*).

Eel (爾): *ńiar (refs. K359; YST.10.12; 2.72440)

(pl.) u.f. and cognate with 邇 *eel* "near."

(gr.) determinant form of the non-status second person pronoun *ruu* (q.v.); (*a*), (*b*), see also (*c*).

(*a*) In syntagma, forms possessives. 2.6.4.1.

(*b*) Form proper to the agential position. 3.5.2; 6.2.1 Note 3.

(*c*) Allegro form of *erl-yii*. 3.9.

Eel (耳): *ńiəg (refs. K981; YST.10.16; 2.73113)

Ear (sign is a drawing of an ear).

Allegro form of *erl-yii* (q.v.). 3.9.

Eh (惡): See *U*.

Erl (而): *ńiəg (refs. K982; YST.10.5; 3.72820)

(pl.) "whiskers" (sign is a drawing of whiskers).

(gr.) see (*a*), (*b*), (*c*).

(*a*) Particle of subordination. 3.7.

(*b*) Conjunction of subordination. 5.2; 3.7.2.

(*c*) Determinant form of the second person non-status pronoun (see *Eel* above). Used in *Erl-how*. 3.7.1.

Erl-yii (而巳): *ńiəg-ziəg.

Particle of sentential mood (see 3.9) for which *Eel* (ńiar and ńiəg) are allegro forms (see *Eel* above).

Fang (方): *piwang (refs. K740; YST. 1.40; 3.01220)

(pl.) a square, square, to square, a district, place, quarter.

(gr.) see (*a*).

(*a*) Aspectual determinant of the verb, momentary aspect. 3.3.2.3.

Farn (凡): *b'iwam (refs. K625; YST. 1.37; 1.88210)

(pl.) everyone, everything.

(gr.) all; see (*a*).

(*a*) In syntagma, collective determinant. 2.6.4.5.

Fei (非): *piwər (refs. K579; YST.1.33; 5.70700)

(pl.) wrong, to disapprove, to reject.

(gr.) is not; see (*a*); this is not; see (*b*); contrary to; see (*c*); is not because; see (*d*).

(*a*) Copula of negation in unqualified categorical predication. 4.4.

(*b*) In determinative sentence, as determined term, used as anaphoric demonstrative plus copula. 4.9; 4.10.3.

(*c*) Forms privatives in sense of "contrary to." 2.6.4.3.

(*d*) Copula of cause. 4.11.

Used in *Fei-wey*. 4.11.
Used in *Fei-jyr-wey*. 4.11.
Used in *Fei-lwu*. 4.11.
Foou (否): *piug (refs. K999; YST.1.36; 3.76881)
Plerematic form of the formal negative *bu* "No!" See 3.5.1; 3.2.1; 6.5 footnote 8.
Fu (夫): *piwo (refs. K.101; YST.1.43; 1.50900)
(pl.) a man, a husband (sign depicts a man, with a stroke through the head, perhaps a hairpin). (Cf. *fuh* *b'iwo "father" which, with reading *piwo* is "honorific second part of personal name," and with this see notes in 1.2 footnote 14—non-free forms).
(gr.) read *Fwu*; see (a).
  (a) Read *b'iwo. Particle of accentuation. 3.12; 3.11.1.
  (b) Particle of sentential mood (allegro form of Foou-hu). 3.9.
  (c) Used as third person pronoun. 6.2.1.
Fuh (復): *b'iôk (Refs. K.1034; YST. 1.48; 5.29942)
(pl.) to repeat, to return, report, reply, restore.
(gr.) (once again). see (a).
  (a) Aspectual determinant of the verb. 3.3.2.8 paragraph (a).
Fwu (非): *piwət (refs. K.500; YST. 1.49; 1.55004)
Emphatic form of the indicative formal negative *bu* (q.v.). 3.3.1.1.
Gaan (敢): *kâm (refs. K607; YST.3.6; 5.77943)
(pl.) to dare, to presume.
(gr.) to presume or dare to . . . ; see (a).
  (a) In verbal syntagma, determining the verb and defining the state of the agent. 3.3.3.2.
Used in *gaan-yii* (3.3.3.2 footnote 24).

Gay (蓋): see *Her* *gâp.
Geh (各): *klâk (refs. K.766; YST.3.1; 2.24881)
Agential distributive, "of the agents, each, both, all." 3.5.3.1.
Goa (寡): *kwâ (refs. K42; 3.02723).
(pl.) a few, a single, the few, lonely.
(gr.) a few . . . ; see (a); our; see (b).
  (a) Determinant of indefinite number. 2.6.4.4.2.
  (b) Determinant status-pronoun "our." 2.6.4.1.
Used in *goa-ren*. 6.2.2.
Goou (苟): *ku (refs. K108; YST.3.4; 3.33221)
(gr.) if indeed . . .; see (a).
  (a) In conditioned sequence, introduces the protasis. 5.3.2 Note 1.
Gu (孤) *kwo (refs. K41; 5.13890)
(pl.) alone, orphan.
(gr.) I; see (a).
  (a) Status personal pronoun. 6.2.2.
Gu (姑): *ko (refs. K49; YST.3.9; 5.34381)
(pl.) mother-in-law.
(gr.) for the moment, in a moment, in a little while; see (a).
  (a) Aspectual determinant, momentary aspect. 3.3.2.3.
Guh (固): *ko (refs. K49; YST.3.9; 2.88381)
(pl.) of long standing, firm, secure, obdurate (cf. *ko "ancient").
(gr.) in fact, really; see (a).
  (a) Modal determinant of the verb, emphatic, indicative. 3.3.1.4.
Guh (故): *ko (refs. K49; YST.3.12; 5.38941)
(pl.) old (of long standing [cf. *Guh*, above], firmly established).
(gr.) it is established that, therefore, the origin, cause or reason for; see (a).
  (a) In determinative sentence, caus-

al copula. 4.11. (See also 6.5.3.6.)
Used in *shyh-guh* 4.11; *her-guh* 6.5.3.6.

Guoo (果): *klwâr (refs. K351; YST.3.20; 1.88604)
(pl.) fruit (sign depicts a tree with fruit), fruition, result, outcome, realization.
(gr.) in reality; see (*a*).
(*a*) Modal determinant of verb, emphatic indicative. 3.3.1.4.

Guu (古): *ko (refs. K.49; 3.30881)
(pl.) ancient, antiquity.
(gr.) in the past; see (*a*).
(*a*) In time phrases, for example, in *guu-jee*, in antiquity. 3.10.

Haan (罕): *xân (refs. K139; 3.02930)
(pl.) a net, rare.
(gr.) rarely; see (*a*).
(*a*) Aspectual determinant of the verb. 3.3.2.8 paragraph (*b*).

Her (何): *g'â (refs. K1; YST.3.32; 5.90721)
(gr.) (*a*) interrogative substitute, substituting singly or in combination in all syntactical positions. See 6.5.1; 6.5.2.3; 6.5.2.5; 6.5.2.7; 6.5.2.8; 6.5.3.5; 6.5.4.
(*b*) indefinite substitute, whatever, whatsoever. 6.8.
Used in *Her-you* 6.5.2.7; *her-tzyh* 6.5.2.7; *her-dwu* 6.5.2.4; *her-yii* 6.5.2.7 and 6.5.3; *her-yong* 6.5.2.5; *her-wey* 6.5.3; *her-ru* 6.5.3.2; *her-guh* 6.5.3.6; 6.5.3.

Her (曷): *g'ât (refs. K.313; YST.3.34; 3.88222)
Interrogative substitute, substituting in time position. 6.5.2.1 and footnote 14.

Her (盍): *g'âp (refs. K.642; YST.3.36; 3.37673 and 3.33373)
(pl.) join, unite.
(gr.) see (*a*).
(*a*) Interrogative substitute (allegro form of *her bu*. 6.5.3.6.

(Cf. 蓋 *g'âp "to thatch, to cover," used for *Her* as interrogative substitute, but from reading *kâb becomes modern *gay*.)

Hu (乎): *g'o (refs. K55; YST.3.43; 1.20300)
(gr.) see (*a*) and (*b*).
(*a*) Sentential modal particle, indicating doubt, surprise, indignation, etc. 3.9.
(*b*) Directive particle of the second post-verbal position. 3.4. (See also 3.4.4. footnote 27 and 6.5.)

Huoh (或): *giwək *g'wək (refs. K929; YST.3.48; 2.50811).
(pl.) read *giwək territory, state (cf. 國 "state"); read *g'wək* doubt (cf. 惑 *g'wək "doubt").
(gr.) someone, some; see (*a*); either/or; see (*b*).
(*a*) Agential distributive, of the agents, some (an unknown quantity) or some one (an unknown person). 3.5.3.1.
(*b*) Modal determinant, alternative mode. 3.3.1.4.

Hwu (胡): *g'o (refs. K49; YST.3.42; 5.38823)
(pl.) dewlap.
(gr.) see (*a*).
(*a*) Interrogative substitute (allegro form of *her-guh*). 6.5.3.6.

I (一): *.iet. (refs. K394; 1.10000)
(pl.) one, the whole, to unite, united, unity.
(gr.) in one act, an act once completed; see (*a*).
(*a*) Aspectual determinant of the verb 3.3.2.9 paragraph (1); 3.3.2.8 paragraph (*a*).
Used in *i-ren* 6.2.2.

Ian (焉): *.ian (refs. K200; YST.7.60; 3.77220)
(gr.) read *yan* *gian to, at, by, from: it, them, he, she, etc.; see (*a*);

read *Ian* where? when? never! see (*b*); at such time; see (*c*).
   (*a*) Allegro form of *yu* (directive particle) and *jy* (anaphoric pronoun). 3.8; 3.11.
   (*b*) Interrogative substitute, time and place position. 6.5.2.1 and 6.5.2.2.
   (*c*) Indefinite substitute. 6.8.
Used in *ian-yeou*. 4.8.1 and 6.5.3.

In (因): *.ien (refs. K370; YST.7.69; 2.88390)
   (pl.) rest upon (sign depicts a man lying upon a mat, cf. 茵 *.ien "a mat"), depend upon, to follow or continue.
   (gr.) causal copula; see (*a*).
   (*a*) Allegro form of *yonq-yii* (instrumental particles) used as copula of cause. 4.11.

Iue (曰): *giwat (refs. K304; YST.9.24; 1.88882)
   to say (restricted in usage to introduce quotations of reported speech only). See 8.3.2.

Jah (乍): *dz'ag (refs. K806; YST.5.16; 4.90700)
   (gr.) now ... now ..., the moment ... etc.; see (*a*).
   (*a*) Aspectual determinant of the verb, momentary aspect. 3.3.2.3.

Jan (旃): *tian (refs. K150; YST.5.23; 5.02930)
   (pl.) a type of flag or banner.
   (gr.) see (*a*).
   (*a*) Allegro form of *jy* (anaphoric pronoun) and *yan* (itself an allegro form of *yu* directive particle and *jy* anaphoric pronoun) *jy yu jy*. 3.8.

Jee (者): *tiă (refs. K45; YST.5.17; 4.33882)
   Particle forming syntagmas from formally complete verbal sentences. 2.7.1; 3.10.

Jeu (舉): *kio (refs. K75; YST.4.32; 3.87950)
   (pl.) to take in the hand, to lift, to raise.
   (gr.) all; see (*a*); all; see (*b*).
   (*a*) Agential distributive, collective 3.5.3.
   (*b*) In syntagma, collective determinant. 2.6.4.5.

Jia (加): *ka (refs. K15; YST.4.20; 5.32881)
   (pl.) to add to, to increase, to apply to.
   (gr.) more so; see (*a*).
   (*a*) Determining a verb, creates a comparative degree. 7.1.

Jiang (將): *tsiang (refs. K727; YST. 6.41; 5.27230)
   (pl.) bring, take, bring or take forth > lead, thus *jianq-jiun* "lead army" u.f. a general. (In military sense modernly read *jianq*.)
   (gr.) about to, will, might; see (*a*); approximately, roughly; see (*b*).
   (*a*) Aspectual determinant of the verb, potential aspect. 3.3.2.1.
   (*b*) Determinant of number. 4.10.4 footnote 15.
Used in *jiang-wei*. 3.3.2.1.

Jiann (見): *kian (refs. K241; YST. 4.18; 3.88213)
   (pl.) to see, to have audience with, read *g'ian* appear before, manifest.
   (gr.) see (*a*).
   (*a*) u.f. periphrastic passive voice. See 3.4.5.

Jiau (交): *kog (refs. K1166; YST.4.14; 3.01940)
   (pl.) to cross (sign depicts man with crossed legs), to cross over, exchange, interchange, have relations with.
   (gr.) mutually; see (*a*).
   (*a*) Particle of reciprocity of agency. 3.5.4.

Used in *jiau-shianq*. See 3.5.4.

Jie (皆): *kɛr (refs. K599; YST.4.15; 3.71282)

Agential distributive, collective. 3.5.3. In determinative sentence, distributive of the determined term. 4.12.

Jie (偕): *kɛr (refs. K599; YST.4.16; 5.90782)

Agential distributive, collective, two agents acting conjointly. 3.5.3.

Jih (既): *kiəd (refs. K515; YST.4.3; 5.21713)

(pl.) to complete, to finish.

(gr.) already, etc.; see (*a*); since; see (*b*).

(*a*) Aspectual determinant of the verb, perfective aspect. 3.3.2.5.

(*b*) In protasis of conditional sequences, indicates fulfilled condition. 5.3.

Used in *Jih... yow...* 5.1 footnote 2.

Used in *Jih-yii* 3.3.2.5.

Jii (己): *kiəg (refs. K953; 1.88810)

(pl.) self, see 3.5.4.1 footnote 49.

Used in *tzyh-jii* See 3.5.4.1 footnote 49.

Jii (幾): *kiər (refs. K547; YST.4.1; 2.65900)

(pl.) a few, nearly, almost.

(gr.) a few...; see (*a*); how many? see (*b*); how often? see (*c*).

(*a*) In syntagma, determinant of numbers or measures. 2.6.4.4.2 and 6.8.

(*b*) In syntagma, interrogative substitute before numbers. 6.5.1.

(*c*) In verbal sentence, interrogative substitute in time position. 6.5.2.1.

Used in *jii-her*, 6.5.1 footnote 11.

Jin (今): *kiəm (refs. K651; YST.4.21; 2.90020)

(pl.) now, the present.

(gr.) now, the present...; see (*a*);

if; see (*b*).

(*a*) In time phrases, used singly or in combination. 3.10.

(*b*) In conditioned sequences, used to introduce protasis. 5.3.2 Note 2.

Used in *jin-ryh*, *jin-shyr*, *jin-jee*, etc. 3.10.

Jinn (盡): *dz'ien (refs. K381; YST. 6.34; 3.57675)

(pl.) finish, exhaust.

(gr.) all; see (*a*); fully; see (*b*); all of; see (*c*).

(*a*) Agential distributive, collective. 3.5.3.

(*b*) Determinant of the verb of intensity or degree. 3.3.

(*c*) Collective determinant (via the verb) of post-verbal elements. 3.5.3 Note.

Jiu (俱): *kiu (refs. K121; YST.4.30; 5.90894)

(pl.) to join with, act conjointly with, both together.

(gr.) both; see (*a*); all; see (*b*).

(*a*) Agential distributive, two agents acting conjointly. 3.5.3.

(*b*) Collective determinant (via the verb) of post-verbal elements. 3.5.3 Note.

Jiuh (具): *g'iu (refs. K121; YST.4.36; 3.87904)

(pl.) an implement.

(gr.) all, the entire; see (*a*).

(*a*) In syntagma, determinant collective 2.6.4.5.

Jiun (君): *kiwən (refs. K459; 4.85883)

(pl.) ruler, prince, used in *jiun-tzyy* "son of a prince" and thus "prince," "gentleman."

(gr.) you Sir! see (*a*).

(*a*) Status pronoun. 6.2.2.

Jonq (衆): *tiông (refs. K1010; 3.27263)

(pl.) the many, the masses (sign depicts three men and ?eye or

?sun).
   (gr.) many...; see (*a*).
   (*a*) Determinant of indefinite number. 2.6.4.4.2.

Jonq (重): *d'iung. (refs. K1188; YST. 5.37; 1.20704)
   (pl.) Heavy, important (to make heavy) to increase, to regard as important.
   (gr.) read modernly *Chorng*, once again; see (*a*).
   (*a*) Aspectual determinant of the verb. 3.3.2.8 paragraph (*a*).

Ju (諸): *tio (refs. K45; YST.5.28; 5.08383)
   (gr.) various; see (*a*); pronoun+particle; see (*b*).
   (*a*) In syntagma, collective determinant. 2.6.4.5 (involves status).
   (*b*) Allegro form of *jy* (anaphoric pronoun) and *yu* (directive particle) or *hu* (particle of sentential mood). 3.8; 3.11.1; 3.9.

Juan (專): *tiwan (refs. K231; YST. 5.33; 3.56304)
   (pl.) to monopolize, use exclusively.
   (gr.) exclusively; see (*a*).
   (*a*) Aspectual determinant of the verb. (3.3.2.9 paragraph 2.

Jy (之): *tiəg (refs. K962; YST.5.1; 1.08900)
   (pl.) To go to (sign depicts a foot).
   (gr.) particle; see (*a*); pronoun; see (*b*); demonstrative; see (*c*).
   (*a*) In syntagma, particle of determination. 2.6.2; 2.7.2; 4.7.
   (*b*) Pregnant form of the anaphoric pronoun. 6.4; 2.6.4.1; 3.8.
   (*c*) Determinative form of the near demonstrative. 2.6.4.2.

Jyh (至): *tied (refs. K413; YST.5.10; 1.08900)
   (pl.) to arrive at, to come to.
   (gr.) most; see (*a*).
   (*a*) As determinant, forms superlative degree. 7.1.
   (*b*) Used with *jyh-yu*. 3.4.5.1 and 3.10.

Jyi (亟): *kiək (refs. K910; YST.4.11; 1.70101)
   (pl.) fast, quick.
   (gr.) read *Chih* *k'iəg, frequently, often; see (*a*).
   (*a*) Aspectual determinant of the verb. 3.3.2.8 paragraph (*b*).

Jyi (及): *g'iəp (refs. K681; YST.4.7; 1.78240)
   (pl.) to come to, to reach to, to overtake (sign depicts a hand grasping a man).
   (gr.) together with; see (*a*); by the time that; see (*b*).
   (*a*) In syntagma, particle of simple connection. 2.5 and 3.5.4.
   (*b*) In time phrases. 3.10.

Jyi (即): *tsiet (refs. K399; YST.6.31; 5.21822)
   (pl.) to go to.
   (gr.) copula; see (*a*); then...; see (*b*).
   (*a*) Copula of unqualified categorical, emphatic. 4.4.2.
   (*b*) Conjunction of conditioned sequence. 5.3.

Jyr (直): *d'iək (refs. K919; YST.5.13; 3.30274)
   (pl.) straight, to straighten (sign depicts an "eye" and "straight line"), to rectify, straightforward.
   (gr.) is merely; see (*a*).
   (*a*) Restrictive copula. 4.4.2.

Jyue (厥): *kiwat (refs. K301; YST.4.37; 4.12990)
   (gr.) his, its, etc. EAC form; see (*a*).
   (*a*) anaphoric pronoun, determinant form. See 2.6.4.1 footnote 17.

Jyy (祇): *tieg (refs. K867; YST.5.7; 5.06830)
   (pl.) an earth spirit.
   (gr.) merely; see (*a*).

(*a*) Aspectual determinant of the verb, restrictive. 3.3.2.9 paragraph 2.

Kee (可): *k'â (refs. K1; YST.3.24; 2.72881)
(pl.) to be permitted, to be possible.
(gr.) can; see (*a*); could; see (*b*).
(*a*) Determinant of the verb defining the state of the agent. 3.3.3.2.
(*b*) Modal determinant of the verb, subjunctive. 3.3.3.2 footnote 23.
Used in *kee-yii*. 3.3.3.2 footnote 24.

Keen (肯): *k'əng (refs. K882; YST. 3.27; 3.27822)
(pl.) to be willing.
(gr.) willing to; see (*a*).
(*a*) Determinant of the verb defining the state of the agent. 3.3.3.2.

Kuanq (況兄): *xiwang (refs. K765; YST.3.28; 5.01811)
(gr.) how much more so? more so; see (*a*).
(*a*) Used in degrees of comparison. 7.1.

Leu (屢): *gliu
See *Lou* *gliu.

Lou (婁): *gliu (refs. K123; YST.2.60; 3.50346)
(pl.) drag, trail, bind, connect.
(gr.) read *Leu*, frequently, often; see (*a*).
(*a*) With *Leu* above: aspectual determinant of the verb. 3.3.2.8 paragraph (*b*).

Meei (每): *mwəg (refs. K947; YST. 1.28; 4.90850)
(pl.) (of growth) flourishing, abundant (sign depicts "woman" [here phonetic] and "branches").
(gr.) each time; see (*a*); each; see (*b*).
(*a*) Aspectual determinant of the verb. 3.3.2.8 paragraph (*a*).
(*b*) In syntagma, distributive determinant 7.3.

Ming (明): *miang (refs. K760; 5.88824)
(pl.) light (sign has "sun" and "moon"), bright, sight, lights, enlightened, immanences, spirits.
(gr.) see (*a*).
(*a*) In time phrases, used in *ming-ryh* "next day." 3.10.

Moh (莫): *mâk (refs. K802; YST.1.24; 3.33892)
(pl.) Evening (sign has "sun" with "grass" above and below).
(gr.) none, no one; see (*a*).
(*a*) Agential distributive, of the agents, none. 3.5.3.1. (See 4.3 footnote 1 and 3.4.8 paragraph 3.)

Nae (乃): *nəg (refs. K945; YST.2.37; 1.78220)
(gr.) ... is indeed ...; see (*a*); "your ...; see (*b*); in this way; see (*c*); thereupon; see (*d*).
(*a*) Copula of unqualified categorical, emphatic form. 4.4.2.
(*b*) Determinant form of non-status personal pronoun *ruu* 2.6.4.1.
(*c*) Allegro form of *Ru-jy*. See 3.3.3.1 footnote 22.
(*d*) Emphatic form of *Erl* 3.7.2.1.

Neng (能): *nəng (refs. K885; YST. 2.46; 5.62712)
(pl.) A species of bear (sign depicts a bear); to be able, ability.
(gr.) can, is able to; see (*a*).
(*a*) Determinant of the verb defining the state of the agent. 3.3.3.2 and 3.3.3.2 footnote 23.
Used in *neng-yii*. 3.3.3.2 footnote 24.

Nuoh (諾): *nâk (refs. K777; YST.2.37; 5.08382)
(pl.) I concur, Yes! (see 6.5 footnote 8). 3.2.2. (Perhaps a specialization of sense of *ruoh* [*ńiak] (q.v.).

Piann (徧): *pian (refs. K246; YST. 1.14; 5.29024)

(gr.) all; see (a); read *biann* everywhere; see (b).

(c) Collective determinant (via the verb) of post-verbal elements. 3.5.3 Note.

(b) Used in place position. 3.5.3 Note.

Ran (然): *ńian (refs. K217; YST.5.94; 3.29600)

(pl.) to burn (sign depicts "flesh," "dog," and "fire"). (This is modernly written 燃.)

(gr.) like-this, quite so! Yes! see (a).

(a) Allegro form of *ru-tsyy* (lit: "like-this" i.e., "thus") and as such: "yes," "it is so." See 6.5 footnote 8 and 3.2.1. Particle placed between determinations of manner and the verb. 3.3.3.1. Used anaphorically as the protasis in conditioned sequences "If the foregoing be so." 5.3.1 Note 1.

Used in *ran-tzer* (5.3.1 Note 1) and *ran-hou* (5.3.1 Note 2, and 3.7.1 footnote 57.) (See also 4.6 footnote 7.)

Reen (忍): *ńiən (refs. K456; YST.5.100; 3.72010)

(pl.) to bear, to endure.

(gr.) to bear to; see (a).

(a) Determinant of the verb defining the state of the agent. 3.3.3.2.

Ru (如): *ńio (refs. K94; YST.5.106; 5.34881)

(pl.) to be like, to resemble (in *Tso*) to go to.

(gr.) subjunctive modal determinant; see (a)); copula; see (b).

(a) Modal determinant of the verb, subjunctive. 3.3.1.3; 5.3.

(b) Copula of partial inclusion. 4.6.

Used in *ru . . . moh ru . . .* 4.6 footnote 8.

Used in *Ru-wuh* 3.3.1.3 Note.

Used in *Buh-ru* 4.6 footnote 8.

Ruoh (若): *ńiak (refs. K777; YST.5.85; 3.33381)

(pl.) to agree, to conform to (the sign depicts a figure kneeling, with dishevelled hair, ?an act of submission). (Cf. here *nuoh* 諾 *nâk "I agree.") To select, to resemble.

(gr.) or; see (a); modal particle; see (b); copula; see (c); pronoun; see (d).

(a) Particle of alternative connection in syntagma. 2.5. Cf. "to select."

(b) Modal determinative of the verb, subjunctive. 3.3.1.3 and 5.3 footnote 6.

(c) Copula of partial inclusion. 4.6.

(d) Used for *Ruu* non-status pronoun (q.v.). 6.2.1. Used in *Bwu-ruoh*. 4.6 footnote 8. Used in *Ruoh-shyy*. 5.3 footnote 6.

Ruu (汝女): *ńio *nio (refs. K94; 5.01340)

Non-status personal pronoun, second person, pregnant form 6.2.1; 2.6.4.1; 6.2.1 Note 3. (See also Appendix 3.)

Ryh (日): *ńiet (refs. K404; YST.5.82; 1.88882)

(pl.) the sun (of which sign is a picture), a day.

(gr.) day by day; see (a); on another day; see (b).

(a) Aspectual determinant of the verb (either singly, or in gemination). 3.3.2.8 paragraph (b).

(b) In time position. 3.3.2.10 Note 3.

Shanq (尚): *diang (refs. K725; YST.5.73; 3.60821)

(pl.) high (cf. 上 "above"). (Sign ? depicts a house with the ridge pole and roof.) (To regard as

high), to exalt.
  (gr.) continues to, still; see (*a*); even so, still; see (*b*); injunctive particle ought? should? see (*c*).
  (*a*) Aspectual determinant of the verb, durative aspect. 3.3.2.4.
  (*b*) Concessive conjunction. 5.4.3.
  (*c*) Modal determinant of the verb, injunctive (cf. cognate *dang*). 3.3.1.2.
  (*d*) Used in *shang-you*. 3.3.2.4.
Shao (Shaw) (少): *śiog (refs. K1149; YST.5.65; 1.60200)
  (pl.) a few, the few.
  (gr.) few; see (*a*); somewhat, rather; see (*b*); gradually; see (*c*); only, just, barely; see (*c*); a few . . .; see (*d*); shortly; see (*c*); read *Shaw* "when young"; see (*e*).
  (*a*) In agential complex, distributive. 3.5.3.1.
  (*b*) In verbal complex, determinant of the verb of quality or degree. 3.3.
  (*c*) In verbal complex, aspectual determinant of the verb. 3.3.2.8 paragraph (*b*) and 3.3.2.9 paragraph 1.
  (*d*) In verbal complex, restrictive determinant (via the verb) of post-verbal elements. 3.5.3.1 footnote 47 and 3.5.3 Note.
  (*e*) In time position, "in a little while" and read *Shaw* "when young, in youth." 3.10. (See also 3.3.2.10. Note 3.)
Shau (稍): *sog (refs. K1149; YST. 5.66; 5.26622)
  (cognate with *Shŧau* and *Shao*).
  (gr.) gradually; see (*a*); a few; see (*b*).
  (*a*) Aspectual determinant of the verb. 3.3.2.8 paragraph (*b*).
  (*b*) Restrictive determinant (via the verb) of post-verbal elements. 3.3.2.10 Note 3.
Shaw (少): See *Shao*.
Sheau (小): *siog (refs. K1149; YST. 6.84; 1.6000)
  (pl.) small, minor, make small (putative: regard as small), belittle, despise.
  (gr.) somewhat, slightly; see (*a*); gradually; see (*b*); a few; see (*c*).
  In verbal complex:
  (*a*) Determinant of the verb of quality or degree. 3.3.
  (*b*) Aspectual determinant of the verb. 3.3.2.8 paragraph (*b*).
  (*c*) Restrictive determinant (via the verb) of post-verbal elements. 3.5.3.1 footnote 47.
  Used in *sheau-ren*. 6.2.2. (See also 3.3.2.10 Note 3.)
Sheng (勝): See *Shenq*
Shenn (甚): *diəm (refs. K658; YST. 5.71; 3.37212)
  (gr.) in an intense degree; see (*a*).
  (*a*) Used in creating superlative degree. 7.1.
Shenq (勝): *śiəng (refs. K893; YST. 5.76; 5.82622)
  (pl.) conquer, vanquish, victory.
  (gr.) read *Sheng*, more than enough; fully equal to; see (*a*).
  (*a*) Aspectual determinant of the verb. 3.3.2.9 paragraph 3.
Shi (奚): *g'ieg (refs. K876; YST.4.55; 3.22690)
  (pl.) slave (sign has "man" and "to bind").
  (gr.) by what means; how? doing what? why? where to? see (*a*); allegro form of *her-yii*.
  (*a*) Interrogative substitute. See 6.5.2.2; 6.5.2.2 footnote 16; 6.5.2.5; 6.5.2.6; and 6.5.3.6.
  Used in *Shi-wey*. 6.5.3.6.
  Used in *Shi-dwu*. 6.5.2.4.
  Used in *Shi-yeou*. 6.5.3.

LEXICON AND INDEX OF WORDS 249

Shi (悉): *siet (refs. K1257; YST.6.82; 3.26010)
(gr.) all; see (*a*).
  (*a*) Collective determinant (via the verb) of post-verbal elements. 3.5.3 Note. See 7.3 for *Shi* and the instrumental.

Shiang (相): *siang (refs. K731; YST. 6.88; 5.36883)
(pl.) to look at, to face (sign has "eye" and "tree"), thus "facing" from which "minister" (facing, and assisting the ruler); reciprocal, reciprocated.
(gr.) mutually, reciprocally; see (*a*).
  (*a*) Particle of reciprocity of agency. 3.5.4.

Shianq (鄉):* xiang (refs. K714; YST. 4.62; 5.62222)
(pl.) read *Shiang* "to face," "to turn towards" (sign depicts two men facing each other across a food vessel), u.f. "village."
(gr.) read *Shianq* "formerly"; see (*a*).
  (*a*) In time phrase. 3.10.

Shin (新): *sien (refs. K382; YST.6.86; 5.06820)
(pl.) new, renew.
(gr.) recently; see (*a*).
  (*a*) Aspectual determinant of the verb. 3.3.2.9.

Shuh (數): *sliu (refs. K123; YST.5.78; 5.54946)
(pl.) a number; read *Shuu*; to count, to number, to rebuke.
(gr.) a number of, many; see (*a*); read *Shuoh* often, frequently; see (*b*).
  (*a*) Determinant of numbers and units of measure. 2.6.4.4.2.
  (*b*) Aspectual determinant of the verb. 3.3.2.8 paragraph (*b*). (Cf. *Lou*; *Leu*.)

Shuoh (數): See *Shuh*
Shuu (數): See *Shuh*
Shwei (誰): *diwər (refs. K575; YST. 5.83; 5.08974)
Interrogative substitute who? whom? what name? See 6.5.1; 6.5.2.3; 6.5.2.8; and 6.8 footnote 26.

Shwu (孰): *diôk (refs. K1026; YST. 5.80; 5.03311)
(pl.) cooked (cf. 熟).
(gr.) which of them? which one? see (*a*).
  (*a*) Interrogative substitute in agential distributive position. 6.5.2.4.

Shyan (咸): *g'ɛm (refs. K671; YST. 4.60; 2.50181)
Agential distributive, collective. 3.5.3.

Shyh (是): *dieg (refs. K866; YST.5.55; 3.88792)
(pl.) right, true, to approve.
(gr.) this; see (*a*); is; see (*b*); this is; see (*c*); this; see (*d*) (see 4.0 ff.).
  (*a*) Determinant form of the near demonstrative *tsyy*. 2.6.4.2.
  (*b*) Copula of unqualified categorical predication. 4.4.1.
  (*c*) As determined term, anaphoric demonstrative plus copula. 4.9.1 and 4.10.3.
  (*d*) Anaphoric substitute in determinative sentence. 4.10.3.
Used in *shyh-you*. 4.6.
Used in *shyh-yii*. 2.6.4.2 and 4.11.
Used in *shyh-guh*. 2.6.4.2 and 4.11.

Shyh (適): *śiek (refs. K.877; YST.5.62; 2.09021)
(pl.) (active) to go to; (cause) to send, despatch.
(gr.) at that moment; see (*a*); by chance; see (*b*).
  (*a*) Aspectual determinant of the verb, momentary aspect. 3.3.2.3.
  (*b*) See 3.3.2.3 footnote 16.

Shyi (昔): *siak (refs. K798; 3.37883)
(gr.) in time past, yesterday, a few days ago, or in the remote past, indifferently.
  (*a*) See 3.10.

Used in *shyi-jee*. 3.10.

Shyy (始): *śiəg (refs. K976; YST.5.54; 5.34681)
 (pl.) to begin.
 (gr.) at first, prior to this; see (*a*); for the first time; see (*b*).
  (*a*) In time phrases. 3.10.
  (*b*) Aspectual determinant of the verb. 3.3.2.8 paragraph (*a*). (See also 3.3.2.10 Note 3.)

Shyy (使): *sliəg (refs. K975; YST.5.53; 5.90502)
 (pl.) to send, to order, an envoy, to cause.
 (gr.) see (*a*)
  (*a*) Used in periphrastic causative. 3.4.5.
 Used in *shyh-ruoh*, to suppose, to imagine, if. (See 5.3 footnote 6.)

Soou (叟傁): *sug (refs. K1097; 3.88840)
 (pl.) an old man.
 (gr.) you Sir! Used to elderly men.
  (*a*) Status pronoun. 6.2.2.

Suoo (所): *sio (refs. K91; YST.6.92; 5.82821)
 (pl.) a place (sign has "door" and "axe") (cf. *t'io 處 "a place").
 (gr.) see (*a*).
  (*a*) Indefinite substitute. 6.6.ff.
 Used in *suoo-tzyh*. 6.6.1.1.
 Used in *suoo-you*. 6.6.1.1.
 Used in *suoo-wey*. 6.6.1.3 and in 6.6.1.3 footnote 25.
 Used in *suoo-yii*. 6.6.1.3.
 Used in *suoo-yeu*. 6.6.1.4.

Swei (雖): *siwər (refs. K575; YST. 6.95; 5.86976)
 (gr.) although; see (*a*); even if; see (*b*); even a; see (*c*).
  (*a*) In concession introduces the concessive clause. 5.4.1.
  (*b*) In conditioned concession. 5.4.2.
  (*c*) In syntagma, determinant in sense of "an extreme case of something more generally implied, even a . . ." 5.4.1.
 Used in *Swei-ran*. 5.4.1.

Sy (斯): *sieg (refs. K869; YST.6.76; 5.39823)
 (pl.) to cleave (sign has "axe" and "basket").
 (gr.) this; see (*a*); then; see (*b*).
  (*a*) Determinant form of the near demonstrative *tsyy*. 2.6.4.2.
  (*b*) Conjunction of conditioned sequence. 5.3.

Ta (他佗): *t'â (refs. K4; YST.2.26; 5.90310)
 (pl.) another, other.
 (gr.) see (*a*).
  (*a*) Demonstrative "other than the thing indicated," contra *bii* and *tsyy*. See 6.3.

Tch (特): *d'ək (refs. K961; YST.2.28; 5.25330)
 (pl.) single.
 (gr.) especially, particularly; see (*a*).
  (*a*) Aspectual determinant of the verb. 3.3.2.9 paragraph 2.

Torng (同): *d'ung (refs. K1176; 2.82181)
 (pl.) together, identical.
 (gr.) unanimously, in concert; see (*a*).
  (*a*) Aspectual determinant of the verb. 3.3.2.9 paragraph 3.

Tsorng (從): *dz'iung (refs. K1191; YST.6.72; 5.29990)
 (pl.) to follow, to obey, to comply or accord with, followers.
 (gr.) at the instigation of; see (*a*); from; see (*b*);
  (*a*) See periphrastic treatment of voice. 3.4.5 footnote 28.
  (*b*) Lexical directive. 3.4.5.1.

Tsyy (此) *ts'iar (refs. K358; YST.6.56; 5.27710)
 (gr.) this; see (*a*); this . . .; see (*b*); this; see (*c*).
  (*a*) Demonstrative, pregnant form.

LEXICON AND INDEX OF WORDS

6.3.

(b) Used as determinant demonstrative. 2.6.4.2.

(c) Anaphoric pronoun in determinative sentence. 4.10.3.

Twu (徒): *d'o (refs. K62; YST.2.32; 5.29390)

(pl.) to go on foot, foot follower, infantrymen (sign depicts "ground," "foot," and "walk"); bare, naked.

(gr.) only; see (a); empty-handed, in vain; see (b).

(a) In syntagma restrictive determinant. 2.6.4.5.

(b) Determinant of the verb of manner. 3.5.3 Note.

Tzai (哉): *tsəg (refs. K943; YST. 6.21; 2.35881)

Sentential modal particle. 3.9.

Tzay (再): *tsəg (refs. K941; YST.6.26; 1.70334)

(pl.) to act twice, two.

(gr.) once again, twice; see (a).

(a) In verbal complex, aspectual determinant of the verb. 3.3.2.8 paragraph (a) and 7.6 footnote 8.

Tzer (則): *tsək (refs. K906; YST.6.12; 5.89223)

(pl.) a pattern, exemplar, a law (sign has "knife" and "ritual vessel"; laws were inscribed on such vessels); to pattern oneself upon, to exemplify.

(gr.) then; see (a); copula, "A rather than B is of the class C"; see (b); and then; see (c).

(a) Conjunction of conditioned sequence. 5.3.

(b) Copula of unqualified categorical, selective. 4.4.2.

(c) Conjunction of narrative sequence. 5.3.

Tzonq (縱): *tsiung (refs. K1191; YST. 6.54; 5.66290)

(pl.) let loose, release.

(gr.) even though; see (a).

(a) In concessive conditioned sequences, introduces protasis. 5.4.2 (for "to loosen" > "to concede"; cf. 舍 *shee* "to loose," "to release," "except").

Tzow (驟): *? (refs. K132; YST.5.22; 5.82766)

(pl.) quick, fast.

(gr.) read *Chow*, frequently, often; see (a).

(a) Aspectual determinant of the verb. 3.3.2.8 paragraph (b).

Tzwu (足): *tsiuk (refs. K1219; YST. 6.48; 3.88791)

(pl.) a foot (sign has "foot" and a circle); sufficient, to be adequate.

(gr.) adequate to . . .; see (a).

(a) Determinant of the verb defining the state of the agent. 3.3.3.2.

Used in *tzwu-yii*. 3.3.3.2 footnote 24.

Tzyh (自): *dz'i (refs. K1237; YST.6.5; 2.28113)

(pl.) self.

(gr.) reflexive particle; see (a); from; see (b).

(a) Reflexive determinant of the verb. 3.5.4.1 and 3.5.4.1 footnote 49.

(b) Lexical directive. 3.4.5.1.

(c) In time indications. 3.10.

Used in *her-tzyh*. 6.5.2.2.

U (惡): *.âk (refs. K805; YST.8.1; 3.77010)

(pl.) read *Eh*; bad, evil; read *Wuh* *.ag to hate.

(gr.) interrogative; see (a); exclamation; see (b).

(a) Read *U* interrogative substitute, in place position. 6.5.2.2.

(b) Interjection. 3.9.1.

Used in *u-hu*. 6.5.2.2.

Uei (微): *miwər (refs. K584; YST. 8.30; 5.29240)

(pl.) small, minute, to hide, hidden, subtle.
(gr.) if it were not for; but for; see (a).
(a) Used in protasis of conditional. 5.3.2 Note 3.

Wei (惟唯): *diwər (refs. K575; YST. 8.24/27; 5.60973; 5.88974)
(gr.) nothing but, only; see (a); merely; see (b).
(a) Determinative restrictive. 2.6.4.5.
(b) Copula of categorical predication, restrictive. 4.4.2. See also 3.4.8. paragraph 4.

Wei (爲): *gwia (refs. K27; YST.8.16; 3.22822)
(pl.) to become (cause to become) > to make, build, create.
(gr.) in subjunctive usages; see (a) and (b). Read *wey* (to become for the time being) > to act as or on behalf of (gr.) particle of delegated agency; see (c) and causal copula; see (d).
(a) Copula of qualified categorical predication, subjunctive. 4.4.3.
(b) Modal determinant of the verb, subjunctive. 3.3.1.3.
(c) Particle of delegated agency. 3.5.5.
(d) Copula of causal predication. 4.11.
Used in *yii-wey*. 4.11.
Used in *buh-wei* 4.4.3.
Used in *wei-ruoh*. 4.6.
Used in *fei-wey*. 4.11.

Wey (未): *miwəd (refs. K531; YST. 8.34; 1.50600)
(gr.) not; see (a).
(a) Formal negative, indicative, universal negation contra *Bu* See 3.3.1.1. See also 4.8.1 footnote 13.
Used in *wey-charng*. 3.3.2.7.
Used in *wey-yeou*. 4.8.1.

Wey (爲): See *Wei*

Woo (我): *ngâ (refs. K.2; 1.25500)
(gr.) I, we, our state; self; see (a).
(a) Non-status personal pronoun, first person, pregnant form. 6.2.1 and notes (cf. 2.6.4.1).

Wu (無) *miwo (refs. K103; YST.8.4; 4.90363)
(pl.) not to possess, to lack (contra *yeou* "to possess").
(gr.) would not; see (a); there is not . . . ; see (b); none, no one; see (c); a— un—; see (d).
(a) Formal negative, subjunctive. 3.3.1.3.
(b) In determinative sentence, as determined term. 4.8.1.
(c) In agential complex, distributive. 3.5.3.1.
(d) In syntagma, forms privatives. 2.6.4.3.

Wu (无): *miwo (refs. K106; 1.70310)
Used as *Wu* *miwo above. See 2.6.4.3 footnote 20.

Wu (毋): *miwo (refs. K107; YST.8.11; 1.88854)
(gr.) do not, should or ought not; see (a).
(a) Formal negative, injunctive, unemphatic form contra *Wuh* (q.v.). 3.3.1.2.

Wu (吾): *ngo (refs. K58; 3.77882)
(gr.) I, my, our; see (a) and (b).
(a) In syntagma, determinant form of *Woo* (q.v.) non-status personal pronoun first person, creating possessives. 2.6.4.1 and 6.2.1 Note 1.
(b) In verbal sentence, agential form of *Woo*. 3.5.2.

Wuh (勿) *miwət (refs. K503; YST. 8.13; 2.22220)
(gr.) do not; see (a).
(a) Formal negative, injunctive, emphatic form contra *Wu* (q.v.).

3.3.1.2.
Wuh (惡): See *U*
Yan (焉): See *Ian*
Ye (邪): *ziă (refs. K47; YST.7.36; 5.77823)
(耶 is a graphic variant).
Sentential modal particle. 3.9.
Yee (也): *dia (refs. K4; YST.7.38; 1.33810)
Particle of accentuation. 3.12; see also 3.11.1; 4.2; and 3.10.
Yeou (有): *giug (refs. K995; YST.7.55; 4.30822)
(pl.) to possess, to have, to be in existence, to occur.
(gr.) some; see (*a*); and; see (*b*); would; see (*c*); there is; see (*d*).
(*a*) Agential distributive. 3.5.3.1.
(*b*) Particle of simple connection in enumeration. 7.6, read *you*.
(*c*) Modal determination of verb subjunctive. 3.3.1.3.
(*d*) See 4.8.1 and 4.8.2.
Yeu (與): *zio (refs. K89; YST.9.11; 3.87900)
(pl.) association (sign is drawing of two hands holding a ?boat ?tray); an association, caucus, ally, to associate with, to accompany, to receive, accept, concede (cf. 許) and (causatively) cause to receive, give, grant, bestow upon.
(gr.) together with; see (*a*).
(*a*) Particle of simple connection in syntagma. 2.5 and 3.5.4.
(*b*) Read *Yu*. Sentential modal particle. (Allegro form of yee-hu.) 3.9.
(*c*) Directive particle. 3.4.7.
Yih (益): *iek (refs. K.849; 2.90173)
(pl.) to add to, to increase.
(gr.) more so; see (*a*).
(*a*) Used in creating comparative degrees. 7.1.
Yih (亦): *ziak (refs. K800; YST.7.27; 3.01220)
(gr.) after all; see (*a*).
(*a*) Co-ordinate conjunction, contingent. 5.1.
Yii (以): *ziəg (refs. K976; YST.7.8; 5.27900)
(pl.) the means, *raison d'être*, to use.
(gr.) instrumental particle "by means of," "by its means," etc.; see (*a*); "because"; see (*b*); directive particle; see (*c*).
(*a*) Instrumental particle. 3.6.1 ff.
(*b*) Causal copula in determinative sentence. 4.11.
(*c*) See 3.4.7.
Used in *yii-wey* (4.11), in *yii . . . wei . . .* and *yii-wei*. 3.6.1 footnote 50.
Yii (已): *ziəg (refs. K977; YST.7.16; 1.18810)
(pl.) to complete, to finish (and causatively) to end, to dismiss.
(gr.) already; see (*a*) .
(*a*) Aspectual determinant of the verb, perfective aspect. 3.3.2.5.
(*b*) Particle of sentential mood. 3.9.
Used in *jih-yii*. 3.3.2.5.
Used in *erl-yii*. 3.9.
Yii (矣): *ziəg (refs. K976; YST.7.21; 3.60990)
Particle of accentuation. 3.12 and 3.12.1.
Yonq (用): *diung (refs. K.1185; YST. 9.36; 2.82504)
(pl.) to use, employ, materials, implements.
(gr.) see (*a*).
(*a*) Instrumental particle. 3.6.1. See also 4.11.
You (猶): *ziôg (refs. K1096; YST. 7.48; 5.42982)
(pl.) similar.
(gr.) Copula "like"; see (*a*); subjunctive particle; see (*b*); continues to, still; see (*c*); even so, still; see (*d*); from; see (*e*).

(a) Copula of partial inclusion. 4.6.
(b) Modal determinant of the verb, subjunctive. 3.3.1.3.
(c) Aspectual determinative of the verb durative aspect. 3.3.2.4.
(d) Concessive conjunction. 5.4.3.
(e) Lexical directive (u.f. *you* 由). 3.4.5.2.
Used in *you-shang*. 5.4.3.
Used in *you-yeou*. 4.8.
You (由): *diôg (refs. K1079; YST.7.51; 1.58884)
(pl.) origin.
(gr.) from; see (a).
  (a) Lexical directive. 3.4.5.2.
  (b) u.f. *you* (猶) copula of partial inclusion. 4.6.
  (c) Used in time indications. 3.10.
Used in *her-you* 6.5.2.2.
You (尤): *giug (refs. K996; YST.7.54; 1.30010)
(pl.) fault, to blame, excess.
(gr.) see (a).
  (a) Forms superlative degree. 7.1.
Yow (又): *giug (refs. K995; YST.7.58; 1.88400)
(gr.) also, too; see (a); once again; see (b).
  (a) Co-ordinate conjunction. 5.1.
  (b) Aspectual determinant of the verb. 3.3.2.8 paragraph (a).
Yu (於): *.io (refs. K61; YST.9.1; 5.02910)
(gr.) particle; see (a) and (c); interjection; see (b).
  (a) Directive particle of the second post-verbal position. 3.4. (See also 3.4.4 footnote 27.
  (b) Interjection. 3.9.1.
  (c) Time and place indications. 3.10 Note.
Yu (于): *giwo (refs. K97; YST.9.7; 1.70300)
(gr.) particle; see (a).
  (a) Directive particle of the second post-verbal position (archaistic in LAC). 3.4 (See also 3.4.4 footnote 27.
Yu (予): *dio (refs. K83; 3.10720)
EAC form of the first person non-status pronoun. 6.2.1 Note 2.
Yu (余): *dio (refs. K82; 2.90760)
EAC form of the first person non-status pronoun. 6.2.1 Note 2.
Yu (與): See *Yeu*
Yuh (欲): *giuk (refs. K1202; YST. 9.20; 5.98291)
(pl.) to wish, want, intend, desire, desires.
(gr.) see (a).
  (a) Aspectual determinant of the verb, desiderative, becoming potential in Han usage. 3.3.2.2.
Yun (云): *giwən (refs. K460; YST.9.28; 3.11600)
"to say," restricted in usage to indicating citations from written works; see 8.4.7.

www.ingramcontent.com/pod-product-compliance
Lightning Source LLC
Chambersburg PA
CBHW080037100526
44584CB00023BA/3252